The Structure of Liberty

The Structure of Liberty

Justice and The Rule of Law

Randy E. Barnett

OXFORD
UNIVERSITY PRESS

OXFORD

UNIVERSITY PRESS

Great Clarendon Street, Oxford OX2 6DP

Oxford University Press is a department of the University of Oxford.
It furthers the University's objective of excellence in research, scholarship,
and education by publishing worldwide in

Oxford New York

Athens Auckland Bangkok Bogotá Buenos Aires Calcutta
Cape Town Chennai Dar es Salaam Delhi Florence Hong Kong Istanbul
Karachi Kuala Lumpur Madrid Melbourne Mexico City Mumbai
Nairobi Paris São Paulo Singapore Taipei Tokyo Toronto Warsaw
and associated companies in Berlin Ibadan

Oxford is a registered trade mark of Oxford University Press
in the UK and in certain other countries

Published in the United States
by Oxford University Press Inc., New York

© Randy E. Barnett 1998

British Library Cataloguing in Publication Data
Data available

Library of Congress Cataloging in Publication Data
Barnett, Randy E.
The structure of liberty: justice and the rule of law / Randy E. Barnett
1. Liberty. 2. Justice. 3. Rule of law. I. Title.
K487.L5B37 1998 3409.11—dc21 97–41149
ISBN 0–19–829324–0
ISBN 0–19–829729–7 (pbk.)

Printed in Great Britain
on acid-free paper by
Bookcraft Ltd,
Midsomer Norton, Somerset

To my parents and grandparents for giving me love,
And to my father for giving me a love of justice and liberty.

ACKNOWLEDGMENTS

It is difficult to acknowledge, without being either neglectful or tedious, all those people and institutions whose influence have contributed to a book about one's deepest convictions. But my debts are such as to oblige me to run these risks. Let me begin with the people.

My gratitude goes, first and foremost, to my parents, to whom this book is dedicated: my father, Ronald, the court of law and justice, and my mother, Florice, the court of equity and understanding. At least those were the roles they played convincingly before I was old enough to have them as my closest friends. My father's overriding concern for principle, right, and liberty certainly was responsible for my goal, acquired at the age of 10, to become a lawyer—a criminal lawyer to be specific—in order to make the world a more just place, and has shaped my intellectual agenda ever since. Though he was distressed when, in college, I was diverted to philosophy, his concern was short-lived for, as he later admitted, philosophy turned out to have been good for me.

I owe that diversion, which for ever changed my life, to Henry Veatch, whose every philosophy course I took when he taught at Northwestern, but who taught me as much outside of the classroom as within. Henry (I still have a hard time calling him anything other than Professor Veatch) devoted an incredible amount of time and energy to me, a lowly undergraduate, patiently enduring my endless questioning, not to mention my flirtations with political and philosophical views which to him could only have seemed like the follies of youth. It was Henry's impassioned Aristotelian-Thomist defense of natural law in both his classes and, especially, in his books, *Rational Man* and *For an Ontology of Morals*, that persuaded me to adopt what was then, in the heyday of analytic philosophy, considered to be an archaic position which time had passed well by. It was also from Henry I first learned that natural law and natural rights were distinct, for when I encountered the latter and rushed eagerly to share with him my discovery, my enthusiasm was met with a fatherly disapproval I would never forget. Imagine my surprise when, some years later, Henry presented an Aristotelean defense of natural rights in his book, *Human*

Rights: Fact or Fancy? I know Henry, now in his 80s, must be disappointed that my explication of natural law in Chapter 1 is not more Aristotelian. I can only plead that it is also not meant to be *anti*-Aristotelian and that my account of natural law is a minimalist one intended to sweep broadly and for a very limited purpose. My objective was to take no position on the merits of a more teleological natural law, given that it was unnecessary to do so to explain the conception of natural rights which I employ here.

I owe that initial discovery of natural rights to a classmate of mine, and future journalist, Jeanette DeWyze. Being unsuccessful, after repeated efforts, in interesting me in this and some other even more heretical notions, she introduced me to a very junior, very earnest classics professor at Northwestern named John Cody. John, who often traveled with a copy of Mises' *Human Action* so well-marked with marginalia that the original typescript was all but obliterated, undertook a nine-month private tutorial conducted at the student union and other such sordid places.

After this instruction had finally begun to sink in, I embarked from the safety of my native Chicago to the heated halls of Harvard Law School where such ideas were treated by my professors and fellow students alike with, well, shall we say, diffidence. As luck would have it, I soon met another first year (1L) student, John Hagel, who shared my deviance, and we quickly became fast friends and collaborators on a number of projects, culminating in our anthology, *Assessing the Criminal: Restitution, Retribution, and the Legal Process*. And it was John, now an influential business consultant and author, who took me to New York and introduced me to such intriguing intellectuals as Walter Grinder, Leonard Liggio, Joe Peden, Ronald Hamowy, Walter Block, Ralph Raico, Bill Evers, Mario Rizzo, Gerry O'Driscoll, Don Lavoie and, above all, the unforgetable Murray Rothbard.

I had first read Murray's writings in college and my attraction to a polycentric legal order of the sort I defend here in Chapters 12 through 14 was strongly reinforced by his book, *For New Liberty*. And it was the day I first met Murray and found myself alone with him and John in his study when I began to suspect the limitations of abstract principles of justice, an issue which I discuss in Chapter 5, and the need for *law*. For, as John and I peppered him with the classroom hypotheticals with which we were being tormented as 1Ls, we discovered that they were as baffling to him as to us. Murray also recommended me to the Institute for Humane Studies (IHS) for a summer fellowship that enabled me to write my earliest work on restitutive justice (discussed in Chapters 8, 10, and 11) in the summer between my first and second years of law school.

It was not too long after that when I met George Smith. For a time, we were something of friendly intellectual rivals. The first indication that we would be more than this came on the heals of a debate we had on the subject of procedural justice. I had commented somewhat critically on a paper by George at a conference held at Princeton. Sometime later, when I was already in practice as a criminal prosecutor in Chicago, the papers were published, along with George's reply. I remember quickly skimming through his response and feeling a bit uneasy. For he had refined his initial position in such a way as to make my argument seem less than entirely persuasive. A bit disconcerted, I tossed the volume aside, being too enthralled by my involvement with the criminal justice system to focus on such matters. When I picked it up again some years later, my initial instincts were confirmed. Without question, he had bested me in that debate and taught me an important lesson about the centrality of *legality*, as distinct from *justice*, in the structure of liberty. It was not to be my last lesson from George.

My instruction continued when, for many years, George and I both taught in the summer seminars organized by the Institute for Humane Studies. Every summer, I would audit his lectures which were fascinating from the beginning and which became increasingly so over time. Though trained in philosophy at Arizona State, George had abandoned his formal schooling to pursue a decade-long course of independent study, a large measure of which was devoted to the long-forgotten classical natural rights theorists. It was his synthesis of their arguments that caused my thinking to take the direction reflected in this book, most importantly in Chapter 1, but also in the argument on the inalienability of certain rights which is presented in Chapter 4. In more ways than I can know or acknowledge, this book has been influenced by George's distillation of the classical approach to natural rights as well as his own theories of justice. I am and will forever be deeply indebted to him.

Then there are two men who influenced me greatly solely through their writings, as will be apparent throughout this book: F. A. Hayek and Lon L. Fuller. I cannot claim to have known either man. While I was once at a conference with Hayek, I confined my contact with him to taking his picture from the safety of an adjacent table. With Fuller, I was little younger and a bit more daring. Long after his retirement, and shortly before his death, he gave a lecture in a law school class I took on law and religion. I called him up afterwards, and he invited me to his house, where we shared an afternoon tea in his parlor. I wish I could remember what we discussed, but the image of that bright sunny afternoon has always remained with me.

So many people have contributed importantly to this work during its long gestation by reading various portions or commenting on oral presentations of these ideas that I will surely overlook someone. Those who have helpfully marked up portions of previous incarnations include Eric Blumenson, David Friedman, Ellen Paul, Michael Zuckert, and my colleagues Ron Cass and David Lyons. I benefited greatly from reactions I received during faculty workshops at the University of Toronto, the Quinnipiac College School of Law, Case Western Reserve School of Law, Bowling Green State University, Institute Euro '92 in Paris, and the Boston University School of Law, as well as during the many years of lecturing on this subject at IHS summer seminars. For the price of a cappuccino, Russell Hardin gave me invaluable advice about seeking a publisher.

Special thanks are due Tom Palmer, for his enormous assistance on the first and last chapters, and to David Schmidtz and Jeremy Shearmur, who read an entire early version and made painstaking critical comments on nearly every page. Many serious errors were avoided due to them and this book was substantially rewritten with their comments in mind.

Lastly, there is my wife Beth. I would not be where I am today without her steadfast support and her ability to temper my more erratic and misguided enthusiasms and instincts. She is my emotional anchor who never fails to remind me of what is truly important. By sharing my life, she makes my happiness possible. And she chose to be the full-time mother of our wonderful, now-teenage children, Laura and Gary, who I hope one day will be able both to appreciate this book and to live in a freer world.

Then there are the institutions that made this book possible and the individuals who administered them. As should already be apparent, a singular role has been played by the Institute for Humane Studies, especially under the leadership of John Blundell, but beginning even before that with the decision by Davis Keeler to award me that summer research grant while I was still in law school and a residential fellowship for the summer after I took the bar exam. Walter Grinder's remarkable confidence in a then-young county prosecutor led him to invite me to lecture in the IHS summer seminar program, an experience that not only impelled me to develop the ideas in this book, but also to leave practice and seek an academic position. Leonard Liggio assisted me in obtaining the grants that led to the first version of this book but, more important, both Leonard and Walter have always been the warmest and most encouraging of friends.

In 1989, Dean Robert Bennett of the Northwestern University School of Law graciously allowed me to set up shop in its comfortable facilities for the sabbatical year that produced the first version of this work. Before that, in 1981, Richard Epstein, whose example of scholarly production, diversity of subject interests, and independence of mind I have tried (alas) unsuccessfully to emulate, helped facilitate a research fellowship at the University of Chicago Law School where I first began reading and writing about the role of consent in contractual obligation.

My editors at Oxford University Press, Dominic Byatt and Sophie Ahmad have been, from the first contact and to the end, incredibly enthusiastic and cooperative. They both believed in this project and worked diligently to bring it to fruition.

Finally there are, ah yes, the grants. I received generous support from the Humane Studies Foundation and the Earhart Foundation whose President, David Kennedy, has always been both supportive and patient as this project developed at a glacial pace. And I have also been well-supported by my home institutions, the Illinois Institute of Technology, Chicago-Kent College of Law, where, until 1993, I was a Norman and Edna Freehling Scholar, and since then, by the Boston University School of Law. Lew Collins, my dean at Kent, and Ron Cass, my current dean, have given me far more than financial support. They both made it clear that I could pursue whatever academic direction my interests might lead—provided I did first-rate work—and encouraged a departmental environment within which creative work was possible. But the generous research money they made available came in more than a little handy and I am grateful for it.

To all of these people, and the countless other friends and colleagues I could not name here, I hope that you will consider this book to be a small return on your many investments in me.

Boston, 1997   Randy Barnett

CONTENTS

ONE

Introduction: Liberty vs. License

Human art in order to produce certain effects, must conform to the principles and laws, which the Almighty Creator has established in the natural world. . . . And every builder should well understand the best position of firmness and strength, when he is about to erect an edifice. For he, who attempts these things, on other principles, than those of nature, attempts to make a new world; and his aim will prove absurd and his labour lost. No more can mankind be conducted to happiness; or civil societies united, and enjoy peace and prosperity, without observing the moral principles and connections, which the Almighty Creator has established for the government of the moral world.[1]

1. The Structure of Liberty

EVERYONE, or nearly so, claims to favor liberty. Yet everyone, even the most "libertarian," also favors constraining people's conduct. One ought not be free to murder, rape, or rob another, for example. Thus nearly everyone carries within them a tension between freedom and constraint.[2] How can this be? Some explain this tension by using the distinction between liberty and license—a distinction commonly made by natural rights theorists. For

[1] Elizur Goodrich, "The Principles of Civil Union and Happiness Considered and Recommended," in Ellis Sandoz, (ed.), *Political Sermons of the American Founding: 1730–1805* (Indianapolis: Liberty Press, 1991), pp. 914–15.

[2] Duncan Kennedy has referred to this as the "fundamental contradiction" of liberalism, although it is not clear how anyone who favors liberty can escape it. See Duncan Kennedy, 'The Structure of Blackstone's Commentaries,' *Buffalo Law Review*, vol. 28 (1979), p. 211: "[I]ndividual freedom is at the same time dependent on and incompatible with the communal coercive action that is necessary to achieve it." See also Joseph W. Singer, "The Legal Rights Debate in Analytical Jurisprudence from Bentham to Hohfeld," *Wisconsin Law Review*, vol. 1982 (1982), p. 980: "Liberalism is founded upon "the contradiction . . . between the principle that individuals may legitimately act in their own interest to increase their wealth, power, and prestige at the expense of others and the principle that they have a duty to look out for others and to refrain from acts that hurt them."

example, in describing the "state of nature" or world without government, John Locke wrote, "though this be a *State of Liberty*, yet it is *not a State of License*."[3] By liberty is meant those freedoms which people ought to have. License refers to those freedoms which people ought not to have and thus those freedoms which are properly constrained. But this distinction merely restates the tension, it does not explain or justify it. And it surely does not tell us where to draw the line.

In this book, I will explain that liberty has a structure and this structure implies both freedom and constraint of actions. The best analogy is to a building. I used to regularly eat lunch in the Sears Tower in Chicago. Every day I would see thousands of persons, enough to populate a small town, moving in an apparently chaotic or "disorderly" fashion throughout the building. They were there for countless purposes and were headed for innumerable destinations: shops, restaurants, offices, the observation "skydeck" from which on a clear day they could view four states. Yet the freedom they exercised was structured by the tower itself, by its lobbies, its corridors, its stairways, its escalators, its elevators. Imagine that the tower was invisible and you could simply view the inhabitants, suspended in space. To explain their movements you would have to hypothesize the existence of a tower with floors, walls, elevators, and stairs, in much the same way as the movement of some visible stars leads astronomers to hypothesize the existence of an invisible collapsed "twin" star or "black hole" which is exerting a gravitational influence on the visible star.

The structure of Sears Tower surely constrains the behavior or "freedom" of its occupants. You cannot, for example, take a single elevator directly from the 20th floor to the 60th floor. Instead you need to change elevators on the 34th floor. The skydeck is only accessible to the public via an elevator that originates in the basement. Yet the structure also permits thousands of persons on a daily basis to pursue their disparate purposes for entering the building. Were it not for the structure provided by the tower the occupants on all 100 floors on any given day could probably not fit within the square block of space on which the tower rests. Even if they could all be jammed into that space, they could not accomplish their purposes or, for that matter, any useful ends. Indeed, though it might never have been built, now that it exists the structure is essential to maintaining the very lives of those within. Imagine being able to push a button and make the structure of the building instantly vanish. Thousands of persons would plunge to their deaths.

Like a building, every society has a structure that, by constraining the actions of its members, permits them at the same time to act to accomplish their ends. Without any such structure, chaos would reign and the current population could not be sustained. But not all "social structures" are the same. Like poorly designed buildings, some impose constraints on action that inhibit rather than facilitate the ability of persons to survive or flourish.

---

[3] John Locke, *Two Treatises of Government* (1690), ed. Peter Laslett (Cambridge, Mentor, rev. edn. 1963), p. 311.

Others are better able to tailor the nature of these constraints to facilitate their inhabitants' pursuit of happiness.

This book is about the principles which provide the structure of liberty. These principles are clustered under the concepts of *justice* and *the rule of law*. Just as the structure of a building solves certain architectural and engineering problems to enable its occupants to pursue their respective purposes, certain principles of justice and the rule of law provide a structure that enables people to pursue happiness by handling the serious and pervasive social problems of knowledge, interest, and power. No society can exist unless it handles these problems to some degree, and the better these problems are handled, the better able are the people who comprise it to pursue happiness, peace, and prosperity.

The structure of this book, then, is straightforward. I will describe in some detail the fundamental problems of knowledge (Part I), interest (Part II), and power (Part III) and how solving these problems requires a *liberty* that is structured by justice—defined by certain rights I shall specify—and the formal procedures associated with rule of law. The precise contours of the rights and procedures that structure liberty, and which distinguish liberty from license, will evolve as the discussion of these various problems unfolds. Then, in Part IV, I will apply this analysis to certain arguments that have been made against relying on these sorts of rights or in favor of other conceptions of justice that conflict with these rights.

While this book is about how a liberty that is structured by certain rights and procedures is needed to handle the problems of knowledge, interest, and power, it is not about the philosophical nature of these rights. Nor do I attempt to survey all the arguments, philosophical or otherwise, that can be offered on their behalf. Nevertheless, in the balance of this introduction I shall briefly detour into more philosophical terrain so as not to be misunderstood by those who care about such matters. Doing so has the added advantage of putting the method of analysis employed here in historical context, for this method has a long and distinguished pedigree which it would be wrong to ignore.

Still, you need not agree with how I shall characterize these rights to accept my thesis that they are necessary to handle the pervasive social problems of knowledge, interest, and power. For those who care more about *why* solving these problems makes adherence to certain "principles and laws"[4] necessary for "mankind to be conducted to happiness; or . . . enjoy peace and prosperity,"[5] than about the philosophical status of this claim, that account begins at Chapter 2.

---

[4] Goodrich, "Principles of Civil Union," p. 914 .   [5] Ibid.

2. The Natural Law Method of Analysis

Let us return to John Locke's distinction between liberty and license in a world without government. "The *State of Nature*," Locke asserted, "has a Law of Nature to govern it, which obliges every one: And Reason, which is that Law, teaches all Mankind, who will but consult it, that being all equal and independent, no one ought to harm another in his Life, Health, Liberty, or Possessions."[6] According to Locke and the other "classical liberals" of his era, even when individuals do not have a common government—say, on the high seas, in the woods of America, or between princes of sovereign states—their relationships ought to be structured by principles which they referred to as the Law of Nature or natural law.[7] These natural law principles, enacted by no legislature, were discernible by reason.

The idea of natural law is mysterious to us today.[8] We are accustomed to thinking of law as the command of the legislature, or perhaps the command of a government official or judge, which is enforced by a government. A natural law, whatever that might be, that was not incorporated into a command enforceable by government seems hardly worth the paper it isn't written on. How can there be a law in any meaningful sense in the absence of government recognition and enforcement?

But when we think of the disciplines of engineering or architecture, the idea of a natural law is not so mysterious. For example, engineers reason that, *given* the amount of force that gravity exerts on a building, *if* we want a building that will enable persons to live or work inside it, *then* we need to provide a foundation, walls, and roof of a certain strength. The principles of engineering, though formulated by human beings, are not a product of their will. These principles must come to grips with the nature of human beings and the world in which human beings live, and they operate whether or not they are recognized or enforced by any government. And though they are never perfectly precise and are always subject to incremental improvements and sometimes even breakthroughs, they are far from arbitrary, and we violate them at our peril.

The disciplines of engineering and architecture are normative in that, unlike the physical sciences on which they may be based in part, they instruct us on how we *ought* to act, given the nature of the human beings and the world in

---

[6] Locke, *Two Treatises*, p. 311.

[7] See Richard Tuck, *Natural Rights Theories: Their Origin and Development* (Cambridge: Cambridge University Press, 1979); and Stephen Buckle, *Natural Law and the Theory of Property* (Oxford: Oxford University Press, 1991).

[8] Though less so than at any time in the past several decades. See e.g. Robert P. George (ed.), *Natural Law Theories: Contemporary Essays* (Oxford: Oxford University Press, 1992); "Natural Law Symposium," *Cleveland State Law Review*, vol. 38 (1990), p. 1; "Symposium: Perspectives on Natural Law", *Cincinnati Law Review*, vol. 61 (1992), pp. 1–222 "Symposium on Natural Law", *S. Cal. Interdisciplinary Law Journal*", vol. 3 (1995), p. 455.

which they live, and the purpose at hand. Nor need one be an engineer or an architect to formulate similar "natural law" normative principles. For example, the existence of gravity and the nature of the human body leads to the following natural law injunction for human action: *given* that gravity will cause us to fall rapidly and that our bodies will not withstand the fall, *if* we want to live and be happy, *then* we had better not jump off tall buildings.

Could it be that the "great first principles of the social compact" are natural "laws" of this type? *If* we want persons to be able to pursue happiness while living in society with each other, *then* they had best adopt and respect a social structure that reflects these principles. In the words of the influential seventeenth-century natural law theorist Hugo Grotius, the "maintenance of the social order, which we have roughly sketched, and which is consonant with human intelligence, is the source of law."[9] According to this way of thinking, "[t]he basic requirements of an organized social life are the basic principles of the natural law."[10]

True, any such natural law principles may be more difficult to discern and consequently more controversial than the principles of engineering or architecture. Partly this is true because human beings are so amazingly complex and, unlike the materials from which buildings are constructed, are self-directed in pursuit of their own purposes. But the mere existence of controversy does not render such principles nonexistent. Nor does the fact that we cannot see, hear, taste, or touch them. After all, we cannot see, hear, taste, or touch the principles of engineering or architecture either. Both sets of principles or "laws" are humanly constructed concepts used to explain and predict the world in which we live.

The idea that the world, including worldly governments, is governed by laws or principles that dictate how society ought to be structured, in the very same way that such natural laws dictate how buildings ought to be built or how crops ought to be planted, was well-accepted by Americans at the founding of the United States.[11] Consider this passage from a sermon delivered by Pastor Elizur Goodrich (1734–97) to the governor and general assembly of Connecticut on the eve of the Constitutional Convention, a portion of which headed this chapter:

[9] Hugo Grotius, *De Jure Belli ac Pacis Libri Tres*, Prol. 8 (Oxford: Clarendon Press, 1925; trans. Francis W. Kelsey), p. 12. The passage continues: "To this sphere of law belong the abstaining from that which is another's, the restoration to another of anything of his which we may have, together with any gain which we may have received from it; the obligation to fulfil promises, the making good of a loss incurred through our fault, and the inflicting of penalties upon men according to their deserts." Ibid. at 12–13.

[10] Buckle, *Natural Law*, p. 19.

[11] See Philip A. Hamburger, "Natural Rights, Natural Law, and American Constitutions," *Yale Law Journal*, vol. 102 (1993), p. 907. Although Hamburger presents a remarkably sensitive analysis of the evidence concerning the founding generation's understanding of natural law and natural rights with which I am in general agreement, I do not share his contention—which is beyond the scope of this book—that this generation thought natural rights were not a source of legal claims to be made in a court.

The principles of society are the laws, which Almighty God has established in the moral world, and made necessary to be observed by mankind; in order to promote their true happiness, in their transactions and intercourse. These laws may be considered as principles, in respect of their fixedness and operation, and as maxims, since by the knowledge of them, we discover the rules of conduct, which direct mankind to the highest perfection, and supreme happiness of their nature. *They are as fixed and unchangeable as the laws which operate in the natural world.*

Human art *in order to produce certain effects*, must conform to the principles and laws, which the Almighty Creator has established in the natural world.[12]

The types of "principles and laws" in the "natural world" that Goodrich had in mind are those which govern agriculture, engineering, and architecture.

He who neglects the cultivation of his field, and the proper time of sowing, may not expect a harvest. He, who would assist mankind in raising weights, and overcoming obstacles, depends on certain rules, derived from the knowledge of mechanical principles applied to the construction of machines, in order to give the most useful effect to the smallest force: And every builder should well understand the best position of firmness and strength, when he is about to erect an edifice. For he, who attempts these things, on other principles, than those of nature, *attempts to make a new world*; and his aim will prove absurd and his labour lost.[13]

The "principles of society" are of the same order as these other natural laws: "No more can mankind be conducted to happiness; or civil societies united, and enjoy peace and prosperity, without observing the moral principles and connections, which the Almighty Creator has established for the government of the moral world."[14]

Notice that, although Goodrich identifies God as the original source of the laws that govern in the moral world, so too does he identify God as the source of the laws that govern agriculture, engineering, and architecture. With both types of principles and laws, once established by a divine power they become part of the world in which we find ourselves and are discoverable by human reason. Thus today one can no more disparage the idea of natural law (or natural rights) because eighteenth-century thinkers attributed their origin to a divine power than one can disparage the laws of physics because eighteenth-century scientists believed that such laws were also established by God.

Whatever the source of natural order on which these moral principles or laws are based—however they came to be inscribed in the world in which we live—Goodrich's argument is that these principles must be respected if we are to achieve the end of happiness, peace, and prosperity. As Hugo Grotius wrote: "What we have been saying [about natural law] would have a degree of validity even if we were to concede what cannot be conceded without the utmost wickedness, that there is no God, or that the affairs of men are of no concern to Him."[15] Richard Tuck characterizes this passage to mean: "Given the nat-

---

[12] Goodrich, "Principles of Civil Union," p. 914 (emphases added).
[13] Ibid. at 914–15 (emphasis added).   [14] Ibid. at 915.
[15] Grotius, *De Jure Belli*, Prol. 11, p. 13. Of this passage Stephen Buckle writes: "This brief remark, by affirming the possibility of at least a partially secularized political

ural facts about men, the laws of nature followed by (allegedly) strict entailment without any mediating premises about God's will (though his will might still be an explanation of those natural facts.)"[16]

When one mentions "natural law" some ask, "where are these natural laws?" Are they "out there" somewhere? Yet we do not speak of the humanly-developed principles of engineering or agriculture as being "out there," though these principles must respected if bridges are to stand and crops to grow. The "principles of society" spoken of by Goodrich are of the same status. They must be respected if people are to pursue happiness, peace, and prosperity while living in society with one another.

This natural law account of moral "principles of society" assumes, of course, that "happiness . . . peace and prosperity" are appropriate ends. While the essence or nature of happiness, peace and prosperity may properly be controversial, should anyone question the assumption that these are desirable ends to be pursued, additional arguments will need to be presented. Every intellectual discipline, however, presupposes a commitment by those within it to certain shared ambitions or problems thought by all members of the discipline to be worthy of solution.[17] As H. L. A. Hart wrote of the human desire for survival: "We are committed to it as something presupposed by the terms of our discussion. . . ."[18] Surely, the normative disciplines of agriculture, engineering, and architecture are also based on the assumption that human existence and happiness are worthwhile.

The normative force of natural law can therefore be seen as the imperative of "if–then." *If* you want to achieve *Y, then* you ought to do *Z.* If you want to live and be happy, then you ought not jump off tall buildings or drink poison. *If* you want to facilitate the pursuit of happiness by those living in society with others, *then* you ought to adhere to certain basic principles. Later in this chapter, I shall return to the issue of whether it is appropriate to characterize as *moral* the normative conclusions reached by a "hypothetical imperative" type of natural law reasoning.

In describing natural law as based on "if–then" reasoning, however, I have omitted one crucial and problematic dimension of this approach. As was seen above, the existence of gravity provides a prefatory "given" before the if–then claim: *given* that gravity will cause us to fall rapidly, *if* we want to live and be

---

theory, exercised a powerful influence on subsequent political thought. In an age of intense political conflict arising from or reflected in religious differences, it also offered the prospect of peace despite religious differences." Buckle, *Natural Law*, p. 23.

[16] Tuck, *Natural Rights Theories*, pp. 76–7.

[17] For a discussion of the nature of intellectual disciplines, see Stephen Toulmin, *Human Understanding* (Princeton, NJ: Princeton University Press, 1972). There he explains that "the existence and unity of an intellectual discipline, regarded as a specific 'historical entity', reflects the continuity imposed on its problems by the development of its intellectual ideals and ambitions." Ibid. at 155.

[18] H. L. A. Hart, *The Concept of Law* (Oxford: Oxford University Press, 1961), p. 188.

happy, *then* we had better not jump off tall buildings.[19] What distinguishes natural law reasoning from other types of if–then reasoning is the particular "given" on which it is based: the nature both of human beings and of the world in which they live. So the fuller argument is: "*Given* that the nature of human beings and the world in which they live is *X*, *if* we want to achieve *Y*, *then* we ought to do *Z*." This adds yet another layer of inquiry and controversy. Do human beings have a "nature"? If so, what is it and how does that nature suggest that, if we want to achieve *Y*, then we ought to do *Z*?

Some today may dispute the idea that human nature is "innate" or natural and insist that human nature is "socially constructed" by which is meant the product of complex interaction with others. For example, what it means to be *a man* or *a woman* may not be entirely biological, but rooted also in the expectations that are imbued in each of us by others from the earliest ages. While there may be much truth to this observation, it misunderstands the claim being made by natural law theorists in two ways.

First, unless one posits that this process of social construction can be willfully manipulated or altered, then the fact that human nature is a product of social processes, as opposed to innate natural qualities, is as immaterial to discerning principles of human action as the belief of classical thinkers that natural law was of divine origin. Even were processes of social construction the source of what is thought of as human nature, if these processes cannot freely be altered in any desired manner, human nature would still affect the means by which we must accomplish our ends.

Some who believe that human nature is a product of social construction may indeed think that it may be deliberately altered or manipulated. That is, they believe that if a particular social construction of human nature is X and we prefer it to be Y, we can change social processes to accomplish this objective. But while it seems clear that some widespread beliefs or prejudices can, with great effort, be changed, the types of human characteristics on which natural law reasoning is or ought to be based cannot be so affected. For example, as I explain in Chapter 2, persons have access to personal and local knowledge and are pervasively ignorant of the personal and local knowledge of others. As I discuss in Chapter 7, people also have a tendency to prefer their own interests and those for whom they have affection to the interests of those who are remote from them. And in Chapter 2 we shall see how and why the physical resources that people need to use in their pursuit of happiness are subjectively scarce. These and other facts of human nature and the nature of the world in which we live that I shall discuss in this book greatly influence

---

[19] There are of course many "givens" implicit in this claim. For example, given the fragility of the human body, it is not the fall that kills but the sudden stop at the end. This simply illustrates the complexity of if–then claims. And this complexity is all the more serious when discussing the structure of liberty. One of the purposes of this book is simply to sort out some of the myriad "givens" that have led to particular conclusions about the nature of this structure.

the principles that order society and, for better or worse, cannot be changed. They can only be dealt with.

Second, some who speak of social construction in this context are objecting to basing claims simply on an alleged natural tendency of persons to act in certain ways. They deny that such behavioral tendencies are "natural" and therefore inevitable or unalterable, much less good. If natural law is based on how human beings "naturally" or normally act, then it is based on a fallacy, for human behavior, they argue, is as much a product of social attitudes and practices as it is of any "innate" human nature. Yet this response to natural law reasoning is based on a misunderstanding of natural law reasoning.

The concept of "human nature" that is the basis of natural law is not limited to how persons "naturally," normally, or instinctively behave. Natural tendencies play only a very small a role in such reasoning, though passages from some writings on natural law can sometimes suggest otherwise. Indeed, John Locke explicitly denied that natural inclinations were the same as natural laws. He rejected the view of those who "seek the principles of moral action and a rule to live by in men's appetites and natural instincts rather than in the binding force of a law, just as if that was morally best which most people desired."[20]

Though classical natural law reasoning is not based on the natural instincts of people, to the extent that such instincts exist and cannot be changed, whether or not such instincts are the product of social construction, they may very well influence what human laws can and cannot accomplish. For example, if humans instinctively do crave survival, a legal system that required tremendous personal sacrifice under ordinary circumstances is likely to be resisted by many. Or because human beings normally try to overcome obstacles put in the way of their chosen projects, the prohibition of certain pleasurable activities is likely to lead to an illegal or black-market to supply these activities and this illegal market, in turn, will likely lead to corruption of law enforcement. Any legal system that ignored these likely human reactions to certain laws will reap unfortunate consequences.

The nature of human beings and the world in which they live that yields "principles of society," goes far beyond whatever natural instincts people may have. In addition to their psychological makeup, this nature includes the physical needs and abilities of human beings and the physical properties of the world in which humans must live. The rest of this book is devoted to describing in some detail, yet still only superficially, these features of people

---

[20] John Locke, *Essays on the Law of Nature*, essay VIII (Oxford: Clarendon Press, 1952; ed. W. von Leyden), p. 213. Although Grotius thought, as did Aquinas and unlike Locke, that human inclinations tended to the good, like Locke he too thought that "[t]he law of nature has its beginnings in instinctive nature, but it is certainly not a mere cloak of rectitude over our instincts. Rather reason is our highest characteristic good, and so the law of nature must in some way reflect our rational nature. . . . The law of nature is, then, the law of our nature, and this of rational nature: it is not merely the transformation of instincts into laws." Buckle, *Natural Law*, p. 25.

and the world and drawing implications therefrom. True, the natural law mode of analysis does require us to generalize about these features of social life—to abstract from the particulars, and I shall do so here. And though this process is very much one of "construction," it is no more nor less so than any other theoretical effort. All theories are constructed, if by constructed is meant that they are the fallible product of human thought and are not somehow "out there" written in the stars.[21]

None of this is simple or easy. To the contrary, natural law reasoning is highly contestable because it depends on what we think are the "facts of human life," both the makeup of human beings and the world in which they live, and what generalizations we choose to make from these facts. Having made these factual generalizations (X), it then depends upon a claim that given X, if you want to accomplish Y, then you must do Z. Each step of this analysis is subject to error and dispute. But it is the nature of human life that we must act (this is one of those pesky generalizations) and, given this imperative, we must decide how to act and we ought to act as best we can. Adopting a natural law mode of reasoning does not guarantee that we will act wisely, but it does I think point in the direction of wisdom. It tells us what we should be looking for. As important, a proper theory of natural law explains what we usually do look for and why.

Though I have drawn a parallel between natural laws in engineering and those which concern the governance of society, this version of natural law does not succumb to H. L. A. Hart's criticism that some natural law proponents confuse two different uses of the term law: so-called natural laws that can be "broken" by human beings and physical laws that cannot. According to Hart, though human beings can disobey so-called natural laws,

[i]f the stars behave in ways contrary to the scientific laws which purport to describe their regular movements, these are not broken but they lose their title to be called 'laws' and must be reformulated. . . . So on this view, belief in Natural Law is reducible to a very simple fallacy: a failure to perceive the very different senses which those law-impregnated words can bear.[22]

In the conception of natural law I have sketched here, "scientific" laws influence the formation of "natural law" principles of society in the same way they bear on the normative principles of agriculture, architecture, and engineering. *Given* facts about human nature and the nature of the world—including, but not limited to, such "scientific" laws as the law of gravity–(X), *if* you want to accomplish certain ends (Y), *then* you should do (Z). While a human actor cannot "break" the law of gravity or the natural law principles that apply to human social interaction in the sense of *repealing* them, one pays a price for violating them none the less.

---

[21] If by "constructed" is meant consciously devised as a whole, then this is rarely true of human theories. Most theories evolve with only incremental refinements contributed by individual theorists. See Toulmin, *Human Understanding*.

[22] Hart, *Concept of Law*, p. 183.

Unsurprisingly then, while Hart rejects the identification of natural law with physical laws, he endorses a conception of natural law whose analytic structure is much the same as the natural law theories I have cited above:

Reflection on some very obvious generalizations—indeed truisms—concerning human nature and the world in which men live, show that as long as these hold good, there are certain rules of conduct which any social organization must contain if it is to be viable. . . . Such universally recognized principles of conduct which have a basis in elementary truths concerning human beings, their natural environment, and aims, may be considered the *minimum content* of Natural Law, in contrast with the more grandiose and more challengeable constructions which have often been proffered under that name.[23]

Hart takes as "given" five contingent facts about "human nature and the world in which men live"[24]: (*a*) human vulnerability, (*b*) approximate equality, (*c*) limited altruism, (*d*) limited resources and (*e*) limited understanding and strength of will.[25] He then assumes, on the basis of observation, the additional contingent fact that most people desire to survive: "survival has . . . a special status in relation to human conduct and in our thought about it, which parallels the prominence and the necessity ascribed to it in orthodox formulations of Natural Law."[26]

Hart concludes that, *given* these five factual conditions, *if* persons desire to survive, *then* their legal systems ought to have such features as rules that "restrict the use of violence in killing or inflicting bodily harm;"[27] "a system of mutual forbearances and compromises;"[28] "some minimal form of the institution of property (though not necessarily individual property), and the distinctive kind of rule which requires respect for it;"[29] rules "that enable individuals to create obligations and to vary their incidence;"[30] and the imposition of sanctions by an "organization for the coercion of those who would . . . try to obtain the advantages of the system without submitting to its obligations."[31]

A natural law method of analysis need not be limited to the facts Hart takes as given, nor to the limited objective of survival. Nevertheless, for a natural law method of analysis to yield answers to the question of how human beings are to survive, pursue happiness, peace, and prosperity while living in society with others, it must be based on some such generalized features of human beings and the world that are common to all persons who are interacting with one another.

Hart's approach and even his list is strikingly similar to that offered by eighteenth-century theorist David Hume, for whom certain principles of justice

are intended as a remedy to some inconveniences, which proceed from the concurrence of certain *qualities* of the human mind with the *situation* of external objects. The qualities of the mind are *selfishness* and *limited generosity*: And the

---

[23] Ibid. 188–9.   [24] Ibid. 188.   [25] Ibid. 190–3.   [26] Ibid. 188.
[27] Ibid. 190.   [28] Ibid. 191.   [29] Ibid. 192.   [30] Ibid.
[31] Ibid. 193.

situation of external objects is their *easy change*, join'd to their *scarcity* in comparison with the wants and desires of men.[32]

Hume conceded that precepts of justice are "artificial" in the sense that they are the product of human invention. Nevertheless he insisted that: "Tho' the rules of justice be *artificial*, they are not *arbitrary*. Nor is the expression improper to call them *Laws of Nature*; if by natural we understand what is common to any species, or even if we confine it to mean what is inseparable from the species."[33] Although modern philosophers question Hume's sincerity in making this claim, Stephen Buckle has argued both that Hume ardently insisted he was staying within the natural law tradition and that he was correct to so insist.[34] Buckle concludes that:

Hume's aim is not to replace natural law, but to complete it, by calling on the powerful resources of the new experimental philosophy. He aims to ground moral obligations firmly in the soil of human nature itself, in the natural workings of the human mind, and thereby fulfil the bold ambitions of the theory of natural law.[35]

In this book, I shall try to avoid the "grandiose" while presenting a somewhat more ambitious elaboration of Hart's "core of good sense"[36] yielded by this type of natural law reasoning. Most of my analysis will consist of evaluating the nature of the human condition (the "given") in considerably more detail than Hart's simple "truisms" to which he devotes a scant six pages. And I shall also take as the shared objective of human social interaction (the "if") not only survival, but also the pursuit of happiness, peace, and prosperity.[37] What then does natural law reasoning tell us about the principles by which society should be organized?

3. Natural Law Ethics vs. Natural Rights

As I have sketched it here, natural law describes a *method of analysis* of the following type: "*Given* that the nature of human beings and the world in which they live is *X*, *if* we want to achieve *Y*, *then* we ought to do *Z*." The subject of any particular natural law analysis fills in the "if." When the subject is agriculture, the "if" might be "if we want to raise crops so that human beings may eat." When the subject is engineering the "if" might be "if we want to build a bridge so that human beings may cross a river." By the same token, the study of *ethics* may be conceived as an inquiry into the question of "given the nature of human beings and the world in which they live (*X*), *if a person wants to live*

---

[32] David Hume, *A Treatise Concerning Human Nature*, 2nd edn. (Oxford: Clarendon Press, 1978).
[33] Ibid. 484. [34] See Buckle, *Natural Law*, p. 243–98.
[35] Ibid. 298. [36] Ibid. 194.
[37] Though I do not assume that these are the only objectives of social interaction.

a good life (*Y*), then he or she ought to do *Z*." Whether we attempt to feed our-selves, build bridges, or live a good life is a matter of choice (though human nature may impel a certain choice[38]). How we go about making our attempts and whether they succeed or fail will be constrained by natural law.

Thus, applying a natural law method of analysis to the ethical question of how people ought to live their lives would begin with an inquiry into the nature of a "good life," resting this judgment, at least in part, on human nature. Then, given a conception of the good life, a "natural law ethics" could potentially address nearly every choice a person confronts. Should I go to school? Which one? What should I study and how hard? Should I use drugs? With whom should I have sex? Each one of these ethical questions can poten-tially be addressed by the natural law method of "given–if–then" analysis.

Does a natural law approach to ethics also entail that human law coercively mandate every ethical or moral action recommended by a natural law analysis and punish every immoral or unethical act? Do the constraints on action rec-ommended by a natural law ethics imply coercively imposed legal constraints on virtue and vice? Because they think the answers to these questions are yes, some associate a commitment to natural law reasoning about virtue and vice with authoritarian political theory. Yet even the father of modern natural law analysis, Thomas Aquinas, did not hold to so conservative a view. In answer to the question, "Whether human law prescribes acts of all the virtues," he wrote:

[H]uman law does not prescribe concerning all the acts of every virtue, but only in regard to those that can be ordered to the common good—either immediately, as when certain things are done directly for the common good, or mediately, as when a lawgiver prescribes certain things pertaining to good order, by which the citizens are directed in the upholding of the common good of *justice and peace*.[39]

And, after asking "whether it pertains to human law to repress all vices," he answered:

Now human law is framed for a number of human beings, the majority of which are not perfect in virtue. Therefore human laws do not forbid all vices, from which the virtuous abstain, but only the more grievous vices, from which it is possible for the majority to abstain, and chiefly those that are to the *hurt of others, without the prohibition of which human society could not be maintained*; thus human law prohibits murder, theft and the like.[40]

In this manner, Aquinas anticipated a distinction that later came to be made by classical liberal political theorists. While a natural law analysis could be

---

[38] Some Aristoteleans and Thomists contend that it is part of man's nature to pursue the good and I take no stance here on this issue. See e.g., Thomas Aquinas, *Summa Theologica*, I–II, Q. 94 A. 2; in Robert Hutchins (ed.), *Great Books of the Western World*, vol. xx (Chicago: Encyclopædia Britannica, 1952), p. 222*b* ("[I]n man there is an incli-nation to good in accordance with the nature which he has in common with all sub-stances; that is, every substance seeks the preservation of its own being, according to its nature.").

[39] Ibid. 232*b* (emphasis added). [40] Ibid. 232*a* (emphasis added).

applied to a variety of questions, including the question of *how human beings ought to act* (i.e. vice and virtue), the question of *how society ought to be structured* is a separate and quite distinct inquiry. Given the various problems that arise when humans live and act in society with others, the classical liberal answer to the latter question[41] was that each person needed a "space" over which he or she has sole jurisdiction or *liberty* to act and within which no one else may rightfully interfere. The concepts defining this "liberty" or moral space came to be known as *natural rights*.

Unlike a natural law ethics, then, natural rights do not proscribe how rights-holders ought to act towards others. Rather they describe how others ought to act towards rights-holders. As explained by seventeenth-century natural rights theorist Dudley Digges:

If we looke back to the law of Nature, we shall finde that the people would have had a clearer and most distinct notion of it, if common use of calling it *Law* had not helped to confound their understanding, when it ought to have been named the *Right* of nature; for *Right* and *Law* differ as much as Liberty and Bonds: *Jus*, or right not laying any obligation, but signifying, we may equally choose to doe or not to doe without fault, whereas *Lex* or law determines us either to a particular performance by way of command, or a particular abstinence by way of prohibition; and therefore *jus natural*, all the right of nature, which now we can innocently make use of, is that freedome, not which any law gives us, but which no law takes away, and lawes are the severall restraints and limitations of native liberty.[42]

Thus it is a mistake, and an all-too-common one, to equate natural law with natural rights. Natural law is a broader term referring to the "given–if–then" *method* of evaluating choices based on the "given" of human nature and the nature of the world. A natural law approach to *ethics* uses a "given–if–then" analysis to evaluate the propriety of any human action. In contrast, a natural *rights* analysis uses a natural law "given–if–then" methodology to identify the *liberty* or space within which persons ought to be free to make their own choices. It seeks to determine the appropriate social structure within which people ought to be free to do as they please.

According to this distinction, when discussing moral virtues and vices—or the problem of distinguishing *good* from *bad* behavior—the imperative for which is supposedly based on human nature, natural law *ethics* is the appropriate term (though such principles are sometimes referred to simply as natural law). When discussing the contours of the moral jurisdiction defined by principles of justice—or the problem of distinguishing *right* from *wrong* behavior—which is supposedly based on the nature of human beings and the world in which they live, the appropriate term would be *natural rights*. Whereas natural law ethics provides guidance for our actions, natural rights define a moral

[41] I am not suggesting that this was Aquinas' answer.
[42] Dudley Digges, *The Unlawfulness of Subjects, Taking up Armes against their Soveraigne* (n.p., 1644), sig. B3v., quoted in Tuck, *Natural Rights Theories*, pp. 102–3.

space or liberty—as opposed to license—in which we may act free from the interference of other persons.

In short, *natural law ethics purports to instruct us on how to exercise the liberty that is defined and protected by natural rights.* Although principles of natural law ethics can be used to guide one's conduct, they should not be coercively enforced by human law if doing so would violate the moral space or liberty defined by natural rights. Thus, one can reject a natural law approach to pro-scribing the *ethics* or propriety of human conduct, and still accept the useful-ness of a natural rights approach to specify the appropriate principles of *justice* that comprise a social structure in which people can pursue happiness, peace, and prosperity. Only the latter of these two inquiries is the subject of this book.

Justice is a concept—a concept that is used to evaluate the propriety of using force. We resort to justice to tell us how persons ought to act, not generally as a natural law ethics may do, but specifically when they seek to use force against others. The classical liberal approach I shall develop here defines just-ice in terms of particular natural rights—for example, the rights of several property, freedom of contract, self-defense, and restitution—for the various reasons I discuss in the balance of this book and others besides. Once devel-oped, this classical liberal conception of justice (and the rule of law) is then used to critically evaluate and correct human laws that are coercively enforced.

Defining justice in terms of rights, especially natural rights, will invite con-fusion, however, unless we are clearer about what it means to call something a right. A nice description is provided by Allen Buchanan:

[A]ssertions of rights are essentially *conclusory* and hence *argumentative*. An asser-tion of right is a conclusion about what the moral priorities are. At the same time, because it is a conclusion, it is an admission that it is appropriate to demand support for this conclusion, reasons why such priority ought to be recognized. And it is vital to recognize that there is a plurality of different kinds of considerations that can count as moral reasons to support a conclusion of this sort and that the conclusion that an assertion of a right expresses will usually be an all-things-considered judgment, the result of a balancing of conflicting considerations.[43]

Thus, to call something a natural right is to assert one's conclusion; it is no substitute for presenting the reasons why this conclusion is justified. What makes natural rights *natural* is the type of "given–if–then" reasons that are offered in support of its conclusions, based as they are on the "givens" of human nature and the nature of the world in which humans live. What makes them *rights* is the "natural *necessity*"[44]—to use H. L. A. Hart's felicitous term—

---

[43] Allen Buchanan, *Secession: The Morality of Political Divorce from Fort Sumpter to Lithuania and Quebec* (Boulder, Colo.: Westview Press, 1991), p. 151.

[44] Hart, *Concept of Law*, p. 195 (emphasis added). Hart uses this term in the context of his discussing the imperative to have coercive sanctions in a legal system and rules protecting bodily integrity, property, and contractual commitments: "We can say, given the setting of natural facts and aims, which make sanctions both possible and necessary

of adhering to them if we are to solve certain pervasive social problems that must be solved somehow if persons are to achieve their objectives.

Why the conclusions reached by a natural rights analysis are properly called rights is more easily grasped if we distinguish between "background" and "legal" rights. *Background rights* are those claims a person has to legal enforcement that are *justified*, on balance, by the full constellation of relevant reasons, whether or not they are actually recognized and enforced by a legal system. *Legal rights*, by contrast, are those claims that some actual legal system will recognize as valid.[45] The legal rights that a particular system of laws recognizes as valid may or may not conform to the background rights specified by the liberal conception of justice. Natural rights reasoning is a method of identifying background rights against which the legal rights of any particular legal system can be assessed.

If done properly, then, a natural rights analysis provides reasons why legal rights *ought* to correspond as closely as possible with natural rights. This book is about the reasons—though certainly not the *only* reasons—favoring the legal recognition of certain background rights. The thesis I will develop in this book is that, if the pervasive social problems of knowledge, interest, and power I examine here are to be addressed, legal rights *ought* to correspond as closely as possible with justice as defined by the natural background rights to acquire, possess, use, and dispose of scarce resources (and other rights as well). As H. L. A. Hart put it:

In considering the simple truisms which we set forth here, and their connexion with law and morals, it is important to observe that in each case the facts mentioned afford a *reason* why, given survival as an aim, law and morals should include a specific content. The general form of the argument is simply that without such a content laws and morals could not forward the minimum purpose of survival which men have in associating with each other.[46]

In my view, a natural rights analysis should also take as its objective, not only the "purpose of survival which men have in associating with each other"—Hart's "if"—but also the pursuit of happiness, peace, and prosperity.

in a municipal system, that this is a *natural necessity*; and some such phrase is needed also to convey the status of the minimum forms of protection for persons, property, and promises which are similarly indispensable features of municipal law. . . . [A] place must be reserved, besides definitions and ordinary statements of fact, for a third category of statements: those the truth of which is contingent on human beings and the world they live in retaining the salient characteristics which they have."

[45] I have loosely adopted this from Ronald Dworkin's distinction between "background" and "institutional" rights: "Any adequate [political] theory will distinguish . . . between background rights, which are rights that provide a justification for political decisions by society in the abstract, and institutional rights, that provide a justification for a decision by some particular and specified political institution." Ronald Dworkin, *Taking Rights Seriously* (Cambridge, Mass.: Harvard University Press, 1977), p. 93. Unfortunately, this helpful distinction has disappeared from Dworkin's later writings, and is nowhere to be found in Ronald Dworkin, *Law's Empire,* (Cambridge, Mass.: Harvard University Press, 1986).
[46] Hart, *Concept of Law*, p. 189.

To structure society so as to pursue these ends, human beings must somehow come to grips with the problems of knowledge, interest, and power. Doing so will require adherence to the rights and procedures that define the conception of justice and the rule of law I shall describe here. In sum, *given* the pervasive social problems of knowledge, interest, and power confronting every human society, *if* human beings are to survive and pursue happiness, peace and prosperity while living in society with others, *then* their laws must not violate certain background natural rights or the rule of law.

4. Natural Rights and The Obligatoriness of Human Laws

Is this "given–if–then" conception of natural rights robust enough to create a *moral* obligation that they be respected? Are those persons who do not accept the "if" in this "given–if–then" analysis morally bound to adhere to natural rights? Michael Zuckert pointedly identifies this difficulty for Hugo Grotius's "given–if–then" conception of natural law:

Grotius appears able, at best, to generate a hypothetical obligation: to live according to one's nature, one ought to obey the natural law. But where is the obligation to live according to nature? . . . As Grotius concedes in a key place, perhaps the best one can really say is that it is "wise" to live according to the promptings of nature; he cannot establish the obligatoriness of natural law.[47]

This difficulty may be recast as follows: in what sense are natural rights, defended in the way I shall do so here, *obligatory* requirements of *justice* as opposed to mere prudential guides to conduct? Are persons obligated to respect them, particularly, if they reject the purposes they serve?

For reasons I shall explain in this section, I think this response overstates the distinction between justice and prudence. In this matter I agree with Phillipa Foote, who wrote: "That moral judgments cannot be hypothetical imperatives has come to seem an unquestionable truth. It will be argued here that it is not."[48] The distinction between a hypothetical imperative and a categorical imperative was made by Immanuel Kant:

All imperatives command either *hypothetically* or *categorically*. Hypothetical imperatives declare a possible action to be practically necessary as a means to the attainment of something else that one wills (or that one may will). A categorical

---

[47] Michael Zuckert, *Natural Rights and the New Republicanism* (Princeton, NJ: Princeton University Press, 1994), p. 191.
[48] Phillipa Foote, "Morality as a System of Hypothetical Imperatives," *Philosophical Review*, vol. 81 (1972), pp. 305–16.

imperative would be one which represented an action as objectively necessary in itself apart from its relation to a further end.[49]

Categorical imperatives "tell us what we have to do whatever our interests or desires, and by their inescapability they are distinguished from hypothetical imperatives."[50]

Foote questions whether categorical imperatives are really any more "imperative" than hypothetical ones. A moral man "has moral ends and cannot be indifferent to matters such as suffering and injustice."[51] He does not have these ends because they are dictated by categorical imperatives, but because he is moral and cares about morality, including the morality dictated by categorical imperatives. Foote argues that, despite the efforts of philosophers to show otherwise, the mere existence of a categorical imperative does not provide a reason for an amoral person to adopt a moral demand.

If he is an amoral man, he may deny that he has any reason to trouble his head over this or any other moral demand. Of course, he may be mistaken, and his life as well as others' lives may be most sadly spoiled by his selfishness. But this is not what is urged by those who think they can close the matter by an emphatic use of "ought." My argument is that they are relying on an illusion, as if trying to give the moral "ought" a magic force.[52]

In short, only if one cares about morality, will one care about a categorical imperative.

I shall not attempt to summarize further Professor Foote's argument here, nor wager an opinion on whether hypothetical imperatives are just as "moral" as categorical ones. Instead, I will supplement her argument with several reasons why, regardless of whether one accepts her conclusion, the hypothetical imperatives provided by the sort of natural rights analysis I shall advance in this book are of moral significance. For the real issue may be not so much whether background natural rights are morally obligatory, but the moral obligatoriness of human laws that infringe upon them.

The term "law" can be used descriptively or normatively. Descriptively, it can refer to commands by a recognized law-maker which, if disobeyed, will result in the imposition of a legal sanction, whether or not such commands are just. Even the natural law theorist Thomas Aquinas was quite capable of distinguishing, as a descriptive matter, between those human laws that were just and those that were unjust when he declared that "Laws framed by man are either just or unjust."[53] Whether just or unjust, Aquinas described both as "laws."

---

[49] Immanuel Kant, *Groundwork of the Metaphysics of Morals*, Sect. II, trans. H. J. Paton (New York: Harper & Row, 1964), p. 82. The meaning of this passage may be clarified by substituting the term "desire" for the word "will" as some translations do.
[50] Foote, "Hypothetical Imperatives", p. 308.   [51] Ibid. 325.
[52] Ibid.   [53] Aquinas, *Summa Theologica*, p. 233.

Rather, for Aquinas and other natural law thinkers, the issue of lawfulness is not purely descriptive or "value-neutral" as it is for modern legal positivists,[54] but normative. Only just laws "have the power of binding in conscience."[55] It is this issue of "binding in conscience" that informs his endorsement of Augustine's statement that "'that which is not just seems to be no law at all;' therefore the *force* of a law depends on the extent of its justice."[56] By "force" he meant *moral* force of a law to bind in conscience. As John Locke wrote, "we should not obey a king out of fear, because, being more powerful, he can constrain (this in fact would be to establish firmly the authority of tyrants, robbers, and pirates), but for conscience' sake."[57] Locke concluded from this that, "[h]ence the binding force of civil law is dependent on natural law; and we are not so much coerced into rendering obedience to the magistrate by the power of the civil law as bound to obedience by natural right."[58] Unless they adhere to natural law, "the rules can perhaps by force and with the aid of arms *compel* the multitude to obedience, but put them under an *obligation* they cannot."[59]

Unlike some philosophers,[60] persons who make laws are not content to employ a merely descriptive "value-neutral" conception of law which proscribes no duty of obedience. When they use the term "law" to describe their commands they typically claim that others *do* have a moral duty to obey them. It is legitimate therefore to assess the validity of their claim. Do their commands really create a duty of obedience? H. L. A. Hart correctly acknowledged that the challenge for legal positivism is to explain how a legal command is different than a command of a gunman, only a "gunman situation writ large."[61] To this he responded by invoking (albeit without acknowledgment) Locke's distinction between *being obliged* to obey a command in the sense that one will be coerced into obedience, and *having an obligation*.[62] While one was obliged—or to use Locke's word, "compelled"—to obey the gunman, one had no obligation to do so. But whence comes an obligation to obey the law?

[54] See e.g. Joseph Raz, *The Authority of Law* (Oxford: Oxford University Press, 1979), pp. 39–40 ("A jurisprudential theory is acceptable only if its tests for identifying the content of the law and determining its existence depend exclusively on *facts of human behavior capable of being described in value-neutral terms*, and applied without resort to moral argument.")(emphasis added).

[55] Aquinas, *Summa Theologica*, p. 233. See John Finnis, *Natural Law and Natural Rights* (Oxford: Clarendon Press, 1980), pp. 360–1.

[56] Aquinas, *Summa Theologica*, p. 227 (emphasis added).

[57] Locke, *Natural Law*, p. 189.   [58] Ibid.   [59] Ibid. 119 (emphasis added).

[60] See e.g. Raz, *Authority of Law*, p. 233 ("[T]here is no obligation to obey the law. . . . [T]here is not even a prima facie obligation to obey it. . . . [T]here is no obligation to obey the law even in a good society whose legal system is just."). I am not here contesting Raz's claim about the duty of obedience, nor his descriptive value-neutral conception of law. Rather, I am examining the conditions that are needed to establish or justify the claim by lawmakers that their laws happen to be binding in conscience. In Chapter 13, I introduce the concept of *legitimacy* that links the descriptive value-neutral conception of *validity* with the normative value-laden concept of *justice*.

[61] Hart, *Concept of Law*, p. 7.

[62] See Hart, *Concept of Law*, p. 80: "There is a difference . . . between the assertion that someone *was obliged* to do something and the assertion that he *had an obligation* to do it."

Hart departed from nineteenth-century legal positivist John Austin (and also Oliver Wendell Holmes[63]) by acknowledging that legal obligation is typically perceived by individuals, not merely as a command from a superior to a subject or as a way to predict the imposition of a legal sanction, but also as a *reason* for personal conduct. This "internal" point of view cannot be explained entirely by the physical coercion attached to noncompliance.[64] For Hart, the perception of obligation was based either on the widespread acceptance of "primary rules" regulating individual conduct[65] or on the widespread acceptance of "secondary rules that regulate the making of primary rules."[66] And what, according to Hart, accounted for such popular acceptance of primary or secondary rules?

Rules are conceived and spoken of as obligatory when the general demand for conformity is insistent and the social pressure brought to bear upon those who deviate or threaten to deviate is great. . . . The rules supported by this serious social pressure are thought important because they are believed to be necessary to the maintenance of social life or some highly prized feature of it.[67]

Legal obligation in Hart's scheme, then, is largely if not entirely, a matter of perception. Legal rules create obligations of obedience when they are "*thought* important because they are *believed* to be necessary. . . ."[68] But at most Hart's account explains the general *perception* in a given society of an obligation to obey the law not whether there truly *is* such an obligation. When a law-making authority claims that we are obligated (not merely obliged or compelled) to obey its commands, we are entitled to ask whether this claim is warranted. When a normative conception of law entailing a moral obligation to obey is invoked, whatever quality a law must have to make it binding in conscience, we are entitled to demand that this *quality goes in before the name "law" goes on*.

In sum, to determine whether legal rules are *really* obligatory we must ask whether they are *in fact,* as Hart put it: "necessary to the maintenance of social

---

[63] See Oliver Wendell Holmes, Jr., "The Path of the Law," *Harvard Law Review*, vol. 10 (1897), p. 459: "If you want to know the law and nothing else, you must look at it as a bad man, who cares only for the material consequence which such knowledge enables him to predict, not as a good one, who finds his reasons for conduct, whether inside the law or outside of it, in the vaguer *sanctions of conscience*." (emphasis added)

[64] See Hart, *Concept of Law*, pp. 86–8. As he summarized this point, for the majority of society, "the violation of a rule is not merely a basis for the prediction that a hostile reaction will follow but a *reason* for hostility." Ibid. 88.

[65] Hart's description of these "primary rules" sounds a lot like the liberal conception of justice described here: "If society is to live by such primary rules alone, there are certain conditions which, granted a few of the most obvious truisms about human nature and the world we live in, must clearly be satisfied. The first of these conditions is that the rules must contain in some form restrictions on the free use of violence, theft, and deception to which human beings are tempted but which they must, in general, repress, if they are to coexist in close proximity to each other." Ibid. 89. My objective in this book is to move beyond "the most obvious truisms" and generate a richer understanding of these "conditions."

[66] See ibid. 77–6.   [67] Ibid. 84–5.   [68] Ibid. 85 (emphasis added).

life." And this is exactly what a natural rights enquiry attempts to do. If adherence to natural rights is indeed essential for the maintenance of social life, as natural rights theorists maintain and as I shall try to explain in the balance of this book, then laws are obligatory only if they are consistent with natural rights. By this account, a command may be a "law" in the descriptive sense that it is issued by a recognized law-maker, but it is only *law* in the normative sense of a command that binds in conscience on the citizenry if it does not violate the background rights of persons. Thus, for human laws to be obligatory, they should not violate natural rights.[69] For human beings in society with others to pursue happiness, peace, and prosperity, enforceable legal rights must not conflict with certain background natural rights.

This account of the obligation to obey the law suggests an additional reason why human law or legal rights should respect the natural rights that I will identify in this book. At the same time law-makers claim that subjects of their law have a moral duty of obedience, they also invariably claim that their laws advance the general welfare or the common good. Indeed, if pressed, many would advance the latter claim in defense of the former—that is, people have a duty to obey the law *because* adherence to such laws does advance the general welfare. Yet if the analysis presented in the balance of this book is correct, then laws that violate the rights specified by liberal conception of justice do *not* advance the general welfare or common good. Indeed they harm it. Thus human laws which violate natural rights are not obligatory and only those human laws that respect natural rights can be obligatory.

Finally, this previous observation suggests yet another basis for legal rights to adhere to natural rights. We have all heard that the legitimacy of law making is grounded on the "consent of the governed" to the law-making regime. Yet the analysis just presented suggests that the obligation of law-makers to respect natural rights rests, at least in part, on the "consent of the governors" to respect these rights. For do not law-makers explicitly or implicitly claim that their laws promote the common good and are not unjust? By doing so are they not consenting to adhere to any principles of justice that, if violated, would thwart the common good? For example, the Preamble to the United States Constitution explicitly claims that its purpose was to "establish Justice, ensure domestic tranquility, . . . promote the general Welfare, and secure the blessings of Liberty to ourselves and our posterity. . . ."[70] Do not law-makers in the United States who take an oath to uphold the Constitution explicitly obligate themselves to pass laws that actually *do* establish justice, *do* ensure peace, *do* promote the general welfare, and *do* secure liberty? Therefore, if the argument presented in this book in favor of certain natural rights holds, then these

---

[69] Although it may be necessary that laws not violate rights for them to be obligatory, this may not be sufficient. Along with requirements of justice, requirements of *legality* specified by the rule of law must also be respected. And we shall begin considering the liberal conception of the rule of law in Chapter 5.

[70] *The United States Constitution*, preamble.

background rights must be respected by law-makers in devising legal rights if for no other reason than because they have promised or consented to do so.

For all these reasons, even if natural rights generated only a "prudential" or "hypothetical" obligation, this would be plenty significant. For the hypothetical obligation at issue is: *if we want a society in which persons can survive and pursue happiness, peace and prosperity*, then we should respect the liberal conception of justice—as defined by natural rights—and the rule of law. Who among us would not accept this as their political goal? What law-maker would deny that he or she desires this objective? Responding to those who would consider as dangerous and subversive a view of justice that depends on the contingent fact that people happen to care about certain shared objectives, Phillipa Foote observed:

> But it is interesting that the people of Leningrad were not similarly struck by the thought that only the *contingent* fact that other citizens shared their loyalty and devotion to the city stood between them and the Germans during the terrible years of the siege. Perhaps we should be less troubled than we are by fear of defection from the moral cause; perhaps we should even have less reason to fear if people thought of themselves as volunteers banded together to fight for liberty and justice and against inhumanity and oppression.[71]

Of course, in suggesting that legal rights should correspond with background rights, I claim neither that we can use natural rights to *derive* legal rights, nor that we can always *know* what a particular person's background rights are independent of the processes that produce legal rights. As I explain in Chapter 6, background natural rights are highly abstract, and many very different sets of rules or laws may be consistent with them. Further, theorists speculating about background rights usually, if not always, take the legal rights with which they are familiar as starting points. A legal system operating according to certain procedures associated with the rule of law may be needed to generate a set of legal rights that can serve as a necessary starting point of any theory of background rights. And, if these rule of law procedures are sound, then the starting points they provide may not be entirely arbitrary.

In determining the content of background rights, legal rights generated by a sound legal process may even be entitled to presumptive legitimacy. Why this might be the case will become clearer in Chapter 6, when we will see how certain features of a "common law" adjudicative process make it likely that rights will be discovered that are compatible with justice. And in Chapters 13 and 14, I examine the constitutional structure that will best ensure that legal rights actually comport with the background rights that comprise the liberal conception of justice.

Yet despite these caveats, a natural rights analysis attempts to provide knowledge of certain "principles of society" that must be respected if persons are to pursue happiness, peace, and prosperity while living in society with others.

---

[71] Foote, "Hypothetical Imperatives", pp. 314–15.

Though they may often be more controversial than principles of engineering, architecture, and agriculture, these principles have the same status.

5. Natural Rights and Utility

Is a natural rights analysis *utilitarian*? Though this type of philosophical question is really beyond the scope of this book, for what it is worth, my answer depends on how the term "utilitarian" is used. If utilitarian is viewed as a *consequentialist* approach that evaluates practices by their consequences, then the conception of natural rights sketched here appears to be consequentialist, though only indirectly.[72] Some rights are thought to be natural because adherence to them is necessary to solve some serious social problems. For this reason, these rights (not an assessment of utility) are then used to evaluate the justice of human laws.

I must hasten to add, however, that though a "given–if–then" argument provides consequentialist reasons to favor natural rights, these reasons may well be reinforced and bolstered by other equally valid "nonconsequentialist" types of analysis.[73] I do not claim that the analysis presented here is the only argument or type of argument that supports these rights. Moreover, the argument presented here takes the goal of enabling persons to survive and pursue happiness, peace, and prosperity while living in society with others as given. If this goal needs to be defended, then it must be on some other grounds and such grounds need not be consequentialist.

If utilitarianism is viewed as a general *theory of ethics* or morality, however, then the natural rights approach presented here, though consequentialist, is not utilitarian. The approach presented here does not provide a theory of how persons ought to pursue the good life, the traditional province of ethics. Many but not all natural rights theorists also take a natural law approach to this question, but historically a natural law approach to ethics is more teleological—that is, based on the natural end or good for human beings[74]—than utilitarian.

[72] See Larry Alexander, "Pursuing the Good—Indirectly," *Ethics*, vol. 95 (1985), p. 315; John Gray, "Indirect Utility and Fundamental Rights," *Social Philosophy and Policy*, vol. 1 (Spring, 1984), p. 73.

[73] See Randy E. Barnett, "Of Chickens and Eggs—The Compatibility of Moral Rights and Consequentialist Analysis," *Harvard Journal of Law and Public Policy*, vol. 12 (1989), pp. 611–35.

[74] See Hart, *Concept of Law*, p. 185 (describing the association of natural law thinking with "the teleological conception of nature as containing in itself levels of excellence which things realize.") For an example of such a natural law approach to ethics, see Henry B. Veatch, *For an Ontology of Morals* (Evanston, Ill.: Northwestern University Press, 1974). For two contemporary examples of teleological, natural law defenses of natural rights, see Douglas B. Rasmussen and Douglas J. Den Uyl, *Liberty and Nature* (La Salle, Ill.: Open Court, 1991); Henry B. Veatch, *Human Rights: Fact or Fancy?* (Baton Rouge, La.: Louisiana State University Press, 1985).

Perhaps most importantly, if utilitarianism is taken as a *method of decision making* in which the effects of various policies are assessed by determining their effects on the sum of all individual's subjective preferences, then the view of natural rights described here is decidedly not utilitarian. For the indirect consequentialist analysis presented here suggests that respecting natural rights, not the calculation and aggregation of subjective preferences, promotes the common good. And the common good is viewed, not as a sum of preference satisfaction, but as the ability of each person to pursue happiness, peace, and prosperity while acting in close proximity to others.

Finally, some who adopt an Aristotelian teleological defense of natural rights consider themselves opposed to utilitarianism and even consequentialism. Nonetheless, they view rights as *conditions* of pursuing happiness or "flourishing," *given* the nature of human beings and the world. For example, according to Douglas Rasmussen and Douglas Den Uyl: "Rights are used to create a legal system which defines a set of compossible territories that provides the *necessary political condition* for the possibility that individuals might carry on a life in accord with virtue."[75] Such an approach is difficult to distinguish in its structure from the analysis I am using here. Therefore, if they are correct in describing their method as nonconsequentialist or "deontological," then so is this one. Perhaps all this suggests that how we describe or categorize the analysis I will present here is less important than the merits of the analysis itself.

6. Moving Beyond Philosophical Issues

Notwithstanding the impression I have given to this point, this is not a book about the nature or existence of natural law or natural rights. I have considered these philosophical matters in this introductory chapter, in part, to get them out of the way, so some readers will not become distracted trying to categorize the analysis I present. As interesting as these issues may be, I want to get beyond them to consider which rights we ought to respect and why. I care less about a topology of the reasons I advance for a particular conception of justice and the rule of law than I do the reasons themselves.

Indeed, what has always frustrated me about contemporary discussions of natural law and natural rights is that they usually focus exclusively on such philosophical issues and never get around to showing how such an approach actually works. Very little attention is paid, even by those who accept a natural law or natural rights approach, to whether and why particular principles of conduct *are* in fact natural laws and whether any particular right *is* in fact a natural right.[76] Beginning in Chapter 2, I will stop talking *about* what a

---

[75] Rasmussen and Den Uyl, *Liberty and Nature*, p. 115 (emphasis added).
[76] Three exceptions to this have already been cited. See Hart, *Concept of Law*, pp. 189–95; Veatch, *Human Rights;* and Rasmussen and Den Uyl, *Liberty and Nature*. I mean no disrespect to others who have done the same.

natural rights analysis is and actually *do* one (whether or not the reader wishes to consider this a natural rights analysis).

Nonetheless, in addition to clarifying the nature of the analysis I am about to present, the preceding discussion of natural law and rights is needed to put this analysis in proper context. For the type of reasoning I advance on behalf of certain rights and procedures is not original to me and it has a long, rich, and distinguished heritage, though a largely forgotten one. And it transformed the world by stimulating and legitimating the American Revolution.

In addition, acknowledging the relationship of this analysis to the tradition of natural law and natural rights theories helps connect the thesis presented here to issues of constitutional theory—in particular the nature of the rights "retained by the people" that the Ninth Amendment says shall not be "denied or disparaged"[77] or of the "privileges or immunities of citizens" protected from state infringement by the Fourteenth Amendment.[78] For the principles I shall identify as comprising the liberal conception of justice can be viewed as natural and inalienable rights which are retained by the people when they form governments.[79] Such rights also help us understand the constitutional requirements that all laws passed by Congress "shall be necessary *and proper*"[80] and that "private property [shall not] be taken for public use without just compensation."[81] Indeed, without an understanding of natural rights, we are very likely to misinterpret the Constitution in crucially important ways.[82]

[77] See *United States Constitution*, amend. IX ("The enumeration in the Constitution of certain rights shall not be construed to deny or disparage others retained by the people."). Elsewhere I have written at length both about the Ninth Amendment and about the relationship of natural rights to constitutional adjudication. See Randy E. Barnett, "Introduction: James Madison's Ninth Amendment," in Randy E. Barnett (ed.), *The Rights Retained by the People: The History and Meaning of the Ninth Amendment*, vol. i (Fairfax, Va.: George Mason University Press, 1989), p. 1; Randy E. Barnett, "Introduction: Implementing the Ninth Amendment," in Randy E. Barnett (ed.), *The Rights Retained by the People: The History and Meaning of the Ninth Amendment*, vol. ii (Fairfax, Va.: George Mason University Press, 1993), p. 1; Randy E. Barnett, "Getting Normative: The Role of Natural Rights in Constitutional Adjudication," *Constitutional Commentary*, vol. 12 (1995), p. 93; and Randy E. Barnett, "The Intersection of Natural Rights and Positive Constitutional Law," *University of Connecticut Law Review*, vol. 25 (1993), p. 853.

[78] See *United States Constitution*, amend. XIV ("No State shall make or enforce any law which shall abridge the privileges or immunities of citizens of the United States. . . .").

[79] By the same token the principles I shall identify as part of the liberal conception of the rule of law inform the meaning of "due process of law" that is mentioned in the Fifth and Fourteenth Amendments. See *United States Constitution*, amend. V ("No person shall . . . be deprived of life, liberty, or property, without due process of law. . . ."); and amend IV ("nor shall any State deprive any person of life, liberty, or property, without due process of law. . . .").

[80] *United States Constitution*, art. I, sect. 8 (emphasis added) ("The Congress shall have Power . . . To make all Laws which shall be necessary and proper for carrying into Execution the foregoing Powers, and all other Powers vested by this Constitution in the Government of the United States, or in any Department or Officer thereof.") See Randy E. Barnett, "Necessary and Proper," *UCLA Law Review*, vol. 44 (1997), pp. 745–93.

[81] *United States Constitution*, amend. V ("nor shall private property be taken for public use without just compensation.").

[82] See *Nomination of Robert H. Bork to be Associate Justice of the Supreme Court of the*

Still, if the idea of natural law or natural rights rubs you the wrong way, don't worry. You need not accept these terms to accept the analysis that follows. (Conversely, some who accept the concepts of natural law and natural rights may well reject some or all of my analysis.) In the rest of this book, I will identify the problems of knowledge, interest, and power that confront all human societies and, given these problems, the structure of liberty that we need, not only to survive, but also to pursue happiness, peace, and prosperity in a social setting. I will argue that the singular ability of the rights and procedures that structure liberty to handle not one but numerous pervasive and otherwise intractable social problems that must somehow be solved, provides a compelling reason—a "natural necessity"[83] to use H. L. A. Hart's term—to reject laws that are inconsistent with these rights and procedures.

In James Madison's words, "the pre-existent rights of nature," are those rights that "are essential to secure the liberty of the people,"[84] and a properly structured liberty is essential to solving the pervasive problems of knowledge, interest, and power. A respect for these fundamental principles of justice and the rule of law is as essential to enabling diverse persons to pursue happiness, peace, and prosperity while living in society with others as a respect for the fundamental principles of engineering is essential to building a bridge to span a chasm. As the medieval poet Abraham Ibn Ezra wrote: "It is a known fact that every kingdom based on justice will stand. Justice is like a building. Injustice is like the cracks in that building, which cause it to fall without a moment's warning."[85]

United States: Hearings before the United States Senate Committee on the Judiciary 249 (1989) (testimony of Robert Bork): "I do not think you can use the ninth amendment unless you know something of what it means. For example, if you had an amendment that says 'Congress shall make no' and then there is an ink blot and you cannot read the rest of it and that is the only copy you have, I do not think you the court make up what might be under the ink blot if you cannot read it."

   [83]   Hart, *Concept of Law*, p. 195.
   [84]   Joseph Gales (ed.), *The Debates and Proceedings in the Congress of the United States*, vol. 1 (Washington: Gales & Seaton, 1834) [hereinafter cited as *Annals of Congress*], p. 454 (statement of James Madison) (emphasis added). In the passage from which these phrases are taken, Madison is arguing that the right of trial by jury enumerated in the proposed amendments, though a "positive right," is as essential to secure the liberty of the people as any natural right.
   [85]   Abraham Ibn Ezra (1092–1167), as it appears in *The Pentateuch and Haftorahs*, 2nd edn., (London: Soncino Press, 1960), p. 856.

PART ONE

The Problems of Knowledge

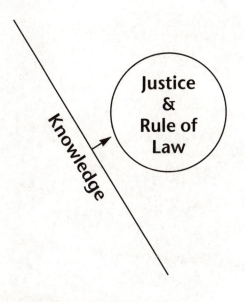

PART ONE

TWO

Using Resources: The First-Order Problem of Knowledge

THE problem of knowledge in society is ubiquitous. So are the means by which we cope with it. Perhaps this is why the knowledge problem is so easily overlooked as a problem in need of a solution. The particular problem of knowledge that I am interested in here concerns the knowledge of how to use physical resources in the world.

All human beings are confronted with a multitude of ways that they may use physical resources, including their own bodies. The challenge of making good choices regarding the use of resources would be difficult enough in an "atomistic" world where one's choices had no effect on the choices of others. Since this is not our world, the problem of a person or association making knowledgeable choices among alternative uses of physical resources is compounded by other persons and associations striving to make their own choices. Indeed, given the number of possible choices persons might make, the number of persons making choices, and the physical proximity of each to the others, it is remarkable that the world is not in complete chaos. The world is not in chaos, I suggest, because concepts and institutions have evolved to harness the diverse knowledge about potential uses of resources in a manner that contributes to harmonious and beneficial interaction.

In this chapter, I discuss what I call the "first-order problem of knowledge." This is the problem of knowledgeable resource use that confronts every person in any society. No one has placed greater stress on this particular knowledge problem than Friedrich Hayek. As he explains:

The peculiar character of the problem of a rational economic order is determined precisely by the fact that the *knowledge of the circumstances* of which we must make use never exists in concentrated or integrated form but solely as the dispersed bits of incomplete and frequently contradictory knowledge which all the separate individuals possess. The economic problem of society is thus not merely a problem of how to allocate "given" resources—if "given" is taken to mean given to a single mind which deliberately solves the problem set by those "data." It is rather a problem of how to secure the best use of resources known to any of the members of society, for ends whose relative importance only those individuals know. Or, to put it briefly, it is *a problem of the utilization of knowledge which is not given to anyone in its totality.*[1]

Hayek's account does not assume that everything that people believe is true. Rather, it maintains that (*a*) there are many things each of us believes that are true and (*b*) access to these truths by others is severely limited. The limited access to each of these different kinds of knowledge gives rise to a problem of knowledge that every human society must cope with in some manner or other.

1. Two Kinds of Knowledge

To get a handle on the first-order knowledge problem of resource use, it is useful to distinguish between two kinds of knowledge: personal knowledge and local knowledge. What distinguishes each of these kinds of knowledge are their different *domains of access*—that is, who exactly has access to the knowledge in question.

Personal Knowledge

As I sit here at my computer, I can see people walking past my window. I can hear people closing doors in the corridor outside my office. I can hear an announcer's voice on the radio behind me and the whine of the computer's hard drive. No one else in the world has quite the same external perspective as I have at this moment. Indeed I venture to say that no one in the world is imagining what I am presently perceiving. It would be quite extraordinary that anyone would even think to do so and quite impossible in any event. I am the only person in the world to know what I am perceiving right now and in this sense this knowledge is intensely personal.

Nor does anyone else in the world have access at this moment to my inner thoughts and feelings. No one else can know that at this moment I feel the need to take a sip of coffee, a beverage that only a few minutes ago I decided I wanted to drink. No one else can know exactly what I long for, what and whom I love, or what I am grateful for. Even if I tried to tell someone everything I think and feel, a verbalized account would not capture the totality of my thoughts and feeling. (Would that I were able to write down exactly what

---

[1] Friedrich A. Hayek, "The Use of Knowledge in Society," *Individualism and Economic Order* (Chicago: University of Chicago Press, 1948), pp. 77–8 (emphasis added). For additional discussion of the knowledge problem, see Don Lavoie, *National Economic Planning* (Cambridge, Mass.: Ballinger, 1985); Don Lavoie, *Rivalry and Central Planning* (New York: Cambridge University Press, 1985); Thomas Sowell, *Knowledge and Decisions* (New York: Basic Books, 1980).

I think about the relationship of the problems of knowledge, interest, and power to the liberal conceptions of justice and the rule of law. Then this book would not be so hard to write!) What I am thinking and feeling, as well as what I remember, is intensely personal.

Nor can anyone else directly experience the choices available to me at this moment. I can continue writing or I can go to my chair and resume reading the book I was reading this morning. Indeed there are literally countless numbers of things I can choose to do at this moment, including getting on an airplane for some other town, abandoning my family, this project, and my academic career. Of course, I have absolutely no desire to do this—and would not even have imagined this possibility had I not been searching for an example to illustrate my point—but it is an option. My options for action at this moment, being in large measure a function of my personal abilities and resources as well as my imagination, are intensely personal. Personal knowledge[2] may thus be defined as follows:

Personal knowledge is the knowledge unique to particular persons of their personal perception, of their personal preferences, needs, and desires, of their personal abilities, and of their personal opportunities.[3]

Now I want to make a paradoxical claim: each living person is in the same position as I am right now, but also that each living person is in a radically different position as well. This means only that *all* persons are confronted with their own intensely personal knowledge of their perceptions, desires, and opportunities. Although the content of each person's personal knowledge is quite different from my or anyone else's personal knowledge, the fact of having our own personal knowledge is something we all have in common.

The paradoxical nature of this claim needs to be recognized or my project will be misunderstood. These days any effort to describe general features of the world on which conclusions about justice can be based is often characterized as either simplistic or imperialist: simplistic because the world is so complex

---

[2] Although I have borrowed the term "personal knowledge" from Michael Polanyi, his use of the term differs markedly from mine as does the type of problems his analysis is intended to address. See Michael Polanyi, *Personal Knowledge* (Chicago: University of Chicago Press, rev. edn. 1962).

[3] The personal knowledge of alternative opportunities is related (but not identical) to the personal or "subjective" costs of choice, the seminal analysis of which is James Buchanan, *Cost and Choice* (Chicago: Markham, 1969). Because each person faces a unique set of opportunities or alternative courses of conduct, it is the individual who must bear the personal and very real "cost" of choosing one activity over another. This cost is reflected by the next most highly valued opportunity forgone. In the act of choice this alternate action is lost forever. This means that when persons make any choice (or have a choice imposed upon them) they unavoidably bear a very personal "opportunity cost" of such a choice. Thus we may distinguish between the personal knowledge unique to a person and the subjective cost that choice based on such personal (and other) knowledge imposes upon a person. The subjective "cost of choice" gives rise to a problem of interest that is discussed in Chapter 8, and which provides a justification, independent of the need to solve the knowledge problem, for the background rights of several property, freedom of contract, and first possession.

that it cannot be captured by such generalities; imperialist since it seems to assume that every society is like ours (or should be). Yet, if properly understood, the general claim that all persons are similarly situated insofar as they have their own perceptions, preferences, and opportunities is neither simplistic nor imperialist. For the flip-side of the claim is that all persons are situated differently, insofar as their perceptions, preferences, and opportunities differ. True, considered in isolation, any particular preference is probably shared by many people. But the constellation of perceptions, preferences, and opportunities is so situation-dependent that there is virtually no chance that the personal knowledge reposed respectively in two different people will be identical in every respect. It is then neither simplistic nor imperialist to describe—and then take seriously—a feature common to all human beings when such a feature allows both for the functional similarities among persons and cultures and for the seemingly infinite individual and cultural diversity that human beings manifest.

Now let me be clear about what I am *not* claiming. I am not claiming that all people invariably make more knowledgeable choices for themselves than others could possibly make for them. We all know of circumstances where persons lack information that would bear importantly on their choices to which others have access. I would not be surprised to learn, for example, that I regularly eat some kinds of food that, unbeknownst to me but known to some nutritionists, are harmful to my health. Yet the fact remains that each person has *access* to personal knowledge that others—including experts and loved ones—lack and cannot possibly obtain. A nutritionist, for example, does not know what foods my family and I like the taste of, are allergic to, or can prepare, store, afford, and find in the local market.

Nor am I claiming that each person is the sole *source* of his or her own knowledge. It is popular these days to observe that knowledge itself is a product of social interaction and that the very concept of a "pre-social" self is impossible.[4] I am saying nothing about such claims. It may well be true that most of what we know is made possible by a shared and "socially constructed" conceptual structure. But however we obtain our personal knowledge, the analysis presented here focusses entirely on the fact that this knowledge is unique to each of us and is largely inaccessible to others. The first-order problem of knowledge arises from the fact that access to personal (and local) knowledge—regardless of its source—is highly restricted.

Why is access to personal knowledge so limited? Why is it possible to convey to others only a tiny fraction of one's personal knowledge? One reason is

---

[4] See e.g., Michael Sandel, *Liberalism and the Limits of Justice* (Cambridge: Cambridge University Press, 1982), p. 172 (emphasis added): "[T]o be capable of a more thorough-going reflection, we cannot be wholly unencumbered subjects of possession, *individuated in advance and given prior to our ends*, but must be subjects constituted in part by our central aspirations and attachments, always open, indeed vulnerable, to growth transformation in the light of revised self-understanding."

that most of what we know is *tacit* or inarticulate knowledge. As Michael Polanyi explained, tacit knowledge contains "an *actual knowledge* that is indeterminate, in the sense that its contents *cannot be explicitly stated.*"[5] Consider some examples. You may be very adept at performing some task, say, driving a car or playing a musical instrument, and be entirely unable to explain to someone else how such a task should be performed. Or you may be intimately familiar with a portion of a city and yet, when asked by a stranger for directions, be entirely unable to explain accurately how to find a place that you would have no difficulty finding yourself.

When we are unable to articulate what we know, we sometimes try to convey our knowledge by showing others how we do it. Law professors, for example, do not normally try to teach the method of legal reasoning by explaining how lawyers reason, but by demonstrating it and compelling their students to try to replicate the method. But this technique—like all techniques of knowledge conveyance—will be of only limited success. That we can sometimes articulate or demonstrate what we personally know and thereby communicate it to others does not mean that we can always do so or that we can do so for more than a small fraction of our store of personal knowledge.

The fact that a large fraction of our personal knowledge is both inarticulate and inarticulable does not mean, however, that *no* information can be communicated to or shared with others. Personal knowledge is only one dimension of knowledge. Let us now consider a form of shared or public knowledge I will call local knowledge.

Local Knowledge

Earlier today I had lunch with a colleague in a very crowded deli. As we sat at our table we had a conversation. Despite the fact that each of us brought our unique personal knowledge to the conversation and were interpreting the experience in our own personal way, we both were participating in and experiencing the same conversation. We both were perceiving the same words we were speaking. We both knew the subject of our conversation. This was

---

[5] Michael Polanyi, *Knowing and Being* (Chicago: University of Chicago Press, 1969), p. 141 (original emphasis). Closely related to tacit knowledge is the phenomenon of tacit assumptions, which has been described by Lon L. Fuller as follows: "Words like 'intention,' 'assumption,' 'expectation' and 'understanding' all seem to imply a *conscious* state involving an awareness of alternatives and a deliberate choice among them. It is, however, plain that there is a psychological state which can be described as a 'tacit assumption' that does not involve a consciousness of alternatives. The absent-minded professor stepping from his office into the hall as he reads a book 'assumes' that the floor of the hall will be there to receive him. His conduct is conditioned and directed by this assumption, even though the possibility that the floor has been removed does not 'occur' to him, that is, is not present in his mental processes." Lon L. Fuller, *Basic Contract Law* (St. Paul, Minn.: West, 1947) pp. 666–7. The difference is that we make countless assumptions about circumstances of which we do not have even personal tacit knowledge.

knowledge of a "public" nature—we were literally "publishing" some of our personal thoughts to each other—but it was public knowledge that was intensely local. Only we had access to this ("our") conversation. No one else in the restaurant, except perhaps the two people at the next table could possibly know what we were saying. And I would wager that even if the couple at the next table could hear our words they would not have appreciated what we were talking about. Nor have I the foggiest idea of what they were saying or talking about, despite the fact that I could clearly hear them talking. I was too involved in our conversation to pay any attention to theirs.

Similarly, at a faculty meeting each person in the room can experience and participate in the same meeting. Those who are not in the room can do neither. Everyone who is in the room can share in a local knowledge of the fact of the meeting and its objectives that is not entirely personal. True, each of us in the room is having a personal reaction to the meeting and interpreting it somewhat differently, but we are interpreting a public, though local, phenomenon. Sharing the same language, hearing the same words, we are engaged in a public, though local, discourse. In sum, while our interpretations may not agree, we have knowledge of the same data. Each person in the meeting has access to (and some of us are participating in) a common and public conversation in progress; each has access to a public phenomenon that everyone else on earth lacks. This sort of publicly accessible but still limited knowledge may be called *local knowledge*:

> *Local knowledge* is that publicly accessible knowledge of resource use, the access to which is limited to certain associations of people.

Although access to local knowledge is limited, it need not be limited to small numbers of people: 65,000 people can watch the same football game and have local knowledge of the game in progress. Millions more can obtain local knowledge of the game in progress while watching it on television. It may seem odd to describe such widely shared knowledge as "local," but such knowledge is local in the sense that the billions of persons who are not watching the game in person or on television will not have knowledge of the game in progress, just as I have no knowledge of whatever games are at this moment being played before audiences in countless arenas throughout the world. In addition to having personal knowledge that I could not possibly have (for example, how much each is enjoying the contest), these audiences have local knowledge of a public event that I might in principle be able to know, but to which in practice I still lack access.

Knowledge of events is not the only type of local knowledge. Knowledge of language is also publicly accessible, but local. I have access to conversations and writings in English, but not to those in Chinese. So too is our conceptual understanding of the world. As Stephen Toulmin has explained, "[e]ach of us thinks our own thoughts; our concepts we share with our fellow-men. For what we believe we are answerable as individuals; but the language in which our beliefs are articulated is public property."[6] Yet, though publicly accessible, access even to this sort of knowledge can be limited and therefore local in the sense used here.

We sometimes refer to those with access to local knowledge, especially those with access to specialized modes of conceptual understanding, as having *expertise*. Thousands of scientific experts may have access to research data of which millions of people are ignorant. They are ignorant not just because they did not (or could not) view the data but also because they could not have understood it if they did. Similarly, though many students enter law school expecting to learn a list of rules or commands, much of what is taught there is actually an interconnected structure of specialized concepts. When they have integrated this conceptual structure into their own, they can better predict and explain the outcomes of legal disputes than the bulk of the "untutored" public. Indeed, the whole notion of "expertise" presupposes the idea that access to specialized knowledge is somehow limited and therefore is local in the relevant sense.

Unlike personal knowledge, then, local knowledge is public and therefore potentially accessible to others. Despite this, because it is costly to gain access to such knowledge, as a practical matter access to all local knowledge is limited. In a very real way, we are all "experts" in some domain of local knowledge to which others lack access. Add to this the vast repository of largely inaccessible personal knowledge dispersed among billions of persons and there arises a problem.

2. The First-Order Problem of Knowledge

With this discussion of personal and local knowledge in mind we can distinguish two dimensions of what I shall call the first-order problem of knowledge. First, we have the problem of everyone being able to make constructive use of their own knowledge. If persons living in society with each other are to pursue happiness and achieve peace and prosperity, how can the personal and local knowledge of individuals or associations be effectively incorporated into their *own* use of resources? Second, the limited accessibility of knowledge in society means that, at any given time, every person and association is and must be pervasively ignorant of all but a small fraction of what is known to others. If persons living in society with each other are to pursue happiness and achieve peace and prosperity, how can the personal and local knowledge of others—of which we are necessarily and hopelessly ignorant—be incorporated into an individual or association's use of resources?

These two dimensions of the first-order problem of knowledge can be summarized as follows:

---

[6] Toulmin, *Human Understanding*, p. 35.

(1) One must be able to act on the basis of one's own personal knowledge, or the knowledge one has acquired as a member of an association with local knowledge;

(2) when so acting one must somehow take into account the knowledge of others of which each person is hopelessly ignorant.

The dispersal of personal and local knowledge can be pictured as a "knowledge glass" each of us possesses that is both half-full (what each of us knows) and half-empty (what each of us is ignorant of)—although a more accurate analogy might be an Olympic-size swimming pool containing a single molecule of water. The problem is for each person to make use of the water that is there, while taking into account the part that is empty.

Even this brief description, however, understates the magnitude of the first-order knowledge problem facing any society. We have yet to consider the effects of changes in knowledge and of resource scarcity.

The Dynamic Features of the Knowledge Problem

So far I have described the knowledge problem in static terms, as though knowledge of potential resource use was "given" either to individuals or to associations and that the problem of knowledge was somehow to harness the "pool of knowledge" that, though widely dispersed, is actually in existence at a particular time. Although the difficulties in solving even a static conception of the knowledge problem are daunting, we can at least imagine that over time more and more of our personal knowledge could be rendered articulable and communicated to others and our store of local knowledge therefore dispersed ever more widely. In short, there is nothing in a static conception of the knowledge problem that prevents us from envisioning progress occurring to the point where the problem of knowledge would cease to be very serious.

Knowledge, however, is far more like a turbulent stream than a tranquil pool. We live our lives in a rush of events in real time. Our personal knowledge of perceptions, preferences, and opportunities is changing by the second. Local knowledge, including our conceptual understanding of the world, is also continuously evolving. What could cause such changes in knowledge? Changes in knowledge occur for at least two quite different reasons.

First, some of our knowledge is temporal. Knowledge of the world of here and now changes because the world of here and now itself changes over time. One minute I have a thirst for coffee, but the cup on my desk is full of coffee that is too hot to drink. A few minutes later the coffee has cooled and my thirst leads me to drink it. A few minutes after this, my coffee cup is empty and I am no longer thirsty. Less transitory but also ever changing is my knowledge of which company is producing the best car for my purposes, how well my students are doing this semester, what writing project I should undertake after this one, and which classes I am interested in teaching next year. Although some aspects of our knowledge remain relatively constant, the entire constellation of our personal knowledge will differ from moment to moment.

Second, even when the world we live in has not changed, our conceptual understanding of it can evolve. Such conceptual evolution does not merely reflect a correction of previously held error, though this is important. Concepts are tools by which we come to understand the world and communicate our understanding to others. Whether or not a conceptual understanding of the world may be thought of as "true" or "false," viewed as tools; concepts can be *superior* or *inferior* to each other. To take the most obvious example, while Newtonian physics was, and to some extent still is, useful to understand the world of our five senses, Einsteinian physics has revealed the limitations of this approach and has proved a superior tool to understand the character of both the subatomic realm and the universe. Our knowledge of the world changes as we develop better conceptual tools with which to grasp it.[7]

Any effort to deal with the first-order knowledge problem must, therefore, confront the fact that harnessing personal and local knowledge poses a dynamic not a static challenge.

The Effect of Subjective Scarcity on the Knowledge Problem

Scarcity of physical resources also plays a role in the knowledge problem, for in a very real sense, there would be no knowledge *problem* with respect to resource use in the absence of scarcity. Because we do not live in a world in which people are like atoms, one person's or one association's actions can affect the actions of others. Indeed the pervasive norm is that everyone's actions potentially affect others. So were everyone to attempt to act on the basis of their personal knowledge of their perceptions, preferences, opportunities, etc., their actions are likely to have effects on others. Were every association to attempt to act on the basis of its local knowledge, these actions would also have effects on others. But this commonplace observation is only the edge of the problem. We must acknowledge why it is that all actions are likely to affect others.

Human action affects others because, among other reasons, human action requires the use of scarce physical resources. The term "scarce physical resources" is a bit misleading since it makes it appear that the problem of resource use is only a problem of *physical* scarcity or the quantitative limits on the stock of a resource. Of course, it is true that the quantity of any physical resource is limited or "scarce" in some sense. But a serious problem of scarcity would still exist if there were no physical limitations of resources. To see why this is so consider the following hypothetical example.

---

[7] See Toulmin, *Human Understanding*, p. 150 ("[T]he task of science is to improve our ideas about the natural world step by step, by identifying problem areas in which something can now be done to lessen the gap between the capacities of our current concepts and our reasonable intellectual ideals.").

Suppose that there was an unlimited supply of any good, say trees, so that the physical quantity of trees was infinite or nearly so. Suppose further that there is a particular tree between my neighbor's house and mine. I like this tree, but it tends to block my neighbor's view of the sunset and she wants to cut it down. Consequently, notwithstanding the unlimited supply of trees, my neighbor's act of cutting down the tree will adversely affect my desired act of viewing the tree from my house. Conversely, my preservation of the tree will affect her desired act of viewing the sunset from her house.

Now an economist would respond that my initial assumption of an unlimited quantity of trees was misleading since the relevant good here is that of "trees between our houses." While my hypothetical assumed that there is an unlimited quantity of "trees," the economist would say that there is only one "tree between our houses" so that the problem of physical scarcity remains. This response is intriguing for it has quietly introduced a new dimension into the problem of scarcity that extends beyond a limitation on the quantity of a physical resource. This new dimension is that of defining the *relevant* good.

What is it that makes a particular good or resource "relevant" for purposes of assessing its scarcity? Relevance, I suggest, is a product of the fact that one or more persons seek to perform two actions that are physically impossible to perform simultaneously. Both actions are not "compossible" in the sense that it is possible to perform both actions at the same time. As Hillel Steiner has explained, "if two actions are such that their joint occurrence requires either (i) the same object being in different places at the same time, or (ii) different objects being in the same place at the same time, then they are incompossible."[8] And relevance is subjective because it requires that one or more people actually desire to perform the acts.

In my example, my neighbor and I both have personal knowledge of how the tree affects the view from our respective windows. My neighbor and I have personal knowledge of each of our preferences concerning the use of this particular tree. Finally, and most significantly, these preferences conflict or, more precisely, each of us subjectively prefers to use the tree in physically incompatible ways. In sum, a problem of subjective scarcity of a relevant good exists when, based on their personal and local knowledge of how particular physical resources may be used to satisfy their desires, (1) one or more persons subjectively desire to use a resource, but (2) the resource in question cannot simultaneously be used to satisfy all of these subjective desires.

Notice that there is no *problem* of scarcity in the absence of an incompatibility of subjective preferences. The "scarcity" that exists in the example of the tree between my neighbor's house and mine is a consequence, not of the fact that there is only one tree between our house, but of the fact that two or more persons have focused their attention on a particular resource that neither can

---

[8] Hillel Steiner, *An Essay on Rights* (Oxford: Blackwell, 1994), p. 37. I shall return to the concept of compossibility and the principle of legality it entails in Chapter 5.

use without adversely affecting the use of the other. The scarcity of a good, then, is subjective in so far as it results from a prior selective focus of attention that defines that good as relevant to more than one physically incompatible use. Moreover, a problem of subjective scarcity may exist even for a single person who subjectively desires to put a resource to two incompossible uses.

Perhaps the nature of subjective scarcity may be illustrated more simply. Imagine a world in which everyone's preferences for resource use were naturally "coordinated" in the sense that no one ever subjectively desired to put a resource to more than one use; that no one ever subjectively desired to use any particular resource at the same time as any other person; that, though individual preferences concerning resource use differed, every preferred use could be acted upon without physically impeding in any way the preferred actions of others; in sum, a world in which all subjectively desired uses were compossible with each other. In such a world, while all resources could be as *physically* scarce as they are in our world, we would face no *subjective* scarcity. If the first-order problem of knowledge is the need to permit people to act on their knowledge while taking the knowledge of others into account, then subjective scarcity engenders a need to render harmonious or to "coordinate" the conflicting personal and associational preferences of real people. This challenge shall be taken up in Chapter 3.

The Relevance of the "External Effects" of Human Action

I have gone to some length to explain how, in light of the subjective scarcity of physical resources, the actions of one person will very likely have what economists sometimes refer to as "external effects" upon the ability of others to put their knowledge into action. What follows from this observation, however, is not at all clear, even were it the case that these effects are often subjectively perceived to be negative. Sometimes people appear to assume that we should prohibit any action that imposes "negative externalities" on others, but the very pervasiveness of subjective negative externalities suggests just the reverse. For, given that some human action is both inevitable and desirable, *if human action will likely affect others negatively, then it must sometimes be permissible to act in such a way as to negatively affect others*. The mere fact that the actions of one person or association will negatively affect others is not enough to justify prohibiting such action for, if it were, then nearly all human action could be prohibited. (Of course, when the effects of an action on another is subjectively perceived to be a positive—a "positive externality"—this fact hardly supports a case for prohibiting that action.)

In sum, while the fact that a particular action will affect others in ways they subjectively perceive to be negative may be *necessary* to justify prohibiting such action, this fact cannot alone be *sufficient* to establish the propriety of prohibition. Assuming that having a subjectively negative effect on others is a necessary condition of prohibiting such actions, the true challenge is to determine, *of all the actions that may potentially affect others adversely*, which should be legally prohibited and which should be permitted.

Summary

In light of the preceding discussion, we may now reformulate the first-order problem of knowledge as follows:

(1) In light of the multitude of individuals and associations, each with their own ever-changing and potentially conflicting personal and local knowledge of potential resource use, how is it possible for individuals to act on the basis of their *own* personal knowledge and for individuals and associations to act on the basis of their own local knowledge without producing irreconcilable and destructive conflict over resource use?

(2) In making their decisions, how are individuals and associations somehow to take into account the ever-changing and potentially conflicting personal and local knowledge of *others*, to which by definition they do not, and often cannot, have access?

THREE

Two Methods of Social Ordering

IN the previous chapter, I described how different people have access to different knowledge, including the personal knowledge of their own perceptions, preferences, and opportunities, and various types of local knowledge. I also explained that this radical dispersion of knowledge—an unavoidable feature of human social life—leads to a knowledge problem when people seek to act on the basis of their differing knowledge in incompatible ways. While the fact of differing personal and local knowledge is a fact we must live with, we want to live with it as comfortably as possible. The pursuit of happiness requires that people be able to develop and to act on the basis of their own personal and local knowledge, but many actions are likely to affect others, sometimes adversely. What is needed then is some way for individuals and associations to develop and act on the basis of their own knowledge, while appropriately taking "into account" the knowledge of others. We seek, in a word, a way of *ordering* those human actions that are likely to affect others in such manner as to permit them to use their knowledge in pursuit of happiness.

1. The Meaning of Social Order

This analysis suggests a useful way of understanding the meaning of "social order." In a perfectly orderly society, no actions of any person would conflict with the actions of any other. In practice, the fewer actions that conflict, the greater is the degree of social order. While each person has knowledge of his or her own preferences,[1] the preferences on which people act are not naturally

---

[1] As was made clear in Chapter 2, personal and local knowledge includes far more than knowledge of personal preferences. Nor are preferences exogenous and "given" as opposed to being in part the product of social interaction. Still, it is the personal preferences that result from the constellation of one's personal and local knowledge (however this knowledge is obtained) that leads him or her to act in ways that conflict with the actions of others. Thus for simplicity this portion of the analysis will refer simply to preferences.

coordinated. Differing preferences for using the same resources can lead some to act in ways that conflict with and impede the ability of others to act on the basis of their knowledge.

One way to achieve an orderly society would be to modify everyone's preferences in such a manner as to reduce or eliminate conflicts over resources use. Because the modification of individual preferences promises to eliminate the phenomenon of conflicting actions at its root, many are attracted to this type of preference or value control and totalitarian regimes pursue such policies with a vengeance. Indeed, its association with totalitarian zealotry has caused the very term "social order" to be viewed with suspicion.

The inclination to modify preferences, however, is not limited to totalitarians. In the name of achieving social order, activists on both the left and right advocate the use of legal coercion to influence personal beliefs and preferences by controlling the content of books, music, movies, and the Internet. The prohibition of sexually explicit books and movies, for example, is sometimes justified on the grounds that such materials allegedly inspire some men to rape or others to molest children. True, prohibitions on speech may also be desired because some ideas or thoughts are considered offensive in themselves or because they lead to actions that are thought to be intrinsically immoral. Still, regardless of the diverse motivations of those who advocate restrictions on speech, these sorts of prohibitions are often publicly *justified* on the ground that the preferences engendered by exposure to the prohibited materials lead to social conflict.

Others who believe that social order requires the resolution of conflicting preferences favor the satisfaction of the majority's preferences when they conflict with the preferences of a minority (including a minority of one). These majoritarians assert that any other mode of achieving social order requires some way of ranking or judging preferences objectively. Since no uncontroversial or nonarbitrary method of ranking preferences is available, the preferences of the majority must prevail—even the majority's preferences as to how those in the minority should live their lives. In the words of Robert Bork, "there is no objectively 'correct' hierarchy to which judges can appeal. But unless there is, unless we can rank forms of gratification, the judge must let the majority have its way."[2] According to this argument, the subjectivity of preferences makes an order imposed by the majority the only alternative to the tyranny of a minority.

The analysis of the first-order problem of knowledge presented in Chapter 2, however, suggests a way to achieve social order that is less drastic than either regulating preferences or imposing the majorities' preferences on minorities. The first-order problem of knowledge is to enable each person to *act* on the basis of their own knowledge while enabling each person to take into account the knowledge of others. The *actions* of some, not their prefer-

---

[2] Robert H. Bork, *The Tempting of America* (New York: Free Press, 1990), p. 258.

ences, are what interfere with the ability of others to pursue happiness by acting on the basis of their own personal and local knowledge. What is sought is a social order in which such knowledgeable actions by everyone are possible.

Although differing preferences and opinions can give rise to conflicting actions we need not control preferences and opinions themselves to handle the problem of conflicting action. We need only control actions. Nor need we control any actions that do not impede the ability of others to put the knowledge in their possession to good use. In sum, to solve the first-order knowledge problem requires only what Hayek called an "order of actions,"[3] not an order of preferences. And, as I shall discuss in Chapter 15, those who advocate regulating preferences or actions to pursue some other objective besides social order must demonstrate that such regulation will not itself impede social order by interfering with the conditions that make an order of actions possible.

Conflicts among human action, then, comprise the disorder that impedes the pursuit of happiness. And by its nature, human action must occur during particular periods of time and in particular spaces. This imperative is reflected in the term "order" itself. An order of actions initially suggests a scheme of *temporal priority*. (First her actions, then his.) But *spatial priority* is another dimension of order. (She acts over here; he acts over there.) An order of actions is achieved when the individual or associational use of resources—that is, human action—is both temporally and spatially coordinated in such a manner as to reduce or eliminate the possibility that two persons or associations will attempt to use the same resource at the same time. If human actions can be suitably regulated, then we need not attempt the potentially tyrannical effort to remold or coordinate personal preferences themselves. To achieve an order of actions one need only regulate the use of physical resources in a society.

Yet although the concept of a social order in which human actions are coordinated is useful to clarify our objective, the concept itself specifies neither the type of order that is most desirable, nor the manner by which such an order of actions can be achieved. Lon Fuller, for example, distinguished between the order "of a morgue or cemetery" and "an order . . . at least good enough to be considered as functioning by some standard or other."[4] Social order could be achieved by allocating the use of resources by a lottery, by brute force, or "by lawless terror, which may serve to keep people off the streets and in their homes,"[5] but what sort of order would this be?

The preceding analysis of the knowledge problem provides a way out of the open-endedness of the concept of social order. For it suggests that, for people

---

[3] Friedrich A. Hayek, *Law Legislation, and Liberty*, vol. 1 (Chicago: University of Chicago Press, 1974), p. 96.

[4] Lon L. Fuller, "Positivism and Fidelity to Law: A Reply to Professor Hart," *Harvard Law Review*, vol. 71 (1958), p. 644.

[5] Lon L. Fuller, *The Morality of Law*, 2nd rev. edn. (New Haven, Conn.: Yale University Press, 1969), p. 107.

to be able to pursue happiness, peace, and prosperity while living in society with others, we need an order of actions in which their personal and local knowledge is developed, disseminated, and acted upon. Not every kind of order will be able to accomplish this equally well.

2. Two Methods of Ordering Actions

Let us now distinguish between two quite different methods of achieving an order of actions: centralized and decentralized ordering. Although I believe that each of these methods has its own distinctive advantages and disadvantages, in this section I want to begin by defining these concepts as neutrally as possible. Then, in the next two sections I will consider the comparative advantages of each ordering method for addressing the first-order problem of knowledge.

This distinction and the discussion that follows is heavily influenced by Friedrich Hayek's distinction between "made" orders (*taxis*) and grown or "spontaneous" orders (*kosmos*),[6] and by Lon Fuller's distinction between "two principles of social ordering,"[7] organization by common aims and reciprocity. Although it is difficult to differentiate sharply between their distinctions and mine, Hayek can be viewed as distinguishing two *types* of social orders and Fuller as distinguishing two kinds of aims or *purposes* of social order. In contrast, I will be discussing two *methods* by which an order of actions can be achieved.

Centralized ordering processes are sometimes referred to as "vertical," or "top down" ordering, while decentralized ordering processes are referred to as "horizontal" or "bottom up" ordering.[8] This hierarchical way of picturing the difference between centralized and decentralized methods of ordering suggests that those who make the decisions in a centralized ordering scheme are in some sense elevated "above" those who are to carry them out. However apt, such hierarchical imagery carries with it certain pejorative connotations that are best avoided at the definitional stage. Hierarchical language suggests that those who are making the decisions from "above" have qualities (apart from

---

[6] See Hayek, *Law and Liberty*, vol. 1, p. 37. Hayek gives language as a pervasive example of a grown or spontaneous, as opposed to a made order. He maintains that a spontaneous order "arises from each element balancing all the various factors operating on it and by adjusting all its various actions to each other, a balance that will be destroyed if some actions are determined by another agency on the basis of different knowledge in the service of different ends." Ibid. 51.

[7] See Lon L. Fuller, "The Forms and Limits of Adjudication," *Harvard Law Review*, vol. 92 (1978), pp. 353, 357–65.

[8] Cf. Fuller, *Morality of Law*, p. 233 (distinguished between "horizontal" and "vertical" forms of order); Wallace Matson, "Justice: A Funeral Oration," *Social Philosophy and Policy*, vol. 1 (1983), pp. 94, 112 (distinguishing between "justice from the bottom up" from "justice from the top down").

their position) that are in some way superior to the inferiors "below" who are to do as they are told. Due to this connotation, hierarchical decision making is viewed pejoratively by those who believe it violates a norm of equality. Conversely, hierarchical decision making is viewed favorably by those who believe that some persons truly are superior decision makers and should therefore be empowered to direct the conduct of others.

In place of a hierarchical conception of these methods of ordering human action let me offer the following, hopefully more neutral and horizontal, definitions:

> *Centralized ordering* orders the actions of diverse persons and associations by delegating to some subset of persons or associations in a society the authority to regulate the conduct of other persons or associations in that society.

In contrast:

> *Decentralized ordering* orders the actions of diverse persons and associations by delegating to each person and association in society a defined authority to regulate their own conduct.

I shall consider each method in turn.

Centralized Ordering

The idea of centralized ordering of society as a whole is both attractive and plausible in light of its familiarity, for we witness centralized ordering in nearly every facet of our daily lives. The first order we ever experience, the family, is organized in this manner, with parents making decisions about the disposition of family assets among the family members. Larger commercial firms are organized this way as well, with a hierarchical association called "management" making decisions about using the resources of the company, subject at times to the approval of a board of directors. Perhaps the military is the most explicitly centralized ordering scheme with extremely well-defined chains of command.

Indeed, much of the intuitive appeal of the centralized ordering of society as a whole stems from its emotional association with these familiar and often desirable institutions. We associate altruistic decision making with the family, efficient decision making with the firm, and crisp, clear lines of authority with the military. What social order could be finer than one that is at once clear, efficient, and altruistic? The emotional appeal of centralized ordering is so powerful, so visceral, that it provides an underlying centralizing tendency to almost every political philosophy, even those that are not purely socialist.

Moreover, centralized ordering is undoubtedly a valuable method of capitalizing upon both personal and local knowledge. Central direction by one individual can effectively order the actions of other persons so as to capitalize on that individual's personal knowledge. For example, it can harness the personal knowledge of a parent of the needs of her child, an entrepreneur's personal knowledge of an unfulfilled demand in a market and a practical way of fulfilling it, or a field officer's personal knowledge of a tactical situation in combat. Or central direction can capitalize upon the local knowledge of an association. For example, it can harness the local knowledge of a husband and wife, the talented managers of a corporation, or a military command.

Suppose a person has an idea for a novel product, say, a computer program or a new magazine, or an innovative way of producing a familiar product. A centralized form of ordering can effectively enable such a person to engage the assistance of others to pursue this vision. Indeed, centralized ordering is most adept at pursuing almost any concrete objective or goal, whether that vision is generated by those in control of an organization as in the case of a corporation, or is supplied from outside an organization as in the case of a military that is directed by civilian authorities. In this way, centralized ordering results in a "made order" (Hayek's term) to achieve a "common aim" (Fuller's term).

As attractive as it may sometimes be to harness the personal and local knowledge of individuals and associations, however, centralized ordering is completely unsuited to handle the first-order problem of knowledge. Suppose we delegate to some person or association the responsibility for coordinating resource use in accordance with the diverse knowledge of all persons and associations so as to achieve an overall order of actions. With such a strategy, some person or identifiable set of persons in a society would somehow have to (*a*) obtain the personal and local knowledge of all persons and associations in that society, (*b*) incorporate this knowledge into a coherent or coordinated "plan" of human actions and then (*c*) transmit instructions on resource use consistent with this plan to everyone in the society so that persons may act accordingly. Intractable problems arise when trying to establish the order of an entire society in such a manner.[9]

The very strength of centralized direction in capitalizing on the personal and local knowledge of central directors (parents, managers, military officers) is at once its weakness as a strategy for solving the first-order problem of knowledge. Centralized ordering is especially effective when those in charge of the ordering scheme have access to useful personal or local knowledge. Although central directors have access to their own personal and local knowledge, however, they lack the access to the knowledge that they would need to reconcile the ever-changing diversity of personal and local knowledge radically dispersed throughout a society. Access to such knowledge is essential if a centralized ordering strategy for the society as a whole is to be implemented, but, as was seen in the previous chapter, such access is simply unavailable. In sum, central directors cannot possibly solve the first-order problem of knowledge in

---

[9] For an historical treatment of efforts to put such central planning into effect and the theoretical debates that surrounded these efforts, see Lavoie, *National Economic Planning*; and Lavoie, *Rivalry and Central Planning*.

society at large because they are hopelessly ignorant of the knowledge such an order of actions requires.[10]

Decentralized Ordering

Centralized direction is such a personally familiar and seemingly effective method of decision making that many overlook or simply do not understand that a powerful alternative to centralized ordering exists.[11] Decentralized social decision making strikes many as anarchistic in both the descriptive sense of "no ruler" and the pejorative sense of "chaos." Because so many believe that no ruler—meaning no central direction—inevitably leads to chaos or disorder, this alternative is swiftly dismissed, if considered at all. Given this belief, the concept of decentralized ordering appears to be a contradiction in terms.

Yet as I will explain in the next chapter, the liberal conception of justice has functioned as a way of harmonizing the diversity of personal and local knowledge of resource use with minimal, if any, need to resort to centralized direction of a society as a whole. Indeed, centralized ordering, when it is employed, may disrupt the order of actions made possible by the decentralized operation of the liberal conception of justice. To appreciate how certain concepts of justice can achieve an order of actions, we must first appreciate how this decentralized strategy differs from one of centralized ordering of resource use. How, we must ask, could the first-order knowledge problem possibly be addressed by anything but central direction without immediately descending into chaos or disorder?

The answer—at the most abstract and general level—involves the concept of *jurisdiction*. A jurisdictional strategy handles the first-order problem of personal and local knowledge dispersed throughout society by using the idea of "bounded individual and associational discretion." Although the term "jurisdiction" is usually applied to judges and other legal decision makers, I am using it in a broader sense applicable to all. This method of social ordering defines a jurisdiction or domain within which individuals or associations are free to act on the basis of their own personal and local knowledge.

---

[10] As explained in Chapter 7, such a centralized direction would also run afoul of the problem of interest—in particular the partiality problem. That is, central directors are likely to be partial to their own interests or the interests of those close to them, at the expense of others who are more remote. This problem provides a wholly independent reason to prefer an alternative to centralized ordering, were one to exist.

[11] Teleological arguments for the existence of god—and arguments from design more generally—reflect this bias. If there is order in the human body, the world, or the universe, then this order must, it is thought, have been the product of a designer. Darwin notwithstanding, the idea that order can be the product of "spontaneous" evolutionary development is counterintuitive. See William P. Alston, "Teleological Argument for the Existence of God," in Paul Edwards (ed.), *The Encyclopedia of Philosophy*, viii (New York: Macmillan and Free Press, 1967), pp. 84–8.

Implicit in this jurisdictional strategy is a crucial distinction between the judgment maker and the judgment to be made. Or, to use the language of sports, such a strategy distinguishes the question, "who makes the call?" from the question, "what is the correct call?"[12] Although both of these questions require knowledge to answer, each question requires substantially different knowledge. To answer the second of these questions requires personal and local knowledge of particular circumstances—knowledge that is inaccessible to centralized mechanisms. The first of these questions requires only that we know who is generally in the best position to have personal and local knowledge.

We may refer to this quality of "being in the best position to know" as the quality of institutional or personal *competence*. The knowledge required to answer the second or "substantive" question differs substantially from that required to answer the "jurisdictional" question of competence. Even when we do not know the correct call to make, we may know who is most likely to have the knowledge that such a decision requires. Instead of requiring that we have access to the knowledge needed to make the decision in question, such an assessment requires only that we determine who is in the best position to obtain the knowledge that such a decision requires. In baseball, for example, without knowing anything about a particular pitch we may know that, of all the people in the stadium, the umpire is in the best position to assess whether or not a pitched ball is in the strike zone.[13]

The discussion of personal and local knowledge in Chapter 2 suggests that individuals and associations have a comparative advantage over centralized mechanisms. Individuals and associations have access to vast amounts of relevant personal and local knowledge that centralized decision makers must lack. The fact that individual persons and institutions are generally in the best position to make the right call does not, however, mean that they will always make good use of their access or that others are never in a better position to make a particular call. Nor does it mean that an analysis of personal and institutional competence would never benefit from a substantive assessment of the right call to make. We may, in fact, bolster our assessment of personal and institu-

---

[12] The phrase "making the call" in American sports, derives from baseball umpires who "call" out whether a pitch is a ball or a strike or whether a runner is safe or out.
[13] Of course, the batter and, especially, the catcher may be as well positioned or "competent" as the umpire to know whether a pitch is a ball or a strike. But, as with centralized direction, allocating decision making to them would run afoul of the *partiality problem*, a problem of interest discussed in Chapter 7. This illustrates that, while the knowledge problem may sometimes narrow our range of options (in this example to the umpire, catcher, and batter), it is insufficient to understanding fully the function of justice and the rule of law. The social problems of interest and of power must also be addressed. Just as such considerations lead us to chose the umpire over the catcher and batter to call balls and strikes, as we shall see, the problems of interest and power may not only reinforce the solutions to the knowledge problem; they may also require more specific or refined conceptions of both justice and the rule of law than is needed to handle the knowledge problem alone.

tional competence by sampling a few decisions to see if they appear to reflect the knowledge we expect these persons and institutions to possess. A pattern of egregious decisions would call into question the competence of the decision maker. In contract law, for example, the competency of a person to enter into contracts is sometimes assessed by examining the "rationality" of various decisions that person has made.

Still, the possibility of second-guessing the wisdom of the decisions of those in the best position to make a call does not change the basic analysis. Given that no decision maker is perfect, we need to make a comparative and generalized judgment when determining the appropriate jurisdictional allocation. A persistent bias in favor of centralized decision making results from our apparent ability to second-guess the wisdom of others' decisions when these decisions go awry. Such a bias falsely assumes that an institutional competence to second-guess the correctness of another's call *on occasion* entails an institutional competence to make correct calls for others *systematically*. The concept of competence does not rest on an ability to make every decision better than anyone else; it rests on being in a better position than anyone else to make knowledgeable decisions.[14]

This was illustrated some years ago by the abortive attempt to use televised "instant replays" to override the decisions of football officials on the field. The fact that such replays occasionally revealed that officiating errors had been made led the National Football League to allow teams to appeal certain rulings to an official in the broadcast booth who would review the contested play from a variety of angles. While a genuinely erroneous decision was reversed on occasion, the process of second-guessing field officials also resulted in a number of unforeseen and untoward consequences: the time it took to review the plays disrupted the flow of the game; the review process undermined the self-confidence of field officials who then became more tentative in their decision making which, in turn, led to more errors and more appeals; and finally, both the failure to reverse plays that the public (and television commentators) viewed as erroneous and the erroneous reversals of rulings the public viewed as correct led to much frustration among football fans. The tumultuous experiment in second-guessing officials was quickly ended,[15] though the temptation to correct decisions by means of video replays has grown as the memory of its practical difficulties has receded.

---

[14] The example of persons being declared incompetent suggests that even when they are in the best position to make decisions about their own welfare, on occasion individuals are unable reliably to make use of their privileged access to personal and local knowledge. For this reason, though individuals are, as a general matter, in the best position to make knowledgeable decisions, *particular* individuals are only *presumed* to be competent. In rare circumstances this presumption can be rebutted by showing that the factual preconditions on which it is based do not exist.

[15] Note that even this experimental failure did not completely supplant the personal judgment of field officials, but allowed only for occasional appeals and reversals of their decisions.

Second-guessing the wisdom of decisions made by individuals and associations acting on the basis of their personal and local knowledge, then, is a far less certain process than theorists commonly assume. In the United States, for example, legislatures and administrative agencies who second-guess citizens, are themselves second-guessed by judges, who are themselves second-guessed by multiple appellate courts, who are themselves second-guessed by academics, journalists, and sometimes even by legislatures (to complete the circle of second-guessers).[16] And this understates the process of second-guessing. The House of Representatives is second-guessed by the Senate (and vice-versa) and both are second-guessed by the President. Within administrative agencies, inspectors and rule-makers are second-guessed by internal appeals processes. Within Congress, committees second-guess each other and are second-guessed by the legislature as a whole. Within federal appeals court circuits, all the appeals judges sitting as a whole can second guess the judgments of three-judge panels. Cities and towns who second-guess individuals are themselves second-guessed by state governments, who in turn are second-guessed by the national government. Of course, everyone is second-guessed by historians. Often, at the end of the day, it is not at all clear that the original decision was really unsatisfactory. The unending quest to correct the judgment of individuals and associations is often illusory and always costly. It clearly underestimates the first-order problem of knowledge.

The idea of jurisdiction based on "bounded individual and associational discretion" is, of course, far too general to define actual conduct as permissible or impermissible. It says nothing about the nature of the domain or the extent of the boundary. Nonetheless, even at this extremely general level, such a strategy is theoretically revealing in several ways. First, it identifies *discretion*—or liberty—as a means of capitalizing on knowledge that cannot be transmitted in this context through a chain of command to centralized rulers. Second, it places discretion in the hands of individuals who are *most likely* to possess personal knowledge and in the hands of associations who are most likely to possess local knowledge. Finally, it immediately suggests that discretion must somehow be *bounded* or constrained, albeit in a manner that does not undermine the purpose for adopting the strategy. The boundaries of this discretion are defined by two distinct concepts: decentralized jurisdiction over physical resources and consensual transfers of these jurisdictions. In the next section, I identify the features of these concepts that, if followed, enables them to address the first-order problem of knowledge.

---

[16] When the issue on appeal is one of statutory interpretation, Congress may override a decision of the Supreme Court.

3. Requirements of Decentralized Ordering

The first-order problem of knowledge has two aspects or dimensions. First, persons need to develop and act upon the basis of their own knowledge. Second, persons need to take into account the knowledge of others of which they are ignorant when making their decisions of how to act. A decentralized approach to this problem consists of an adherence to decentralized jurisdiction and consensual transfers. I shall explain here and in Chapter 4 how decentralized jurisdiction addresses the first aspect of the knowledge problem, while consensual transfers addresses both.

Principles of Decentralized Jurisdiction

The first requirement of a decentralized approach to the knowledge problem is *decentralized jurisdiction*. Before briefly sketching the principles underlying this requirement that flow from the preceding discussion, two caveats are in order.

First, I do not contend that the following rather abstract principles of decentralized jurisdiction are capable of yielding specific allocations of jurisdiction to particular individuals. As will be explained in Chapter 5, abstract theoretical principles decide few actual cases or controversies. Rather, the principles that follow serve as functional criteria for evaluating the set of conventional rules that is needed to determine specific allocations. In other words, these general (natural rights) principles cannot take the place of posited or conventional *laws* to govern the allocation of resources, but any such laws should be critically assessed to determine if they function in a manner that is consistent with these principles.

Second, the rationale for each of the principles presented here is limited to its relationship to the first-order problem of knowledge, the only problem I have examined to this point. Further support for these principles is provided by their ability to handle other problems of knowledge, interest, and power. The full force of the imperative that these principles ought to be respected depends on the claim that, when instituted, they address a host of pervasive social problems far better than any competing set of principles. Readers will miscalculate the need for these principles if they think this need is limited to addressing the problem of knowledge.

With these caveats in mind, let me now identify the principles that ought to govern decentralized ordering.

> *Jurisdiction or discretionary control over resources must be delegated to identifiable individuals and groups.*

The fact that access to personal and local knowledge is dispersed throughout society gives rise to the first-order problem of knowledge. Knowledgeable decisions cannot be made concerning the use of resources if the decision maker lacks access to this vital personal and local knowledge. If decisions concerning resource use are to be knowledgeable, decision-making authority concerning resource use must be delegated to the persons and associations in possession of such knowledge. Conversely, those who, by assumption, lack the requisite knowledge of resource use should also lack the authority to interfere with the decisions made by those with knowledge—at least as a general matter. All else being equal, the distribution of jurisdiction over physical resources should mirror as closely as possible the distribution of access to knowledge in society.

> *The allocation of jurisdiction should reflect an assessment of who is in the best position to have personal and local knowledge of the resources in question.*

It is impossible to say systematically which persons or associations have knowledge about the potential uses of particular physical resources. If a centralized institution, or political theorists for that matter, knew what it would need to know to make particular allocations of jurisdictions, we would not need a decentralized jurisdictional strategy in the first place. The best we can hope for is to determine the general characteristics of those who are in the best position to have knowledge of potential resource uses, regardless of whether in fact they always do have the best knowledge. By virtue of their privileged access to the personal and local knowledge pertaining to their situation, individuals and groups ought to be accorded a *presumption of competence* in exercising their discretion. As was noted above, this presumption can sometimes be overcome by evidence that a particular person is not capable of making use of his or her privileged access to personal and local knowledge.[17]

> *The domain accorded any particular individual or group must be bounded.*

If the distribution of jurisdiction over physical resources should mirror as closely as possible the distribution of knowledge in society, then this also means that such jurisdiction must be limited or bounded. Because access to personal and local knowledge is limited, no one has access to all such knowledge. Consequently, no person or group should have jurisdiction over all resources. Indeed, the distinction between liberty and license mentioned in the first chapter is the terminology that classical liberal natural rights theorists used to acknowledge the bounded nature of liberty.

> *Because the knowledge of individuals and associations is dynamic, not static, the boundaries of domains must be subject to revision.*

---

[17] Although the analysis presented here allows, in principle, for a rebuttal of the presumption of competence, any implementation of this "exception" would require safeguards against potentially serious problems of enforcement error and abuse. These problems of power and the need to guard against them are discussed in Part III.

As was discussed in Chapter 2, knowledge is constantly changing and, consequently, jurisdiction cannot be allocated once and for all. Although the dynamic nature of the first-order problem of knowledge makes changes in jurisdictions necessary, allowing jurisdictional boundaries to change gives rise to a very ticklish knowledge problem. If a potential user were permitted to displace the present user simply on the basis of a mere assertion that he has knowledge of how resources may "best" be used, this would provide no way of assuring that the prospective user is really in any better position to use the resources than the present user. Interpersonal comparisons of knowledge (or interests[18]) cannot reliably be made by the parties themselves or by third parties. What is crucial to understand is that some systemic means of transferring jurisdiction must exist that reflects the knowledge (and interests) of both parties. As I explain in the next section, consent performs this vital function.

Principles of Consensual Transfer

The requirement of bounded individual and associational discretion is crucial to harnessing the local and personal knowledge that is dispersed throughout society. Recall the two dimensions or aspects of the first-order problem of knowledge discussed above: (1) one must be able to act on the basis of one's own personal knowledge or the knowledge one has as a member of an association with local knowledge; (2) when so acting one must somehow take into account the knowledge of others of which each person is hopelessly ignorant. The requirement of consensual transfers addresses both dimensions of the first-order problem of knowledge. There are two principles of consensual transfer, each of which addresses a different dimension of the knowledge problem.

First, a principle of *permitting* consensual transfers of jurisdiction enables persons to act on the basis of their personal and local knowledge by authorizing them to exchange jurisdictions they currently have for jurisdictions they believe they can put to better use. In this way, a transfer of one's jurisdiction reflects one's local and personal knowledge. Second, a principle of *requiring* that all transfers of jurisdiction be by consent enables (and forces[19]) persons to take into account the knowledge of others when making their decisions. For changes in boundaries to reflect the knowledge of all affected parties, such

[18] The first-order problem of knowledge cannot be entirely divorced from interest if for no other reason than because one of the things that persons and associations have knowledge of is their interests.

[19] The fact that a person *must* take the knowledge of others into account addresses, not the problem of knowledge, but a pervasive problem of interest discussed in Part II: the *partiality problem*. The set of resource prices, discussed later in this next section, that results from this requirement, however, does address the second aspect of the first-order problem of knowledge by enabling persons to take the knowledge of others into account when they decide whether and how to act. In this respect, the ability of the requirement of consent to address the knowledge problem depends to some extent on its ability also to address the problem of interest.

revisions must be based on the consent of the individuals or associations whose boundaries are changed. By requiring consent,[20] the new claimant is compelled to take the knowledge of the present jurisdiction-holder into account—including the present holder's knowledge of her own perceptions, preferences, opportunities, etc.

For example, if a woman, call her Ann, based on her knowledge of her situation, would prefer to maintain her jurisdiction over particular resources than see it transferred to a man, call him Ben, then to obtain Ann's consent to a transfer, Ben must offer Ann something he thinks she would value more. In other words, the onus falls upon Ben to provide Ann with jurisdiction over some *other* resources that she could put to better use than the resources over which she currently holds jurisdiction. So, for example, in exchange for her jurisdiction over a book she has already read, Ben could offer Ann jurisdiction over a book she has yet to read. Only if Ben must obtain Ann's consent is there any assurance that his claim to jurisdiction will take her knowledge into account.

But the requirement of consensual transfers affects our ability to take into account the knowledge of others far more profoundly than this simple "micro" example suggests. Such a requirement also makes possible the evolution of a powerful "macro" institution that enables personal and local knowledge to be "encoded" and transmitted worldwide in a form that can be easily understood by others and incorporated into their decisions without centralized direction. In short, the requirement of consent permits the evolution of a set of resource *prices*.

Prices are by far the most neglected form of knowledge we have. Although some economic literature stresses the importance of prices,[21] the knowledge-disseminating function of prices is largely unknown—or, if known, then widely ignored—in political and legal theory. The reason for this is that the knowledge embedded in prices is not explicit; we are never conscious of it as knowledge. It is encoded knowledge, and we are conscious only of the code.

Prices reflect the vast personal and local knowledge of the many competing uses to which any physical resource may be put. My computer is constructed

---

[20] That consent ordinarily be objectively *manifested*, as opposed to merely subjective, is a requirement resulting from the need to address the second-order problem of knowledge—communicating justice—that I will discuss in Chapter 5. Were it not for that problem, a subjective conception of consent would suffice to handle the first-order problem of knowledge.

[21] The role that market prices play in conveying information was first stressed by Ludwig von Mises and then greatly amplified by Hayek. See e.g. Ludwig von Mises, *Human Action* (Chicago: Henry Regnery, 3rd edn., 1963)("It is the very essence of prices that they are the offshoot of the actions of individuals and groups acting on their own behalf. . . . A government can no more determine prices than a goose can lay hen's eggs."); Hayek, *Law and Liberty*, vol. 1, p. 86 ("We must look at the price system as . . . a mechanism for communicating information if we want to understand its real function."). My contribution is merely to stress that consent to transfers of jurisdiction must be both permitted and required if prices are to convey the information that can be conveyed effectively in no other manner.

of plastic, glass, various metals, and other resources. My desk is made of wood. These resources could have been used in a variety of other ways by people throughout the globe. I have not the slightest way of knowing even a small fraction of the specific alternative uses that others might find for these resources. And yet without a comprehensive knowledge of all the alternative uses of these resources, how can a knowledgeable decision be made on how these resources should be used?

I have already explained how, in light of the dispersed nature of personal and local knowledge, the problem of knowing alternative uses of resources is immense. It would require the compilation of all persons' personal knowledge of perceptions, interests, and opportunities and all local knowledge of associations as to their shared interests and opportunities, the integration of this knowledge into a coherent plan, and the communication of everyone's allocated role. This is a knowledge problem of such enormous proportions that *less information is preferable to more*. That is, even if we could have direct access to all the knowledge we require, the sheer volume of such knowledge would prevent us from putting it to use. We need somehow to condense this knowledge into a usable form. We need to convert it to a form of local knowledge that can itself be integrated into each person's personal knowledge. And this process of condensation need not be perfect to be superior to the only alternative: near-total ignorance that results from the general inaccessibility of personal and local knowledge. Only the device of resource prices can perform this vital function.

Resource prices condense the personal and local knowledge of each one of us into a form of local knowledge that can be integrated into the personal knowledge of all of us. Resource prices are local knowledge insofar as they are communicated from one person to another in an intelligible form. Once communicated, they may be integrated into the personal knowledge of individuals concerning their available opportunities. For example, a trip to Aix-en-Provence has a resource price attached to it. When I consider this choice, I must consider the subjective cost to me of paying this price. This cost is the most highly valued set of opportunities that I will forgo by choosing to go to Aix.[22] Less formally, I must consider what I will have to sacrifice to make the trip. By requiring me to forgo opportunities I could obtain with the same amount of money, the price of travel to Aix will strongly influence the subjective cost to me of such a trip, and this price reflects the uses to which *others* may put the resources that it would take to get me to Aix.[23] Of course, even

[22] For a discussion of the subjective costs of choice, see Buchanan, *Cost and Choice*. I shall return to the implications of the subjective cost of choice when discussing the incentive problem in Chapter 8.

[23] I do not consider here how the medium of exchange that also is needed for a price system to operate is chosen. Historically, the most popular and useful media of exchange—gold and silver—have evolved from the countless consensual choices of consumers. The evolution of money from consensual exchange has long been recognized: "[I]f he would give his Nuts for a piece of Metal, pleased with its colour; or exchange his Sheep for Shells, or Wool for a sparkling Pebble or a Diamond, and keep those by him

with a market price of zero, there is no such thing as a truly cost-free trip to Aix because such a trip will require me to forgo other potential uses of my time and time is all too scarce. But these are subjective costs to which I have access (personal knowledge) and which I can combine with the monetary price (local knowledge) to reach a decision about whether to make the trip that takes into account both my knowledge and the knowledge of others.

Prices are able to communicate this information, however, *only because the consent of those with jurisdiction over particular resources is required before jurisdiction may be transferred* to another. None of this calculation would have been performed had I not been required to obtain the airline's consent to fly me to France and had the airline not been required to obtain the consent of all those whose cooperation is needed to make the flight possible. The need of others to obtain the consent of a jurisdiction-holder means that anyone wishing to obtain a transfer of jurisdiction must offer the present jurisdiction-holder jurisdiction over other resources that the present holder believes he or she would put to better use. The types of offers, as well as the number of persons offering to make exchanges, educate the holder of the value that others place on the resources. When this value reaches a certain level, the holder is induced to make an exchange, thereby revealing that the value she placed on the resource was less than the value to her of the resources offered. Without the requirement of consent, this information would never be revealed and any prices that may exist will lack *meaning*.[24]

With a set of resource prices, a person is able to—indeed must[25]—decide whether to use a resource, save it for later use, or exchange it for another resource by comparing her knowledge of the different uses she has with the knowledge and preferences of countless others that are encoded in the market price for the good. If the market price is higher than the value she places on the resource then she will be induced to exchange it. If the market price is lower, she will either use the resource or conserve it for later use or exchange.

The process is dynamic in that the holder of jurisdiction is incorporating price signals—a form of local knowledge—into the personal knowledge on which she bases her decision. In turn, her decision (to hold or sell) will influence the price signals received by others and will then be incorporated

---

all his Life, he invaded not the Right of others, he might heap up as much of these durable things as he pleased; the *exceeding of the bounds of his* just *Property* not lying in the largeness of his Possession, but the perishing of any thing uselesly [*sic*] in it. And thus came *in the use of Money*, some lasting thing that Men might keep without spoiling, and that *by mutual consent* Men would take in exchange for the truly useful, but perishable Supports of Life." Locke, *Two Treatises*, pp. 318–19 (fourth emphasis added). See also, F. A. Hayek, *The Denationalization of Money* (London: Institute for Economic Affairs, 1976).

[24] But see Hayek, *Law and Liberty*, vol. 1, p. 86 ("Even when prices have become quite rigid, however, the forces which would operate through changes in prices still operate to a considerable extent through changes in other terms of the contract.").

[25] Once again, by forcing—as opposed to enabling—persons to take into account the knowledge of others, the requirement of consent also addresses the *partiality problem*.

into their personal knowledge. For example, my ongoing decision not to sell my house both influences the market price of housing and, simultaneously, is influenced by the market price of my house and by the market price of alternative housing. True, the effect of my decision alone is unlikely to "move the market," but, in the aggregate, the current market price is a product of everyone's decision either to sell or not to sell.

There is a great deal more to say about information dissemination and resource prices than I have said here. For example, the information embedded in a price depends on where the jurisdictional lines are drawn. After all, there once were market prices for slaves that did not reflect the knowledge or interest of the slave. And prices will also depend on the liability rules in place for actions that impede upon other jurisdictions. A manufacturer might be willing to pay a higher price for jurisdiction over land if liability rules for jurisdiction-holders permitted it to emit noxious fumes into the air than if liability rules required the manufacturer to compensate surrounding jurisdiction-holders.[26]

Still, none of these additional factors influencing the meaning of resource prices contradicts the basic point being made here: the process of knowledge generation and transmittal made possible by resource prices could not occur if consensual transfers were not both *permitted* and *required*. In this way, though they may not be sufficient, both principles of consensual transfers are necessary to address the first-order problem of knowledge. Nonconsensual transfer of jurisdictions "short-circuit" the price system of knowledge transmittal and make it impossible for individuals and associations to take the knowledge of others into account when putting their own knowledge into action. I am not assuming that the process of information dissemination made possible by consensual resource prices is "perfect." Far from it. I contend only that such a process is both necessary to the pursuit of happiness, peace, and prosperity, and superior to any known alternative.

The Relationship Between Centralized and Decentralized Ordering

My earlier disclaimers notwithstanding, the length of my treatment of decentralized ordering may cause some readers to think that I have underestimated the importance of centralized ordering. Let me rectify this impression. Centralized ordering is absolutely vital to implementing the personal and local knowledge of individuals and associations. For this reason, if no other, centralized ordering is inescapable and indispensable to the pursuit of happiness, peace, and prosperity. The university at which I teach would be in chaos were there no administration to schedule classes, assign teachers to subjects and time-slots, collect tuition fees and dispense scholarships, procure maintenance of the buildings and grounds, etc. In the classroom, I serve as a "central

---

[26] If such emissions are prohibited then we would say that one's jurisdiction did not include this activity, and this would therefore fall under the category of where jurisdictional lines are drawn.

director" deciding what readings to assign and directing the discussion along lines I determine.

Further, Ronald Coase has argued that central direction within a company or "firm" is sometimes preferable to decentralized ordering because it reduces the transaction costs of contracting.

The main reason why it is profitable to establish a firm would seem to be that there is a cost of using the price mechanism. The most obvious cost of "organising" production through the price mechanism is that of discovering what the relevant prices are. . . . The costs of negotiating and concluding a separate contract for each exchange transaction which takes place on the market must also be taken into account. . . . It is true that contracts are not eliminated when there is a firm but they are greatly reduced.[27]

Coase also observes that long-term contracts which leave a lot of discretion in one or both parties start to look like firms within which each transaction is not explicitly and separately negotiated. "A firm is likely therefore to emerge in those cases where a very short-term contract would be unsatisfactory."[28] Under such circumstance, "entrepreneur[s] . . . take the place of the price mechanism in the direction of resources."[29]

Yet the very pervasiveness of different and overlapping centrally-ordered institutions, such as firms, makes an overall decentralized order all the more essential. Some means of interaction *among* centralized associations is needed. Superimposing a centralized ordering mechanism on top of the myriad centralized organizations would undermine rather than enhance their value. Consider religion. The fact that churches, mosques, and synagogues require some internal centralized ordering to function in no way suggests that "religion" in the abstract requires an overarching external centralized ordering scheme to direct all churches, mosques, and synagogues (though some religions, Catholicism for example, have a more centralized relationship among their churches than others). To the contrary, it is the decentralized order provided by religious toleration that enables congregation members of different faiths to reap the benefits of their centrally-ordered religious institutions. This holds true as well for every other example of centralized ordering, from education to health care, from publishing to sports.

The same considerations that led us to the principles of decentralized order for individuals discussed in this chapter hold true as well for centrally-ordered institutions. Because the knowledge reposed in its managers is necessarily limited,[30] the jurisdiction of centrally-ordered institutions must be bounded. And

---

[27] Ronald H. Coase, "The Nature of the Firm," *Economica*, vol. 4 (1937), pp. 386, 390–1.

[28] Ibid. 392.   [29] Ibid. 388.

[30] Cf. ibid. 397: "[T]he costs of organising and the losses through mistakes will increase with an increase in the spacial distribution of the transactions organised, in the dissimilarity of the transactions, and the probability of changes in the relative prices." Coase referred to these and other such limiting factors as "diminishing returns to management." Ibid. 396.

addressing the first-order problem of knowledge requires that a centrally-ordered institution arise by the consent of its constituents. Based on the personal and local knowledge at our disposal, I consent to teach at my university and accept the governance of the administration and my students consent to attend and accept my governance in addition to that of the administration. Our consent, coupled with the consent of all others who comprise the university to join and accept central governance, along with the imperative of obtaining the consent of all who have physical resources which the university needs, is a precondition for a beneficial relationship existing among its constituents and between it constituents and others.

While self-direction or "autonomy"[31] may not always be needed to pursue happiness, a self-rule embracing a mix of both self-direction *and* consent to the governance of others, including centralized authorities, is essential to handle the first-order problem of knowledge. Only by *permitting* centrally-ordered organizations to arise by the consent of their constituents can the personal and local knowledge of managers within associations be harnessed. But only by *requiring* the consent of constituents of centrally-ordered organizations institutions and those whose physical resources is needed by these organizations, can we be confident that the decisions of central authorities reflect the dispersed knowledge of all other persons and associations. In this respect centralized organizations represent "islands of conscious power in [an] ocean of unconscious co-operation."[32]

From the perspective of the first-order problem of knowledge, then, centralized and decentralized ordering are not on an equal footing. For only by adhering to the principles of decentralized ordering can we be at all sure that a choice to use centralized ordering is a knowledgeable one.

Adam Smith's term for the decentralized spontaneous order, or what Hayek called "catallaxy,"[33] within which both individuals and centrally-ordered institutions can thrive was the Great Society.[34] The Great Society composed of individuals, associations, and centrally-ordered organizations is made possible by adherence to the principles of decentralized ordering identified in this

---

[31] Careful readers will notice that nowhere in this book do I appeal to the value of "autonomy." Because the term autonomy, as distinct from heteronomy, entails complete self-direction, I use instead the term liberty, or sometimes discretion, to refer to the exercise of consent, which can include the consent to have one's actions directed by others.

[32] D. H. Robertson, *Control of Industry*, (New York: Harcourt, Brace & Co., 1923), p. 85.

[33] See Hayek, *Law and Liberty*, vol. ii, pp. 108–9 (defining catallaxy as "the order brought about by the mutual adjustment of many individual economies in a market.")

[34] See Adam Smith, *The Theory of Moral Sentiments* (London, 1759), part 6, sect. ii, ch. 2 (Indianapolis: Liberty Classics, 1976), pp. 233–34: "The man of system . . . is apt to be very wise in his own conceit. . . . He seems to imagine that he can arrange the different members of a great society with as much ease as the hand arranges the different pieces upon a chessboard. He does not consider that the pieces upon the chessboard have no other principle of motion besides that which the hand impresses upon them; but that, in the great chessboard of human society, every single piece has a principle of motion of its own." I follow Hayek in capitalizing the Great Society.

chapter. In the next chapter, I shall explain how these principles of decentralized ordering are embodied in the rights that define the liberal conception of justice. In this manner, as we shall see, a respect for these rights is a prerequisite to the achievement of the Great Society.[35]

Two Types of Coordination

The type of *coordination* provided by what Smith refers to as the Great Society and that Hayek refers to as "catallaxy" must be distinguished from another common use of the term. As Dan Klein explains:

Coordination is first and best understood as something we hope to achieve in our actions with others. I hope to drive on the same side of the road as others, I hope to use the same semantics as my listeners, I hope to go to the same place in Manhattan as the persons I wish to meet. In these cases, we hope to coordinate our actions *with* the actions of others, by coordinating *to* some common principle or focal point.[36]

You say, "Make it Grand Central Station at noon," and I coordinate to that remark, and hope to coordinate my actions with yours.

In response to the writings of Thomas Schelling,[37] an important literature has arisen to answer the question of whether and how coordination in this sense can arise spontaneously—that is, without central direction.[38] This kind of coordination requires "a common principle or focal point. . . . Individuals make a conscious effort to coordinate with each other. They strive for and see a meshing of action in their own activities. Schelling coordination is manifest."[39] It is achieved by the use of conventions or rules.

The coordination—or "order of actions"—described by Hayek is different. "He means that when the blacksmith forges a pair of clipping shears, that activity is well coordinated to the activities of the weaver, who some time later works with the wool that was clipped from sheep with those shears."[40] Klein points out numerous differences between these two types of coordination. "First of all, the blacksmith and weaver do not even know of each other's existence, and have no manifest sense of coordinating their actions with the actions of others."[41] Rather, their actions are "coordinated," not in the sense that each has an expectation of how the other will act, but in the sense that each person's actions complement the others. The blacksmith can use the

---

[35] Cf. ibid. 109 ("A catallaxy is thus the special kind of spontaneous order produced by the market through people acting within the rules of the law of property, tort, and contract.")

[36] Daniel B. Klein, "Convention, Social Order, and the Two Coordinations," *Constitutional Political Economy*, vol. 8/4 (1997).

[37] See Thomas C. Schelling, *The Strategy of Conflict* (Cambridge, Mass.: Harvard Univ. Press, rev. edn. 1980); Thomas C. Schelling, *Micro and Macrobehavior* (New York: W.W. Norton, 1978).

[38] See e.g. Robert Sugden, *The Economics of Rights, Co-operation and Welfare* (Oxford: Blackwell, 1986), pp. 34–54.

[39] Klein, "Convention".   [40] Ibid.   [41] Ibid.

knowledge at his disposal in pursuit of his purposes in a manner that facilitates the weaver in using her knowledge in pursuit of her purposes and vice versa.

Klein refers to this as *metacoordination*. "The distinction between coordination and metacoordination lines up with the distinction between conventions and social concatenations or orders."[42] Metacoordination, or social order, embraces myriad individuals who do not know of each other's existence and who may even be in rivalrous competition with each other. Their actions are coordinated, not only in the sense that they are not in conflict with each other, but *also* in the sense that they are pursuing their disparate purposes while acting on their personal and local knowledge.

The coordination provided by conventions and norms is quite important to the achievement of the metacoordination or social order described by Hayek. The principles described above, and the rights embodying them, that make social order in the Hayekian sense possible, are abstract. For reasons I shall explain in Chapter 6, their exact requirements are not always manifest in complex day-to-day transactions. To implement these principles requires persons to converge on certain conventional rules to govern their conduct. But these coordinating (in the Schelling sense) rules must be consistent with more abstract principles described above that coordinate (in the Hayekian sense) by enabling persons to handle the first-order problem of knowledge as well as the problems of interest described in Part II. In Chapter 6, I will describe features of a legal system that are capable of discovering such coordinating rules.

Summary

In this chapter, I have suggested that actions harnessing personal and local knowledge can be ordered by either centralized or decentralized decision-making processes. Centralized decision making works when the decision maker has access to the relevant personal and local knowledge. Since such access is limited, such decision making must be limited as well. In any society, personal and local knowledge is widely dispersed. This means that decision making must be decentralized within any society. Jurisdiction over resources must be delegated to individuals and associations who have access to the relevant knowledge and who can then use centralized decision making within their jurisdictional domain. In sum, centralized ordering—of families, associations, companies, etc.—needs to take place within a decentralized framework.

I have tried to show how the idea of individual and associational jurisdiction over resources and the requirement that transfers of jurisdiction be consensual helps to solve the first-order problem of knowledge. The first of these

---

[42] Ibid.

attributes addresses the ability of individuals and associations to act on the basis of their personal and local knowledge. The second addresses the ability of individuals and associations to incorporate into their decisions the personal and local knowledge of others. This approach has the following characteristics:

(1) Jurisdiction or discretionary control over resources by identifiable individuals and groups must be recognized.
(2) The allocation of jurisdiction should reflect an assessment of who is in the best position to have personal and local knowledge of the resources in question.
(3) The domain accorded any particular individual or group must be bounded.
(4) Because the knowledge of individuals and associations is continuously changing, the boundaries of domains must be subject to revision.
(5) In order that changes in boundaries reflect the knowledge of all affected parties, such revisions must be based on the manifested consent of the individuals or associations whose boundaries are changed.
(6) Consensual transfers of jurisdiction should be both permitted and required.

In the next chapter, I shall relate these features to the liberal conception of justice and suggest still further refinements of this strategy.

FOUR

The Liberal Conception of Justice

W HEN liberties are naked, a person may be free to do as he wishes, but others are similarly free to interfere with his actions. As Hillel Steiner has observed: "Like other naked things, unvested liberties are exposed to the numbing effects of cold fronts: in the case of liberties, to the obstructive impact of others' exercise of their powers and liberties."[1] Liberty (capital "L") requires the protection of liberties (small "l"),[2] but given that the world is one of subjective scarcity, not all liberties or freedom can be protected, however nice that would be. Rights are concepts that define a domain within which persons ought to be at liberty or free to do as they please free of interference by others.[3] In this sense "No one ever has a right to do something; he only has a right that some one else shall do (or refrain from doing) something. In other words, every right in the strict sense relates to the conduct of another."[4]

The liberal conception of justice is the respect of rights.[5] Some rights are natural in so far as the domains they define are prerequisites for the pursuit of

---

[1] See Steiner, *Essay on Rights*, p. 87. Adopting H. L. A. Hart's refinement of the Benthamite distinction between *naked* and *vested* liberties, Steiner defines a "vested liberty [as] one surrounded by a 'protective perimeter' formed by others' duties which, though not specifically correlative to any right in the liberty-holder to exercise that liberty, nonetheless effectively prohibit their interference." Ibid. 75.

[2] Because of the confusion that may arise from distinguishing Liberty from liberties, classical liberals sometimes distinguish between Liberty (meaning those liberties that are protected) and Freedom (meaning all liberties whether protected or not). See e.g., ibid. 60 n. 4: "Liberty in this *normative* or *evaluative* or *rule-constituted* sense, is to be distinguished from the *descriptive* or *empirical* concept—absence of prevention—which . . . I shall henceforth refer to as 'freedom' where confusion between the two might otherwise occur." I shall do the same.

[3] See ibid. 76: "A vested liberty is *internal* to a person's rights—contained by them because protected by their correlative duties—while a naked liberty is *interstitial* to respective persons' rights, suspended in whatever action-space is left between them. Vested liberties exist in one-man's land; naked liberties inhabit no-man's land."

[4] Glanville Williams, "The Concept of Legal Liberty," in Robert Summers (ed.), *Essays in Legal Philosophy* (Oxford: Blackwell, 1970), p. 139.

[5] See Steiner, *Essay on Rights*, p. 109: "[M]oral reasoning is reasoning about moral actions. And moral actions are ones directed towards our various ends which we believe should be pursued and sustained by everyone and ought not to be obstructed or abolished by anyone. One such end may be justice: the requirement that moral rights be respected."

happiness, peace, and prosperity in light of the nature of persons and the world in which they live. In Chapter 3 it was seen that addressing the pervasive problem of knowledge requires an order of actions that is achieved by means of two components: decentralized jurisdictions and consensual transfers of jurisdiction. In Chapter 1, I discussed how a structure of liberty is needed to facilitate freedom of action and also to constrain it. In the next section, I explain how the rights recognized by the liberal conception of justice facilitate the freedoms described by these two components. After that, I explain how these rights also provide constraints on the actions that people may "rightfully" take. Bear in mind, however, that the case for recognizing such rights does not rest solely on their ability to address the first-order problem of knowledge. As we shall see in Parts II and III, these same rights (and more) are also needed to address the pervasive problems of interest and power.

1. Fundamental Natural Rights

The Rights of Several Property and Freedom of Contract

The discussion in Chapter 3 reveals two prerequisites of achieving a decentralized social order:

(1) *Decentralized jurisdiction*: Recognize the bounded jurisdiction of individuals and associations over physical resources so as to permit them the freedom to act on the basis of their own personal and local knowledge. This enables individuals and associations to harness the knowledge in their possession.
(2) *Consensual transfers*: Permit the freedom to transfer a person or association's jurisdiction and require that such transfers be consensual. This permits changes in jurisdictions to reflect changes in knowledge, while enabling persons who are deciding how to act to take the knowledge of others into account in their decision.

These principles also allow people to consent to having their actions directed by others within centrally-managed institutions.

This two-part strategy is reflected in the rights that are recognized by the liberal conception of justice. The first part of the strategy—decentralized jurisdiction—is reflected in the nature and scope of these rights. Within the classical liberal approach, the rights that concern jurisdiction over physical resources are called property rights. Since our bodies are physical entities or resources they are included in the term. As John Locke famously noted, "every Man has a *Property* in his own *Person*. This no Body has any Right to but himself."[6] According to the classical liberal view, to have property in a physical

---

[6] Locke, *Two Treatises*, p. 28.

resource—including one's body—means that one is free to use this resource in any way one chooses provided that this use does not infringe upon the rights of others.

Because this concept of property protects the freedom of private persons, as opposed to government officials, this idea is often referred to as "private" property. However, for present purposes, *several property*—a term favored by Friedrich Hayek—may be more apt.[7] The term "several property" makes it clearer that jurisdiction to use resources is dispersed among the "several"— meaning "diverse, many, numerous, distinct, particular, or separate"[8]—persons and associations that comprise a society, rather than being reposed in a monolithic centralized institution.

The second part of the strategy—permit consensual transfers and consensual transfers only—is reflected in the right of "freedom of contract." Freedom of contract has two components which may be thought of as distinct rights: the right of freedom *to* contract and the right of freedom *from* contract. Freedom to contract holds that persons may consent to legally enforceable transfers of their property rights;[9] freedom from contract holds that transfers of property rights should not be imposed upon them without their consent.[10]

---

[7] See Hayek, *Law and Liberty*, p. 121. See e.g. John Locke, *Two Treatises*, p. 338 ("[W]e see how *labour* could make Men distinct titles to *several* parcels of [land], for their private uses; wherein there could be no doubt of Right, no room for quarrel.") (second emphasis added).

[8] The *Oxford English Dictionary* identifies one meaning of "several" as "[e]xisting apart, separate" and a second meaning as "[p]ertaining to an individual person or thing." As a special instance of the second meaning it gives the following: "Chiefly Law. (Opposed to common.) Private; privately owned or occupied." *Oxford English Dictionary*, 2nd edn., vol. xv (Oxford: Clarendon Press, 1989), p. 97.

[9] Ian Macneil refers to this aspect as the "power of contract." See Ian R. Macneil, "Power of Contract and Agreed Remedies," *Cornell Law Quarterly*, vol. 47 (1962), p. 495: "Power of contract is one of the two sides of freedom of contract. On one hand, freedom of contract is a freedom from restraint, an immunity from legal reprisal for making or receiving promises. On the other hand, it is not really a freedom of contract, but a power of contract, a power to secure legal sanctions when another breaks his promise." Ibid. 495. I discuss how this characterization of contractual freedom has led Macneil to neglect the crucial function of freedom from contract in Randy E. Barnett, "Conflicting Visions: A Critique of Ian Macneil's Relational Theory of Contract," *Virginia Law Review*, vol. 78 (1992), p. 1175.

[10] See Richard E. Speidel, "The New Spirit of Contract," *Journal of Law and Commerce*, vol. 2 (1982), p. 193: "In fact, the spirit of a people at any given time may be measured by the opportunity and incentive to exercise 'freedom to' and the felt necessity to assert 'freedom from.' Similarly, the nature of a society and its legal order may be determined by the force and permissible scope of these two concepts of liberty and how the inevitable tension between them is resolved." Ibid. 194. Some commentators have resisted the term "freedom from contract" on the ground that an obligation imposed without one's consent is not properly called "contractual." By this view, a better term would be "freedom from obligation." Although I am obviously sympathetic to equating semantically the term "contract" with consensual obligation, there is a virtue in adopting a more neutral version of the word in order to communicate with those who are sympathetic to the "death of contract" movement that equates contractual obligation with that imposed by tort. The term "freedom from contract" rhetorically highlights the injustice of imposing so-called "contracts" on persons without their consent.

Against a backdrop of several property rights, these two components of freedom of contract regulate the transfers of the several property rights persons have. The manifested consent of the right-holder is, under normal circumstances, sufficient to transfer a property right; and property rights may not normally be transferred without the consent of the right-holder.

In light of the analysis presented in Chapter 3, the rights of several property and freedom of contract can be seen as enabling us to deal with the problem of knowledge in society. By delegating discretion to make choices concerning the uses of resources, several property rights enable persons and associations to act on the basis of their personal and local knowledge. The right of freedom *to* contract enables persons to exchange their several property rights on the basis of their knowledge that other rights would better serve their purposes; it also enables them to give their rights away on the basis of their knowledge that others could make better use of these rights. In this way, rights to use resources are permitted to flow to those who believe that they know best how to use them. These advantages of several property and freedom to contract are hardly unknown, although often inadequately appreciated. Less well-known is the important role played by freedom from contract in addressing the knowledge problem.

The right of freedom *from* contract not only protects current right-holders, it also forces those who wish to use resources belonging to others to take the knowledge of the current right-holders into account when deciding whether to acquire these rights. The fact that property rights may not transfer without the consent of the current owner means that, to acquire the right to use these resources, prospective owners must somehow induce the current right-holder to consent to a transfer. The amount and kind of this inducement reflects the personal and local knowledge of the current right-holder as to how these resources may be used. In this way, the knowledge of the current right-holder is reflected in the price that the prospective owner must pay to obtain control over the resource. Since the price reflects the current owner's knowledge, a prospective owner must take this knowledge into account.

Simultaneously, this process of knowledge dissemination also works in reverse. An offer to purchase certain rights presents the current owner with information about the knowledge that others possess about potential uses of the resources in question. In deciding whether to accept or reject the offer, the present owner is forced to take this knowledge into account. Thus, even a decision by the current owner to retain ownership will reflect the knowledge of both the owner and of prospective owners. In this way, the right of freedom from contract makes possible the development of prices—the extremely elaborate, though largely unappreciated, system of knowledge encryption and transmittal. The price system of knowledge transmittal would be short-circuited by the forced exchange of rights.

The rights of several property and freedom of contract correspond to a traditionally powerful conception of rights—those rights that are sometimes called "negative rights" (as distinct from "positive rights") or, more informatively, "liberty rights" (as distinct from "welfare rights").[11] Representing the idea of jurisdiction based on bounded individual and associational discretion by the term "right" makes a great deal of sense. It conforms to common usage to say that a person who is exercising her jurisdiction to regulate the use of particular resources is exercising her rights and that others have a duty to refrain from interfering with her actions.

However, a serious problem with the rhetoric of rights arises when rights are conceived, as modern philosophers are wont to do, merely as "justified" or "valid" claims.[12] Since anything can be made the subject of a claim, *a fortiori*, anything can potentially be the subject of a right. By permitting *any* claim to be cast in the form of a rights- claim, the modern conception of rights can mislead us into validating invalid rights claims.

In contrast, the idea of jurisdiction based on "bounded individual or associational discretion" offers a much more specific conception of rights. Unlike the entirely open-ended modern concept of a right as a justified or valid claim, the liberal conception of justice ties the concept of a right to jurisdiction over particular physical resources. Such property rights are "natural" insofar as, given the nature of human beings and the world in which they live, they are essential for persons living in society with others to pursue happiness, peace, and prosperity. And part of what it takes to accomplish these ends is the ability to solve the first-order problem of knowledge.

It is appropriate to characterize several property and freedom of contract as background rights, because they provide a method of evaluating the scheme of legal rights that may be recognized in a given legal system. If people are to be able to pursue happiness, peace, and prosperity while living in society with others, we must come to grips somehow with the problems of knowledge, interest, and power. Handling these problems requires the legal recognition of the background rights of several property and freedom of contract, as well as other rights yet to be discussed.

As explained in Chapter 1, to claim a "natural right," is to claim that a legal system ought not violate such a right if its commands are to bind in conscience. While a claim based on natural rights does not make a regime of legal rights disappear in a puff of smoke, one consequence of violating natural rights is that legal commands may not bind the citizen in conscience, in which

[11] See e.g. Loren E. Lomasky, *Persons, Rights, and the Moral Community* (New York: Oxford University Press, 1987), p. 84. I greatly prefer Lomasky's terminology for its moral neutrality. Both liberty and welfare are generally considered good things, whereas the rhetoric of negative and positive rights is biased in favor of the positive and against the negative.

[12] See e.g., Joel Feinberg, "The Nature and Value of Rights," in *Rights, Justice, and the Bounds of Liberty* (Princeton, NJ: Princeton University Press, 1980), pp. 151–2: "Some identify right and claim without qualification; some define 'right' as justified or justifiable claim, others as recognized claim; still others as valid claim. My own preference is for the latter definition."

case citizens may obey the law only to avoid punishment. In some circumstances, physical resistance, secession, or even revolution may also be warranted.

I am not here presenting the conditions that must be satisfied to make any of these actions appropriate. The violation of natural rights may be necessary but not sufficient to justify resistance, secession, or revolution. Just as natural law theorist Thomas Aquinas thought that obedience even to an unjust law that did not bind in conscience might still be warranted "to avoid scandal or disturbance, for which cause a man should even yield his right,"[13] the American founding generation thought that "[p]rudence, indeed will dictate that Governments long established should not be changed for light and transient Causes."[14] For this reason they felt the need to establish "a long Train of Abuses and Usurpations, pursuing invariably the same Object, [which] evinces a Design to reduce [the People] to absolute despotism" before asserting "their Right, . . . their Duty, to throw off such Government, and to provide new Guards for their future Security."[15] In sum, they thought it necessary to show, in effect, a criminal conspiracy whose purpose was to destroy the "unalienable rights" of the people to "Life, Liberty, and the Pursuit of Happiness."[16]

But while I will not consider when any particular acts of resistance, secession, or revolution are justified, I did offer in Chapter 1 several reasons why the commands of a legal system that failed to recognize the rights that are essential to the pursuit of happiness, peace, and prosperity might fail to bind in conscience. These reasons, combined with the analysis presented in Chapters 2 and 3 (as well as the analysis, yet to come, of the problems of interest and power), suggest that a failure to respect the "bounded individual discretion" or liberty that is essential to the pursuit of happiness, peace, and prosperity can deprive a legal command of its power to bind in conscience. And if this conclusion is warranted, then it is appropriate to call the concepts that define the structure of liberty, and that distinguish liberty from license, *rights*.

The Right of First Possession

An important aspect of the liberal conception of justice is yet to be considered. We have discussed at considerable length the rights of several property and freedom of contract. The right of several property suggests that the control of resources should reflect the dispersal of personal and local knowledge, and the right of freedom of contract governs how rights to already owned resources are to be transferred. Still, we have yet to specify any principle to govern how physical resources come to be owned in the first instance.

The principle of property acquisition associated with classical liberalism is that of first possession.

[13] Aquinas, *Summa Theologica*, p. 233*b*.
[14] *The Declaration of Independence* (1776), para. 2.   [15] Ibid.   [16] Ibid.

The *right of first possession* specifies that unowned resources come to be owned by the first person or association to establish control over them.[17]

The principle also embraces self-proprietorship—the ownership of one's body—since only the person controls his or her own body. Although the most important and best-known function of the right of first possession is its ability to address the problems of interest—in particular the incentive problem that I discuss in Chapter 8—it also plays a generally overlooked role in addressing the first-order problem of knowledge which is best considered at this juncture.

Consider what happens when Ann first comes upon a resource that is unowned, perhaps a section of ocean floor that can be mined for minerals. The first function of a right of first possession is to enable Ann to act on the basis of her knowledge by asserting control over the resource. And, because the resource is unowned—that is, no one else maintains a prior claim to the resource—her actions do not disturb the order of actions in her society; her actions do not interfere with the actions of others. Though important, this is not the only way that the right of first possession reflects the need to address the first-order problem of knowledge.

Second, since Ann's time and other resources are scarce, her efforts to establish control over the seabed come at the expense of other opportunities she must necessarily forego. The fact that Ann incurs these opportunity costs by using resources she already owns—for example, her body—to establish control over this resource reveals that she has knowledge of how it may be used, in much the same way that the requirement of consensual transfers reveals such knowledge. She would rather invest this portion of her time and energy on using this resource than for any other purpose. Because Ann is the first, she is also the only person to demonstrate such knowledge in so reliable a fashion. At this point, by her committal of her own scarce resources to establish possession of the unowned seabed, Ann is the only potential claimant who is demonstrating that she knows of good uses for it. The right of first possession acknowledges this fact by allocating the ownership of this resource to Ann.

Third, and crucially, when Ben comes later to the seabed, unless Ann and Ben agree to share the resource, some way of deciding between his claim and hers must be established or a conflict will occur that will interfere with the order of actions. From the perspective of the ongoing order of actions, however, the two claims are quite different. That Ann's possession was first in time is salient. Ann's first possession—solely because it was first—did not jeopardize

---

[17] One must be careful to distinguish the right of first possession that has long dominated the law of property from theories that seek to explain or *justify* the right, such as the "labor-mixing theory" of John Locke. In contrast, offered here is a functional theory of the right of first possession that stresses its role in handling the problems of knowledge and interest. For a concise account of how this right is embodied in the law of property, see Richard A. Epstein, "Possession as the Root of Title," *Georgia Law Review*, vol. 13 (1979), pp. 1221–43.

the existing order of actions by dispossessing a previously lodged claim of any other person. Ben's claim, on the other hand, does threaten to dispossess Ann's previously lodged claim, entailing a loss of her prior investment of time and resources and the defeat of her previously formulated plans that depend upon her continued possession of the resource. In this respect, favoring the claim of the first possessor is less disruptive to the order of actions that permits persons and associations to act on the basis of their knowledge. Time is of the essence.

Fourth, unless Ben is obliged to obtain Ann's consent to use the resource, we have no way of knowing that Ann's previously demonstrated knowledge is being taken into account when Ben decides to make his claim. Put another way, without a requirement of obtaining the consent of the first possessor, any subsequent claimant will not "internalize" the cost imposed in the first possessor by dispossession. In this respect, the right of first possession performs the same general function as the right of consensual transfers—that is, it assures that the knowledge of others will be taken into account when one acts on the basis of one's own knowledge. This should not surprise since the right of first possession can be viewed as a specific application of the right of consensual transfers. All the functions performed by the latter are performed by the former as well. Indeed, the resource price mechanism (which has to begin somewhere) begins when Ben is required to "bid" for Ann's previously established claim to the resource and Ann must decide whether to transfer her rights perhaps in exchange for something that Ben has offered or to hold on to them. Requiring Ben to bid for Ann's rights causes him to take into account her opportunity costs; conversely and simultaneously, when evaluating whether to accept Ben's bid, Ann will take into account Ben's opportunity costs. Assuming that Ann's right of first possession is respected, whichever person ends up in possession of the resource will have taken into account the opportunity cost of that possession to the other claimant.[18]

Although the right of first possession can be seen as addressing the first-order problem of knowledge in these ways, I want to emphasize that I am not suggesting that the first possessor necessarily has "better" knowledge than any subsequent claimant, any more than the requirement of consensual transfers is based on a claim that a present right-holder is necessarily "more knowledgeable" than every potential transferee. The analysis of the function of several property and freedom of contract presented here entails no such effort at interpersonal comparisons of knowledge. Rather, it is precisely because as observers or as claimants we are unable to make such comparisons that some

---

[18] This argument differs from the famous Coase Theorem which posits that resources will end up in the hand of the "highest value user" regardless of which of two competing parties is required to bid for the resources. See Ronald H. Coase, "The Problem of Social Cost," *Journal of Law and Economics*, vol. 3 (1960), p. 1. Unlike Coase, I am not here concerned with the efficient distribution of resources, but rather with the quite different problem of ensuring that the knowledge (and interests) of both parties are taken into account before resources change hands.

criterion such as first possession is needed to handle the two-fold knowledge problem arising from the radical dispersion of personal and local knowledge.

Of course, if a consensual transfer of rights occurs between the first possessor and a subsequent claimant, then this is *prima facie* evidence that each party to an exchange of rights could put the resource that each gains rights over to better use than what each gives up in exchange. Adhering to the right of first possession addresses the knowledge problem, in part, by *revealing* this information. In contrast, any principle of allocation that requires for its operation that such information first *be obtained* runs afoul of the knowledge problem.

Beyond the First-Order Problem of Knowledge

It would be a serious error to characterize the thesis of this book as resting entirely on the first-order problem of knowledge. I begin with this problem because I must begin somewhere and can only discuss one problem at a time. I claim neither that this is the only pervasive social problem that must be solved if persons are to pursue happiness, peace, and prosperity while living in society with others, nor that the need to handle this problem is the sole rationale for the rights of several property, freedom of contract, and first possession. These rights have other important functions and appreciating these functions is as important as understanding how these rights handle the first-order problem of knowledge. A more accurate characterization of my thesis is that the very *multiplicity* of *different* serious social problems handled by these rights provides confidence that adherence to them is imperative, even when one is tempted to restrict the exercise of these rights in order to achieve some other objective.

So, for example, a more concrete version of the right of first possession—"first to stake a claim, first in right"—addresses the problem of communicating justice (the second-order problem of knowledge) that is handled by the liberal conception of the rule of law. Only a more concrete expression of the right of first possession can provide a useful guide to action *before* costly investment is made by two conflicting parties. And, as I discuss in Chapter 8, the right of first possession also addresses the important problem of incentives. Ann will have the incentive to use her knowledge only if she can be assured that she will not be dispossessed by latecomers. The more different problems are handled by a purported right the more confident we can be that this claim of right is justified.

The first-order problem of knowledge, therefore, does not unequivocally determine the entire scope of the liberal conception of justice because this problem is just one among several pervasive social problems addressed by the liberal conception of justice. From the perspective of this particular knowledge problem or any other problem considered in isolation, it may be possible to imagine alternative conceptions of justice or other types of solutions that may work as well as the rights of several property, freedom of contract, and first possession. But the fact that the liberal conception of justice (and the rule of law) are seen as handling several different social problems means that ties at the level of the first-order problem of knowledge can be broken by taking into account further stages of analysis involving other problems.[19]

Indeed, one weakness of previous accounts of liberalism is their tendency to focus exclusively on a single problem or on only a small number of the problems that the rights comprising the liberal conception of justice are needed to handle. The basic tenets of liberalism become more authoritative as the number of pervasive social problems they address increases. When the answers liberalism provides to one set of problems are refined in light of other pervasive problems, the importance of liberalism becomes much clearer as does the comparative weaknesses of alternative approaches.

For example, my analysis of the first-order problem of knowledge has stressed that knowledge is dispersed, that individuals and associations are usually in the best position to make knowledgeable decisions, and, therefore, that individuals and associations should be accorded a presumption of competence and a jurisdiction over resources that will effectuate their decisions. It would be easy, however, to identify instances where individuals and associations seem incompetent to make decisions for themselves and others more competent. If this were the only problem we faced we might imagine other institutions intervening, perhaps only in exceptional circumstances, to correct the errors that individuals and associations will inevitably make.

However, permitting such interventions gives rise to a serious partiality problem—one of the pervasive problems of interest. Once the power of intervention is legitimated, interveners are quite likely to serve their own interests rather than the interests of the person allegedly being protected. Moreover, because individuals and associations will not always think they have made a mistake, the intervening decision makers will often have to impose their decisions by force. Using force aggravates both the problems of knowledge and of interest by raising the costs of both enforcement error and enforcement abuse; these are the problems of power that I discuss in Part III.

To argue for such interventions on the grounds that they will address the first-order problem of knowledge better than adherence to the liberal conception of justice is, therefore, insufficient. Advocates of such intervention must also show how the *other* serious problems handled or avoided by the liberal conception of justice but exacerbated by such interventions can be adequately handled.

---

[19] Recall the baseball example discussed in Chapter 3 in which a tie between the umpire, batter, and catcher in their respective abilities to handle the knowledge problem is broken by an assessment of the problem of interest, in particular the partiality problem.

2. Two Constraints on Freedom

Just as the natural rights of several property, freedom of contract, and first possession circumscribe a protective domain within which persons are free to acquire, possess, use, and transfer rights to scarce physical resources, they also define appropriate constraints on these actions.

Constraining the Freedom to Use Resources

Up to this point we have identified how rights to possess and use physical resources may be acquired and transferred. We have yet to specify the way in which resources can rightfully be used and the constraints, if any, on such use. At first blush the answer is easy: if the purpose of recognizing property rights is to permit people to put their personal and local knowledge into action in pursuit of happiness, peace, and prosperity, then they should be able to use their rightfully owned resources in any manner they wish. Only in this way will they be able to put their knowledge into action; and no third party will usually know better than they how to do this. At a minimum, this suggests that freedom of action is to be presumed rightful and that any constraints on this freedom require justification.

Yet upon reflection, the answer cannot be this easy. For rights are relational. Rights impose duties on others; in the absence of other persons, rights serve no purpose. They are an essential means for establishing a relational order of actions when persons live in society with others. To live in society with others is to affect others by one's actions and to be affected by the actions of others. It cannot be the case, then, that persons can do anything they wish with their rightfully owned physical resources. For should they act in such a manner as to prevent others from using their rightfully owned resources then the purpose of having rights in the first place would be defeated.

Classical liberals have long dealt with this by adopting what Herbert Spencer referred to as the law of equal freedom: "Every man has a freedom to do all that he wills, provided that he infringes not the equal freedom of any other man."[20] The objective is to define a set of choices that every person can make without interfering in the like choices of others. John Stuart Mill expressed this sentiment in terms of what has come to be called the "harm principle":

The object of this Essay is to assert one very simple principle, as entitled to govern absolutely the dealings of society with the individual in the way of compulsion and control, whether the means used be physical force in the form of legal penalties, or the moral coercion of public opinion. That principle is, that the sole end for which mankind are warranted, individually or collectively, in interfering with the liberty of action of any of their numbers is self-protection. That the only purpose for

[20] Herbert Spencer, *Social Statics* (New York: Robert Schalkenbach Foundation, 1970), p. 95.

which power can rightfully be exercised over any member of a civilized community, against his own will, is to prevent harm to others.[21]

The problem with the harm principle is well-known. As Joel Feinberg notes, "in its present form, the principle is too vague to be of any potential use at all. Clearly not every kind of act that causes harm to others can be rightly prohibited."[22]

One reason for this is provided by the framework presented here. A definition of harm that makes an individual "worse off" as determined by that person's subjective scale of preferences will fail to facilitate an order of actions. For, as was discussed in Chapter 3, subjective preferences will often be in conflict, and were it not for these conflicts we would not need to recognize rights to own and use physical resources in the first place. In a world of conflicting subjective preferences, an order of actions will not be achieved unless we adopt a more limited conception of "harm."

Moreover, assuming an objective assessment of a person's "true" interest were possible (which I doubt), and a "harm" was considered a diminution of that person's interest, this would still fail to establish an order of actions. For there is no reason to suppose that everyone's true interests were in harmony; that there existed no genuine conflicts of interest. But if the permissibility of actions were based on the true interest of the actor and the interests of different actors conflicted, then their actions will also conflict and an order of actions will not be achieved.

For these reasons, we require a conception of "harm" that is compatible with achieving an order of actions. The common law of private nuisance developed one useful standard: the invasion of a land owner's *use and enjoyment* of land.[23] To facilitate an order of actions, we may adopt this standard as follows: Persons should be free to do whatever they wish with their own justly acquired resources provided that this use does not (*a*) *physically* interfere with (*b*) another person's *use and enjoyment* of his or her resources.

This conception of harm rules out prohibitions on a number of types of action. For example, suppose Ann opens a restaurant across the street from Ben's restaurant and attracts many of Ben's customers. As a result, Ben makes much less money than before, perhaps even goes out of business. Though Ann's actions have "interfered" with Ben's "use and enjoyment" of his

---

[21] John Stuart Mill, *On Liberty*, in Hutchins, *Great Books*, vol. xliii, p. 271*b*.

[22] Joel Feinberg, *Harm to Others* (Oxford: Oxford University Press, 1984), p. 12.

[23] See e.g. Restatement of the Law Second, Torts 2d (The American Law Institute, 1979), §821D: "A private nuisance is a nontrespassory invasion of another's interest in the private use and enjoyment of land." In the short discussion that follows, I cannot recreate the law of torts that has evolved to govern the use of one's person or external property. For a series of articles that treats these issues in some detail, see Richard A. Epstein, "A Theory of Strict Liability," *Journal of Legal Studies*, vol. 2 (1973), p. 151; *id.*, "Defenses and Subsequent Pleas in a System of Strict Liability," *Journal of Legal Studies*, vol. 3 (1974), p. 165; *id.*, "Intentional Harms," *Journal of Legal Studies*, vol. 4 (1975), p. 391; *id.* "Causation and Corrective Justice: A Reply to Critics," *Journal of Legal Studies*, vol. 8 (1979), p. 477.

property, her interference was not physical and thus would be permissible under this standard of harm. In contrast, if Ann were to have exploded a bomb in Ben's restaurant, her actions would be an impermissible use of her own resources. As Robert Nozick observed, "[m]y property rights in my knife allow me to leave it where I will, but not in your chest."[24] Nozick's thought echoed that of an early American state legislator: "[T]hough the law allows a man the free use of his arm, or the possession of a weapon, yet it does not authorize him to plunge a dagger in the breast of an inoffensive neighbor."[25]

Suppose instead that Ann operates a radio station that transmits radio waves through Ben's body. Though these waves are physically passing through his body, unless it could be shown that such radio waves interfere with Ben's use and enjoyment of his body (perhaps by causing cancer), here too Ann's actions would be permissible under this standard. In contrast, were Ann to blow cigarette smoke into Ben's face this act might well be a physical interference that interfered with Ben's use and enjoyment of his body.

Limiting constraints on use to physical interferences with the use and enjoyment of another's physical resources protects freedom of choice and action while at the same time avoiding social conflict better than any alternative. In this way, it helps facilitate an order of actions that addresses the first-order problem of knowledge. As important to these advantages, however, is that such a criterion of harm also addresses the second-order problem of knowledge that will be discussed in Chapter 5: the problem of communicating the requirements of justice. Restricting only physical interference provides a relatively clear and discernable criterion of harm, thereby providing useful guidance for both the affected persons and third parties as to the limits of their freedom.

Once we move beyond common examples such as these, however, things can get pretty dicey. Would Ben be able to object to smelling Ann's perfume? What if he is allergic to perfume? Too subjective a conception of "use and enjoyment" may overly restrict the actions of some to engage in truly benign conduct; too objective a conception will certainly impede the ability of some to use and enjoy their property. Yet no rule or principle is entirely without difficulties. The fact that a legal rule produces many hard cases does not mean that it does not also handle most cases with relative ease:[26] cases of murder, rape, robbery, and theft, for example.

---

[24] Robert Nozick, *Anarchy, State, and Utopia* (New York: Basic Books, 1974), p. 171.

[25] Republica v. Oswald, 1 US (1 Dall.) 319, 330 n* (Pa. 1788) (statement of representative William Lewis to the Pennsylvania General Assembly).

[26] See generally Frederick Schauer, "Easy Cases," *Southern California Law Review*, vol. 58 (1985), p. 399. With regard to constitutional law, for example, Schauer writes: "By ignoring the innumerable instances in which potential disputes are not litigated, and by ignoring the infinitely larger class of actions governed by the Constitution but not thought subject to any controversy regarding application, the contemporary agenda has neglected an enormous portion of constitutional law. It has forgotten the easy case." Ibid. 407.

As I explain at length in Chapter 6, it is a mistake to think that abstract principles, such as those provided by natural rights, can decide all cases. A principle that one should have the right to use one's property in ways that do not physically interfere with the use and enjoyment of another's resources provides a "frame" by which conventional rules are evaluated.[27] While the enumerable rules lying outside the frame are excluded, the frame does not determine which of the possible rules lying within its four corners we should select. This is a matter of convention or agreement, like deciding which side of the road we should drive on, and I will describe the features of a legal system that enables it to make this selection. The principles or rights which provide the "frame" do not determine a choice made within the frame. Moreover, as I shall also explain, the process of selecting these rules in a system of common-law adjudication contributes to a better understanding of our principles or rights and even, on occasion, to their reform. Of course, none of this is peculiar to the particular rights and principles that comprise the liberal conception of justice, and this conception of justice should not be held to a higher standard than all other theories.[28]

Whatever gaps or uncertainties remain after conventional rules are chosen to implement the abstract requirements of justice are commonly handled in practice by the right of freedom of contract. Herbert Spencer made a similar point concerning the principles of equal liberty: "Though further qualifications of the liberty of action thus asserted may be necessary, yet . . . in the just regulation of a community no further qualification of it can be recognized. Such further qualifications must ever remain for private and individual application."[29] So, for example, while it would be unjust for Ann to blow smoke in Ben's face but unclear whether she should be allowed to wear perfume, Ben may allow smoking or prohibit the wearing of perfume in his own restaurant for anyone who consents to eat there. Prohibiting this form of consensual *centralized* order would violate the background rights of Ben and his customers. The rule prohibiting physical interference with use and enjoyment is simply a "default rule"[30] or baseline which specifies who bears the obligation to seek (and possibly pay for) the consent of another.

There is considerable irony in the tendency of some who stress the importance of centralized ordering of society as a whole to deny or disparage the

[27] The metaphor of a "frame" is Schauer's. See ibid. 430.

[28] See e.g. John Rawls, *Political Liberalism* (New York: Columbia University Press, 1996), p. 228: "[T]he scheme of basic liberties is not specified in full detail in the original position. It is enough that the general form and content of the basic liberties be outlined and the grounds of their priority understood. The further specification of the liberties is left to the constitutional, legislative, and judicial stages."

[29] Spencer, *Social Statics*, p. 95. Indeed, the analysis presented here suggests that individuals and associations are in the best positions to consensually adopt such qualifications.

[30] For an explanation of default rules, especially in the context of contract law, see Randy E. Barnett, "The Sound of Silence: Default Rules and Contractual Consent," *Virginia Law Review*, vol. 78 (1992), p. 821.

exercise of centralized ordering by people exercising their rights of several property and freedom of contract. Given the serious constraints imposed by a decentralized regime, the control exerted by owners or managers of several property over those who actually manifest consent to their authority is far less dangerous than imposing the authority of central rulers on subjects without their consent.

Constraining Consensual Freedom

In the liberal conception of justice developed here, rights are construed as enforceable claims to acquire, use, and transfer resources in the world—claims to control one's person and external resources. The right of freedom of contract requires the consent of a rights-holder to effectuate a rights transfer. There are reasons, however, why certain property rights may be *inalienable*.[31] An inalienable right is a right that cannot be extinguished or transferred even by the consent of the right-holder. "That which is inalienable . . . is not transferable to the ownership of another. So an inalienable right is one that can never be waived or transferred by its possessor. . . . Thus what is proscribed by inalienable rights are certain relationships or agreements."[32]

A claim that a right is inalienable must be distinguished from a claim that it is nonforfeitable. "A person who has forfeited a right has lost the right because of some offence or wrongdoing."[33] One who wishes to extinguish or convey an inalienable right may do so by committing the appropriate wrongful act and thereby forfeiting it.[34] But notwithstanding the consensual nature of such an action, it is the wrongfulness or *injustice* of the right-holder's act, and not the right-holder's consent, that justifies the conclusion that an inalienable right has been forfeited.[35]

The notion that some rights are inalienable was not shared by all classical liberals, nor by all those who today subscribe to the liberal conception of justice, and one can immediately see why. For to hold that a right is inalienable is to restrict the freedom of contract of the right-holder. Any philosophy that places a high regard on freedom generally and freedom of contract in particular is likely to be skeptical of such restrictions. Why prevent persons from

---

[31] Elsewhere, I examine four distinct reasons for inalienability of certain rights, only one of which I develop here. See Randy E. Barnett, "Contract Remedies and Inalienable Rights," *Social Philosophy and Policy*, vol. 4 (Autumn, 1986), pp. 186–95.

[32] Terrance McConnell, "The Nature and Basis of Inalienable Rights," *Law and Philosophy*, vol. 3 (1984), p. 43.

[33] Ibid. 28. See also Joel Feinberg, *Rights, Justice*, pp. 240–2.

[34] See Diane T. Meyers, *Inalienable Rights: A Defense* (New York: Columbia University Press, 1985), pp. 13–15.

[35] See McConnell, *Nature of Rights*, p. 28: "When a person has forfeited a right, others are permitted to treat him in a way that would otherwise be inappropriate *simply because* of his *wrong action*. But when a right has been waived, others are permitted to behave in an otherwise unacceptable manner *simply because* of the *consent* of the original possessor."

pursuing happiness, peace, and prosperity by exchanging *any* of the their rights?

Consider the validity of a contract to sell oneself into slavery.[36] Many reasons have been given for why such a contract of servitude is unenforceable, while others maintain that a truly voluntary agreement of this kind ought to be enforced.[37] The property rights component of the liberal conception of justice provides a previously unrecognized reason why consent of the right-holder is sometimes ineffective to transfer a right. For, if one views all rights as property rights then some of these rights might be inalienable due to the literal impossibility of the commitments entailed by certain purported property rights transfers. Once rights are viewed as enforceable claims to control physical resource and contracts viewed as enforceable transfers of these rights, then, when control of a resource cannot in fact be transferred, a right to control the resource also cannot be transferred.[38]

Suppose that Ann consented to transfer partial or complete control of her body to Ben. Absent some physiological change in Ann (caused, perhaps, by voluntarily and knowingly ingesting some special drug or undergoing psychosurgery[39]) there is no way for such a commitment to be carried out. True, Ann could conform her conduct to Ben's orders, but her agreement notwithstanding, she would still retain control over her actions and would willfully have to act so as to conform her actions to Ben's orders. Because Ann cannot in fact transfer the control of her body to Ben, despite Ann's alleged transfer of her right to control her body to Ben, Ben would in fact be forced to rely on

---

[36] This discussion concerns only so-called voluntary slavery. Historically, this more closely applies to certain widely-practiced forms of indentured servitude as opposed to, for example, the involuntary enslavement of Africans. See Abbot Emerson Smith, *Colonists in Bondage: White Servitude and Convict Labor in America, 1607–1776* (Chapel Hill, NC: University of North Carolina Press, 1947) at p. 336 ("If we exclude the Puritan migrations of the 1630's, it is safe to say that not less than one-half, nor more than two-thirds, of all white immigrants to the colonies were indentured servants or redemptioners or convicts").

[37] Robert Nozick, for example, asks "whether a free system will allow [an individual] to sell himself into slavery. I believe that it would. (Other writers disagree.)." Nozick, *Anarchy, State and Utopia*, p. 331. See also Buckle, *Natural Law*, pp. 48–9 (identifying natural rights theorists, such as Grotius, who thought that voluntary slavery was, under certain conditions, morally permissible.).

[38] For what it is worth, contract law has long recognized a defense of impossibility. See e.g. Taylor v. Caldwell, 3 B. & S. 825, 122 Eng. Rep. 309 (1863) (no damages for failure to deliver occupancy of a music hall which had been destroyed by fire).

[39] Arthur Kuflik offers these examples to undercut this type of argument for inalienability. See Arthur Kuflik, "The Inalienability of Autonomy," *Philosophy and Public Affairs*, vol. 13 (1984), p. 281: "This suggests that the impropriety of an autonomy-abdicating agreement has more to do with the impropriety of autonomy-abdication itself than with some general fact that we have no right to make commitments we know we will be unable to keep." But arguments based on impropriety and one based on the impossibility of such agreements are not mutually exclusive. Kuflik's examples only show that this reason for inalienability is *limited* to those commitments to alienate the future control over one's person which are not made possible by mind-altering drugs, brainwashing techniques, or psychosurgery.

Ann's actual control of her body to carry out his orders.[40] Ben's "control" of Ann's body would, then, be metaphorical rather than actual. This is not to say that force is *ineffective* in getting slaves or servants to obey the orders of their putative masters but, rather, that force would be *unnecessary* if the actual control of servants' bodies could be transferred to the masters as specified by the terms of the agreement.

George Smith has put the argument as follows:

Given its physical nature, my car can be transferred to another person, so I can alienate my right (i.e. my title) to it. I can sell it, give it away, or abandon it. This is not true, however, of my self-sovereignty, or "right to life." Why? Because the property to which this right is attached is metaphysically incapable of being transferred, abandoned or forfeited. . . . [O]ne person's moral agency cannot be transferred to another person. And if that faculty cannot be transferred, then neither can the title (i.e., the claim of ownership) to that faculty.[41]

A voluntary slavery contract makes no more sense than if the "slave" had agreed to transfer "an absolute property right in his subjective beliefs and values. Regardless of whether he 'consented' or not, a right cannot be alienated unless the object of that right is capable, in principle, of being transferred from one person to another."[42] Because they retain their moral agency, "slaves" can be held accountable for their actions. As Smith observes,

I find it curious that most critics of inalienable rights have no trouble accepting the idea of inalienable duties. Yet these are merely two sides of the same coin. To argue that all rights can be voluntarily alienated is to maintain that a human being can, by nothing more than an act of will, cease to think and choose—and therefore cease to act in any sense that is recognizably human.[43]

This distinction between alienable and inalienable, transferable and non-transferable rights corresponds to the distinction recognized in civil law countries between contracts "to give" and contracts "to do."[44] The former kind of contract transfers a right to control external resources; the latter calls for some future act involving the use of one's person. Surely, the former kind of transfer is possible. What is *my* house or car could equally well be *your* house and car. But bodies are different from other kinds of things. What is *my* body

---

[40] Similarly, a promise to undergo a dependency-inducing procedure would be an unenforceable attempt to transfer an inalienable right: the right to control whether or not to submit to the operation. But third parties might have no right to forcibly interfere with some one who voluntarily undergoes such a procedure. (The claim, for example, that members of religious "cults" may rightfully be kidnapped and "deprogramed" is properly controversial.) A person who voluntarily submitted to such a procedure (assuming that such a procedure actually worked) might be committing a nonfatal kind of "suicide" (zombicide?) and the "master" or guardian *would* then become legally responsible for his ward.

[41] George H. Smith, "Inalienable Rights?" *Liberty*, vol. 10 (July 1997), p. 52.

[42] Ibid. 53–4.   [43] Ibid. 54.

[44] See Barry Nicholas, *French Law of Contract* (St. Paul, Minn.: Mason, 1982), p. 149; Gunther H. Treitel, "Remedies for Breach of Contract," in Arthur T. Mehren (ed.), *International Encyclopedia of Comparative Law*, vol. vii (Paris: J. C. B. Mohr, 1976), p. 13.

cannot literally be made *your* body. Because there is no obstacle to transferring control of a house or car (of the sort that is unavoidably presented when one attempts to transfer control over one's body), there is no obstacle to transferring the right to control a house or car.[45] But if control cannot be transferred, then a right to control cannot be transferred. One may as well consent to transfer a right to control the movement of the stars.

Some will respond that, because it is not impossible to obtain effective enforcement of this purported rights transfer, voluntary slavery contracts are quite possible indeed. Such a claim is a *non sequitur* in a theory of background natural rights. According to a theory of background rights, we do not have background rights because our claims are enforced as legal rights. Nor does might make right. To the contrary, legal rights should not be enforced if they violate background rights. If for some reason—in this case the literal impossibility of the transfer of the control over one's person—the subject of a purported rights transfer simply cannot be transferred, then the right is inalienable and legal rights and remedies should be adjusted to correspond to this facet of background rights. In sum, the issue is not the impossibility of enforcing such a "contract," but the impossibility of transferring the rights that *justify* contractual enforcement.

Another response would be to point to labor contracts short of slavery which are and have long been held enforceable. If these restrictions on liberty are properly enforced, notwithstanding the inability to transfer control over one's person, then does this not undermine the argument for inalienability presented here? Most who make this argument do not realize that contracts for personal services are rarely, if ever, specifically enforced.[46] That is, no per-

---

[45] Transferring ownership in animals may be seen as presenting a special difficulty. Cannot animals refuse the orders of the master? But the problem of control here is less than meets the eye. The second owner gets no more control and hence no more rights than those held by the original owner. Suppose the promisor attempted to transfer the right to a horse that would cuddle up with you in bed. Unless the first owner actually possessed such a horse, *the right to this kind* of horse could not pass. While the failure to tender this kind of horse would not alone constitute a breach of contract, the possibility of an action for fraud or breach of warranty remains. In contrast, the issue of inalienable human rights concerns the rights an individual *retains* despite the fact that consent to transfer these rights may have been expressed. Therefore, the truly analogous problem with animals is whether or not sentient animals themselves have rights—inalienable or otherwise—in the first place, an issue that is well beyond the scope of this treatment.

[46] Indeed, until late in the nineteenth century the thought that labor contracts (other than those for indentured servitude which was permitted and regulated by statute) might be specifically enforced was adamantly rejected by American courts on the ground that it violated the "free labor" rights of persons. See Lea S. Vandervelde, "The Gendered Origins of the *Lumley* Doctrine: Binding Men's Consciences and Women's Fidelity," *Yale Law Journal*, vol. 101 (1992), pp. 784–7 "During the colonial and revolutionary periods of American history, there were no known instances of employers restricting the mobility of individuals retained under general employment contracts. . . . [In the early nineteenth Century], the contractual relationships of . . . talented or skilled tradesmen could not be specifically enforced, nor could they be enjoined from quitting and going elsewhere. The relationships between these free individuals were

son is actually compelled to service as would be expected if the right to one's person had actually been alienated. Rather a breach of personal services contract gives rise to the remedy of money damages.[47] In no way does this remedy necessarily entail that a right *to the labor itself* had been alienated. Rather, monetary relief could be as well accounted for by saying that it is the right *to the money*—an indisputably alienable right—that has been conditionally transferred; the condition being the nonperformance of the services. In other words, every labor contract is implicitly a commitment to perform or pay damages for nonperformance.

True, Ann may choose to exercise her inalienable rights for Ben's benefit. She may consent to let him touch her or, if Ann and Ben were both prize fighters or movie stunt performers, even to strike her. The crucial question, however, is whether Ann's current consensual choices can limit her right to revoke her consent in the future. Having consented to let Ben touch her or to enter the ring with him, may she be forced to carry through with her commitment after she has changed her mind?

Perhaps then the most salient characteristic of inalienable rights may be that, while right-holders may *exercise* their inalienable rights consistent with the wishes of others, a right-holder may never surrender *the right to change her mind* in the future about whether to exercise such rights or not. Restrictions on alienability govern which of two inconsistent expressions of assent by the same party will determine the rights of both parties to an agreement. With alienable rights (absent some agreement to the contrary) *ex ante* consent irrevocably transfers rights to control resources and binds the transferor *ex post*; with inalienable rights, the right to exercise control over the resource is never transferred by consent, so *ex post* consent takes precedence over *ex ante* consent.

Of course, extreme situations warranting different treatment can always be hypothesized. For example, may a pilot be compelled forcibly to complete a journey he has contracted to fly and be prevented from parachuting out of the plane? May a person who agrees to sell a kidney to another change his mind on the operating table once it is too late to obtain a kidney from another

easily created and fairly easily dissolved. Once one of the parties to the relationship chose to repudiate the contract, he was free to go his own way, subject only to the limitation of possible damages for breach of the agreement." The only change to this rule has been to allow the enforcement of labor contracts by prohibiting or "enjoining" workers in breach from working elsewhere. Specific performance is still not allowed. See E. Allan Farnsworth, *Contracts*, 2nd edn. (Boston: Little, Brown, 1990) §12.7, p. 868 ("A court will not grant specific performance of a contract to provide a service that is personal in nature.").

[47] In this century, courts have also on rare occasions enjoined workers who break their labor contracts from working elsewhere. This remedy may or may not be just. See Christopher T. Wonnell, "The Contractual Disempowerment of Employees," *Stanford Law Review*, vol. 46 (1993), pp. 87–146. But though Wonnell favors the injunction remedy when (and only when) it prevents opportunistic behavior by employees, he does not propose compelling these employees to specifically perform for their original employer and he advocates an employee's right to avoid an injunction by paying damages.

source? The endangerment involved in these examples, however, introduces a new element in addition to the *ex ante* consent of the right-holder. The better analogy would be to ask whether a pilot who safely lands a plane short of completing a designated route can be compelled to finish the trip or whether the purchaser of a kidney can insist upon specific performance when the cost of obtaining a kidney from a different donor is markedly increased.

Still, we cannot conclude on the basis of the analysis presented here for inalienable rights that *all* our rights are inalienable. Far from it. Except in the most rare and extreme of circumstances, rights to external resources are not inalienable. The transfer of rights to control external resources is not undermined by the argument concerning the impossibility of alienating control of certain resources. On the other hand, the alienability of rights wholly or partially to control the future use of one's person has been called into question. In a regime of several property, the transfer of even limited rights of bodily control may be barred in principle by the literal impossibility of transferring control over one's person. Thus, we may conclude that (*a*) rights to possess, use, and control resources external to one's person are (generally) alienable, and (*b*) the rights to possess, use, and control one's person are inalienable. John Stuart Mill made similar distinction when he wrote that, "there are perhaps no contracts or engagements, *except those that relate to money or money's worth*, of which one can venture to say that there ought to be no liberty whatsoever of retraction."[48]

The practical implications of this analysis may appear far-reaching. It may appear that the legitimacy of *all* commitments to perform personal services in the future has been undercut. When a promisor who has promised to perform services in the future refuses to perform, because no right to performance has been transferred to the promisee by the promise, no right of the promisee is violated by nonperformance. But as has already been suggested, the actual consequence of such analysis is only to limit relief for nonperformance of personal service commitments to money damages. Because it is quite possible to transfer control over money, the reason given here for inalienable rights does not apply to a consensual commitment by Ann to transfer a certain sum of money to Ben should she fail to perform a personal service. Although she cannot be compelled to perform, Ben may obtain an enforceable right to money damages from Ann—precisely the normal remedy now given for breach of a personal services contract.[49] What the liberal conception of justice excludes, as does the common law of contract, is the extraordinary relief of specific performance for breach of a personal services contract.

---

[48] Mill, *On Liberty*, p. 316*b*.

[49] See Farnsworth, *Contracts*, p. 864 ("Even if these limitations bar specific relief, the contract is nevertheless enforceable and damages can be recovered for its breach.").

Summary

In this chapter, the liberal conception of justice was introduced and refined in light of the need to address the first-order problem of knowledge. We may now offer a tentative formulation of this conception of justice based on the fundamental natural rights identified to this point:

FORMULATION 1. *Justice is respect for the rights of individuals and associations.*
(1) The *right of several property* specifies a right to acquire, possess, use, and dispose of scarce physical resources—including their own bodies. Resources may be used in any way that does not physically interfere with other persons' use and enjoyment of their resources. While most property rights are freely alienable, the right to one's person is inalienable.
(2) The *right of first possession* specifies that property rights to unowned resources are acquired by being the first to establish control over them.
(3) The *right of freedom of contract* specifies that a right-holder's consent is both necessary (freedom *from* contract) and sufficient (freedom *to* contract) to transfer alienable property rights.

We are not yet finished refining the liberal conception of justice. In Parts II and III, we shall see that further additions to this formulation are required to handle the problems of interest and power. Before shifting gear to consider these pervasive social problems, however, we must first turn our attention to the second-order and third-order problems of knowledge that are handled by the liberal conception of the rule of law. We shall also discover in the next chapter that the second-order problem of knowledge necessitates adding to our list of background rights that define justice.

FIVE

Communicating Justice: The Second-Order Problem of Knowledge

SUPPOSE it to be true that respecting justice as defined by the fundamental natural rights discussed in Chapter 4 is the best way to address the first-order problem of knowledge. This strategy would still fail if no one in the world had knowledge of these rights or what conduct they require or prohibit. Without this knowledge no one's conduct could be influenced by the dictates of justice, an order of actions would not be achieved, and the first-order problem of knowledge would go unaddressed. Assuming widespread acceptance of this strategy, the rights of several property, freedom of contract, and first possession that to this point comprise the liberal conception of justice may be intuitively obvious to some of the people most of the time, and to all of the people some of the time. But unless acting consistently with natural rights is instinctive to all of the people all of the time, we need a way to disseminate knowledge of these rights in such a manner as to make its requirements accessible to everyone in a society.

This is, moreover, to understate the problem. For the difficulty lies not merely in gaining knowledge of the substance of natural rights, but in the very nature of these rights. For, as will be discussed at greater length in Chapter 6, the natural rights of several property, freedom of contract, and first possession (and the other rights to be identified later) are extremely *abstract*. By this I mean that they cannot be applied automatically and logically to any but the most simple of actual disputes. The natural right of several property and the right of first possession, for example, does not specify in sufficient detail all the permissible or impermissible ways that property can be used or acquired. The right of freedom of contract does not tell us how to identify those actions which constitute consent to transfer rights. More specific guidance is required.

Where knowledge of justice is not instinctive or the implications of abstract natural rights are not obvious, the requirements of justice must be communicated and, for this to be accomplished, justice must take a certain form. These formal characteristics make up an important part of the liberal conception of the *rule of law*. (The other part of the rule of law is the type of legal processes that are needed to resolve disputes.) Unless the formal precepts of the rule of law are respected, the knowledge of justice that is needed to address the first-order problem of knowledge will not reach individuals and associations and consequently will not inform their decisions.

In sum, we need a way to disseminate knowledge of justice in such a manner as to make its requirements accessible to everyone in a society. This is the second-order problem of knowledge:

> The *second-order problem of knowledge* is the need to communicate knowledge of justice in a manner that makes the actions it requires accessible to everyone.

The problem of communicating justice is *"second-order"* because it must be faced only once we use a conception of justice to address the first-order problem of knowledge.

Suppose, while Ann is away working, Ben enters the apartment in which she has been living and begins to fix himself some dinner with the food he finds in the refrigerator. When Ann returns and demands that Ben leave the apartment, how are they to know who has the stronger claim to the apartment or that they must share? Or suppose that Ann cultivates some land for crops. While she is away negotiating a loan for equipment, Ben comes along and, seeing no one around, begins to build a house in the clearing. Ann returns, informs Ben of her prior activities, and asks him to leave. Ben refuses. In the absence of a voluntary compromise, how is this conflict to be resolved? Whatever the just resolution of this dispute may be, unless they have some way of knowing whose claim is stronger, or that they must share, Ann and Ben do not know which of them must yield to the other.

Or suppose that Ben wishes to have sexual relations with Ann, but Ann refuses. Although the very idea that Ben could make a claim of right here is repugnant to us, I think that this example deserves to be included. For we must somehow have come to know the injustice of Ben's claim and, given the history of the subordination of women (and others) by otherwise well-meaning persons, we cannot take this knowledge of justice for granted. There was a time in the United States and elsewhere when a male master was thought to have a right to the sexual favours of a female slave. In each of these examples, Ann and Ben have a knowledge problem, but of a different kind than we have studied previously. Their problem is not in knowing the uses to which resources can be put so as to serve their interests. Their problem is in knowing who the resources belong to. Nor is the second-order problem of knowledge limited to such simple examples. Without adequate advance knowledge of what justice requires, complex economic activity is nearly impossible. No business, for example, will invest substantial sums in building an office tower unless they have confidence that their investment will not be expropriated by someone claiming to be the true owner of the land on which they are to build. Nor will they do so unless they have confidence that they will be free to occupy and charge rent for leasing the office space. And without complex commercial activity, life for everyone would truly be nasty, brutish, and short.

In each of these examples I have assumed that Ann and Ben or commercial enterprises desire only to do the just or right thing, provided that they know what this is. Assuming that Ann and Ben or the managers of a company do not instinctively or intuitively know who should prevail, however, some way must be found to communicate the answer to them. This is what I am calling here the second-order problem of knowledge.

Of course, there are people who would act unjustly even if they had perfect knowledge of what justice required. The only thing that matters to such people, if anything matters, is whether they will be injured by the physical resistance of their victims or will be punished for their unjust actions. That some people are like this led Oliver Wendell Holmes, Jr., to posit what has come to be called the "bad man" theory of law:

If you want to know the law and nothing else, you must look at it as a bad man, who cares only for the material consequences which such knowledge enables him to predict, not as a good one, who finds his reasons for conduct, whether inside the law or outside of it, in the vaguer sanctions of conscience.[1]

H. L. A. Hart, describing this as "the external point of view,"[2] rejected the idea that it accurately explained the whole of law:

At any given moment the life of any society which lives by rules, legal or not, is likely to consist in a tension between those who, on the one hand, accept and voluntarily co-operate in maintaining the rules, and so see their own and other persons' behaviour in terms of the rules, and those who, on the other hand, reject the rules and attend to them only from the external point of view as a sign of possible punishment. One of the difficulties facing any legal theory anxious to do justice to the complexity of the facts is to remember the presence of both these points of view and not to define one of them out of existence.[3]

I contend that each of these "points of view" identified by Hart reflect distinguishable social problems. A proper conception of justice and the rule of law should be based on neither undue optimism, nor undue pessimism about human nature and the human condition, but a proper mixture of the two. Adopting Hart's distinction, the "internal" view of law should realistically address the second-order problem of knowledge (while "optimistically" assuming good intentions); the "external" view of law should realistically address the problem of compliance by those who are motivated solely by interest (while "optimistically" assuming such people have knowledge of the behavior that justice requires). The first of these problems—how "good

---

[1] Wendell Holmes, "The Path of the Law," p. 459.
[2] H. L. A. Hart, *Concept of Law*, pp. 86–7.   [3] Ibid. 88.

people" who find their reasons for conduct "in the vaguer sanctions of conscience" come to know what justice requires of them—is the subject of this chapter and is addressed by the liberal conception of the rule of law. The second problem—how "bad people" who care "only for the material consequences which such knowledge enables him to predict" can be made to comply with the requirements of justice and the rule of law—is a problem of interest I shall call the "compliance problem" and is the subject of Chapter 9.

1. The Need for *Ex Ante* Communication

Knowledge of justice can be communicated either before (*ex ante*) persons take action that may bring them into conflict with others or after (*ex post*) such action is taken. There are advantages to each approach. The advantage of communicating *ex post* is that only after the fact can the information conveyed about justice take into account all the particular circumstances of an actual dispute over resource use. Presumably, an *ex post* decision can be much more exactly tailored to fit what really occurred than an *ex ante* decision. For example, only *ex post* can we know exactly why and how much Ann and Ben desire to control the apartment, the clearing, or Ann's body. For this reason *ex post* communication of justice is favored by those legal theorists who think that justice requires case-by-case decision making based upon extensive fact-finding. The Legal Realist writer Jerome Frank referred to this as "individualization" (which he contrasted with "generality"):

The task of the judge, if well done is no simple one. He must balance conflicting human interests and determine which of several opposing individual claims the law should favor in order to promote social well-being. As each case comes before him, he must weigh the claims of the parties. . . . [T]he power to individualize and to legislate judicially is the very essence of [a judge's] function.[4]

While legal theorists have for years debated the advantages of individuation versus generality and whether judges should or even can be bound by abstract rules announced in advance, a serious drawback to *ex post* decision making based on the particular facts of a dispute is generally neglected. A purely *ex post* system unavoidably requires that *a dispute first occurs*. This means that *ex post* decision making actually requires both a disruption of social life and an expenditure of scarce resources on an *ex post* adjudicative process. Without a real dispute in which two or more persons assert conflicting claims for particular resources, one cannot know the particular facts on which to base an *ex post* judgment. No authoritative judgments are possible without engaging in some kind of *ex post* adjudicative process. In principle, then, an *ex post* approach is incapable of *avoiding* or *preventing* costly social disruption. Most advocates of *ex post* decision making probably assume that individuals will

---

[4] Jerome Frank, *Law and the Modern Mind* (New York: Tudor, 1936), pp. 120–1.

predict future decisions from very detailed accounts of the factual bases of past *ex post* judgments,[5] but this is really to advocate a form of *ex ante* judgment based on precedent (a topic to which I shall return in Chapter 6 when I discuss the advantages of a "common law" process of adjudication).

Despite the social disruption it causes, an *ex post* approach might be acceptable if a legal system were able to undo completely and costlessly the wrong *ex post*—to turn back the clock and adjust the situation. In our world, however, this is quite impossible. When a dispute takes place, costs that can never be fully compensated, such as the costs of adjudication itself, must be borne by the disputing parties. I am not here speaking of monetary costs. The subjective costs of any action are borne by the actor in the form of opportunities for alternative conduct that can never be recaptured. Because they cannot go back in time, persons who lose a dispute *ex post* can never arrange their affairs so as to avoid the conflict in the first instance. If Ann loses, she can never use her expended time and energies to clear a different piece of land. If Ben loses, he can never use his expended time and energies to build another house on land from which he will not be displaced. Once her body is violated, Ann can never be returned to the *status quo ante*. She can never be "unraped."

Moreover, even an *ex post* analysis is not infallible. A legal system faces its own knowledge problem. As will be discussed at greater length in Chapter 10, adjudicative errors are inevitable. The costs of such enforcement errors are magnified when they occur after it is too late to avoid the conflict. Perhaps a decision that the clearing belongs to Ann is unjust. The injustice is magnified, however, if the decision comes after, rather than before Ben has built a house on the land. Even if Ann keeps the house and compensates Ben for his loss *ex post*, it means that the time it takes her to produce the compensation may not be used in the manner she would have preferred had Ben not built the house in the first place. Do we really want to wait until after the fact to adjudicate the justice of Ben's claim to Ann's body? If not, perhaps this sentiment is due to our strong *ex ante* convictions concerning the injustice of Ben's claim, the serious costs to Ann of withholding judgment until after the fact and, to a much lesser extent, the risk of an adjudicative error in Ben's favor.

In sum, whatever an *ex post* system may gain by its ability to render more particularistic judgments is jeopardized by its inability to avoid imposing *conflict costs* on the guilty and innocent alike. Assuming it is possible to do so, such information should be communicated *ex ante*, for only *ex ante* communication can avoid a conflict that will disrupt the lives of both Ann and Ben. When the full costs borne by the parties of *ex post* adjudication are considered, an *ex ante* mode of communication need not be perfect to be preferable. But how is information to be conveyed *ex ante*?

---

[5] See e.g., Jerome Frank, *Law and the Modern Mind*, p. 275: "What courts have done, how they have done it, and why, are important to the lawyer, because such knowledge will enable him more adequately to predict how and what the courts will do in future concrete cases."

2. *Ex Ante* Communication and Rule of Law Principles

To address the second-order problem of knowledge, we need a way to convert the substance of justice into a form that is somehow accessible to the general population of a society in advance of a dispute. My thesis is that, while requirements of justice address the first-order problem of knowledge, the rule of law—or formal requirements of *legality*—addresses the second-order problem of knowledge, the problem of communicating knowledge of justice. The idea of the rule of law or legality immediately presents two questions: what are the requirements of legality?; how do these requirements relate to the requirements of justice? The conception of justice described in Chapter 4 provides us—at least in general terms—with the substance of the message we want made accessible: the natural rights of several property, freedom of contract, and first possession (as well as other rights we have yet to consider). The medium for conveying this message is provided by institutions that conform to principles of legality associated with the liberal conception of the rule of law. These principles raise two issues: The first, the subject of this chapter, is the *form* that this message should take. The second, the subject of Chapter 6, is the *process* by which this form of message is determined and disseminated. It is to the first of these issues I now turn.

A well-known and still the best summary of the formal principles of legality was provided by Lon Fuller:

[T]he attempt to create and maintain a system of legal rules may miscarry in at least eight ways; there are in this enterprise, if you will, eight distinct routes to disaster. The first and most obvious lies in a failure to achieve rules at all, so that every issue must be decided on an ad hoc basis. The other routes are: (2) a failure to publicize, or at least to make available to the affected party, the rules he is expected to observe; (3) the abuse of retroactive legislation, which not only cannot itself guide action, but undercuts the integrity of rules prospective in effect, since it puts them under threat of retrospective change; (4) a failure to make rules understandable; (5) the enactment of contradictory rules or (6) rules that require conduct beyond the powers of the affected party; (7) introducing such frequent changes in the rules that the subject cannot orient his actions by them; and, finally, (8) a failure of congruence between the rules as announced and their actual administration.[6]

What about a system that fails to adhere to one or more of these principles of legality? Fuller wrote:

A total failure in any one of these eight directions does not simply result in a bad system of law; it results in something that is not properly called a legal system at all, except perhaps in the Pickwickian sense in which a void contract can still be said to be one kind of contract.[7]

This claim is not one of semantics—that is, a quibble about how the word "legal" or "law" is to be used—but of function. Each of these "desiderata," as

---

[6] Lon L. Fuller, *Morality of Law*, pp. 38–9.   [7] Ibid. 39.

Fuller called them, can best be understood, in my view, as formal requirements of legality that make it possible to handle the second-order problem of knowledge.

To coordinate human action, the requirements of justice must be communicated in advance of a conflict so as to permit people to act consistently with its dictates. To enable persons to avoid conflicting actions, we cannot rely on *ex post* ad hoc decision making, but must try to communicate in advance however imperfectly with general rules or principles (#1) that, if adhered to, would coordinate their behavior. To be grasped by people seeking to act properly (or to avoid sanctions), these rules must be communicated or publicized (#2) in an understandable form (#4). If the objective is to coordinate individual actions, then persons must not only be apprised of this information in advance of their taking action, they must also be reasonably confident that the information will not be changed after the fact (#3). Obviously, requirements that recommend conflicting courses of action (#5) or that are impossible to follow (#6) will not serve to coordinate behavior; nor can requirements that change too frequently (#7). Finally, coordination will not occur once it is discovered that the communicated rules differ from their actual administration (#8).

Although the relationship between these principles of legality and our ability to handle the second-order problem of knowledge is evident, two of these requirements merit a lengthier treatment. The fifth of Fuller's requirements—the avoidance of contradictory rules—deserves a more extensive discussion because it has important implications for our conception of justice that are generally neglected. The first of his requirements—"the failure to achieve rules at all, so that every issue must be decided on an ad hoc basis"—deserves a more extensive treatment because it has received considerable scholarly attention in recent years and remains controversial.

The Requirement of Compossibility

Fuller's fifth requirement of legality bars "the enactment of contradictory rules."[8] This hardly seems a radical suggestion, particularly in light of the obvious role that consistency plays in conveying usable information to persons seeking a knowledge of just conduct. Persons who are told that just conduct requires that they act in two mutually incompatible ways cannot know how to act. Without more guidance they are as likely to act unjustly as justly. Yet when discussing justice, some have lost sight of this insight.

In Chapter 4, the liberal conception of justice was defined as respect for the *rights* of individuals and associations. Two kinds of rights were distinguished: *background rights* are those claims a person has to legal enforcement that are valid, right, or just, whether or not they are actually recognized and enforced

---

[8] Lon L. Fuller, *Morality of Law*, pp. 39.

by a legal system; *legal rights* are those claims that an actual legal system will recognize as valid, right, or just. Justice requires that the legal rights that actually result from a system of laws correspond as closely as possible with the background rights to possess, use, and dispose of scarce resources that persons have.

It is commonly thought, however, that valid rights may conflict with each other.[9] According to this view, the responsibility of the political and legal processes is to mediate between conflicting rights; rights are mere claims, which must be assessed and compared with each other rather than the conceptual means by which the validity of claims are assessed. This view results from an inflation of rights. The more different kinds of rights that are recognized, the more there is potential for conflict between alleged rights and the more that rights start to look like mere claims rather than *valid* or dispositive claims. If asserting a right does not establish the validity of one's claim over that of another then some other way must then be found to settle the conflict among competing rights. Obviously, rights themselves provide no basis for such a settlement.

Yet when understood as facilitating the communication of justice to achieve an order of actions, Fuller's fifth requirement of legality argues for a parsimony of rights. The liberal conception of justice uses rights as the way of allocating jurisdiction for making decisions concerning the use of resources in a manner that achieves an order of actions. If rights are to play this function, then ideally rights should not conflict. If rights were to conflict then persons would be receiving conflicting information concerning their jurisdiction and an order of actions would not be achieved. For example, if both Ann and Ben are said to have rights to the same clearing, the same house, or Ann's body that bring their actions into conflict, then an analysis of their rights cannot resolve the conflict between them about how these resources should be used.

Whatever particular formulation of rights we settle upon to explicate the requirements of justice, to handle the second-order problem of knowledge, these rights must be *compossible*. Hillel Steiner explains this concept:

A right denotes a range of actions that its possessor may perform. It further implies a duty, on the part of persons other than the possessor, not to act in such a way as to interfere with or prevent those actions. . . . Actions interfering with or preventing the performance of rightful actions are themselves impermissible. Suppose there is a set of rights such that action A_1 falls within the range of rightful actions denoted by a right that X possesses, and action A_2 falls within the range of rightful actions denoted by a right that Y possesses. And suppose that the occurrence of A_1 constitutes an interference with or prevents the occurrence of A_2. What is the

---

[9] See e.g. Joseph Raz, *The Morality of Freedom* (Oxford: Oxford University Press, 1986), p. 184 ("Rights can conflict with other rights or with other duties. . . ."). See also Jeremy Waldron, "Rights in Conflict," in *Liberal Rights* (Cambridge: Cambridge University Press, 1993), pp. 205–6 (Because "individual interests often conflict with one another," Raz's interest theory of rights "indicates that conflicts of rights, though not logically necessary, are in the circumstances of the real world more or less inevitable.")

deontic status of A_1? It is at once a permissible action because it is an exercise of X's right, and an impermissible action because it is a violation of X's duty not to interfere with or prevent the exercise of Y's right. This contradiction implies that the set of rights in question is logically impossible.

I shall call a set of rights devoid of such contradictions a set of *compossible* rights.[10]

In a perfectly compossible set of rights, every right could be exercised according to its terms without any right in the set conflicting with any other. In short, with a set of compossible rights, no right may sanction an action in conflict with the action sanctioned by another right.

The compossibility of rights is functionally necessary to achieving an order of actions, because people need the information that rights provide as to how they may act to pursue happiness while avoiding conflicts with the actions of others. For this reason, the purely formal requirement of legal consistency is linked to substantive considerations of justice. If two purported background rights authorize two simultaneous actions that are in conflict, then when the two persons holding these "rights" act as their "rights" permit them to, they will still come into conflict and interfere with each other's actions. Even a perfect knowledge of their rights will not enable the "good men and women" to avoid a conflict over resource use. The coordination—or social order—that rights are formulated to secure would not be obtained. The need to resolve such a dispute by appealing to higher principles (or someone's discretion) instead of the rights of the parties would mean that we would not have succeeded in providing a framework that coordinates the conduct of persons living in society with each other. To the extent that it failed in its basic mission, such a scheme of background rights would be substantively deficient.

At this point form has placed important constraints on substance.[11] However attractive a particular claim of right may be, if it conflicts with other rights that are essential to solving the knowledge problem—such as the rights to several property or to freedom of contract—it violates the requirement of compossibility and its validity is highly suspect. As Steiner explains:

The elementary particles of justice are *rights*. . . . We learn something about justice by examining the formal or characteristic features of rights. These features constrain the possible content of justice principles in much the same way as architectural precepts must be informed by the properties of the construction materials they orchestrate. . . . Any justice principle that delivers a set of rights yielding contradictory judgements about the permissibility of a particular action either is unrealizable or (what comes to the same thing) must be modified to be realizable. Particular applications of such a principle would too frequently drive us to say,

[10] Hillel Steiner, "The Structure of a Set of Compossible Rights," *Journal of Philosophy*, 74 (1977), pp. 767–8.

[11] *Cf.* Waldron, "Rights in Conflict", pp. 203–4 (Although a set of rights which constrain "the actions that are morally available to any agent" is compossible, "the price for this tidiness is a severe limitation on the types of moral concerns that can be articulated [as rights].")

"Leave it to the judge/the legislator/heaven to sort this one out." And they, after all, seem sufficiently busy already.[12]

This is yet another reason to prefer the liberal conception of justice based on background property rights over the conception of rights as any "justified claim." Since any right could potentially be justified, this conception of right is extremely open-ended and conducive to generating conflicting "rights." Property rights are limited to claims to particular resources and thereby reduce the range of possibly conflicting claims that may be made. An exclusive focus on conflicting claims to control physical resources also makes potential conflicts easier to identify and to resolve.

All of this is missed by theorists who ignore the informational role played by a compossible set of rights. For example, in his lengthy treatment of rights in conflict, Jeremy Waldron, argues that with theories of rights based on interests, conflicts of rights are nearly inevitable and require "trade-offs" among rights. Waldron would make some of these trade-offs by "establish[ing] the relative importance of the interests at stake, and the contribution each of the conflicting duties may make to the importance of the interest it protects,"[13] and by "try[ing] to maximize our promotion of what we take to be important."[14] In other cases, he would establish an "internal relation between moral considerations"[15] to handle conflicting claims of rights.

Even were it possible for a rights theorist like Waldron, or all the rights theorists in the world working together, to perform this task—he does not actually attempt it—one thing is for sure. Individual persons living in society with each other could not hope to do so. Those "good" people who want only to know what conduct is required of them so as not to create conflicts with others would be given no guidance by a knowledge of their "rights." And in this respect, such a rights theory would fail to fulfill its function of establishing an order of actions. Nowhere in his lengthy treatment of compossibility does Waldron consider the epistemic function of rights.

None of this suggests that any real legal system will escape the discovery of conflicts between legal rights it acknowledges. The analysis presented here does suggest, however, that no just legal order should tolerate such conflicts when they are discovered, and Waldron acknowledges that compossibility is possible in principle for the type of rights theory presented here.[16] Judged by

---

[12] Steiner, *Essay on Rights*, pp. 2–3. [13] Waldron, "Rights in Conflict," pp. 223–4.

[14] Ibid. 224. Waldron apparently thinks that at least some claims of interest can be "weighted quantitatively in relation to one another (so that we allow a right to life to be worth five rights to free speech, or whatever)." Ibid. 219. The practicality of systematically valuing even a small fraction of everyone's interests in this way is, shall we say, doubtful.

[15] Ibid. 223.

[16] Ibid. 213: "A conception of rights which regarded each right as simply a correlative of some independently justified duty might not have this characteristic [of incompossibility]." In this case the duties are "essentially negative in character, requiring each agent to *refrain* from performing actions of the specified type: they can never require anything other than an omission. And they are *agent relative*, in the sense that each

its ability to handle the second-order problem of knowledge, then, this conception of rights is superior to any other conception. Contrary to the modern
popular view that conflicts between background rights are normal and that we
resolve such conflicts by determining legal rights on some other grounds, both
our conception of the background rights required by justice and the legal
rights specified by a legal system should be as compossible as humanly possible.

The Need for Specific Precepts of Justice

The first requirement of legality given by Lon Fuller was the achievement of a
system of rules that avoids the need to decide every issue on an ad hoc basis.
Under the influence of Ronald Dworkin, legal theorists today draw a distinction between rules and principles.[17] Principles are explicit reasons for or
against acting in a particular manner. There may be several principles or reasons favoring a particular action and several principles against taking the same
action. What action is appropriate may depend on selecting the most persuasive set of principles or reasons. Though legal principles may conflict in the
sense that they argue in favor of conflicting outcomes, the rights that are
determined by the weightier *set* of legal principles ought not conflict with
other similarly determined rights.

According to Dworkin's account, principles are seen as general maxims of
conduct. An example of a principle would be that one who causes injury to
another ought to provide compensation for that injury. A principle that might
sometimes yield a contrary result would be that when a victim is violently
attacked, the attacker should not receive compensation for injuries caused by
the victim in self-defense. Rules, on the other hand, recommend action in an
all-or-nothing fashion. An example of a rule would be that a will is invalid and
unenforceable if it bears the signatures of fewer than three witnesses.
According to this distinction between rules and principles, if an applicable rule
is followed, the rule alone specifies the appropriate action. To reject the recommended action is to reject the rule. To enforce a will with two signatures is
to reject the rule requiring three. In contrast, with principles when one principle or set of principles outweighs another, this is not a refutation or rejection
of the outweighed principles.

Having acknowledged this now well-accepted and important distinction I
wish to set it aside, at least for now. This section concerns the need for *ex ante*
guidance for conduct. Such guidance can be provided either by rules or principles or a combination of both, although each approach has its strengths and
weaknesses. Therefore, in this work I shall employ the term *legal precept* to refer

agent is taken to be concerned only with his own observance of the constraints. . . . On
this conception, rights are more or less incapable of conflicting". Ibid. 204.

[17] See Ronald Dworkin, "The Model of Rules," *University of Chicago Law Review*, vol.
35 (1967), pp. 22–9.

to an explicit canon of conduct, whether in the form of a rule or a principle. So recast, Fuller's point is that the first requirement of legality is the achievement of a system of decision making governed by a set of discernable legal precepts.

Legal precepts are needed because, while imperfect, they are the best available way to address the second-order problem of knowledge. In the absence of some instinctive grasp of the requirements of justice, individuals attempting to act in a just manner need some way of knowing when their actions are unjust. Such information must be conveyed in some manner before people act. There are two general methods of communication one can imagine.

The first would be a system of instructions that are "custom made" to reflect the particular facts of a given decision. One could call a central authority and ask whether or not a particular act was appropriate. Given that the number of actions taken every day are literally countless, such a method would be strictly impossible; the problem of knowledge makes such a system almost inconceivable. The authority would need somehow to acquire knowledge of the particular situation and such knowledge would be impossible to obtain. Even if this were possible, such a system would require some mechanism of coordinating the advice given to different persons so that people would not be brought into conflict when acting on conflicting advice. A system of custom-made instructions is a pure fantasy. Of course, a central authority might rely on precepts that govern similar classes of conduct, but this would actually be a resort to the second method of conveying knowledge of justice.

The second method is to attempt to classify different kinds of actions that commonly are taken and then to formulate general precepts to distinguish those actions that are consistent with the requirements of justice from those that are not. So, for example, we may identify a "verbal commitment to perform an action" as one kind of conduct that is quite common and then formulate legal precepts to identify the circumstances that characterize legally effective commitments, or contracts. How are such specific precepts discovered in a manner that is consistent with the requirements of justice? I shall discuss this in the next chapter. But first let me consider some objections to governing human action by means of legal precepts.

Criticisms of Using Legal Precepts

The practice of using legal precepts to decide disputes was criticized by American Legal Realists as either redundant or pernicious. Disputes, it is said, should be decided justly. Where legal precepts dictate the same outcome as that of justice, then legal precepts are redundant—acting justly will achieve the same results as following the precept. Where legal precepts recommend a different result than that recommended by justice then following the rules is pernicious. The result is, in the words of Jerome Frank, "injustice according to law."[18] Most people are of a similar opinion when confronted with what appears to be the "unjust" application of a rule to a particular situation.

One assumption underlying this objection is that, because they are formulated before a dispute arises, legal precepts cannot take into account the specific facts of a dispute that may argue in favor of a different "just" result than that recommended by the legal precept. Only after the fact can we know enough about the actual dispute to do real justice between the parties. As Frank argued,

The judge, at his best is an arbitrator, a "sound man" who strives to do justice to the parties by exercising a wise discretion with reference to the peculiar circumstances of the case. He does not merely "find" or invent some generalized rule which he "applies" to the facts presented to him. He does "equity" in the sense in which Aristotle—when thinking most clearly—described it. "It is equity," he wrote in his Rhetoric, "to pardon human failings, and to look to the law giver and not to the law, and for this an arbitrator was first appointed, in order that equity might flourish."[19]

When based on this assumption, however, the objection against legal precepts amounts, then, to an argument in favor of *ex post* decision making. As was just discussed, the costs of *ex post* decision making are exceedingly high. Even a highly imperfect application of *ex ante* legal precepts is usually preferable to an *ex post* determination. Nonetheless, as discussed in Chapter 6, the common-law process of adjudication does provide for a method of taking changed circumstances into account by modifying or refining (as opposed to discarding) legal precepts.

Moreover, this assumption views legal precepts as distinct from and at least sometimes opposed to the requirements of justice. However, the analysis presented here offers a quite different picture of this relationship. Justice, at least in its first derivation, is extremely abstract and general. For justice to be brought to bear effectively on individual decision, specific legal precepts are needed to guide conduct. Such precepts are the necessary means by which just results or ends are to be achieved in practice, and they are also the means by which persons decide how to act justly so as to avoid a dispute that requires resolution.

Most importantly, perhaps, this objection to the use of legal precepts assumes that persons deciding how to act or judges deciding how to resolve a dispute have access (independent of legal precepts) to a conception of justice that is specific enough to decide the outcomes of disputes. Where this assumption is false and a conception of justice, such as one based on natural rights, does not provide specific enough guidance, as is commonly the case, legal precepts are the inescapable means of putting the abstract requirements of justice into practice. Where this assumption holds true and abstract natural rights do recommend for or against certain conduct, legal precepts generally have no

---

[18] Frank, *Law and Mind*, p. 154.   [19] Ibid. 157.

difficulty mirroring the requirements of justice. Where the just result is very clear and a legal precept violates it, this is an argument for changing or refining the precept at issue, not discarding the use of precepts altogether. Indeed, as I explained in Chapter 1, the primary function of background natural rights is, to provide a means of evaluating and reforming legal rights.

The practice of using legal precepts is also sometimes criticized as being impossible. Some argue that the meanings of the words used to express legal precepts are too indefinite to provide useful guidance to actors or to judges assessing the justice of actions. "Law has no interior rationality," writes James Boyle, "nothing in the rules themselves dictates any particular result."[20] Others contend that legal rules are inevitably contradictory. Joseph Singer contends that

the question is whether it is possible to set up a legal system based on the rule of law. If legal reasoning is internally contradictory and therefore indeterminate, there are no objective limits on what judges or other governmental officials can do. Thus the goal of constraining government or regulating interpersonal conduct by previously knowable general rules seems impossible. Is the realm of judicial action, then, inevitably governed by whim and caprice?[21]

While these arguments advanced by "critical legal scholars" have been much debated,[22] their appeal is rapidly eroding. "Judges are, to a significant extent, practically 'bound' by law," writes Duncan Kennedy, "and often, often, often declare and apply rules that they would never vote for if they were legislators."[23] Indeed, it may come as a surprise to many that any legal scholar would deny that legal precepts are capable of conveying information in advance of action. Those who know that they must pay a fare before they may ride a bus (and how much the fare will be), those who know they are supposed to drive on the right-hand side of the street and to stop at a red traffic light, those who know that they are not supposed to smoke in a no smoking section of an airplane or restaurant, those who know that they must be admitted to law school before they may attend and that to be admitted they must take an admissions test, are quite familiar with the ability of general precepts to guide

---

[20] James Boyle, "The Politics of Reason: Critical Legal Theory and Local Social Thought," *University of Pennsylvania Law Review*, vol. 133 (1985), p. 728

[21] Joseph William Singer, "The Player and the Cards: Nihilism and Legal Theory," *Yale Law Journal*, vol. 94 (1984), p. 7.

[22] For two criticisms of the indeterminacy thesis, see e.g. Kenny Hegland, "Goodbye to Deconstruction," *Southern California University Law Review*, vol. 58 (1985), p. 1203; Lawrence B. Solum, "On the Indeterminacy Crisis: Critiquing Critical Dogma," *University of Chicago Law Review*, vol. 54 (1987), pp. 462–503.

[23] Duncan Kennedy, *A Critique of Adjudication* (Cambridge, Mass.: Harvard University Press, 1997), p. 275. While Kennedy says he never advocated a radical indeterminacy thesis (ibid. 60), he does report that, "[i]n the latter days of [critical legal studies], postmodern crits sometimes thought they knew, without ever reading a judicial opinion that, 'law' just 'had to be' indeterminate, because deconstruction had 'proved' that all texts are indeterminate." Ibid. 276.

conduct.[24] Of course everyone also knows that novel or unusual situations do arise that are not clearly covered by any known precept, but few would conclude from this that the exceptions prove the inefficacy of all legal rules.

Most critical legal scholars, such as Boyle, do not ultimately deny that we can find a determinate noncontradictory meaning for legal precepts, but only that this meaning results from our background political and other assumptions. For this reason the use of legal precepts is not "neutral," a neutrality which the liberal conception of the rule of law supposedly requires.[25] "But content enters law through the back door, not through the pure linguistic connections envisaged by formalist theory but through the limitations imposed by a deeply political set of assumptions about the social world."[26] Meaning results from "the collective consciousness of the interpreting community."[27]

When qualified in this way, however, it is not entirely clear that the criticism has the same bite against the function of the rule of law presented here. For my argument on behalf of relying on legal precepts is that they are necessary to convey information about the requirements of justice in advance of acting. That this information is conveyed by words whose meaning is determined by "the socially constructed reality that filters the infinite meanings we could derive from a text"[28] does not undermine the fact that legal precepts are playing a vital information disseminating role. Nor does the fact that the "socially constructed reality" that allegedly makes shared meaning possible includes political or ideological assumptions. The issue is *whether* legal precepts are able to convey information, not *how* they do so.

Some argue that legal precepts are unable to "constrain" the conduct of legal decision makers and, therefore, it is illusory to purport to be basing a legal system on such precepts. "There is no rule," asserted Jerome Frank, "by which you can force a judge to follow an old rule."[29] This observation confuses two very basic, but quite distinct social problems. True, everyone knows that precepts can be disregarded by decision makers. Though this would violate Fuller's

---

[24] See e.g. ibid. 160: "[I]t is a constant of everyday life that directives are experienced as having a single obvious meaning. To proceed as though they had different meanings, or many possible meanings, is bad faith, or disobedience, or evasion. When you ask me to close the door, I don't, typically, see myself as having to make a difficult interpretation. I know what you mean without thinking about it. You don't hesitate to say I haven't closed the door when I close the window."

[25] See e.g. Gary Peller, "The Metaphysics of American Law," *California Law Review*, vol. 73 (1985), p. 1168: "The purported distinction in liberal thought between reason and will—and, I will contend, law and politics—depends on the denial of the contingency of representational categories. . . . Meaning is traced to a source supposedly immediate and pure rather than socially produced through contingent mediating categories." I take up the issue of neutrality in Chapter 15.

[26] Boyle, "Politics of Reason," p. 728.

[27] Ibid. See also Peller, "Metaphysics", p. 1164: "To the extent we understand a speaker, intelligibility depends, at least in the first instance, on shared conventions and codes of meaning built into the language structure, rather than on any natural tie between representational terms and the concepts they signify."

[28] Boyle, "Politics of Reason," p. 728.   [29] Jerome Frank, *Law and Mind*, p. 128.

tenet bars the use or threat of force to obtain a manifestation of consent; thus, a contract signed or "consented to" under duress is void. In addition to prohibiting force to obtain consent, liberalism has always barred persons from obtaining consent by means of fraud.

Although the equivalence of force and fraud is both long-asserted and well-accepted by classical liberals, its theoretical basis remains obscure. This is because, as I shall now explain, the two doctrines perform distinct functions. The prohibition of force or duress addresses the first-order problem of knowledge, while the prohibition of fraud addresses the second-order problem of knowledge.

Force is prohibited as a means of obtaining consent, in important part, because its use would legitimate transfers of resources that do not reflect the knowledge of the rights-holder regarding the potential uses and value of the resource in question. (It would also create serious problems of interest and power.) Permitting forcible transfers disrupts the complex, but vital, mechanism of information dispersal that only consensual transfers make possible. In this regard, the prohibition on the use of force reflects an effort to handle the first-order problem of knowledge, which consists of permitting persons and associations to act on the basis of their diverse local and personal knowledge while taking into account the knowledge of others about which they are pervasively ignorant.

The function of the prohibition against fraud is related, but nonetheless different. This prohibition reflects an effort to handle a problem of interpersonal communication that is part of the second-order problem of knowledge. Unlike the case of force or duress, a manifested consent that is fraudulently induced *does* reflect the knowledge of the person consenting, but the resources actually received by the defrauded transferee do not conform to the description communicated by the transferor. A defrauded buyer may know that she values the use of the resource she is supposed to be obtaining from the seller—for example, a used car with 10,000 miles—more than those she is transferring to the seller, but the resource she actually receives—a car with 50,000 miles—does not conform to the description communicated to her by the deceiving party. In other words, as with the objective approach discussed in the previous section, the fraudulent seller is telling the buyer that she will receive certain rights, but the resources actually delivered do not conform to this description. Due to the transferor's failure to deliver resources conforming to the rights he communicated and conveyed by his manifestation of consent, a legal remedy is needed to close the gap that has arisen between the distribution of resources and the distribution of rights.

In sum, though force and fraud operate to frustrate an order of actions somewhat differently, they are equally problematic. When a seller uses force or duress to obtain the buyer's manifestation of consent, the transfer may not reflect the buyer's knowledge; with fraud, the buyer's manifestation of consent *does* reflect her knowledge but the resulting distribution of resources does not reflect the consent that was communicated. We may therefore add the following to the formulation of justice we have developed thus far:

FORMULATION 3. *Justice is respect for the rights of individuals and associations.*
(1) The *right of several property* specifies a right to acquire, possess, use, and dispose of scarce physical resources—including their own bodies. Resources may be used in any way that does not physically interfere with other persons' use and enjoyment of their resources. While most property rights are freely alienable, the right to one's person is inalienable.
(2) The *right of first possession* specifies that property rights to unowned resources are acquired by being the first to establish control over them and to stake a claim
(3) The *right of freedom of contract* specifies that a rightholder's consent is both necessary (freedom *from* contract) and sufficient (freedom *to* contract) to transfer alienable property rights. A manifestation of assent is ordinarily necessary unless one party somehow has access to the other's subjective intent.
(4) Violating these rights by *force or fraud* is unjust.

Does this analysis of fraudulently obtaining consent by conveying false information extend to the *failure* to convey *true* information that, if known, would influence the decision of the other party to consent to a transfer? This situation presented itself in the famous case of *Laidlaw v. Organ*[35] which involved a tobacco purchase contract made during the war of 1812. At the time the contract was executed, the buyer had advance information that the treaty ending the war had been signed, promising an end to the naval blockade of New Orleans that had been suppressing the price of tobacco in the blockaded region. When asked by the seller if he knew anything that might affect the price of tobacco, however, the buyer failed to disclose this information. The legal issue was whether the seller could avoid the contract because of this failure to disclose. Chief Justice John Marshall, speaking for the Supreme Court, endorsed a rule of nondisclosure that reflects a distinction between information concerning the *intrinsic* qualities of a resource and that concerning *extrinsic* circumstances affecting the market price:

The question in this case is, whether the intelligence of extrinsic circumstances which might influence the price of the commodity, and which was exclusively within the knowledge of the vendee, ought to have been communicated by him to the vendor? The court is of the opinion that he was not bound to communicate it.[36]

The foregoing analysis confirms the correctness of Marshall's judgment. It suggests that a duty to disclose information exists when the failure to disclose creates a disparity between the rights transferred and the resources received. This may occur, for instance, when (*a*) an item, as it appears, would normally have

---

[35] Laidlaw v. Organ, 15 US (2 Wheat.) 178 (1817).   [36] Ibid. 195.

certain intrinsic characteristics, (*b*) a reasonable inspection will not reveal the absence of these characteristics, (*c*) the seller knows that these characteristics are absent, and (*d*) the seller has reason to know that knowledge of this fact is "material," that is, it would likely influence the manifestation of assent by the buyer. An example of this is a product with a latent defect, such as a house infested with termites. When these circumstances obtain, the resources conveyed to the buyer do not conform to the substance of the rights implicitly or explicitly conveyed by the seller.

On the other hand, a duty to disclose is not warranted by this analysis of fraud when the seller remains silent about a fact which does not concern the substance of the rights being transferred. In such a case, the seller does deliver resources that conform to the rights that were represented as being transferred. For example, (to reverse the facts of *Laidlaw v. Organ*) when a seller sells grain at a high price due to the shortages caused by a war. Although the seller fails to communicate his knowledge that the war has ended and consequently that prices are about to fall, he commits no fraud provided that he delivers grain of a quality and quantity conforming to the rights that were communicated and transferred.

Permitting transfers of rights motivated by disparities of knowledge (other than the substance of the rights being transferred) actually increases, rather than diminishes, the flow of information by providing an incentive to make exchanges that will eventually move prices to a level that is consistent with the facts. So-called "speculative" profits reward those who correctly anticipate new information and thus provide a powerful incentive to produce new information. Moreover, the transactions that yield these profits help convey the information developed by speculators to others.

At first glance, a rule permitting those in possession of information concerning the demand for particular scarce resources—what Marshall called "intelligence of extrinsic circumstances which might influence the price of the commodity"—to withhold it from their trading partners would seem inimical to the dissemination of such information. Closer analysis, however, reveals that a nondisclosure rule does indeed promote that end. To put the matter paradoxically, permitting persons to conceal certain types of information best promotes the dissemination of that information.

The resolution of this paradox lies in the fact that, their verbal silence notwithstanding, the aggregate *actions* of persons in possession of Marshall's extrinsic intelligence disseminate more information than mere words ever could. Both consenting to trade and withholding one's consent importantly affect the market price of a resource. In this context, many persons often seem to forget that the prevailing market price reflects the price at which the marginal seller is willing to transact with the marginal buyer. The market price of, for example, a house is as influenced by the decisions of all homeowners who prefer to hold on to their property than accept the prevailing market price as it is influenced by those at the margin who consent to such transfers.

The movement of resource prices caused in the aggregate by the actions of those who trade and those who withhold their consent to trade conveys invaluable and otherwise unobtainable knowledge. As was discussed in Chapter 3, resource prices represent a summation of innumerable amounts of radically-dispersed information concerning the competing alternative uses of scarce resources and the relative subjective desirability of these uses. Therefore, a person in possession of "windfall" information concerning a particular scarce resource still contributes importantly to the welfare of others by causing the price of that resource to move in an information-revealing direction, whether the direction is up, down, or unchanged. The price-effect of the decision to trade or refrain from trading results notwithstanding the fact that the trader may neither have produced the information nor intentionally disclosed it. As before, I do not claim that this information process is perfect, but only that it is both vital and irreplaceable.

Imposing a duty to disclose on persons in possession of information that concerns a future change in market demand for a resource eliminates the possibility of profiting from the information, and thereby greatly reduces any incentive for potential traders to engage in an information-revealing transaction. Consequently, a legal duty to disclose extrinsic intelligence to the other party would greatly reduce disclosures of this information to the society at large. Moreover, such a disclosure rule would cause countless persons to be misled. By eliminating the incentive to trade on information, enforcing a duty to disclose would induce persons in possession of extrinsic intelligence inadvertently to convey to the market by their silence the inaccurate impression that future demand will be lower or higher than they know it to be.

In his landmark article on the duty to disclose, Anthony Kronman argued that imposing such a duty undermines the incentive to deliberately *acquire* information concerning resource use that is vital to the price mechanism. He would thus privilege trading on deliberately-acquired information, as opposed to casually-acquired information.[37] Omitted from Kronman's otherwise insightful analysis is the fact that trading upon this information, however the information is acquired, *disseminates* that information by affecting the resource price. Without protecting trades on the basis of casually-acquired "extrinsic" information concerning market demand, the incentive to disseminate this information by means of trading is eliminated, and this information is lost to the market. As a result, resource prices would be less meaningful than necessary, undermining our ability to handle the first-order problem of knowledge.

---

[37] See Anthony T. Kronman, "Mistake, Disclosure, Information, and the Law of Contracts," *Journal of Legal Studies*, vol. 11 (1978), pp. 1–34.

Summary

The analysis of this chapter can be summarized as follows:

(1) The *second-order problem of knowledge* is the need to communicate knowledge of justice in a manner that makes the actions it requires accessible to
everyone.

(2) The need for this message to be conveyed in advance of persons taking
action (*ex ante*) influences the form of the message in at least eight ways:
(*a*) general rules or principles that are (*b*) publicized, (*c*) prospective in
effect, (*d*) understandable, (*e*) compossible, (*f*) possible to follow, (*g*) stable, and (*h*) enforced as publicized.

(3) These formal requirements that are needed to communicate the message
of justice *ex ante* are part of what is known as the rule of law. (The other
part concerns the process by which legal precepts are discovered and
applied, which is the subject of Chapter 6).

(4) The need for *ex ante* information about allocation of several property
rights also influences the substance of these rights. The boundaries defined
by several property rights must normally conform to the objective meaning that attaches to human conduct. Only if human conduct is channeled
into certain forms will it be legally effective. This enables persons to rely
on the appearances created by others.

(5) Forced exchanges of rights are prohibited by a liberal conception of justice, in part, because such exchanges do not take into account the knowledge of the coerced right-holder. (Such exchanges also may not serve the
right-holder's interest.)

(6) Fraud is prohibited by a liberal conception of justice because it creates a
gap between the manifestation of consent to transfers of rights and the
resources actually transferred, resulting in holdings of resources that do
not reflect the revealed knowledge of one of the parties to a transfer.

(7) The duty to disclose applies only to information pertaining to the intrinsic qualities of resources which are the subject of a rights transfer and not
to extrinsic circumstances affecting market demand.

The fact that legal precepts can convey information in advance of acting does
not tell us how any particular set of legal precepts is to be discovered and
applied. For this we will need to expand the conception of the rule of law to
include the processes by which cases and controversies are adjudicated. This is
the subject of Chapter 6.

SIX

Specifying Conventions: The Third-Order Problem of Knowledge

IN the previous chapters, we saw how the first-order problem of dispersed personal and local knowledge is addressed by a conception of justice with three distinct dimensions. First is the dimension of several property: the jurisdiction or right to decide questions of resource use is decentralized to the level of individuals and voluntary associations—those who have access to personal and local knowledge. Second is the dimension of freedom of contract: (*a*) permit persons to consent to transfer their rights to others (freedom to contract) and (*b*) require the manifested consent of the rights-holder for all interpersonal rights-transfers (freedom from contract). Third, permit persons to acquire unowned resources by first possessing them. We then saw how the second-order problem of providing *ex ante* knowledge about justice to affected persons is handled by putting this message into a form consistent with principles associated with the rule of law, and how these formal requirements, in turn, influence the substance of justice.

So far this discussion of justice and the rule of law has been extremely abstract. I have offered no specific precepts that are to be used to decide the actual contours of persons' jurisdiction or the precise circumstances that reflect consent. The formal requirements of the rule of law described earlier are a bit more specific, but to be applicable to real cases these tenets require still further specification. How are such concrete precepts developed? This is the "third-order problem of knowledge":

> The *third-order problem of knowledge* is the need to determine specific action-guiding precepts that are consistent with both the requirements of justice and of the rule of law.

One way to accomplish this is to examine more closely the natural rights of several property, freedom of contract, first possession, and the rule of law principles discussed in Chapter 5 and to try to deduce from these rights and principles more specific precepts that can be used to address the first-order and second-order problems of knowledge. We can call this the deductive or *theoretical method* in so far as specific precepts are being logically deduced from more general principles and from a theoretical understanding of the social problems we are trying to solve. Although I do believe it is possible to generate in this way precepts that are considerably more specific than those presented thus far, at some point the ability to specify legal rules or principles in this theoretical manner is limited. Understanding these limits is important to appreciate the need for decision making processes that I have yet to consider.

1. The Limits of Theoretical Methods of Discovery

Our ability to deduce from a theory of justice a unique set of specific precepts is limited for two reasons. First, in some respects the general principles that animate this theory of justice are "underdeterminate." Second, theorists who attempt to deduce specific action guiding precepts from general principles face a daunting problem of knowledge.

The Underdeterminacy of Abstract Theory

A theory of justice is *underdeterminate* when it narrows down our choice of legal precepts but does not determine a unique precept to address the social problems at issue.[1] This contrasts with a theory that it is "indeterminate" insofar as it does not narrow down our choices at all.[2] Though he does not use this term, when describing the efficacy of legal rules (as opposed to theory), Frederick Schauer explains the concept of underdeterminacy as follows:

[T]he existing articulation of rules, even if only presumptive, guides us away from some answers that would otherwise be included. By identifying and thus presumptively excluding those answers that are unacceptable, the rules embodied in language decrease the size of the field of potentially right answers. Even if the size of the field never reduces to one uniquely correct answer, the articulated rules have played a significant role in eliminating the enormous number of answers that might otherwise have been acceptable. This presumptive exclusion thus gives us, in most instances, a more manageable range of choices with which to deal.[3]

The same could be said of the abstract requirements of justice. As Loren Lomasky has observed, "The abstraction of a defensible natural law precludes

---

[1] See Solum, "Indeterminacy Crisis," p. 473: "The law is *underdeterminate* with respect to a given case if and only if the set of results in the case that can be squared with the legal materials is a nonidentical subset of the set of all imaginable results."
[2] See ibid.: "The law is *indeterminate* with respect to a given case if and only if the set of materials is identical with the set of all imaginable results."
[3] Schauer, "Easy Cases," p. 428.

its direct application to concrete situations that are immersed in a sea of particularity."[4] For this reason, "[b]asic rights cannot be expected to function as legal rights do, entailing imperatives that are directly applicable to human affairs. It must not be supposed that there is one unique instantiation of basic rights that is everywhere optimal."[5] There are probably any number of different sets of specific legal doctrine that could satisfactorily specify the contours of the liberal conception of justice and the rule of law.

In the context of constitutional interpretation, Schauer illustrates the underdeterminacy of language with the metaphor of a "frame":

[L]inguistically articulated rules . . . [exclude] wrong answers rather than point[ ] to right ones. . . . The language of a [constitutional] clause, whether seemingly general or seemingly specific, establishes a boundary, or a frame, albeit a frame with fuzzy edges. Even though the language itself does not tell us what goes within the frame, it does tell us when we have gone outside it.[6]

By this metaphor, when specifying legal precepts, justice as defined by natural rights and the formal principles of the rule of law provide a theoretical frame or boundary. More than one set of legal precepts lie within the frame and natural rights and rule of law principles do not specify a single or unique choice among them. These theoretical considerations do, however, help identify the many sets of rules that are outside the frame and therefore inconsistent with either justice or the rule of law or both. Abstract natural rights and rule of law principles exclude wrong answers rather than definitively establish right ones.

To better appreciate the underdeterminacy of abstract principles of justice and the rule of law we may analogize this to the design of passenger cars. The purpose of passenger cars is the transportation of persons and their belongings and this requires that a car, among other things, be able to accelerate, turn, stop, and move in reverse at the command of the driver. Most cars satisfy these and other basic "theoretical" requirements. Moreover, from behind the wheel, they appear to operate in a very similar manner. Under the hood, however, there is a tremendous diversity among the engines and other mechanical parts that are used to accomplish these functions. Most engines operate according to the same set of principles but only if these principles are kept reasonably general or abstract.

For example, an internal combustion engine requires chambers in which to ignite a mixture of air and gasoline so that the force of this explosion can be converted into motion. This may be accomplished either by a rotary combustion chamber or by a set of pistons. The fuel may be mixed with air and injected into the combustion chamber either by a carburetor or by a fuel injector. The electricity used to ignite the fuel-air mixture in the combustion chamber must be distributed to the correct chamber at just the right time so that all the explosions are synchronized, but this may be accomplished by either a mechanical "distributor" or by an electronic ignition. It is apparent that the

---

[4] Lomasky, *Persons, Rights*, p. 105. [5] Ibid. [6] Schauer, "Easy Cases," p. 430.

basic theory or functional principles of automotive engine design underdetermines the precise design of any particular engine. Although current production engines operate according to a common set of principles, the exact design of an automobile engine cannot be logically deduced from these principles. Let us refer to this as the *principle of nondeducibility*.

The fact that specific engine designs cannot be logically deduced from a knowledge of the functions of passenger cars or from principles of automotive engineering does not mean that this knowledge is irrelevant to the process of engine design. Instead, understanding these functions and principles provides a basis for critically evaluating engine designs that are developed in some other manner. Furthermore, the fact that any number of engine designs accomplish the basic mission of automobile engines does not mean that every engine design works as well as any other. For example, rotary engines have had a problem maintaining a good seal on the rotating combustion chambers, a problem that piston engines avoid. For this reason, piston engines are overwhelmingly favored by car manufacturers despite the early theoretical promise of rotary designs. Similarly, it is rare to find a mechanical distributor on a car today. For reasons of cost and fuel efficiency, all new cars have electronic ignitions. General principles of automotive engineering help distinguish those designs that work better than others—especially after testing the performance of prototypes—and help explain why an infinite number of designs would fail to work at all. Let us refer to this as the *principle of rational criticism*.

Much of a particular car's specific design can neither be deduced from general principles of automotive design nor subjected to rational criticism on the basis of these principles. Especially with the controls used by the driver there are probably many equally acceptable designs, but there is a substantial advantage in adopting a common design for all cars. For example, all four-speed manual transmissions employ an "H" shifting pattern: to change gears you move the gear stick up for first gear; down for second; over the middle, to the right, and up for third gear; down for fourth. While this pattern probably reflected the early engineering requirements of manual transmissions, clearly it would now be disadvantageous to deviate from this pattern. By adopting a common shift pattern for all four-speed transmissions, every person who can drive a four-speed can drive all such cars with four-speed transmissions without having to learn a new pattern for every different car.

The advantages of uniformity extend to all phases of life. The "qwerty" keyboard on which I am typing this text gets its name from the first six of its top row of letters and is the standard keyboard arrangement in use today. Obviously, the keyboard could be rearranged in an infinite variety of ways. Some arrangements have been designed that are supposed to have efficiency advantages over the qwerty arrangement. (Some say that the qwerty keyboard was originally intended actually to slow down typists whose typing speed would jam early manual typewriters.) Yet any advantages of an alternative arrangement would have to outweigh (in the minds of prospective users) the considerable advantage of keyboard uniformity. Once we have acquired a knowledge of one arrangement, it is very costly to learn another (although sometimes the benefits to us of learning a new arrangement can outweigh the costs). We can call this the *principle of uniformity*.

How do these three principles apply to law? The principle of nondeducibility suggests that, as with engineering, a unique set of specific action-guiding precepts may not be logically deduced from the general principles of justice and the rule of law. So the process by which we discover legal precepts must include some mechanism in addition to logical deduction from first principles. Nonetheless, the principle of rational criticism suggests that whatever sets of specific precepts are discovered in some nondeductive manner may still be subjected to criticism on the grounds that they are inconsistent with more general principles of justice and the rule of law. Finally, the principle of uniformity suggests that when there is no reason to prefer one specific precept to another—even when there is some reason to prefer one to another—there is generally an advantage to uniformity.

Let me illustrate these principles with an example. Consider the situation where Ann abandons her claim to the clearing. Clearly, principles of justice generally permit persons who no longer wish to exercise control over resources to consensually relinquish their rights. Others such as Ben are then free to acquire rights in these now unowned resources by exercising the right of first possession. A problem arises when, as is quite common, Ann abandons her land but does not manifest her intention to do so in some clear way. Typically, persons who are abandoning land simply leave and do not return. How is Ann's act of abandonment to be distinguished from that of a person who intends to return, but who leaves her land alone for a period of time? When Ben comes to the land, how is he to know if it has been abandoned and whether and when the land becomes his by the right of first possession?

To handle this case, some jurisdictions adopt the following rule: if a person openly asserts control over apparently abandoned land without objection from the original owner for a period of fourteen years, this person acquires the rights to the land by "adverse possession." Other jurisdictions make the period seven years. Consistent with the principle of nondeducibility, there is no way to logically deduce from the liberal conception of justice or from the rights of several property and first possession the exact number of years that must pass before title to the land transfers to the adverse possessor. Neither seven years, nor fourteen, nor any other specific number is logically required by the theory. In this respect the liberal conception of justice that permits abandonment and adverse possession is underdeterminate.

Still, the principle of uniformity suggests that some specific number should be determined so that persons such as Ben who exert control over land adverse to the original owners would know when and if they have acquired legal title by adverse possession. Such a conventional rule is also required so that owners of land who intend to retain title can know that they had better check on their land at least once during the specified period to oust anyone who is attempting to establish ownership by adverse possession.

Nonetheless, the principle of rational criticism suggests that, while a conventional rule is needed and cannot be logically deduced from the abstract background right of several property, some specific rules can be rationally criticized as inconsistent with this right.[7] For example, a rule that specified that adverse possession transferred title after seven hours or seven days would clearly undermine the ability of several property to address the social problems this right has evolved to handle. With such a short period, Ann could never leave her land for fear that she would lose her rights before she returned. Such a rule would undermine rather than facilitate Ann's or any property owner's ability to make effective use of their personal and local knowledge.

The first limit on our ability to derive specific precepts from general principles, then, is the underdeterminacy of general or abstract background rights principles. To render abstract principles specific enough to govern conduct requires some process of arriving at a conventional choice of precepts. Although such precepts may not be deduced from abstract principles, they can run afoul of these principles and when this occurs may be characterized as inconsistent with the requirements of justice or the rule of law. The process of arriving at a conventional set of precepts must somehow be able to discern when such conflicts exist so the offending conventions may be modified or replaced with new precepts that better harmonize with the requirements of justice and the rule of law.

The Ignorance of Theorists

Let us now turn briefly to a second limitation of justice that reflects, not the inherent limitations of abstract principles of justice and the rule of law, but the inherent limitations of those who attempt to formulate such principles. Due to the wide diversity of problems arising in practice, human interactions can become highly complex. Theorists have extremely limited access to this complexity. When I teach contract law, I take three hours a week for twenty eight weeks to examine different problems that can arise when one person makes (or is claimed to have made) a commitment to another and the rules and principles that have evolved to resolve these problems.[8] And, sad to say, this only provides students with a superficial exposure to the difficulties that may arise in practice or the legal precepts that cover the field of contract law.

---

[7] See Lomasky, *Persons, Rights*, p. 105. (Explaining how "[b]ecause basic rights abstract from particular forms of social life and from particular project attachments, basic rights do serve as a moral standard by means of which various social arrangements can be evaluated.").

[8] For an introduction to these intricacies, see Randy E. Barnett, *Contracts Cases and Doctrine* (Boston: Little, Brown, 1995).

Those philosophers (who are not also lawyers) who speculate about the morality of promise-keeping are oblivious to the myriad of problems that can arise when one person makes a commitment to another. Without some knowledge of the intricacies of practice it is next to impossible to generate useful action-guiding precepts governing contractual relationships. What, for example, does an abstract moral duty to keep one's promises tell us about the circumstances to which the doctrine of anticipatory breach, the substantial performance doctrine, the parol evidence rule, or the doctrines of consideration and promissory estoppel apply?[9]

One cannot formulate a specific precept to solve a problem to which one is oblivious. Yet, as with other questions of knowledge, access to the intricacies of practice is limited. Such knowledge is both personal and local. Even were abstract rights and principles not underdeterminate, this limitation on our knowledge would prevent us from simply deducing a completely specified set of precepts from a general understanding of the knowledge problem or from an understanding of how several property and freedom of contract address this general problem. For an institution or institutions to be competent to formulate legal precepts to handle these problems, they must have access to the nuances of the complex problems that actually arise in practice. But how?

2. The Common Law Process of Adjudication

Both the underdeterminacy of theory and the ignorance of theorists create two barriers to generating specific action-guiding precepts from abstract considerations of justice or the rule of law. These barriers indicate a need for institutions that can bridge this gap between theory and practice—a gap that creates a third-order problem of knowledge. Such institutions must be able to look both backward and forward. Because we can learn from the details of a particular dispute only after it occurs, it is necessary to be able to look back and somehow discover these facts. Because specific conventions are needed to influence and coordinate future behavior, in formulating these conventions we must somehow project ourselves into the future. As it happens, the evolutionary process known as the common law system of adjudication handles both of these needs, although the features I shall offer to define a "common law" system can be found in many "civil law" systems as well. Indeed, as Lon

[9] The doctrine of *anticipatory breach* applies to instances where, before the time for performance arrives, the party whose performance is outstanding gives the other party reason to believe that his performance will not be forthcoming. The doctrine of *substantial performance* concerns the appropriate measure of damages when the cost to repair a defect that is caused by a breach of contract is greatly in excess of the diminution of market value of the defective item. The *parol evidence rule* governs when evidence of contractual intent that is extrinsic to a written contract may be used to contradict what is contained in the writing. The doctrines of *consideration* and *promissory estoppel* attempt to distinguish enforceable from unenforceable promises.

Fuller noted: "The two great systems of law that dominate the world today—the common law and the civil law—took their origins in a case-by-case evolution of doctrine."[10]

The Need for an Evolutionary Process

Given that the principles of automotive engineering are underdeterminate, how are the extremely elaborate engines in today's cars designed? The answer is that they are not designed—at least not from scratch. The development of the internal combustion engines has been evolutionary. Each device we associate with modern engines was invented against a comparatively stable background of other devices. First there were manual crank-operated starters; then appeared starters turned by an electric battery-powered motor. At first, drivers wore goggles; then windshields caught on; finally safety glass—a piece of plastic laminated between two pieces of glass—replaced plate glass in windshields. Now the safety glass is also tinted to cut down on glare. First there were wooden wheels; then came solid rubber tires on wooden wheels; then came inflated rubber tires on wooden wheels; eventually came wheels made out of steel and inflated tires reinforced with nylon or steel belts. No single component of a car has remained untouched by the process of automotive evolution, with each change slightly improving the operation of automobiles until the cars of today are comparable to cars of fifty years ago in general principle only.

This evolutionary process consisted of two components. One is conceptual. The concept of headlights is to illuminate the road ahead as well as to be visible to oncoming traffic. At first kerosine-fueled lanterns performed this task; then the idea of electric lights was conceived as an improvement over gas; then the idea of sealing the light avoided nagging problems experienced by earlier designs; then came the idea of injecting halogen gas into the sealed bulb to produce a more powerful beam. All the while the idea of two headlights remained constant (although Tucker unsuccessfully experimented with three).

The second component is institutional. The institutional component must provide the prerequisites for innovation. Persons capable of devising each incremental improvement need an incentive to do so, knowledge of the current practices and past failures, and some process by which their imaginings can be tested and eventually implemented. The incentives of today's automobile designers are their salaries (and stock options?) and their employer's

---

[10] Fuller, *Morality of Law*, p. 373. Fuller goes on to elaborate how common law and civil law legal systems are not as different as they are made to seem: "In the civil law countries the codes from which courts purport to derive their principles often provide little beyond a vocabulary for stating legal results. They are filled with clauses referring to 'good faith,' 'equity,' 'fair practice,' and the like—standards that any court could apply without the aid of a code. One of the best modern codes, the Swiss Code of Obligations, lays down very few rules and contents itself largely with charting the range of judicial discretion and with setting forth what might be called checklists for the judge to consult to make certain that he has overlooked no factor properly bearing on the exercise of his discretion". Ibid.

incentive to pay them salaries and supply them with the facilities they require is provided by the prospect of future profits from car sales made possible by successful innovation. The institutional component must also provide the prerequisites for selecting among potential innovations. This is furnished by car manufacturers seeking to anticipate and influence a marketplace in which numerous purchasers choose which of the available cars to buy.

An account of automotive evolution that ignored either the conceptual or institutional component would be incomplete. For evolution to occur, each component requires the existence of the other. Evolution in law is no different. For legal evolution to succeed there needs to be a progression of conceptual improvements and an institutional framework that provides incentives to produce innovation and is able to select among potential innovations.

One such institutional framework has come to be known as the common law process of adjudication. It has a long pedigree. Chancellor George Wythe, a distinguished Virginia judge and holder of the first Law Chair in the United States, in the 1793 case of *Page v. Pendleton* referred to the "unwritten or common law, that is, of the law of nature, called common law, because it is common to all mankind."[11] But though it is based on the law of nature, the common law rules were still contingent on circumstances. Here is how Alexander Addison, a Pennsylvania judge who lived from 1759 to 1807, described the process:

The law of England is of two kinds written and unwritten. The written law is called the *statute law*, because composed of statutes or acts of parliament. The unwritten is called the *common law*, because founded on an implied common consent, from long acquiescence in its authority. The authority of both is thus equally the will of the community. The *common law* is founded on the law of nature and the revelation of God, to which all men are subject; on the law of nations, to which every nation is, as a nation, and the individuals composing it, subject towards every other; and on certain maxims or usages, as naturally rising out of the circumstances by which the subjects of that government are connected with each other, and therefore imposing duties on the individuals of that nation toward each other. Of these maxims or usages some are general, and prevail in every part of England; and some, from the separate authorities formerly existing there, or from other circumstances, are particular, and prevail only in certain parts. Parliament may adopt some part of this *common law*, and, by putting it in an act of Parliament, make it *statute law*; or may alter or annul it by act of parliament. Any part of the common law may also cease, or become obsolete, by the circumstances ceasing to exist, which manifestly were the reasons for its establishment. . . . Thus the circumstances of each colony more or less differing, and each having a distinct legislature; the common law throughout the colonies would be, in part, general maxims or usages prevailing in all the colonies; and, in part, maxims or usages prevailing only in one or several of the colonies.[12]

---

[11] Page v. Pendleton (1793), in George Wythe, *Decisions of Cases in Virginia by the High Court of Chancery* 214 n.(*e*) (ed. B. B. Minor; 1852) as it appears in Suzanna Sherry, "Natural Law in the States," *Cincinnati Law Review*, vol. 61 (1992), p. 186.

[12] Alexander Addison, "Analysis of the Report of the Committee of the Virginia Assembly" (1880) in Charles S. Hyneman and Donald S. Lutz (eds), *American Political Writing during the Founding Era, 1760–1805*, vol. ii (Indianapolis: Liberty Press, 1983), pp. 1077–8.

Notice how Addison distinguishes between "general maxims" and those which prevail more locally based on differing social circumstances. Neither of these descriptions makes clear, however, exactly how the common law process works. What are its basic procedural characteristics that enable a common law adjudicative process to discover in an evolutionary fashion conventional legal precepts that lie within the frame provided by abstract rights and principles, and not outside the frame?

Characteristics of Common-Law Adjudication

The competence of common-law processes to generate conventional precepts that are capable of handling the complex nuances of practice stems from a number of its distinctive procedural characteristics that, along with the formal ones discussed in Chapter 5, are aspects of the rule of law. These characteristics of the rule of law stipulate, not the *form* of the message, but the nature of the *processes* that formulate the message. These characteristics can be clustered around two distinct functions. The first concerns the need to gather and integrate facts about a particular dispute on which to base a decision. The second concerns the need to formulate a particular legal precept and to disseminate this precept to other decision makers.

Fact-finding procedures. Common-law adjudication has three features that provide facts to enable those charged with formulating conventional rules to make knowledgeable decisions. First, common-law processes are only supposed to resolve (*a*) actual "cases and controversies"[13] between persons who are (*b*) directly affected by a dispute. The latter of these two limitations is known by lawyers as the requirement that persons have "standing" to bring a lawsuit. These two limitations of common-law adjudication are sometimes considered by observers to be artificial and unduly confining restrictions on the ability of courts to achieve justice. Yet, although often unappreciated, these requirements are crucial to the common law's ability to take the actual nuances of practice into account in developing precepts to guide conduct. Both help ensure that precepts are devised with the particular facts of actual disputes in mind. Requiring that an actual dispute has arisen ensures that concrete facts—rather than speculation—about the circumstances of the dispute will exist. Requiring that only persons directly affected by the dispute can be parties to a lawsuit ensures that the parties to the proceeding will be in a position to provide the court with access to the knowledge they have of the circumstances surrounding the dispute.

---

[13] The phrase "cases and controversies" is used to describe the clause of the US Constitution that specifies the jurisdiction of the judicial power of the United States. See *United States Constitution*, Art. III, sect. 2 ("The judicial Power shall extend to all Cases, in Law and Equity, arising under this Constitution, the Laws of the United States, and treaties made . . . ;—to all Controversies to which the United States shall be a Party").

Second, common-law processes require that facts concerning the dispute be obtained—usually by the parties to the dispute and their lawyers. A certain amount of fact-finding must be done by the parties before they initiate a common-law action. Once a case is initiated, common-law courts provide various mechanisms—such as subpoenas and depositions—for the "discovery" of pertinent information. Powerful incentives for private parties to invest resources to uncover the details of the dispute are provided by such rules as the "attorney–client privilege" that protects the confidentiality of some kinds of facts disclosed by a client to an attorney and the "work product doctrine" that protects the confidentiality of some kinds of facts disclosed by an attorney's investigation.

Third, common-law processes have developed elaborate procedures to air and assess the information produced by the parties. Particular individuals or groups—called "judges" and "juries"—are empowered to decide factual disagreements insofar as they bear upon an actual case or controversy. These persons are supposed to familiarize themselves with and assimilate the nuances of the factual situation facing two parties to a dispute. A body of legal precepts—called the "law of evidence"—helps the fact-finder sort through a potentially enormous volume of information and to focus on only those deemed relevant to the resolution of the dispute. Moreover, knowing in advance that these evidentiary precepts will be used by the fact-finder also directs and limits the discovery of facts by the litigants.

By requiring the litigants to generate "evidence"—a special form of local knowledge that is made accessible to a judge or jury—these three characteristics of common-law adjudication enable the persons—called "judges" or "justices"—who are responsible for developing specific conventions to gain some access, however limited, to the intricacies of real conflicts over resource use that have already occurred. These procedures have other functions, of course. For example, by requiring each litigant to generate a form of local knowledge that is accessible to the other litigant, these procedures also enable the parties to reach knowledgeable settlements of their dispute. Valuable as settlements are to resolving the dispute at hand, however, they do not contribute much, if anything, to the end of producing precepts more specific than can be provided by deduction from general principles.

Law-determining procedures. Still another set of procedural characteristics enables common-law courts to generate specific conventions to guide future conduct. First, common-law processes typically require the publication of decisions—especially by appellate courts reviewing the merits of the precepts that guided a trial court action. Published decisions contain summaries of the facts of a dispute that were disclosed by the operation of the procedures just discussed. In this way, access to the local knowledge produced by a particular litigant is made accessible to a much wider audience. Publication of truncated versions of the facts of many cases provides a practical way of comparing the facts of a particular dispute with facts of other disputes that have arisen in the past. Only if prospective parties (through their lawyers) and courts (through their clerks and competing counsel) have access to the facts of previous cases is it possible for a specific convention to develop to govern similar cases in the future.

Second, in addition to a summary of the facts of the case, published decisions also contain (*a*) the "result" of an adjudication—who won and who lost, and (*b*) some explanation of the reasons for adopting this holding. Disseminating the facts of a particular case enables a court deciding a case to learn of similar cases that have been decided by others. Once a similar case has been identified, to determine a conventional legal precept, the inquiring court will also need to learn the result of the case and the reasons given by the prior court in support of the result. Knowing the result permits the court to decide the case in the same manner as similar cases have been decided in the past. Knowing the expressed rationale for the decision permits a court to accept or help refine an articulated basis for the decision that can eventually be shaped into a workable specific legal precept that supports their decision and can be used to guide the decisions of future similar disputes. Once formulated, this legal precept too becomes a part of the published opinion, accessible to other lawyers and judges.

Third, common-law processes have traditionally included what is called a "doctrine of precedent." Although the exact content and function of this doctrine is much discussed by legal philosophers, the nuances of this debate need not concern us here. For present purposes it suffices to say that this doctrine imposes a *duty* on judges to strive to do what the previously described procedures make possible: decide similar cases in a similar manner. It is not enough that judges have access to the facts, results, and reasoning of previous disputes if they have no intention of using this knowledge. The doctrine of precedent imposes a duty on judges to make use of the local knowledge provided by prior reported decisions.

These last three features of the common-law process enable courts to make use of the intricate details they glean from the three fact-finding procedures I described previously. Taken together these six "rule of law" characteristics of common law adjudication—(1) actual cases and controversies between persons with knowledge of dispute, (2) information discovery procedures, (3) evidence presentation and assessment procedures, (4) published reports that summarize the facts, result, and holding of a decision, (5) which also include reasons for the decision, and (6) a doctrine of precedent in which holdings of previous cases are typically followed—enable different courts to converge upon a common set of rules and principles of decision. Hence the term "common-law" proccss.

The Comparative Advantage of Lawyers and Judges

Legal precepts are conventional and, for this reason, they cannot be logically derived from political or philosophical theories. Though political or philosophical theories can be used to criticize these precepts, they cannot generate them in the first instance. The rules and principles produced by the common-law process are the specific conventional solutions to the diversity of problems generated by practice. They give decentralized decision makers such as judges and juries access to some of the knowledge available to the parties to particular disputes. Further, this knowledge enables judges to produce specific conventional precepts—legal rules and principles—that can be used to guide the conduct of similarly situated persons and to resolve similar disputes that may arise in the future.

Because they have access to the knowledge generated by the parties who are before them, and because they have access to the decisions of judges who have come before them and the rationales for these decisions, common-law judges are in a far better position than philosophers, economists, and even legal theorists to discover and agree upon specific precepts that can handle the myriad practical problems of knowledge. Lawyers and judges, employing distinctive methods of reasoning called "legal reasoning" perform a function that cannot be performed by theorists. Their methods can knowledgeably generate conventional rules and principles to provide *ex ante* guidance to those who seek to act justly provided they know in advance what justice requires. Charles Fried has offered a similar sentiment about the analogical reasoning of lawyers:

The picture I have . . . is of philosophy proposing an elaborate structure of arguments and considerations that descend from on high but stop some twenty feet above the ground. It is the peculiar task of the law to complete this structure of ideals and values, to bring it down to earth; and to complete it so that it is firmly and concretely seated, so that it shelters real human beings against the storms of passion and conflict. Now that last twenty feet may not be the most glamorous part of the building—it is the part where the plumbing and utilities are housed. But it is an indispensable part. The lofty philosophical edifice does not *determine* what the last twenty feet are, yet if the legal foundation is to support the whole, then ideals and values must constrain, limit, inform, and inspire the foundation—but no more. The law is really an independent, distinct part of the structure of value.

So what is it that lawyers and judges know that philosophers and economists do not? The answer is simple: the law. They are masters of "the artificial reason of the common law." . . . The law is to philosophy, then as medicine is to biology and chemistry. The discipline of analogy fills in the gaps left by more general theory, gaps that must be filled because choices must be made, actions taken.[14]

In addition to their role in handling the second-order problem of knowledge, in Chapter 7, we shall see how lawyers also help mitigate a serious and pervasive problem of interest: the partiality problem.

[14] Charles Fried, "Rights and the Common Law," in R. G. Frey (ed), *Utility and Rights* (Minneapolis, Minn.: University of Minnesota Press, 1984), pp. 231–2.

Still, although all of the six traits of a common law system of adjudication (or some adequate substitute) are essential to render the general principles of several property and freedom of contract in a form that is specific enough to handle the knowledge problem in actual practice, they are not sufficient to perform this task. We need yet another link between substance and process, between justice and the rule of law.

3. The Links Between the Common-law Process and Justice

While the institutional features just described enable persons to coordinate (in the Schelling sense[15]) on certain rules or conventions, how can we be sure that the norms so chosen facilitate a social order (in the Hayekian sense) that addresses the first-order problem of knowledge, as well as the problems of interest we have yet to consider? What assurance do we have that the precepts developed by courts governed by these formal features of the rule of law will be consistent with the general conception of justice based on the background rights of several property, freedom of contract, first possession (and other rights we have yet to encounter)? Two links between the rule of law in common-law adjudication and justice are needed. One is internal and the other is external to the common-law process. Each link has both a conceptual and an institutional dimension.

Internal Linkage: Requiring Parties to Make Claims of Right

The internal link between justice and the common law is the requirement that parties to a common law action make claims of right—that is, both parties to a common-law suit must articulate to the court why it is that they have either a legal or background right to a particular resource. Though legal arguments are typically confined to legal rights, arguments about background rights are not uncommon, especially when legal rights are undefined, ill-defined, in conflict with each other, or alleged to be unjust. Lon Fuller contended that the requirement that parties make claims of right distinguished adjudication from other forms of dispute resolution such as arbitration and mediation:

(1) Adjudication is a process of decision that grants to the affected party a form of participation that consists of the opportunity to present proofs and reasoned arguments. (2) The litigant must therefore, if his participation is to be meaningful, assert some principle or principles by which his arguments are sound and his proofs relevant. (3) A naked demand is distinguished from a claim of right by the fact that the latter is a demand supported by a principle; likewise, a mere

---

[15] The distinction between Schelling coordination and Hayekian social order or meta-coordination is described in Chapter 3.

expression of displeasure or resentment is distinguished from an accusation by the fact that the latter rests upon some principle. Hence, (4) issues tried before an adjudicator tend to become claims of right or accusations of fault.[16]

Whether or not Fuller is correct to say that adjudication is distinguished from other modes of dispute resolution by this feature, I am claiming that requiring parties to cast their arguments as rights claims links adjudication with the background requirements of justice. Consider what it means to make a claim of right:

> If I say to someone, "Give me that!" I do not necessarily assert a right. I may be begging for an act of charity, or I may be threatening to take by force something to which I admittedly have no right. On the other hand, if I say, "Give that to me, I have a right to it," I necessarily assert the existence of some principle or standard by which my "right" can be tested.[17]

If a common-law process of adjudication requires parties to state their claims in terms of rights, then this will limit the range of permissible bases for resolving a dispute.

To appreciate the profound impact of this practice, assume that, instead of making rights claims, parties to a lawsuit were supposed to make claims based on their respective desert (and irrespective of their rights[18]). Each party would try to articulate why he or she deserved the resource in question more than the other party. In such a system, we can expect that the substance of precepts developed to resolve claims of desert—if indeed it were possible to develop such precepts at all—would be far different than the precepts developed by a system in which parties must assert their rights to prevail. Requiring that parties offer rights claims provides an internal conceptual link between the legal rights determined by a court and the background rights that define justice. These legal rights claims need not be "absolute," but need only support a finding that the prevailing party's claim of right is superior to the claim made by the other party. When courts are seeking to discern the relative strength of the rights claims of parties to a dispute, judicial decisions are far more likely to conform to the background rights of the parties than if courts were looking for something entirely different.

At the root of every lawsuit is a contest over the use of resources—if only the resources needed to provide monetary compensation. Judges know that a decision in favor of one party is a decision against the other. The question they must ask is which of the several parties is "entitled" to the resource in question. The underlying assumption of the dispute is that one of the parties to a case has such a right. Consequently, it should not be surprising that the conventional doctrine resulting from adjudication tends to reflect a concern with the contours of several property—a concern that is informed by the particular

---

[16] Fuller, "Forms and Limits", p. 369.   [17] Ibid. pp. 367–8.
[18] I offer this qualification to exclude from this example theories of rights that include within them some concept of desert.

facts of a dispute over rights to resources. To the extent that the parties and judges have an intuitive grasp of the problems facing any society—especially the problems of knowledge, interest, and power—and to the extent that the conception of justice based on several property and freedom of contract is sound, we can expect that decisions made by judges forced to decide claims of right will be generally consistent with this conception.

Moreover, the legal requirement that, to prevail, a party must assert a rights claim superior to that asserted by the other side also creates an institutional incentive for parties to formulate rights claims on the basis of the facts of the dispute as well as those of other disputes in the past. To win their cases, they must argue that past cases support a particular formulation of a right that inures to their benefit. Similarly, this requirement places a burden upon the judge to assess critically the conflicting rights claims in light of the evidence and prior cases, to choose one claim as superior, and to defend this choice in a written and signed opinion. In this manner both the parties and the judge are forced by the institutional roles they occupy to arduously sift through the information at their disposal to determine which claim of right is superior. As Lon Fuller noted:

[L]ife is complicated, and that is especially so of the problems with which lawyers have to deal, which generally involve situations where things have become badly entangled and snarled, or threaten to become so. Men do not readily summon the energy necessary to deal properly with problems of this sort unless they have what psychologists call adequate motivation. Digging up facts, thinking up arguments, tracing out the full implications of proposed solutions—all these things are very hard work. This is where the game spirit comes in. Without it work that is vital to the public interest would not get done. . . .

Viewed in this light the zeal of advocacy is one of those tricks of nature by which man is lured into serving the public interest without knowing it, by which he is made to work and think harder than he really wants to. . . . It is the zeal of advocacy . . . that supplies the court with the facts and the thinking without which an intelligent decision is impossible.[19]

And the judge must then attempt to convey this decision to other parties in the future by casting the legal right in a form that is intelligible to others.

While the internal link between justice and the rule of law embedded within common-law processes impels these processes towards specific precepts that are consistent with imperatives of justice, these processes still can err. Although entire bodies of specific precepts cannot be deduced from the general principles of justice, conventional legal doctrine can be examined to see if it is generally consistent or inconsistent with requirements of justice. This sort of critical inquiry provides an external link between justice and the results of the common law, a link that, once again has both a conceptual and an institutional dimension. A critical scrutiny of the legal precepts produced by a

---

[19] Lon L. Fuller, "Philosophy for the Practicing Lawyer," in Kenneth I. Winston (ed.), *The Principles of Social Order: Selected Essays of Lon L. Fuller* (Durham, NC: Duke University Press, 1981), pp. 289–90.

common-law process is made possible by an understanding of such concepts as justice and rights, property and contract, and many others. For it to shape the direction of legal conventions, this sort of conceptual analysis requires an institutional forum.

External Linkage: The Electorate of Law

Even when all the foregoing features of a common-law process are in operation, this process can still fail, and sometimes fail badly. Judges are only human and they can err. They can also abandon on occasion features of the rule of law that they find unduly confining. A virtue of the common-law process is that a single error is unlikely to "take." Many people must concur before a particular precept becomes a prevailing convention. A weakness of the common-law process is that once a particular rule has become enshrined as a "majority rule," the very same practices that enable it to establish a stable convention make conventions difficult to dislodge.

For a long time such errors were supposed to be corrected by occasional acts of legislation. Recall the description of the common law by Judge Addison: "Parliament may adopt some part of this *common law*, and, by putting it in an act of Parliament, make it *statute law*; or may alter or annul it by act of parliament."[20] Judges who thought a particular legal precept to be wrong but who considered themselves constrained by the conceptual and institutional features of the common-law process sometimes urged legislatures to change the rule. However well this process of extraordinary correction by legislation may once have worked, it has eroded considerably. Today, legislation is hardly extraordinary and is hardly confined to correcting doctrinal errors of courts. Indeed, for some time now the legislative process has tended to overshadow and even to supplant common-law processes as the principal engine of legal discovery and change. This has meant that legal evolution has sometimes been replaced by legal revolution—and the disruption and hubris that typically accompanies revolutions—as the dominant approach to legal change.

Concurrently with the decline of legislation as a means of doctrinal correction, in the United States we have witnessed the rise of external evaluation of common-law doctrine by professional, full-time academic legal scholars, philosophers, and economists and by such influential groups as the American Law Institute, a nonprofit organization comprised of judges, professors, and practitioners. By teaching students and by writing articles and books criticizing common law rules and proposing reforms, these observers comprise an *electorate of law* that gets to vote on the efficacy and justice of common law judges' decisions, but its members' votes are weighted according to the respect each has earned from peers and from succeeding generations, as well as the status of the institutions from which they speak.

[20] Addison, "Analysis of Report."

As a result of the collective decision of the faculty of my law school to hire me to teach contract law, my decision to write, and a journal's decision to publish my writings, I have a vote on the justice of current contract law doctrine. But my vote is not weighted as heavily as, for example, E. Allan Farnsworth, a contracts professor at Columbia Law School, author of a casebook and treatise on contract law, and reporter for the Restatement (Second) of Contracts published by the American Law Institute. Nor is my vote weighted as heavily as that of the late Grant Gilmore, Lon Fuller, or many other prominent contracts scholars. They may be gone, but they are not forgotten and the votes they cast while alive have survived them.

The shift of legislation from correcting to supplanting the common-law process of doctrinal discovery and the rise of the electorate of law is probably not coincidental. For a very long time academics from most every discipline have generally supported centralized, uniform, legislative reform as far more "rational" than the decentralized diversity or "anarchy" of common-law processes. Where the legal system has moved away from a conception of justice based on several property and freedom of contract it has been largely a result of legislation inspired by academic, self-styled reformers. Sweeping legislative "reform" of common-law doctrine has often been formulated and favored by academics who inadequately appreciated how the conception of justice based on the rights of several property and freedom of contract and the procedural features of the rule of law are needed to address the problems of knowledge, interest, and power. In many cases, it was not the evolutionary common-law process that was wrong, but its academic critics who wished to hard-wire their favored precepts into the legal system.

Notwithstanding the potential for error, external criticism can and should provide a potent mechanism for correcting mistakes produced by the evolutionary process of the common law. Although not directly deducible from general principles of justice, specific doctrines can be subjected to rational scrutiny to see if they are consistent with these principles. Academics have long performed an important function in providing this critical assessment, a function that is reflected in the judicial practice of considering and citing what judges refer to as "learned authorities" on a given subject in support of their decisions. What makes an authority learned is the breadth of study that he or she has given a particular area of the law that usually requires the time that only a full-time academic specialist can provide. Common-law judges' traditional and routine reliance upon the opinions of academic experts in the field creates a powerful feedback mechanism to correct judicial errors.

While judges have access to the particularities of many cases and a consequent ability to develop a situation sense of a case, the comparative advantage of academics who are legally inclined is the concentrated attention they can afford a body of doctrine to map its precise contours and its internal inconsistencies. Academics who are economically inclined can assess the likely consequences of a legal precept. Academics who are philosophically inclined can assess the information gleaned by these other academics to see how a legal precept and its consequences squares with abstract principles of justice. Philosophers and economists write in journals that are read by legal scholars who in turn combine their insights with those of legal theory in articles published in law journals (edited by students still under the influence of their teachers) and treatises that are read by judges (or their postgraduate clerks). Increasingly, economists and philosophers are writing in law journals as well. Moreover, academics exert considerable influence on judges through judicial law clerks who have only just emerged from their professors' tutelage.

Moreover, the legal codes in some civil law countries make it explicit that judges are to be bound by the Right or principles of justice (*Recht, droit, derecho, prava, jog*) as well as enacted law (*Gesetz, loi, ley, zakon, törvény*),[21] which means that scholars' opinions of justice are considered to be relevant to judicial decisions. George Fletcher has noted how in Germany, for example, the basic law

makes it clear that the "law" that binds judges includes not only the enacted law but also principles of Right. Therefore, in asserting conceptions of the Right, German scholars engage in discourse about the criteria that in fact bind the courts. This does not mean judges follow the opinions of scholars, as they follow legislative directives. Yet being bound by Right, they are obligated to follow it.[22]

Sometimes this connection between the theories of scholars and judicial decisions is made even more explicit.

Judges are bound by the Right, and therefore must pay careful attention to those theories that become dominant in the literature. The Swiss civil code testifies to the impact of legal theories on the legal process. The first section of the code provides that if the code fails to resolve a legal dispute, the judge should act as though he "were a legislator" in fashioning an appropriate rule. The second half of the provision curtails this grant of legislative freedom: the judge is required to follow "customary law" and "those theories that have stood the test of time" . . . . Thus the Swiss judge assesses the leading scholarly theories and attempts to gauge their substantive merit.[23]

There is no guarantee that the outcome of the intricate balloting process of the electorate of law will be correct, or that the process will inevitably produce genuine progress. While all the law that survives may be "fit," all that survives may not be just. The moral knowledge conveyed by the common-law process as criticized by the electorate of law, however, makes real progress possible. For better or worse, one judge's (or one professor's) ability to influence the electoral tide is clearly marginal: his or her opinion must be accepted by other judges and observers before it becomes "the law." While the decisions of aberrant (and corrupt) judges can work injustice in particular cases—a reason why appellate judicial review of lower court decisions is necessary—individual

---

[21] See George P. Fletcher, "Two Modes of Legal Thought," *Yale Law Journal*, vol. 90 (1981), p. 980.

[22] Ibid. 986 (citations omitted).   [23] Ibid. 990 (citations omitted).

judges cannot "make law" that will effectively bind parties in other cases unless their decisions survive the socio-legal filtration mechanism described here. Judges deciding particular cases are accountable to the electorate of law.

4. Does Common-law Adjudication Violate the Rule of Law?

Some may have noticed that, in Chapter 5, I dwelled on the virtues of specific precepts of law that were capable of providing *ex ante* guidance, while, in this chapter, I stressed the virtues of a common-law process that operated retro-spectively on the basis of its knowledge of factual disputes that had already occurred. The apparent conflict between the virtue of prospectivity and the retrospective nature of the common-law process has long provided grist for the mills of legal philosophers. How are the messages of these two chapters to be reconciled? While it may not definitively resolve the issue, the analysis of the knowledge problem presented here sheds new light on this old debate.

In Chapter 5, prospectivity was shown to be a rule-of-law virtue. In this chapter, the common-law process was defended as a mechanism for deter-mining specific conventions. The common-law process has for centuries proven its ability to generate a body of specific conventional precepts that are capable of providing *ex ante* guidance. Once discovered by this evolutionary process, the rule-of-law doctrine of precedent imposes a presumptive duty on the court to adhere to these precepts. When these precepts are systematized or modified by legislation, the rule of law also stipulates that any legislative change in these precepts should only operate prospectively.

Ex ante guidance is needed to prevent disputes, but the common-law process is largely confined to those exceptional interpersonal transactions in which *ex ante* guidance has failed to avoid a dispute. *Ex ante* guidance can fail because one or both parties (or their lawyers) acted in ignorance of accessible *ex ante* precepts that, had they availed themselves of this access, would have enabled them to avoid the dispute. *Ex ante* guidance can also fail, not because parties (or their lawyers) have no access to *ex ante* precepts that would inform them how to act, but because they are motivated by interest to disregard the rele-vant *ex ante* precepts. In neither case will the *ex ante* precept need to be modified *ex post*. When such disputes are resolved according to a preexisting precept, a court does not violate the rule-of-law virtue of prospectivity.

Even a vintage *ex ante* precept, however, had to be devised and imposed *ex post* for the first time in some case. In light of the rule-of-law virtue of prospec-tivity, how is the *ex post* imposition by a common-law court of a *new* legal pre-cept on the parties ever justified? The analysis of the knowledge problem presented here suggests two reasons why a decision may justifiably apply a new precept retroactively to a particular case or controversy.

First, when the set of *ex ante* precepts fails for some reason to identify the party with the superior claim, the prospective reach of existing precepts is exhausted and a new precept that can avoid a similar dispute in the future is needed. There is simply no alternative to deciding such a case on the basis of a new principle. Although the parties to such a case are faced with a retroactive imposition of a new precept, their dispute involves a failure of the previously discovered set of precepts to handle the problem of communicating justice that constitutes the second-order problem of knowledge. One of the two parties will necessarily be disappointed and we choose between them on the grounds of a new precept consistent with the requirements of justice that will avoid such disputes in the future.

In sum, such a decision does not violate the rule of law because there is no satisfactory *ex ante* precept available. In such a case, the existing body of precepts fails adequately to handle the second-order problem of knowledge and the first criterion of rule of law—that disputes be resolved by general rules and principles—requires that a new legal precept be formulated to handle future cases. As Hayek explains:

The reason why the judge will be asked to intervene will be that rules which secure the matching of expectations are not always observed, or clear enough, *or adequate to prevent conflict if observed.* Since new situations in which the established rules are not adequate will constantly arise, the task of preventing conflict and enhancing the compatibility of actions is of necessity a never-ending one, requiring not only the application of already established rules but also the formulation of new rules necessary for the preservation of the order of actions.[24]

Thus, judges should uphold those existing "rules which, like those which have worked well in the past, make it more likely that expectations will not conflict."[25] When old rules prove to be inadequate to preserve an order of actions the judge who formulates a new legal precept "is not a creator of a new order but a servant endeavoring to maintain and improve the functioning of an existing order."[26]

Second, when a reasonably clear *ex ante* precept is overruled by a court and a new rule is then used to decide the case, such a decision may still be justified although it contradicts an *ex ante* precept if the substance of the *ex ante* precept seriously undermines our ability to solve the first-order problem of knowledge. In rare cases, a decision that breaches the formal rule-of-law virtue of prospectivity (that addresses the second-order problem of knowledge) may still be supported by the substantive requirements of justice (that address the first-order problem of knowledge). In Hayek's words, "[i]f the judge were confined to decisions which could be logically deduced from the body of already articulated rules, he would often not be able to decide a case in a manner appropriate to the function which the whole system of rules serves."[27]

---

[24] Hayek, *Law and Liberty*, vol. i, p. 119 (emphasis added).
[25] Ibid.
[26] Ibid.
[27] Ibid. 116.

The common law of contract, for example, refuses to enforce a commitment supported by a clear manifestation of a right-holder to transfer her rights to another when such a commitment lacks "bargained-for consideration,"[28] has not yet been relied upon by the promisee,[29] or is not under seal.[30] Two examples of this would be a promise of a pension to a valued employee formally approved by the company's board of directors in a resolution stating that it intends to be legally bound,[31] or a promise by a father to his daughters to pay them an amount of money left to him by their deceased mother.[32] In 1925, the Commissioners on Uniform State Laws proposed that state legislatures adopt a statute reading:

A written release or promise hereafter made and signed by the person releasing or promising shall not be invalid or unenforceable for lack of consideration, if the writing also contains an additional express statement, in any form of language, that the signer intends to be legally bound.[33]

Only Pennsylvania has adopted this statute so if this case arose in any other state, courts that followed established doctrine would find such a promise unenforceable. Since the parties clearly are consenting to transfer rights, a refusal to enforce their consent would be an unjust violation of the parties freedom to contract. Considerations of justice therefore would argue for changing the *ex ante* precepts barring enforcement to recognize the enforceability of such commitments. Yet doing so would seemingly violate the rule of law requirement of prospectivity.

What should a court do when faced with a conflict between justice and the rule of law? Such conflicts are bound to occur when multiple modes of analysis are being employed to handle the difficult problems of knowledge, interest, and power. Yet such conflicts can actually be productive. For the degree of confidence we have in any of our beliefs largely depends upon the degree to which the different methods we use to critically assess our beliefs converge on the same conclusion. The greater the number of different sound methods of evaluation that converge on a single conclusion, the more confident we can be in that conclusion. Conversely, a conflict between competing sound modes of analysis, such as justice and the rule of law, over a particular conclusion should lessen our confidence in it and motivate us to search for a better

---

[28] See *Restatement (Second) of Contract* §17(1) ("Except as stated in Subsection (2), the formation of a contract requires a bargain in which there is a manifestation of mutual assent and a consideration."); and ibid. §71(1)("To constitute a consideration, a performance or a return promise must be bargained for.").

[29] See ibid. §90(1) ("A promise which the promisor should reasonably expect to induce action or forbearance on the part of the promisee or a third person and which does induce such action of forbearance is binding if injustice can be avoided only by enforcement of the promise.")

[30] See ibid. §95(1)(*a*) ("In the absence of a statute a promise is binding without consideration if . . . it is in writing and sealed.").

[31] See Feinberg v. Pfeiffer Co., 332 S.W.2d 163 (1959).

[32] See Aller v. Aller, 40 NJL 446 (1878).

[33] *Uniform Written Obligations Act*, §1 (1925).

approach. When the requirements of justice appear to conflict with that of the rule of law, this should induce us to achieve convergence by reconsidering what we think is just or what we think is legal or both. In this way, conflicts between modes of analysis lead us to improve both our conceptions of justice and of the rule of law. The virtue of adopting multiple or redundant modes of analysis is, then, two-fold: (*a*) convergence (or agreement) among them supports greater confidence in our conclusions; and (*b*) divergence (or conflict) signals the need to reexamine critically the issue in a search for reconciliation. In sum, *convergence begets confidence, divergence stimulates discovery.*[34]

Yet when a clear conflict between our conceptions of justice and the rule of law is irreconcilable at least for the time being, I think justice must be given priority. We have seen how the rule of law serves the important objective of concretizing and communicating the background rights that define justice when these rights are too abstract to decide particular cases. (Were the requirements of justice obvious and readily applicable to cases and controversies there would be no need for a rule of law.) So persons may decide how to act so as to avoid conflicts with others, a prior determination of a particular convention that lies *within* the frame provided by the requirements of justice ought to be respected in future cases, even though a different convention also within the frame might have been chosen. Unless a convention is shown to be unjust, the doctrine of precedent should be quite strong within the frame.

When, however, a particular doctrine can be shown to be clearly *outside* the frame defined by background rights, then justice, which addresses the first-order problem of knowledge (and also, as we shall see, problems of interest and power), must take priority over the *ex ante* requirements of the rule of law, which addresses only a second-order knowledge problem. Indeed, this is what the background rights that define justice are for: criticizing and correcting pre-existing legal rights. And judges, no less than legislators, are obliged to do justice, not solely follow the (preexisting) law.

I should hasten to add that conflicts between the rule of law and the liberal conception of justice should be rare. For the liberal conception of justice is a relatively modest one that does not purport to justify a long, and complicated list of detailed background rights. The abstract character of its background rights acknowledges a great range of choice among permissible legal precepts. Justice is not seen as determining the outcomes of very many specific disputes, but is viewed instead as a means for identifying the occasional unjust precept. Nevertheless, because the rule of law is instrumental to the achievement of justice, when a conflict between justice and the rule of law is clear and demonstrable, then justice should triumph if justice is to perform its essential social functions.

---

[34] This paragraph summarizes an argument I have made elsewhere in much greater detail. See Randy E. Barnett, "The Virtues of Redundancy in Legal Thought," *Cleveland-State Law Review*, vol. 38 (1990), pp. 153–68. There I provide examples of how we revise our conceptions of justice and the rule of law to resolve conflicts arising between them.

Summary

(1) The abstract background rights that define justice are underdeterminate in that more than one set of specific action-guiding precepts can often satisfy their theoretical demands. These rights can, however, provide a basis for criticizing specific precepts that are discovered in some other way.

(2) Theorists who would attempt to deduce from abstract rights a set of specific action-guiding principles face a serious problem of knowledge.

(3) Specific conventions to guide conduct can evolve in a common-law process that has certain characteristics enabling judges (*a*) to obtain information about the complexities of practice and (*b*) to formulate rules to decide future cases in a manner that is both consistent with each other and with underlying principles of justice.

(4) To ensure a link between the common-law process and the liberal conception of justice requires both an internal and an external link. The internal link is the requirement that disputants make claims of right; the external link is the "electorate of law" that rationally evaluates the product of common-law adjudication to see if its precepts are consistent with the requirements of justice. Professional academics directly through their writings and indirectly through their influence on law clerks and law review editors have combined with judges to constitute an electorate of law. This electorate subjects each new legal precept produced by the common-law process to critical scrutiny based, at least in part, on the conceptions of justice and the rule of law prevailing among its constituents.

(5) Apparent conflicts between justice and the rule of law can be resolved in a variety of ways, but when the conflict is clear and demonstrable, justice— which addresses the first-order problem of knowledge (and also problems of interest)—should take priority over the rule of law.

PART TWO

The Problems of Interest

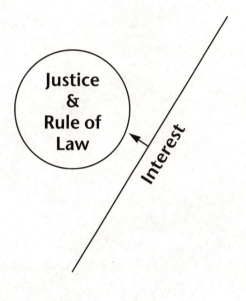

SEVEN

The Partiality Problem

1. Introduction: When Interest Becomes a Problem

THE problem of interest takes many forms but traces from the common tendency of persons to make judgments or choose actions that they believe will serve their interests. Put another way, people tend to try to satisfy their subjective preferences (although these preferences may not always be self-regarding). Natural rights theorists acknowledged the pervasiveness of this phenomenon by according the impulse towards self-preservation a central place in their theories. As seventeenth-century natural rights theorist, Samuel Pufendorf wrote:

[I]n investigating the condition of man we have assigned the first place to self-love, not because one should under all circumstances prefer only himself before all others or measure everything by his own advantage, distinguishing this from the interests of others, and setting forth as his highest goal, but because man is so framed that he thinks of his own advantage before the welfare of others for the reason that it is his nature to think of his own life before the lives of others.[1]

In an essay on natural law, Pufendorf expanded on his last point:

In common with all living things which have a sense of themselves, man holds nothing more dear than himself, he studies in every way to preserve himself, he strives to acquire what seems good to him and to repel what seems bad to him. The passion is usually so strong that all other passions give way before it.[2]

The fact that people make choices on the grounds of interest is not, by itself, a problem. Rather, acting out of interest can be considered a problem only against some normative background that distinguishes objectionable from unobjectionable actions. For natural rights theorists, this normative background was supplied by the human need for peaceful social interaction with which self-interested actions can sometimes interfere:

Man, then, is an animal with an intense concern for his own preservation, needy by himself, incapable of protection without the help of his fellows, and very well

---

[1] Samuel Pufendorf, *De Jure Naturae at Gentiun Libri Octo* (1672), trans. C. H. and W. A. Oldfather (New York: Oceana Publications; London: Wildby and Sons, 1964), Prol. 39.

[2] Pufendorf, *De Jure Naturae,* p. 33.

fitted for the mutual provision of benefits. Equally, however, he is at the same time malicious, aggressive, easily provoked and as willing as he is able to inflict harm on others. The conclusion is: in order to be safe, it is necessary for him to be sociable; that is to join forces with men like himself and so conduct himself towards them that they are not given even a plausible excuse for harming him, but rather become willing to preserve and promote his advantages.[3]

Consequently, for Pufendorf: "The laws of this sociality, laws which teach one how to conduct oneself to become a useful member of human society, are called natural laws."[4]

In this Part, I discuss how the liberal conception of justice and the rule of law helps address three distinct problems of interest. In this chapter, I discuss the *partiality problem*, while the *incentive problem* is considered in Chapter 8 and the *compliance problem* in Chapter 9. Handling these additional problems may require that we further refine the conception of justice and the rule of law that was adequate to handle the very different first-, second-, and third-order problems of knowledge.

Nevertheless, the need to handle these problems of interest provides independent support for the liberal conception of justice and the rule of law. Those who urge that these fundamental rights and procedures be abandoned or highly qualified must explain how this vital function can be performed in some other manner. The fact that the discussion of the problems of interest is shorter than the discussion of the knowledge problems reflects, not their relative importance, but the degree to which the problems of interest are far better known and easier to explain than are the problems of knowledge, and the fact that the way the problems of interest are handled by the liberal conception of justice and the rule of law is more widely understood.

2. The Problem of Partiality

The *partiality problem* is extremely fundamental and would exist whether or not we faced the sort of knowledge problems I described in Part I. It arises from the fact that people tend to make judgments that are partial to their own interests or the interests of those who are close to them at the expense of others. The word "partial" reflects both the cause and consequence of this problem. One meaning of the term is: "Pertaining to or involving a part (not the whole); 'subsisting only in a part; not general or universal; not total'; constituting a part only; incomplete."[5] In this sense, it is inevitable that individuals can have only partial or incomplete view of the facts that go into reaching any decision. It is very hard to avoid seeing the world from one's own particular and therefore partial vantage point. Partial judgment in this sense closely resembles the

---

[3] Pufendorf, *De Jure Naturae*, p. 35.   [4] Ibid. 35.
[5] *Oxford English Dictionary*, vol. xi, p. 265.

first order problem of knowledge. We know only a fraction of what there is to know and are ignorant of the rest.

But this partiality or incompleteness of vision also leads to a tendency to favor one's own interest that comprises the other meaning of the term partial: "'Inclined antecedently to favour one party in a cause, or one side of the question more than the other'; unduly favouring one party or side in a suit or controversy, or one set or class of persons rather than another; prejudiced; biased; interested; unfair. . . . Favouring a particular person or thing excessively or especially; prejudiced or biased in some one's favour."[6] Partiality, in this sense, is judgment affected by interest.

The dual meaning of partiality suggests that the partiality problem, like the first-order problem of knowledge has two dimensions that are in tension with each other. On the one hand, the pursuit of happiness requires that people pursue their own "partial" vision and serve their own "partial" interests (including the interests of those to whom they are partial). On the other hand, their actions are likely to affect, sometimes adversely, the partial interests of others. Just as the knowledge problem is to permit people to act on the basis of what they know while, somehow, taking their ignorance into account, the partiality problem is to permit people to act in pursuit of their own partial interests while, somehow, taking the partial interests of others into account. We may summarize this problem of partiality as follows:

> The *partiality problem* refers to the need to (1) allow persons to pursue their own partial interests including the interests of those to whom they are partial, (2) while somehow taking into account the partial interests of others whose interests are more remote to them.

The need to cope with the partiality problem would exist even if the knowledge of potential resource use was entirely accessible to everyone.

To appreciate the inescapable nature of both the first-order problem of knowledge and the partiality problem, try to imagine a race of beings that did not confront them. These beings would have complete knowledge of everyone's particular circumstances, including each persons's subjective needs, aspirations, and opportunities; and they would act completely impartially, neither favoring their own interests, nor the interests of those they care for. Assuming such a race of beings were imaginable, in my view, they would hardly be attractive. Even if considered attractive, however, we are not and can never be like them. We live in a world of radically dispersed knowledge and partiality of interests and the liberal conception of justice and the rule of law helps us cope with these features of this world.

Though the partiality problem pervades every aspect of human life, it becomes particularly acute when some persons whose viewpoints are influenced by their own interests are called upon to make judgments that are

[6] Ibid.

supposed to take into account the interests of other persons remote to them as well as their own. This type of impartial or objective decision is required when deciding among conflicting claims of right in a system of adjudication, such as described in Chapter 6. Yet it is simply very difficult for persons charged with making such decisions to set their own interests in proper perspective in order to make an impartial assessment.[7]

Here too the tendency of interest to render persons' judgments partial would create a need for the liberal conception of justice and the rule of law even in the absence of any serious knowledge problem. That is, even if, contrary to my thesis, persons with centralized jurisdiction over resources can gain sufficient access to the personal and local knowledge of others to address the knowledge problem, we would still need to confront the problem of partiality. Assuming that these persons have access to the local and personal knowledge of others, what assurance do we have that their decisions concerning resource use will be based impartially on this knowledge, rather than based on a partial judgment of what is in their own interest? What is to preclude these judgments concerning resource use from being made on a partial rather than a complete view of all the knowledge at their disposal?

In what follows I explain how both justice and the rule of law play important roles in handling this problem of partiality.

3. Justice and the Problem of Partiality

The degree to which the partiality of one's actions becomes a problem depends upon the extensiveness of the jurisdiction one has over physical resources. Consider the extreme case of one person having jurisdiction over all the resources in the world including other people's bodies. Quite obviously, a partial decision by this ruler will have far more serious consequences for the interests of all others—and will overlook vast amounts of personal and local knowledge—than a regime in which each person had jurisdiction over his own body and some comparatively small fraction of the world's resources. In the former regime, a partial judgment will reflect the interest of just one person, whereas in the latter regime a multitude of partial judgments will reflect a multitude of interests.

To better appreciate this point, consider a submarine with many different compartments that can be sealed off from the others should a leak occur.

---

[7] Within the public choice school of economics, "interest group theory" explains much about the behavior of government actors by assuming it to be the result of interest rather than as the result of impartial judgment. For a sympathetic portrayal of this approach, see e.g. Iain McLean, *Public Choice* (Oxford: Basil Blackwell, 1987); Jerry L. Mashaw, "The Economics of Politics and the Understanding of Public Law," *Chicago-Kent Law Review*, vol. 65 (1989), pp. 123–60. For a critical appraisal, see Daniel A. Farber, "Democracy and Disgust: Reflections on Public Choice," *Chicago-Kent Law Review*, vol. 65 (1989), pp. 161–76.

Normally, of course, people on the submarine are free to move unimpeded from one area of the ship to another. When leakage threatens, however, the compartment with the leak can be closed off quickly to limit the extent of the damage to the ship. The problem of partial judgment concerning resource use is analogous to the leak of water in the sub, except that partiality is the norm, not an exception. When it inevitably occurs, it is important to limit the area it can affect. Were there no compartmentalization of decision making, a single exercise of partiality—like a single leak of water in the submarine—could seriously jeopardize the interests of everyone else.

The concept of several property reflects a strategy of decentralizing jurisdiction over resources to the level of those individuals and associations that are most likely to be in possession of personal and local knowledge. Such a regime not only makes possible the utilization of personal and local knowledge as I discussed in Chapters 3 and 4; it also limits the impact of judgments on the basis of only partial information.

We may summarize this as follows: *Decentralized jurisdiction through the device of several property makes possible the effective compartmentalization of partiality.* The term *several* property is preferable to private property precisely because it emphasizes the plurality and diversity of jurisdictions in a regime governed by the liberal conception of justice. Like the submarine with separate compartments, in such a regime the jurisdiction of any particular individual or association will be bounded or limited. In most (but clearly not all) circumstances, a partial exercise of such bounded jurisdiction will mainly affect the person exercising this judgment.

Where the exercise of jurisdiction on the basis of partial judgment does affect others, the extent of these "external" effects will be limited. Indeed, the thrust of much of liberal legal theory is to cause actors to "internalize" the costs of their actions by making them liable for the harm their actions cause to others. For example, whole categories of external effects caused by the use of physical force or fraud are prohibited. What "external effects" of partiality remain can often be adjusted by the consummation of mutually satisfactory consensual exchanges that the liberal principle of freedom to contract makes possible. Compartmentalization does not eliminate partiality—something that would be both impossible and undesirable. Instead it dampens the *problem* of partiality by limiting the range of resources over which a single partial interest will prevail.

To be sure, compartmentalization not only limits partiality, it can also insulate its exercise. To a large degree this is desirable as it enables individuals to pursue their personal "projects."[8] The ability to pursue personal projects is

---

[8] In his extensive treatment of this subject, Loren Lomasky offers the following definition of "projects": "Those [ends] which reach indefinitely into the future, play a central role within the ongoing endeavors of the individual, and provide a significant degree of structural stability to an individual's life I call *projects*." Lomasky, *Persons, Rights*, p. 26.

essential to the pursuit of happiness[9] and, as Loren Lomasky explains, necessarily partial: "Project pursuit . . . is partial. To be committed to a long-term design, to order one's activities in light of it, to judge one's success or failure as a person by reference to its fate: these are inconceivable apart from a frankly partial attachment to one's most cherished ends."[10] And yet in at least two ways, the rights of several property and freedom of contract mitigate the insularity of partiality without seeking to end the pursuit of personal projects.

By requiring consent to rights transfers, decentralized jurisdiction impels people to take the interests of others into account. The most obvious way that the liberal conception of justice mitigates partiality and renders it beneficial to others has been known for centuries. Several property coupled with freedom from contract requires that any individual who seeks jurisdiction over resources owned by another must obtain the owner's consent. And to obtain this consent, he usually must take the owner's interest into account. As Adam Smith noted in the *Wealth of Nations*, if properly constrained,[11] the pursuit of one's own interest and the interest of those one cares about can be a powerful motive for conduct that is beneficial both to self and others.

If Ben wants to build a home on a corner of the land that Ann has cultivated for crops, then he must offer Ann something she would prefer to that which he is asking her to give up. In this way, Ann's partial interests are incorporated into Ben's cost of choice. When pursuing his personal projects, Ann's rights of several property and freedom from contract require Ben to act "impartially" with respect to Ann's interest whether he wants to or not. These principles of justice propel a marketplace of consensual exchanges in which each person, acting partially, incorporates the interests of others into their decisions to act or refrain from acting.

Of course, Ann's several property rights also enable her to act "impartially" with respect to Ben by making him a gift of the land. But as Adam Smith recognized, because partiality is so much a part of human nature, we cannot rely on such beneficence.

Whoever offers to another a bargain of any kind, proposes to do this: Give me that which I want, and you shall have this which you want, is the meaning of every such offer; and it is in this manner that we obtain from one another the far greater part of those good offices which we stand in need of. It is not from the benevolence of the butcher, the brewer, or the baker, that we expect our dinner, but from their regard to their own interest. We address ourselves, not to their humanity but to

---

[9] Lomasky contends that project pursuit is an important constituent of personhood itself: "When we wish to understand or describe a person, to explicate what fundamentally characterizes him as being just the particular purposive being that he is, we will focus on his projects rather than on his transitory ends." Ibid.

[10] Ibid. 27–8.

[11] "Every man, *as long as he does not violate the laws of justice*, is left perfectly free to pursue his own interest in his own way, and to bring both his industry and capital into competition with those of any other man, or order of men." Adam Smith, *The Wealth of Nations* (5th edn., London, 1789), in Hutchins, *Great Books*, vol. xxxix, p. 300*a* (emphasis added).

their self-love, and never talk to them of our own necessities but of their advantages.[12]

Decentralization also makes possible a system of effective checks and balances on partiality. At the constitutional level, checks and balances were part of James Madison's solution to the problem of "faction" by which he meant "a number of citizens, whether amounting to a majority or minority of the whole, who are united and actuated by some common impulse of passion, *or of interest*, adverse to the rights of other citizens, or to the permanent and aggregate interests of the community."[13] Madison's response to this instance of a partiality problem was, in part, to divide powers so that each institution could resist the others.[14] While the idea of dividing powers to create checks and balances is well-known among constitutional theorists, that several property plays the same function at the level of individuals and associations is usually overlooked.

The fact that persons retain jurisdiction over their respective resources—including especially their bodies—means that they often have a way to retaliate in kind with actions that undercut the interests of a person whose partial judgment has adversely affected others. (How institutions can effectively harness this potential of retaliation will be discussed in Chapters 13 and 14.) In this way, the decentralized jurisdiction resulting from several property permits undue partiality that affects the interests of others to be discouraged by a strategy of "tit for tat." When I take action that adversely affects the interests of others, those whose interest I have hurt are in a better position to retaliate in kind than they would be in a regime in which all jurisdiction resided in a single person or association or in very few. The demonstrated ability to retaliate in this way has proved to be a powerful deterrent to the initiation of conduct that adversely affects the interests of other. The existence of such a deterrent also can lead to a general and quite powerful norm of cooperation.[15]

---

[12] Ibid. 7*b*.

[13] *The Federalist No. 10* (James Madison) (New York: Modern Library, 1937), p. 54 (emphasis added). Indeed, one dictionary includes "faction" in its definition of partial: "favoring one person, faction, etc. more than another; biased; prejudiced." *Webster's New Twentieth Century Dictionary*, 2nd edn. (Collins+World Publishing Co., 1975)

[14] More broadly Madison pioneered the concept of the "extended republic" which was large enough to ensure that no single interest or coalition of interests could successfully dominate the polity. See ibid. at 60–1: "The smaller the society, the fewer probably will be the distinct parties and interests, the more frequently will a majority be found of the same party; and the smaller the number of individuals composing a majority, and the smaller the compass within which they are placed, the more easily will they concert and execute their plans. Extend the sphere, and you take in a greater variety of parties and interests; you make it less probable that a majority of the whole will have common motive to invade the rights of other citizens; or if such a common motive exists, it will be more difficult for all who feel it to discover their own strength, and to act in unison with each other". In some important respects, the polycentric constitutional order I discuss in Chapters 13 and 14 enjoys advantages similar to those ascribed by Madison to the extended republic.

[15] See Robert Axelrod, *The Evolution of Cooperation* (New York: Basic Books, 1984); Robert Sugden, *The Economics of Rights, Co-operation, and Welfare* (Oxford: Basil Blackwell, 1986).

By compartmentalizing the exercise of partial judgment, the liberal conception of justice takes the dangers posed by self-interested action seriously—more seriously perhaps than political theories that seek to repose in a few hands a broad jurisdiction to constrain interested behavior or coercively mandate disinterested behavior. Because whoever holds this broad jurisdiction is a human being, we can expect them eventually to engage in interested behavior that may very well be worse than that which they are supposed to prevent. This leads to the age-old problem of "who guards us from the guardians." In Chapters 13 and 14, we shall examine how compartmentalization can be instituted far more extensively than at present to address this classic problem.

4. The Rule of Law and the Problem of Partiality

While the liberal conception of justice addresses the general problem of partiality, more obvious, perhaps, is how the liberal conception of the rule of law also helps us to handle the problem of partiality in its most acute form: the partiality of decision makers who ascertain the rights of others. As was discussed in Chapter 5, the rule of law requires the formulation of general precepts that can be publicly communicated. To the extent that such precepts are general, they are less likely to be bent by those administering justice to serve the particular or partial interests of a few individuals or associations. The liberal conception of justice and the rule of law is "impartial" in so far as its precepts address the fundamental problems of social life affecting every person in society and that every person has an interest in solving. (Although this is not to deny that some people will prosper more than others in a regime governed by these principles.)

The Rule of Law as a Warning Sensor

The rule of law requires that knowledge of justice be publicly communicated by means of general precepts. Such publicly-accessible precepts can then be used to assess the judgments made by persons charged with administering justice to see if they are deviating from the requirements of the rule of law. When a deviation is detected, further inquiries can be made to see if partiality is the cause. In sum, a duty to conform to the rule of law makes it easier to detect partiality and thereby more difficult for persons responsible for administering justice to act partially.

The way that the rule of law permits us to detect partiality is illustrated by a case my partner and I prosecuted when I was a criminal prosecutor assigned to the auto theft preliminary hearing court for Cook County, Illinois. The case involved a "chop shop" operation in which stolen cars were disassembled in a garage so that the parts, which could not be easily traced, might be sold separately. The judge in this courtroom, John Devine, was normally rather strict in limiting the scope of the defendant's cross examination during a preliminary hearing. (A preliminary hearing is a proceeding in which a judge finds whether or not there is "probable cause" to hold a case for a full trial.) During this particular hearing, however, Judge Devine unexpectedly and over our objection greatly expanded the scope of cross-examination. During cross-examination of the arresting police officer, surprising information pertaining to the legality of the search was disclosed that damaged our case and of which we had been unaware. Judge Devine found "no probable cause" and the case was ultimately dismissed.

Although we could not prove it, we were convinced that Judge Devine's aberrant behavior (and the police officer's damaging testimony) had been induced by a bribe from the defendant's lawyer. In other words, we believed that a monetary bribe caused Judge Devine's judgment to be partial towards the defendant. For this and other cases in which he accepted bribes, the rule of law ceased to operate in his courtroom and injustice was the consequence.

Judge Devine had a duty to adhere to the rule of law and, for this reason, when he failed to do so we were able to infer from his flagrant disregard of the rule of law that he was acting partially. This knowledge we obtained of Judge Devine's partiality was the first step toward removing him from the bench—a step that was eventually accomplished when, unbeknownst to me, another of my partners in this court, Terry Hake, later became an undercover agent for a federal investigation known as Operation Greylord.[16] Because Terry knew that Judge Devine was acting in a partial manner, he was later able to alert federal investigators to Judge Devine's activities and evidence of his partiality was eventually uncovered. Judge Devine was ultimately indicted, convicted, and sent to prison for numerous instances of official corruption.[17] Although Devine was never prosecuted for his handling of our chop-shop case, the lawyer he retained to defend him against charges of corruption was none other than the very same lawyer who had represented the chop-shop operators in our case.

The problem of obtaining compliance with the rule of law is not usually this extreme. Often the desire to deviate from the impartial adherence to the rule of law results from sympathy for one party or antipathy for the other. Sometimes, as with compassion for a crime or accident victim, such sympathy is natural and otherwise laudable; other times, as with the case of hostility towards a particular ethnic or racial group, such antipathy is reprehensible. A gap between interest and the rule of law may also arise when a judge is

---

[16] See generally James Touhy and Rob Warden, *Greylord: Justice, Chicago Style* (New York: Putnam 1989). John Devine is discussed, ibid. pp. 20–3. Terry Hake is discussed throughout the book and especially ibid. 58–74.

[17] On Oct. 8, 1984 John Devine was convicted on one count of racketeering/conspiracy, 25 counts of extortion, and 21 counts of mail fraud. He was sentenced to 15 years in federal prison. See ibid. 259. He died while serving his sentence.

personal friends with a lawyer for one of the parties or when judges have ideo-logical or religious and moral beliefs that argue for or against one of the par-ties to a case regardless of what legal precepts of justice require. Obtaining adherence to the rule of law presents a particular problem when judges must run for reelection. Judges may fear an adverse rating from a bar association of which a party's lawyer may be a member or that a finding in favor of the accused in a well-publicized criminal case may be disliked by the electorate.

In each of these examples, while the rule of law imposes duties upon a judge, these duties clash with the personal interest of the judge. Corruption is far more likely to take these insidious forms than to take the form of outright bribery. And judges will often be unconscious of their partiality or that they are acting upon it. Still, the story of Judge Devine illustrates how adhering to the rule of law serves to protect justice by helping participants and observers to detect partial judgements.

First, if Judge Devine had indeed taken a bribe to decide our case, then he had an interest in finding for the defendant even if the evidence showed that there was probable cause to believe that the defendant was guilty of commit-ting an unjust act. Second, to earn his bribe, Judge Devine found it expedient, perhaps even necessary, to violate the rule of law by changing the rules of evi-dence just for this case. Had he adhered to the rule of law, it would have been more difficult for him to make an unjust finding that there was no probable cause to pursue the case. Indeed, other judges might adopt an expanded scope of cross examination without raising a suspicion of corruption because they do so consistently. It was the *inconsistency* of the judge's ruling in our case as compared with his judgment in other cases, rather than the content of his rul-ing, that led us to conclude that he was acting out of an illicit interest. Even when their partialities are unconscious, compelling judges to adhere to the rule of law helps them constrain their biases.

In Chapter 5, I discussed the ability of *ex ante* precepts of justice to prevent disputes from occurring. We can now appreciate another important reason why *ex ante* precepts are to be preferred to an *ex post* decision making: dis-cernable *ex ante* precepts of justice enable us to detect partiality in a legal sys-tem. When the precepts that communicate justice are sufficiently clear—as the law governing auto theft and the rules of evidence were to my partner and me—deviations from these precepts can indicate that a judge is not acting impartially. Just as Judge Devine's deviation from his normal interpretation of the rules of evidence enabled us to identify him as corrupt, *ex ante* precepts enable other persons observing the operation of a legal system to detect cor-ruption. Such precepts "constrain" a legal system to adhere to requirements of justice, not because *ex ante* precepts are self-enforcing, but because they make enforcement possible.

The Role of Lawyers in Mitigating Partiality

Another dimension of the rule of law also helps address the partiality problem. In Chapter 6, I discussed certain aspects of the rule of law that inform and constrain a system of common law adjudication. Some will be surprised to learn that one particular feature of this system enables us to mitigate partiality: its *reliance on lawyers*. We are not accustomed to thinking of lawyers as combating partiality. On the contrary, lawyers are commonly thought to contribute to partiality by the zealous pursuit of their client's interest at the expense of justice. As Lord Brougham famously argued in *Queen Caroline's Case*:

An advocate, in the discharge of his duty, knows but one person in all the world, and that person is his client. To save that client by all means and expedients, and at all hazards and costs to other persons, and amongst them, to himself, is his first and only duty; and in performing this duty he must not regard the alarm, the torments, the destruction which he may bring upon others.[18]

Yet this vision of advocacy notwithstanding, when their institutional and ethical responsibilities are considered, we may find that lawyers serve to mediate between the extreme partiality of their clients and the need of the legal system to strive for impartial justice.

Clients are especially partial because they are exclusively concerned (in their capacity as clients) with their own interest. They have little or no vested interest in the just operation of the legal system, which is to say they have little or no vested interest in the impartial administration of justice beyond their interest as a citizen. Clients' immediate interests in the outcome of their cases dwarf their diffused interests as citizens in the administration of justice, in the same way that a domestic industry's immediate interest in receiving protection from international competition usually dwarfs its diffused interest in the benefits of free trade.

Clients are exclusively interested in the outcome of their case, not the fairness by which the outcome is reached, because they are usually one-time players in the legal system or one-sided players who repeatedly find themselves on the same side of legal disputes. For example, a defendant in a criminal case has no interest in viewing the legal system from the perspective of the prosecutor. There is no chance in a million that he will ever be a prosecutor. The same is often true of an individual plaintiff in a civil suit against a large company. There is very little chance that any individual plaintiff will ever be a defendant in a major lawsuit (at least not in any suit that his insurance policy will not cover).

One-time or one-sided players in the legal system, then, have little reason to view their lawsuit impartially. But such players are almost always represented by lawyers—and lawyers are *repeat players* in the legal system as well as players

---

[18] *Trial of Queen Caroline*, vol. ii (London: J. Robins & Co., 1820–1), p. 8.

who often find themselves on both sides of legal disputes.[19] I suggest that, in their nature as repeat players in the legal system, lawyers dampen the partiality of clients and assist in the impartial administration of justice.

There is a common saying that "a lawyer who represents himself has a fool for a client." But what does it mean? Perhaps it means that even a legally-trained client lacks something when attempting to represent himself in a lawsuit. What is that something? I suggest it is a sense of impartiality. True, a lawyer is under an explicit ethical obligation to serve the interests of her client and even to put these interests ahead of her own, as reflected in the quote from Lord Brougham. Yet such an explicit ethical obligation would be unnecessary if it was entirely natural for a lawyer to so act. In other words, if a lawyer's true interests were always entirely the same as a client's, there would be no need to impose upon the lawyer a duty to act *as though* this was the case. Precisely because lawyers are repeat players in the legal system their interests inevitably tend to diverge from those of their clients. Let me explain why this is so.

Studies of conflict have shown that there is a strong tendency in even the most hostile and competitive of systems for repeat players to seek means of cooperation rather than continued hostility.[20] In World War I, for example, troops permanently garrisoned on opposite sides of the trenches learned to cooperate with each other by coordinating attacks so as to minimize the injury to the other side.

For instance, if A persistently fired a weapon at B without regard for range and accuracy . . . and perhaps "aimed high", then B attributed A's lack of zeal to choice not chance, for the choice of accurate fire was always possible. By ritualized weapon use, A signalled a wish for peace to B, and if B was of the same mind as A, he reciprocated and ensured that A was not harmed in the subsequent exchange of ritualized fire. Thus, with the most unlikely of means, either adversary could communicate the inclination to live and let live to each other, which, if and when required, established a mutually reinforcing series of peace exchanges. What an outsider might perceive as a small battle, entirely consistent with the active front policy, might be in fact merely a structure of ritualized aggression, where missiles symbolized benevolence not malevolence.[21]

The same number of artillery shells might be fired at the same spot each day so the opponent would know to get out of the way.[22] Patrols would take routes calculated to avoid the enemy and, if confronted accidentally, would give each other a wide berth.[23] The regime of cooperation was reenforced by stern retaliation whenever the peace was broken.[24] And each side developed ways of disciplining their own compatriots who might breach the peace.[25]

---

[19] To the extent that lawyers specalize in particular types of lawsuits as either plaintiffs or defense counsel, their ability to mitigate partiality is greatly reduced.

[20] The theoretical explanation for this is provided by Axelrod, *Evolution of Cooperation* and Sugden, *Economics of Rights*.

[21] Tony Ashworth, *Trench Warfare 1914–1918: The Live and Let Live System* (New York: Holmes & Maier, 1980), p. 102.

[22] Ibid. 126.   [23] Ibid. 103.   [24] Ibid. 151–2.   [25] Ibid. 153–75.

Likewise, lawyers who use high-handed or illicit tactics face retaliation from other lawyers. Lawyers who get a reputation for using such tactics will pay in countless ways. For this reason lawyers have a strong stake in their reputation, which is the way that most information about them is conveyed to others. Reputations are often quite specific and surprisingly accurate. I dare say that I rarely met a lawyer who did not live up to (or usually down to) his or her professional reputation. A bad reputation costs a lawyer in countless ways that he or she will never know—which is why many lawyers pay inadequate attention to their reputation. Yet enough lawyers appreciate this phenomenon that they jealously guard their reputation and worry a good deal about it.

Reputations arise as a result of repeated exposure to participants in the legal system. To protect one's reputation requires that one acts in a generally trustworthy way and that one treats others as one would want to be treated. This is not to say that lawyers must or do act prissily. As I already noted, every lawyer also has duties towards her client and knows that all other lawyers share a similar duty. Yet the fact that lawyers are repeat players with a considerable investment in their reputations means that they have the very delicate task of mediating between the exclusively partial view of their clients and the impartial perspective of the legal system. They must tread a difficult path between their responsibility as an agent of a client and their responsibility as an officer of the court.

This means that, for example, although they may be forced by their ethical responsibilities to knowingly allow their clients' to testify falsely at trial,[26] they must also attempt to dissuade the client from committing perjury, and certainly must not suborn or encourage the idea. Although they may be obliged to represent a client who has caused extensive injuries to a plaintiff, they must also disclose to the other party pertinent information that may damage their clients' interests as part of the discovery process (discussed in Chapter 6). They may also encourage their clients to agree to a fair settlement of their claims rather than to prolong lawsuits with a series of procedural maneuvers. In these and countless other situations, lawyers pursue their clients' interests while at the same time mitigating their extreme partiality and enabling disputes to be resolved, often by voluntary settlement.

Although I think the lawyer's role as a mediator between the partiality of the client and the impartiality of the legal system is both important and generally neglected, too much should not be made of it. The lawyer should not be blamed whenever the legal system fails to act justly simply because she zealously pursued her client's interests. The inability of even the best legal system to reach infallible results cannot be rectified by forcing the lawyer to disregard completely her client's interest to see that a just outcome is achieved. Forcing

---

[26] For a well-known defense of this practice on ethical grounds, see Monroe H. Freedman, *Lawyers' Ethics in an Adversary System* (Indianapolis: Bobbs-Merrill, 1975), pp. 27–41.

the lawyer to assume complete impartiality is simply no substitute for improving the impartial rules governing the operation of the legal system.

The widespread repugnance expressed toward lawyers who represent the guilty truly amazes me. An inability of the police to collect—or the prosecution to convincingly present—sufficient evidence of guilt cannot be solved systemically by forcing the defense lawyer to reveal the truth or to represent the guilty less effectively than they represent the innocent. Indeed, by reducing the pressure on police and prosecutors to do their jobs well, imposing such an obligation on defense attorneys would have the perverse effect of undermining rather than enhancing the incentives to find and effectively present reliable evidence of guilt. That is, police and prosecutors would act far more partially than they currently do if they did not face the prospect of an adversary scrutinizing their actions at some future date.

Although the lawyer cannot assure that a legal system acts impartially, and although it may often appear that the partiality of lawyers is principally responsible when the legal system goes awry, the lawyer occupies a vital middle ground between complete partiality and complete impartiality. Lawyers in a system governed by the rule of law provide a mediating buffer between the interest of the legal system to sacrifice the individual client and the interest of the individual client to sacrifice justice.

Summary

Two objections may be made to my claim in Part I that the liberal conception of justice and the rule of law is necessary to solve the knowledge problem. Some may challenge the seriousness of the knowledge problem. They may question whether access to personal and local knowledge is as limited as I have suggested. Others may criticize the claim that only the liberal principles of justice and the rule of law are capable of handling this problem. They may argue that a regime of justice based on bounded discretion will necessarily give preference to the right-holder's knowledge at the expense of others who may also know something about how the resources owned by another may best be used.

Yet the analysis of the partiality problem just presented represents an independent reason to adopt the solution to the knowledge problem provided by the fusion of justice and the rule of law. For only this strategy can handle both the problems of knowledge and the problem of partiality. It does so as follows:

(1) The liberal conception of justice based on a decentralized regime of several property rights and consensual transfers addresses the general problem of partiality by compartmentalizing the effects of partial decision making, requiring that persons seeking to use the resources under the jurisdiction

of others take their interests into account, and permitting a checks and balances system of tit-for-tat to operate among right-holders.

(2) The liberal conception of the rule of law based on publicly accessible and generally applicable legal precepts addresses the acute problem of partiality that arises in the administration of justice by triggering a warning when these formal tenets are violated that a partial exercise of judgment may have occurred.

Assuming that the fusion of justice and the rule of law addresses the problems caused by partiality, further problems of interest arise from adopting this approach. As Aristotle knew, to be virtuous and happy, it is not enough to know the good, one must also be willing to act on the basis of one's knowledge. While the liberal conception of justice and the rule of law provides us with a way to handle the knowledge problem, the next two problems of interest involve ensuring that we also have the will.

EIGHT

The Incentive Problem

1. The Cost of Choice

HAVING knowledge of potential uses for resources is one thing. Putting that knowledge into action is another. Human action is costly. For every action we take, we necessarily forgo taking innumerable others. When I chose to write this morning, this choice foreclosed me from working in my yard, reading a book, or going shopping—all things that I would also have liked to do. I chose to write because I thought that, all things considered, on balance, the benefits that would accrue to me from writing would make me happier than those that would result from doing any of these alternatives, not to mention the countless other actions that I would like even less. By allowing me the jurisdiction to make this choice, the rights of several property and freedom of contract permit me to pursue my partial interests by putting into action my personal knowledge of how I might best pursue happiness.

My choices might well turn out to be wrong—the benefits that would have accrued to me by reading that book may have been subjectively greater than those which I gained from writing. For example, reading might have led to an intellectual discovery that would have profited me more than even a productive day at the word-processor. Of course, I will never know for sure. Because time is scarce, by acting, I made a choice that cannot be reversed. I have forever lost the opportunity to have done something different with my today.

This is what James Buchanan has called the subjective "cost of choice": "Cost is that which the decision taker sacrifices or gives up when he makes a choice. It consists in his own evaluation of the enjoyment or utility that he anticipates having to forego as a result of selection among alternative courses of action."[1] Buchanan identifies six features of this choice-bound conception of cost:

(1) Most importantly, cost must be borne exclusively by the decision-maker; it is not possible for cost to be shifted to or imposed on others.
(2) Cost is subjective; it exists in the mind of the decision-maker and nowhere else.
(3) Cost is based on anticipations; it is necessarily a forward-looking or *ex ante* concept.

[1] Buchanan, *Cost and Choice*, pp. 42–3.

(4) Cost can never be realized because of the fact of choice itself; that which is given up cannot be enjoyed.
(5) Cost cannot be measured by someone other than the decision-maker because there is no way that subjective experience can be directly observed.
(6) Finally, cost can be dated at the moment of decision or choice.[2]

This subjective choice-bound conception of the cost of action has important implications for our conception of justice. Not only are individuals (and voluntary associations) in possession of the personal and local knowledge on which to base choices, they must also bear the cost of any choice among potential actions in the form of forgone opportunities that can never be measured or reclaimed. Like the knowledge possessed by individuals, the costs incurred by action are also inherently and unavoidably their *own*. Just as they and only they are in possession of their own personal knowledge, they and only they incur the opportunity cost of putting their personal knowledge into action.

None of this is to deny that sometimes people make choices that do not turn out as they expect. Sometimes people regret the choices they made and wish they could reclaim the opportunities they gave up. And, as was discussed in Chapter 3, sometimes others are in a better position to make decisions than oneself. Moreover, a sole focus on the costs of choice does not take into account the adverse effects that individual choices might have on others (though any such adverse effects are not "costs" as Buchanan is using the term).

Nonetheless, as was also discussed in Chapter 3, the nature of personal and local knowledge supports a presumption that persons and associations with access to information are generally best able to make knowledgeable decisions (though it is sometimes necessary to make individual exceptions for demonstrated incompetence). And, as was discussed in Chapter 7, the impact of choices on third parties is "compartmentalized" by the disparate nature of several property rights, as well as the general prohibition on interfering by force or fraud with the jurisdiction that others have over what is theirs.

The subjective cost of choice suggests another reason, wholly apart from the need to solve the first-order problem of knowledge and the partiality problem, why the jurisdiction to make choices over resource use—the natural rights of several property, freedom of contract, and first possession—should be allotted to individuals and associations. Since they alone must bear the cost of their actions in the form of forgone opportunities, their ability to pursue happiness depends upon being able to make these choices for themselves. The order of preferences which determines a person's cost of choice is highly personal knowledge and what constitutes a forgone opportunity is also subjective in that it reflects what the choosing party would have chosen second. Those who incur the costs of choice are in the best position to know what their

---

[2] Ibid. 43.

alternative opportunities are and how they rank them. For this reason, their interests are likely to be harmed by having choices imposed upon them by others.

In sum, while the recognition of rights of ownership and freedom of contract is initially explicable in terms of the need to solve the first-order problem of dispersed knowledge, violating these rights is also likely to adversely affect the interests of those whose freedom of choice is overridden by the choices of others. We are now in a position to see that the right to own oneself and external resources as well as the right to transfer consensually alienable property rights to others have, not one, but at least two distinct bases in the nature of human beings and the world in which they find themselves:

> (1) the personal and local knowledge possessed by individuals and associations is inescapably their own and largely inaccessible by others; and
> (2) the cost of action is inescapably incurred by those who act and cannot be shifted onto another.

If individuals are to pursue happiness, then they ought to be afforded the opportunity to put the knowledge that is at their disposal into practice by making the best choices they can under the circumstances. For they will have to bear the costs of any choices imposed upon them.

Suppose, for example, that a Ann and Ben are a childless couple because Ann has a medical condition that would make pregnancy dangerous to her health. They would be willing to have an egg from Ann that has been fertilized by Ben's sperm implanted into the womb of another woman who would then bring the resulting fetus to term and give birth to their baby. They come to learn that there is a woman, Cynthia, who would be willing to perform this wonderful service, but only in return for payment of a substantial sum of money. Ann and Ben agree to pay Cynthia $20,000 and all her medical expenses, and Cynthia agrees to become impregnated, give birth to the baby, and waive any parental rights she might claim in the child.[3] Now suppose that a statute exists that makes it illegal for Ann and Ben to offer or for Cynthia to accept the $20,000 and Cynthia refuses to perform the service for free. The statute in question has imposed a choice on Ann, Ben, and Cynthia that they would not otherwise have made. The opportunity forgone by Ann and Ben is the chance to be parents of their biological child; the opportunity forgone by Cynthia is the chance to earn $20,000 and spend it as she chooses. Their interests have been adversely affected in two closely related ways.

---

[3] These facts are loosely based on that of *Johnson v. Calvert*, 19 Cal. Rptr. 2d 494, 851 P.2d 776 (1993), in which the Supreme Court of California upheld the enforceability of a contract between a couple, Mark and Crispina Calvert, and a woman Anna Johnson, who had been impregnated with the couple's fertilized egg, in which Anna had agreed to forgo any parental claims in the child to whom she gave birth. In the actual case, there was no California statute barring such contracts, but such statutes have been enacted elsewhere.

First, of course and most obviously, they have lost the happiness that this particular opportunity might have afforded each of them. Ann and Ben will never know the joy of bringing life into being, and Cynthia will not be able to enjoy that which she might have obtained with the money, perhaps a new car, a down payment on a house, or a college tuition fund for her own child. True the choice to proceed with the implantation might have caused great unhappiness. The child might have been still-born or born with a severe disability, or Cynthia might have developed health complications during pregnancy or emotional trauma from having to give up the child she gave birth to. The important issue is jurisdictional: who is to decide? Unless they are shown to be incompetent, given that they are in the best position to know their own preferences and that they will bear the cost of choice—for better or for ill—it would seem that the choice should belong, jointly, to Ann, Ben, and Cynthia.

Second, imposing a choice on Ann, Ben, and Cynthia undermines substantially their incentive to use their knowledge in such a way as to enhance their well-being by discovering this opportunity. Ann and Ben would have no interest in consuming their scarce time and efforts to seek out a physician and enquire about the feasibility of such a procedure, nor of contacting a fertility center about locating a woman who would be willing to become impregnated. And there would be greatly reduced incentive for anyone to set up a fertility center to locate women who would be willing to perform this service, if they and the women they located were unable to collect a fee for their time and efforts. Moreover, in the absence of this "market" or demand, biologists and physicians would have little reason to develop such procedures.

Thus the subjective cost of choice yields the following problem of interest that I shall call the incentive problem:

> *The Incentive Problem*: ensuring that persons have an adequate incentive to make choices reflecting the knowledge to which they have access and to discover new information; it is the need to close the gap between the conduct that justice *permits* and a right-holder's interest to act knowledgeably with his or her resources.

Let us briefly consider how the background rights of first possession and freedom of contract—both freedom from and freedom to contract—that comprise part of the liberal conception of justice address this problem.

2. How Justice and the Rule of Law Affect Incentives

The principle of first possession ensures that someone investing scarce resources in establishing control over a resource will not be divested of the benefits of this investment at some later time when another person makes a claim for the same resource. Without such a principle, the person first in possession would lack a right to continued possession on which they could rely. Depriving them of the opportunity to benefit from their investment would undermine any incentive to make full use of the claimed property by, for example, improving it in some permanent way.

The principle of freedom from contract helps ensure that changes in control of resources reflect the interests of the original right-holder. Only if the right-holder consents to a transfer will it be recognized as valid. Consent to a right transfer will not be given unless the right-holder subjectively values (*ex ante*) the resulting distribution of rights more highly than the original distribution of rights that preceded the transfer. Only by requiring consent to transfer rights can we be reasonably sure that negative incentives are not created by transfers of control. The principle of freedom to contract provides positive incentives for beneficial transactions by enforcing agreements motivated by the prospects of receiving a benefit or "profit." The prospect of such gains creates powerful incentives to investigate and discover previously unknown opportunities for beneficial transfers.

Entrepreneurship is the ability to identify previously unknown or neglected opportunities for beneficial transactions. If contracts producing so-called "speculative" gains were unenforceable, then the incentive for such entrepreneurial activity would be eliminated. Entrepreneurship is not merely making use of the personal and local knowledge one already possesses—what I have been calling the first-order problem of knowledge. Entrepreneurship is the activity by which previously unknown information about resource use is brought into being; it is a way of reducing ignorance. As explained by Israel Kirzner:

If all market participants were omniscient, prices for products and prices for factors must at all times be in complete mutual adjustment, leaving no profit differential; no opportunity for the worthwhile deployment of resources, through any technology knowable or for the satisfaction of any consumer desire conceivable, can be imagined to have been left unexploited. Only the introduction of ignorance opens up the possibility of such unexploited opportunities (and their associated opportunities for pure profits), and the possibility that the first one to discover the true state of affairs can capture the associated profits by invigorating, changing, and creating.[4]

Pure entrepreneurship is the activity of revealing previously unknown information about the use of resources:

The pure entrepreneur . . . proceeds by his alertness to discover and exploit situations in which he is able to sell for high prices that which he can buy for low prices. Pure entrepreneurial profit is the difference between the two sets of prices. It is not yielded by exchanging something the entrepreneur values less for something he values more highly. It comes from discovering sellers and buyers of something for which the latter will pay more than the former demand.[5]

---

[4] Israel M. Kirzner, *Competition and Entrepreneurship* (Chicago: University of Chicago Press, 1973), p. 67.
[5] Ibid. 48.

The first-order knowledge problem discussed in Chapter 1, concerned the use of knowledge people already have while taking into account the knowledge that other people have. The incentive problem is, in part, to ensure that people have adequate incentive to use the knowledge they already have. But it is also the problem of ensuring that some people will take it upon themselves to improve upon the existing supply and distribution of knowledge. This is what Kirzner calls entrepreneurship and the incentive for engaging in this costly activity is the ability to reap entrepreneurial profits:

Alertness toward new opportunities is stimulated by the heady scent of profits. Profits are to be found where available bits of information have not yet been coordinated. The exploitation of profit opportunities consists in identifying and correcting uncoordinated groups of plans. And, of course, as the process of correction proceeds the profit opportunities themselves dwindle away. . . . The lure of profits, and fear of losses can be counted upon, in some measure, to attract at least some entrepreneurs. . . . The profit incentive (including, of course, the disincentive of loss) operates most significantly by sparking the alertness of entrepreneurs—by encouraging them to keep their eyes open for new information that will lead to new plans. And its powerful effect in this regard acquires normative significance because of the market's prior failure to coordinate sets of decisions.[6]

There are, then, two distinguishable aspects of the incentive problem: (1) the incentive people have to incur the cost of choice to use the information in their possession; and (2) the incentive people have to incur the costs of choice to discover new information about how resources may be used. The liberal conception of justice addresses both of these problems of incentives by inhibiting transfers adversely affecting interest and encouraging beneficial transfers. The rights of first possession and freedom from contract—that is, no transfers without consent—ensure that rights transfers will not create negative incentives; that people can put their knowledge into use without fear of the resultant benefits being expropriated by others. The principle of freedom to contract—that is, consensual transfers are valid—makes entrepreneurship possible by ensuring that positive incentives exist for beneficial rights transfers; that people can retain the entrepreneurial profit yielded by their discovery. In these ways, the rights that define the liberal conception of justice identified in Chapter 4 address not only the knowledge problem, but the problem of interest as well.

The liberal conception of the rule of law also helps address the incentive problem. In Chapter 6 we saw how specific conventions were required to give content to the requirements of justice. In Chapter 5 I discussed the various formal requirements of legality, the seventh of which barred "introducing such frequent changes in the rules that the subject cannot orient his actions by them." Given that different conventions may be equally consistent with justice, the incentive problem argues in favor of stable conventions, even where some marginal improvements may be possible. When different legal precepts

---

[6] Ibid. 223.

governing rights are generally consistent with basic principles of justice, repeatedly changing the precepts would still undermine both the knowledge of justice that specific rules are needed to convey and the incentives to invest and conserve resources. To the extent that frequent changes in legal precepts deprive people of their ability to reap the benefits of conservation, they would have the same deleterious affect on the ability to knowledgeably decide between present and future consumption as would a failure to recognize rights of several property and freedom of contract.

3. Takings and Just Compensation

The incentive problem arises most graphically when the benefits of exercising knowledgeable control over resources do not accrue to the person or persons exercising such control—that is, these benefits are taken away from the person who is incurring costly action without her consent and given to someone else. To appreciate the nature of the incentive problem created by such takings, let us imagine a world of several property where control over resources was decentralized in much the same manner as we witness in western countries—perhaps even more so. Now imagine that any monetary benefits accruing from a knowledgeable exercise of control were routinely taken and given to others. The inability to reap any of the monetary benefits resulting from using one's knowledge to exercise control over resources would greatly reduce the incentive to exercise knowledgeable control in the future. Unless one can profit from one's efforts, the incentive to produce any effort is greatly diminished.

What about takings that occur after one's death? After all, one can hardly require incentives to exercise knowledgeable control over resources after one has died. Yet a policy of post-mortem takings is likely to create serious incentive problems for people when they are still alive. Persons and associations possess personal and local knowledge concerning both present and future uses of resources. Resources may be quickly exploited or they may conserved for later use. Because most people psychologically project their lives into the future, they take a mixed view of resource use, choosing to trade some short-run benefits for the prospects of greater benefits in the future. (It is revealing that the reward demanded for deferred consumption is sometimes referred to as "interest.") The ability to command an interest premium provides incentives to conserve resources for later consumption by the right-holder. It also provides an incentive to shift the present control of resources to others in return for control of different resources in the future.

As people age, however, their "time horizons"[7] are likely to drop. Absent

[7] The term "time horizon" is taken from Edward Banfield, who used it to explain criminal behavior. See Edward Banfield, *The Unheavenly City Revisited* (Boston: Little, Brown, 1974), p. 5. For a critique and expansion of his insight see Gerald P. O'Driscoll,

some other incentive, they would have a continually decreasing interest in conserving resources for their own later use. In a regime of takings after death we can anticipate that, as people age, they will accelerate their consumption of resources beyond that which they would otherwise choose or, perhaps even more dangerously, they will make increasing numbers of gifts to others. Unlike post-mortem transfers, such *inter vivos* (during life) gifts would be irrevocable and, should an aged donor miscalculate his or her life span or income, would increase the risk that a donor's resources would be exhausted before death. Moreover, to the extent that these *inter vivos* gifts were viewed as deliberately evading the policy of post-mortem takings, they would most likely be restricted as well. Any restrictions on *inter vivos* transfers would then further reinforce the incentive to consume as opposed to conserving resources.

Finally, it is well-known that many persons are strongly motivated to amass an estate that will benefit their children. This desire would be defeated by a policy of takings after death. Such a policy creates a serious incentive problem by undermining the natural incentive people have to be altruistic towards those they love and encourages the consumption of any resources a person may accumulate during his life.

In a regime of post-mortem transfers governed by principles of consent, however, these incentive problems are greatly diminished. To the extent that persons contemplate passing their rights to their loved ones who survive them, their time horizons are extended, approaching the horizons of their earlier years. Those whose wealth is particularly great or who have no loved ones to whom they desire to transfer their estate are sought out by charitable institutions whose interest provides them with an incentive to solicit post-mortem bequests. In either case, in a regime in which the recipient of estates may be governed by the consent of the testator, persons are comparatively more likely to conserve resources knowledgeably for later use that they would in a regime of post-mortem takings. Moreover, the power to consent to post-mortem transfers enables persons to act upon their altruistic sentiments by accumulating wealth to be given to others rather than consumed by themselves.

This phenomenon has been noticed by Robert Ellickson, who writes:

Although the assertion may seem counterintuitive, the key to land conservation is to bestow upon living persons property rights that extend perpetually into the future. The current market value of a fee in Blackacre is the discounted present value of the eternal stream of rights and duties that attach to Blackacre. A rational and self-interested fee owner therefore adopts a [*sic*] infinite planning horizon when considering how to use his parcel, and is spurred to install cost-justified permanent improvements and to avoid premature exploitation of resources. The fee

Jr., "Professor Banfield on Time Horizon: What has he Taught Us About Crime?" in Randy E. Barnett and John Hagel III (eds.), *Assessing the Criminal: Restitution, Retribution, and the Legal Process* (Boston: Ballinger, 1977), pp. 143–62; and Mario J. Rizzo, "Time Preference, Situational Determinism, and Crime," ibid, 163–77.

simple in land cleverly harnesses human selfishness to the cause of altruism toward the unborn, a group not noted for its political clout or bargaining power.[8]

Ellickson observes that the device of perpetual rights to land which can either be alienated during life or conveyed to heirs after death, has been discovered and adopted by successful societies.

Throughout history, many close-knit agricultural groups have recognized that perpetual private ownership makes for better land stewardship. As land in a preliterate society becomes scarcer and its economic development advances, it is increasingly likely to confer potentially infinite entitlements in croplands and homesites upon kinship lines. Especially until a group masters literacy, it may honor a variety of non-Blackstonian rules, such as that private parcels are descendible only to kin, inalienable to outsiders, and forfeitable for nonuse. But once it develops a written language, a group will almost invariably recognize unending private rights in some of its lands. For example, the ancients in Egypt and Greece, two cradles of Western civilization, conferred perpetual land entitlements on private owners. In medieval England, farmers' copyholds were inheritable. And when private plots were parceled out at Jamestown and Plymouth, settlers received infinitely long interests. Perpetual private land rights are most emphatically not a uniquely Western institution, however. Land interests of potentially infinite duration evolved separately among the Japanese, the Ibo of Nigeria, and the Navajo of the American Southwest. In sum, the inherent efficiencies of perpetual private land rights have led to their spontaneous appearance on every continent.[9]

A regime of consensual transfers, both during one's life and after one's death, is more likely than a regime of takings to provide the incentives needed for a knowledgeable mix of consumption, savings, and donative decisions during people's lives. This analysis suggests that the incentive problem has another implication for the liberal conception of justice. When incentives to act productively are diminished by takings, it is not enough simply to condemn such a taking as unjust. Condemnation will not preserve the incentives for productive activity that are undermined by transfers without consent. Some form of *compensation* to the victim of a taking is needed to restore the benefits taken from the right-holder. Unless compensation is made, persons will have a greatly reduced incentive to use their knowledge to increase the value of the resources they control. The Fifth Amendment to the United States Constitution reads, in part, "nor shall private property be taken for public use without just compensation."[10] This formulation is very close to the more general principle of justice that is needed to address the incentive problem: just compensation is required whenever several property is taken for any use without the consent of the rights-holder.[11]

---

[8] Robert C. Ellickson, "Property in Land," *Yale Law Journal*, vol. 102 (1993), p. 1369.

[9] Ibid. 1369–71.

[10] *Constitution of the United States*, amend. V. For a comprehensive theory of how this clause should be interpreted, see Richard A. Epstein, *Takings: Private Property and the Power of Eminent Domain* (Cambridge, Mass.: Harvard University Press, 1985).

[11] As an instrument constraining the exercise of government power, the takings clause prohibits takings *for public use*. The clause also appears to presuppose both that

Where is this compensation to come from? In a world of completely decentralized jurisdictions there are really only two choices. Compensation can come from the person who received the benefits of the taking or it can come from someone else who did not. If compensation is taken from persons who did not receive the proceeds of the taking, a new and equally debilitating forced transfer will occur. From the standpoint of the incentive problem there is no reason to prefer the first victim of a taking to the second. It would seem that as between the victim of a forced or fraudulent transfer, all persons in the world who received no benefit from the unjust taking, and the person who received a benefit, the compensation should come from the person who perpetrated the forced or fraudulent transfer. While no compensation can ever eliminate the cost imposed by the original rights violation, only by taking resources from the perpetrator of an unjust taking can incentives be restored to the victim of the injustice without at the same time depriving others of the incentives attached to the exercise of their own knowledge.

The justified claim of a victim of injustice (or her representative) to compel the perpetrator of an unjust taking to make compensation is called the *right of restitution*:

> The *right of restitution* specifies that one who violates the rights that define justice must compensate the victim of the rights violation for the harm caused by the injustice.

This principle is largely noncontroversial.[12] While it once was the animating principle of "criminal" justice,[13] it is today still embraced in the private law system of torts.

We are now in a position to refine further the liberal conception of justice in light of the need to address the incentive problem by supplementing the right of several property and by recognizing an additional background right:

FORMULATION 4. *Justice is respect for the rights of individuals and associations.*
(1) The *right of several property* specifies a right to acquire, possess, use, and dispose of scarce physical resources—including their own bodies. Resources may be used in any way that does not physically interfere with other persons' use and enjoyment of their resources. While most property rights are freely alienable, the right to one's person is inalienable.

takings for public use are permissible when just compensation is made, and that takings for private use are impermissible entirely.

[12] While the principle of restitution has traditionally been widely accepted, limiting the remedy for rights violations to restitution is quite controversial. I take up this issue in Chapters 10 and 11.

[13] I put the word criminal in quotes because when compensation or "composition" was the animating principle in the Anglo-Saxon legal world of what we think of today as crimes, there was no distinction between crime and tort. See generally, Harold J. Berman, *Law and Revolution* (Cambridge, Mass.: Harvard University Press, 1983), pp. 49–84; Bruce L. Benson, *The Enterprise of Law: Justice Without the State* (San Francisco: Pacific Research Institute, 1990), pp. 11–36.

(2) The *right of first possession* specifies that property rights to unowned resources are acquired by being the first to establish control over them and to stake a claim.
(3) The *right of freedom of contract* specifies that a right-holder's consent is both necessary (freedom *from* contract) and sufficient (freedom *to* contract) to transfer alienable property rights—**both during one's life and, by using a "will," upon one's death**. A manifestation of assent is ordinarily necessary unless one party somehow has access to the other's subjective intent.
(4) Violating these rights by *force or fraud* is unjust.
(5) The *right of restitution* **requires that one who violates the rights that define justice must compensate the victim of the rights violation for the harm caused by the injustice.**

Of course, if as is likely to be the case the perpetrator is unwilling to make compensation voluntarily, some way must be found to induce compliance with this principle. The problem of compliance will be discussed in the next chapter. And in Chapters 13 and 14 I will discuss the institutional features of a legal system in which restitution is the norm.

4. Public Goods: Incentives and Free Riders

In recent years it has become popular to claim that the rights of several property, freedom of contract, first possession, and restitution which define (to this point) the liberal conception of justice are not adequate to handle certain incentive problems arising in special circumstances. In particular, with some types of goods, owners who offer it to the public are unable to exclude those who do not pay for its use from consuming it along with those who do pay. Without the ability to exclude, potential consumers will have little or no incentive to pay for a good they can otherwise get for free. Consequently, there will be reduced incentive for any producer to provide the good in question.

The classic example of a nonexcludable public good is a lighthouse, which was offered as an example of a public good by such eminent economists as John Stuart Mill, Henry Sidgewick, A. C. Pigou, and Paul Samuelson.[14] Because the lighthouse owner cannot prevent passing ships from viewing the beacon, there will be little or no incentive for ship owners to pay lighthouse owners for their services and consequently little or no incentive for anyone to produce lighthouses. This is considered a problem because of the assumption that, were it possible to exclude potential users from using the lighthouse, sufficient

[14] See Ronald H. Coase, "The Lighthouse in Economics," *Journal of Law and Economics*, vol. 17 (1974), p. 357, (providing examples of each of these theorists describing lighthouses as public goods).

numbers of them would pay to make it feasible to provide the service. Thus the inability to exclude, which leads to a reduced incentive to provide light-houses, renders ship owners who would be willing to pay for the use of the beacon worse off than they would be if exclusion were possible.

Because the reduced incentive to supply such nonexcludable goods is cre-ated by the ability of some to "free ride" on the production of others, this is referred to as the "free-rider problem." And nonexcludable goods are some-times referred to as "public goods."[15] In sum, free riding is said to create a gap between the knowledge people have of productive resource use, including their knowledge of potential demand for a good or service, and their incen-tives to actually produce the good or service. Although the precepts of justice may *permit* people to act productively, in circumstances where a free-rider problem exists, adherence to justice is insufficient to provide adequate incen-tives to actually do so.

Some economists have maintained that, to overcome the free-rider problem and provide these goods, we must make exceptions to the right of freedom from contract that requires the consent of the right-holder before enforcing a transfer of rights. As Samuelson explains: "Take our earlier case of a lighthouse to warn against rocks. Its beam helps everyone in sight. A businessman could not build it for a profit, since he cannot claim a price from each user. This cer-tainly is the kind of activity that government would naturally undertake."[16] So, for instance, we could involuntarily take resources from—that is, tax— those owners who would be willing to pay to use lighthouses but who lack the incentive to consent because they or others may ride for free, and give this money to the providers of lighthouses. Providing adequate incentives to build and operate lighthouses requires, it is claimed, takings from ship owners.

But the theoretical existence of free-rider problems does not immediately support overriding the right of freedom from contract. Before we can justify compelling potential consumers to pay for goods from which they cannot be excluded, it must also be shown that there exists a sufficiently reliable method to measure both the consumer demand for such goods and the appropriate level of expenditures that should be made to supply them. Given the nature of human beings and the world in which they live, however, any such effort would face enormous problems of knowledge and interest.

---

[15] The technical term "public good" is only supposed to be applied when goods or services are nonexcludable *and* when a person's ability to consume the good is not diminished by allowing additional individuals to consume it. With the lighthouse, for example, not only can potential users not be excluded by the lighthouse owner, but the light is not diminished as more and more ships view it. This last characteristic is referred to as "nonrivalrous consumption." See Tyler Cowen (ed.), *The Theory of Market Failure* (Fairfax, Va.: George Mason University Press, 1988), pp. 3–4. This volume is a very use-ful collection of articles which call into question the seriousness of the public goods problem.

[16] Paul A. Samuelson, *Economics: An Introductory Analysis*, 6th edn. (New York: McGraw-Hill, 1964), p. 159.

In the absence of the revealed preferences provided by the manifested consent of suppliers and consumers, how can central authorities accurately determine the potential demand for the good in question? How could they determine the appropriate level of expenditures to be made on such goods? How could they determine the exact manner by which such goods should be supplied? The answers to all these questions are ordinarily supplied by the consent of consumers and suppliers of goods and services but the taking power overrides this consent and consequently deprives us of this information. Lacking access to the personal and local knowledge of others, how are we to know that enough people would be willing to pay for a particular good or service in the absence of their demonstrating their preferences in a genuine transaction?[17]

Moreover, once the mechanism for coercive takings is established, how can we be sure that they will be used impartially to provide public goods rather than to serve the partial interests of either consumers or suppliers at the expense of those from whom the resources are taken? The requirement of consent is ordinarily how we compartmentalize partiality and ensure that the actions of any one person take into account the partial interests of all others. Using a takings power to override the requirement of consent deprives us of this assurance.

In sum, if central authorities really could do all this efficiently, which is to say *both* knowledgeably *and* impartially, there would be no knowledge problem or problem of partiality, and we could do away with the right of freedom from contract altogether. There is, however, no evidence that any of this is possible. Of course, government has supplied goods and services that are thought to be "public" or nonexcludable goods. But we have no way of being sure that these goods are in fact public goods or that they are being supplied at the *socially optimal* level. And this is the appropriate standard against which to judge proposals to institutionalize takings, since economists cannot, and typically do not, claim that nonexcludable goods are not provided at all in the absence of such takings. They cannot make this claim because, notwithstanding the existence of free riders, nonexcludable goods are routinely provided without overriding the right of freedom from contract.

In practice, the free-rider problem is much less serious than it may at first appear, ironically because the potential to free ride is far *more* common than one may think. When I looked out the back window of my previous home, I

---

[17] Could such information be provided by market research surveys of the sort often undertaken by businesses? Those familiar with such techniques will testify that, while helpful, they are hardly reliable. If dependable advance knowledge of consumer demand were truly available, there would be no need for entrepreneurship and businesses would never fail. Entrepreneurship is required and businesses fail regularly precisely because there is no route independent of trial and error on a marketplace to determine accurately consumer demand. Moreover, if the purpose of the study was known we could expect the answers given to reflect the partial interests of the participants either to avoid the taking or receive the subsidized good or service.

could see the beauty of the well-maintained private golf course that adjoined my back yard. Although the price I paid for the house reflected a premium for this view, the golf course did not receive a share of this. Nor could they charge me for my enjoyment. Yet the fees they charge their members were sufficient incentive for them to maintain the course without my contribution. Similarly, I kept my house and yard attractive despite the fact that I could not charge passing golfers (or my neighbors) for my efforts. When one begins to think about it, one realizes that free riding is pervasive and sufficient incentives for production of desired goods usually exist nonetheless.

Because it is undeniable that the provision of nonexcludable goods is pervasive notwithstanding the existence of free riders, those concerned about a "free-rider problem" argue that, although the "market" for rights to use resources that is governed by justice and the rule of law provides these goods to some extent, free riding can lead to a "sub-optimal" production of a good or service. What needs to be shown, however, is not only that, in the absence of a taking, the supply of a good or service is less than "socially optimal," but also that a mechanism for takings can supply the socially optimal level of nonexcludable goods given the nature of human beings and the world in which they live. Once one appreciates the problems of knowledge and interest, however, there is no reason to be confident that this can actually be done.

When deciding on whether the theoretical possibility of "market failure" due to free riding warrants overriding the right of freedom from contract that is needed to handle the problems of knowledge and interest, we would do well to keep in mind several respects in which this market-failure analysis overstates the practical problem of adhering to a liberal conception of justice. First, particular allegations of market failures often reflect "imagination failures" on the part of analysts rather than a genuine incentive problem. These analysts are usually lawyers, economists, philosophers, or politicians—persons whose expertise does not require them to be entrepreneurs outside their disciplines.

The case of lighthouses described above was long used by economists as a textbook example of the free-rider problem—until economist Ronald Coase discovered that many lighthouses were supported by fees charged by nearby ports.[18] After all, ships could be excluded from ports, so the "good" provided by the lighthouse was tied to the "good" provided by the port and a single fee charged for both, just as a price for the "good" provided to airplane pilots by electronic landing guidance beacons at airports are (or easily could be) included in airport landing fees. Although this may not have eliminated every free rider, like the golf course behind my house which had an adequate incentive to maintain its grounds though I enjoyed the view for free, tying arrangements eliminated enough free riders to permit the profitable operation of lighthouses.

---

[18] See Coase, "Lighthouse", pp. 360–2.

There is hardly an example of a hypothetical free-rider problem that historical investigation did not reveal to have been somehow supplied in a marketplace governed by rights of several property, freedom of contract, and restitution.[19] Indeed, sometimes the contribution of entrepreneurs lies precisely in their ability to devise creative ways to exclude persons from using a particular good. Consider broadcast radio and television, a technology that should be a paradigm of the free-rider problem. Quite obviously a broadcaster is unable to exclude free-riding listeners or viewers.[20] Anyone with access to a radio or television receiver can view broadcast programming, so the broadcaster is unable to induce people to pay for programs by threatening to exclude them if they refuse. Yet we do not consider the inability to exclude potential viewers a problem because entrepreneurs of radio broadcasting hit upon the idea of excluding not viewers but potential *advertisers* unless they paid a fee that is then used to pay for the broadcast. Had broadcast advertising not been discovered early on by an entrepreneur, no doubt some economists, philosophers, lawyers, and politicians would have insisted that broadcast technology poses a "classic" free-rider problem.

Second, adherence to several property rights and freedom from contract creates incentives to develop exclusionary technology. Cable television (narrowcasting) and scrambled broadcast signals are two ways that viewers can be excluded from receiving a video signal, making it less necessary to rely on advertising. Fences are erected around drive-in movie theaters to exclude potential free riders, but even those who can still see over the fence cannot hear the audio track which is provided by individual speakers in each car. Such exclusionary technology is largely taken for granted. Once it is developed, a good is no longer identified as "public" in nature, though without such technology it would have remained nonexcludable. The difficulty of obtaining a financial return in the absence of the ability to exclude provides an incentive to develop this technology. Figuring out how exactly to exclude potential consumers of a good or service so as to capture the potential gains from providing a desired good or service may be viewed as an aspect of entrepreneurship in the broad sense of the term. Like the ability to procure scarce resources from which to make products, the ability to solve the free-rider problem is simply a crucial part of the productive process.

Third, this market failure analysis underestimates both the pervasiveness and value of nonexcludable goods. There is a saying that the best things in life

---

[19] See e.g. Steven N. S. Cheung, "The Fable of the Bees: An Economic Investigation," *Journal of Law and Economics*, vol. 16 (1973), pp. 11–33 (debunking the provision of beekeeping services to apple farmers as an example of market failure, by investigating how bee-keeping is actually supplied to orchard owners). Cheung was responding to the example offered by Francis Bator to refute what he called Adam Smith's "dream world." See Francis M. Bator, "The Anatomy of Market Failure," *Quarterly Journal of Law and Economics*, vol. 72 (1958), pp. 351–79.

[20] And the consumption of broadcasting is also nonrivalrous. The quality of reception by one consumer is not diminished by the addition of many other consumers who also receive the same signal.

are free. These "free" things include manners, attractive people and buildings, interesting ideas, great songs, good jokes, even the English language itself. In writing this book, I am undoubtedly free riding on several centuries of know-ledge of justice and the rule of law, only a small fraction of which I can expressly acknowledge. For me, the best thing that can come out of writing this book is not the royalties I may earn, but that many others may eventually free ride on the ideas presented here (though royalties are certainly something I value, so thanks if you purchased the copy you are now reading; and if you ever write something on this subject, a citation would be much appreciated). A world of complete excludability and no free riders would surely be the atom-istic world that critics of liberalism and markets repeatedly condemn.

Fourth, legal arrangements such as conditional transfer commitments or *assurance contracts* can reduce the severity of some free-rider problems that exclusionary technology cannot solve. David Schmidtz describes these con-tracts as follows:

An assurance contract is a contractual agreement to contribute to a public goods project. . . . The purpose of the contract is to give each party an assurance that his contribution will not be wasted on a public goods project that is financially under-supported. . . . To provide such an assurance, the contract incorporates a feature similar to a "money-back guarantee": The contract is enforceable against a con-tractor if and only if the rest of the total funding is sufficient to produce a return . . . that exceeds the contractor's cost. . . .[21]

Persons who would be willing to pay for a public good if others also pay could be asked to consent to a transfer of rights to an amount of money on the con-dition that a stated percentage of the relevant set of potential users also con-sent.[22] Such people would be bound to pay for the good or service only if an acceptable percentage of their fellow consumers also commit to pay as well. So, for example, an entrepreneur wishing to build a dam for irrigation could finance the project by obtaining conditional rights transfers from a high enough proportion of potential users of the water to make the project feasible. Schmidtz concludes that, though it does not eliminate the free-rider problem entirely, "the assurance contract can be used to provide levels of public goods deemed adequate by the people involved."[23]

[21] David Schmidtz, *The Limits of Government: An Essay on the Public Goods Argument* (Boulder, Colo.: Westview Press, 1991), p. 66.

[22] Schmidtz distinguishes between this "assurance problem" and the free-rider prob-lem in which some people will not pay because they can ride for free. See ibid. 56: "A second reason not to contribute arises if a person believes it would be futile to contribute because the good will not be provided anyway. Unless the person receives reasonable assurance that other people will contribute enough to ensure that his own contribution will not be wasted on a hopelessly underfunded cause, the person may decide to save his money. This is an *assurance problem.*" The connection between the two problems occurs when some persons are willing to pay for a public good, provided enough other people pay also, but they lack assurance that others will pay because the good is nonexcludable and others may think they will ride for free when it is produced.

[23] Ibid. 68.

But what if none of these methods work to provide a particular good or service, or they work "sub-optimally"? Even if we set aside the problems of knowledge and interests that confront any authorities charged with identifying the existence of such a "market failure," and even if we adopt the conception of aggregate "social welfare" that underlies the concept of "market failure," we cannot conclude from this alone that the requirements of justice should be ignored or overridden. For a full "social welfare" analysis must also include the consequences of this course of action. In other words, to justify overriding the rights that define justice from the perspective of social welfare it is simply not enough to establish that adherence to these rights has led to the underproduction of some good or service due to the potential to free ride. We must also know the potential consequences of solving a free-rider problem by setting justice to one side.

In Part I, we examined the important social function uniquely performed by the rights of several property, first possession, and freedom of contract. In Chapter 6, we saw how these rights also address the partiality problem. In this chapter, I explained the need for a right of restitution to handle the problem of incentives. In Part III, we will see how they address the problems of power. To what extent, we must ask, will all these functions be undermined by establishing an exception to this conception of justice just so a particular good or service can be produced at a socially-optimal level? It cannot be assumed and must somehow be shown that the end—the provision of some nonexcludable good or service—justifies the use of illicit means as defined by a standard of justice that is crucially important to our ability to handle the serious and pervasive problems of knowledge, interest, and power.

Yet it is far from clear that any individual or association is competent to make such an assessment or, if such competent persons exist, that we can reliably identify who they are. Certainly it is not economists. I am not speaking now of the problem of identifying nonexcludable goods and the level at which they should be provided. I am speaking of making the judgment that providing the socially-optimal level of some nonexcludable good warrants making an exception to the normal requirements of justice.

Consider the example of broadcast radio and television. It would have been easy for an economist to demonstrate that these are public goods. Yet it would have been considerably more difficult to determine the amount of tax money that should have been taken from potential viewers to pay for this service. And no economist would be qualified to tell us whether creating the power to tax for the sole purpose of providing broadcast radio and television was worth the "social costs" of such a decision; that the world would really be a better place with tax-financed broadcasting, as in Great Britain, than it would be with a system financed by advertising, as in the United States.

In the absence of a competent decision maker or some way of reliably identifying one, it seems quite dangerous to set justice aside to solve a supposed free-rider problem. And, assuming that a decision maker with some knowledge

of a genuine free-rider problem can be found, any process of delegating decisions to that person must confront the partiality problem: how can we ensure
that this decision maker will impartially decide that justice should be set aside
to solve a free-rider problem? How can we ensure that a person or institution
with the power to set justice aside for this purpose will not do so for partial
reasons of interest that have nothing to do with solving the free-rider problem? I will return to this problem when considering the problems of power in
Part III.

When advancing the existence of potential free riders as a justification for
overriding the principles of justice, none of these serious problems can simply
be wished away.

Summary

(1) The incentive problem concerns ensuring that persons have an adequate
    incentive to make choices reflecting the knowledge to which they have
    access and to discover new information.
(2) The principle of first possession addresses this problem by enabling the
    person who first invests scarce resources in controlling a previously
    unowned resource to rely on continued possession.
(3) Freedom from contract prevents negative incentives by requiring the con-
    sent of the rights-holder to any transfer thereby compelling those who
    seek a transfer to induce consent by offering something the right-holder
    values more highly.
(4) Freedom to contract enables persons to transfer rights to resources they
    have in exchange for rights to resources they would rather have, thereby
    inducing transfers of rights that benefit both parties to the exchange as
    well as the recipients of gifts.
(5) The rule of law also addresses the incentive problem by providing a set of
    legal precepts that do not change too frequently and can therefore be
    relied upon.
(6) Takings of property without the consent of the right-holder reduce the
    incentives to use one's knowledge to the fullest or to reduce one's igno-
    rance.
(7) To preserve the incentives created by justice and the rule of law, takings
    must be compensated by requiring the perpetrator of the transfer to make
    restitution to the victim.
(8) The incentive problem created by free riding is less serious than some sup-
    pose and can usually be addressed in a number of ways without the need
    for nonconsensual rights transfers.

NINE

The Compliance Problem

THE second kind of gap between interest and the liberal conception of justice and the rule of law arises when some persons subjectively desire to use resources that lie within other persons' rightful domains. To the extent that people faced with such a conflict choose to satisfy their preferences, they exceed their rightful jurisdiction and cross the boundaries defined by justice. When someone else's domain is invaded, a taking of the sort described in Chapter 8 occurs and the ability of justice to solve the first-order problem of knowledge and the problems of partiality and incentives is seriously compromised. In the absence of a willingness to adhere to the requirements of justice and the rule of law, some way must be found to secure compliance with its dictates lest justice and the rule of law cease to perform their crucial social functions.

Accordingly, we may call this dimension of the problem of interest the *compliance problem*. It can be summarized as follows:

> The *compliance problem* concerns conduct that conflicts with the rights that define justice or the requirements of the rule of law; it is the need to close the gap between the conduct that justice and the rule of law requires and what people perceive to be in their interest to do.

There are then two distinguishable aspects of the compliance problem. The first is compliance with justice, a problem that potentially applies to any person and which I shall consider in this chapter. Second is the special problem of obtaining compliance with the rule of law, a problem that applies only to those persons charged with administering justice, and to which I shall return in Chapter 13.

1. Sources of the Gap Between Justice and Interest

In most facets of life, people take a "live and let live" approach. They believe that their interests will be well-served if others adhere to the boundaries defined by precepts of justice and, in return, they are willing to adhere to these boundaries themselves. This *quid pro quo* attitude toward justice is quite power-ful and accounts for the appeal of political theories based on the idea of a "social contract." Such theories attempt to defend as "just" those principles of justice to which all or most persons would agree (whether or not an actual agreement to such precepts ever occurred).

Moreover, as was explained in the discussion of freedom of contract in Chapter 4, a willingness to agree to constraints not only suggests that con-straints are in one's interest, it also strongly suggests that such constraints reflect the diffused knowledge of the participants. Just as requiring consent before transferring entitlements is an effective means of ensuring that such transfers reflect the knowledge and interests of all parties to the transaction, the fact that persons actually consent to the constraints of justice is strong evidence that such constraints do the work that we need justice to perform. Nonetheless, there are times when people perceive a conflict or gap between the requirements of justice and their short- or long-range interests. Sometimes the perception of a gap is spurious and sometimes it is war-ranted.

There are at least two sources of apparent gaps between justice and interest that do not involve a genuine conflict. First, persons will incorrectly perceive a gap between justice and interest when they fail to understand how adhering to principles of justice serves their interests. This misunderstanding is highly likely when conventional precepts of justice evolve in a common-law process while the important social functions of these precepts remain tacit and obscure. The most common product of this perception of conflict is the enact-ment of legislation that violates liberal precepts of justice and the rule of law while purporting to accomplish some worthwhile end. Presumably if people better understood how adhering to justice and the rule of law served their interests, they would cease to perceive a conflict between their interest and the requirements of justice and the compliance problem would dissolve. This may be the most common and important source of a false perception of a gap between justice and interest.

Second, and far more rarely, a perception of conflict may arise when people find themselves in emergency situations—such as the occurrence of a natural disaster or a personal calamity. As was discussed in Chapter 1, the analysis of natural rights presented here employs a *given–if–then* type of reasoning: given certain facts about human beings and the world in which they live, if we want persons to be able to pursue happiness, peace, and prosperity while living in society with others, then we should respect certain rights. What happens when those facts markedly change?

Consider the classic example of two persons swimming for a floating wooden plank after their ship sinks. The plank can only support one of them. Who gets to use the plank? Does it matter who owned the wood before the ship sunk? Would it be murder for one person to push the other off the plank? If the "given" on which the liberal conception of justice depends is no longer true, then it may well be that the liberal conception of justice is inapplicable to this situation and either that there is no "just" solution or that another theory of justice or morality comes into play. If the normal fact of human social existence were like that of the two persons stranded at sea, then I doubt very much that the liberal conception of justice, much less the rule of law, would be of very much assistance in solving our problems.

To appreciate this implication of natural rights based in given–if–then reasoning consider vampires. According to the oft-told story, vampires *must* live by drinking human blood. Sometimes the tale is told in such a way as to eliminate the possibility of living off blood-bank or stored blood; blood must be taken from a living person. In a world of humans and vampires, would vampires be violating human rights by preying on them? Would human beings be violating vampire rights by defending themselves from attack? I suggest that the answer to both of these questions is no. An important assumption of justice is changed: the assumption that mutual coexistence, peace, and prosperity is possible, provided that the rules of justice are respected. Vampires may have rights against each other—e.g. an ownership claim against other vampires to prey on specific humans—and humans may have rights against each other, but members of each species have no rights against the other since mutual coexistence is made impossible by their basic natures. None of this is to deny that both vampires and humans might have moral duties towards each other, but only that they do not have rights against each other.[1]

Now consider Ben, a hiker in the wild, who has been seriously injured by a rockslide and who comes across an unoccupied cabin in which he seeks shelter. Can he break in without violating the rights of Ann, the cabin owner? Can he eat any food he may find within? When adhering to justice in such exceptional circumstances genuinely threatens a person's interests, some argue that this fact justifies making exceptions to the normal requirements of justice. A departure of the facts from what were assumed by the general precepts of just-

---

[1] I do not think that this analysis of coexistence renders the account of rights a "Hobbesean" one (though I am not much concerned with how it is labeled). According to Hobbes, in a "state of nature"—that is in the absence of a central authority—"every man has a right to everything, even to one another's body" (Thomas Hobbes, *Leviathan*, pt. I, ch. 14 [1651] (Indianapolis: Bobbs-Merrill, 1958), p. 110) and the need for peaceful coexistence justifies the creation of a central authority to whom a portion of these rights must be surrendered. Another way to formulate this is that, in the state of nature, there really are no rights at all to circumscribe boundaries on our freedom—there is no distinction between liberty and license—and peaceful coexistence requires the creation of a central authority to create such freedom-restricting rights. In other words, "first comes government, then come rights."

According to the view presented here, even in the absence of a central authority certain rights are needed to solve the problems of knowledge, interest, and power *on the assumption that mutual coexistence is possible*—though some would argue that the power to *enforcement* of these rights is best delegated from right-holders to a central authority. In other words, "first come rights, then comes government." In contrast with Hobbes, the rights that preexist the creation of a central authority provide the basis by which its behavior is to be assessed. But if peaceful coexistence is impossible, so are rights.

ice are said to rebut the normal presumption in favor of these precepts. While emergency situations may create a perception of a perceived conflict between justice and interest, then, if this argument is sound, no genuine conflict exists because, in just such emergency circumstances, the normally applicable precepts of justice are greatly altered or even inapplicable. In other words, if those who urge emergency exceptions to the regime of justice are correct, then these exceptional situations do not describe a genuine gap between justice and interest because in these circumstances the normal requirements of justice properly yield to interest.

There is another, and I think better, way to describe this situation. Ordinarily laws consistent with natural rights, such as those prohibiting burglary and theft, are binding in conscience, but under emergency life-threatening circumstances, some of these laws cease to have this binding effect. We might say that ordinarily one has a moral duty to adhere to the requirements of justice, but under emergency life-threatening situations, this moral duty is overridden by one's moral duty to preserve oneself. So in the example of the cabin, justice still requires that Ben refrain from breaking in, but morality does not. If he breaks in, we could hold Ben responsible for violating the rights of Ann, but not condemn him for acting immorally.

Drawing a distinction between justice and morality helps resolve two additional problems: does Ann, the cabin owner, have a background right to restitution from Ben, the hiker? Would Ann be violating the hiker's background rights by preventing him from occupying the cabin? If the rules of justice were entirely overridden by Ben's emergency, then Ann would have no background rights against him. Ben would not, for example, owe Ann any payment for the food he takes or the damage caused by his break-in—a conclusion that most who would permit the hiker to take the food would reject.

I think that this situation is not of a kind with that of the two persons swimming for the same plank. In the former example *both* persons are in an emergency situation that cannot be resolved by adhering to requirements of justice. In their situation, the liberal conception of justice might well perform no useful function and, for this reason, be inapplicable. In the latter case, the hiker is in an emergency situation, but the cabin owner is not. All the reasons for respecting the cabin owner's rights that have been examined to this point still hold, with respect to her and others in society (besides the hiker). True, because of the emergency, the hiker may have no *moral* duty to respect the cabin owner's rights and the cabin owner may have a moral duty to render assistance to the hiker. However, a legal system should still recognize and enforce the cabin owner's background rights—and she may do so on her own behalf—out of a concern to address problems of knowledge and interest in normal cases.

The implication of this analysis is that Ben would have no moral duty to respect the property rights of Ann and could break in and take shelter and food. If the cabin was unoccupied, Ben would still owe restitution for its use and any damages he caused.[2] If Ann was present, however, she would be "within her rights" to deny access to the cabin—that is, Ben would have no cause of action against her for preventing his entry. Perhaps she fears Ben might be dangerous; perhaps she is not sure Ben is really in desperate straits; perhaps she has just enough food for herself and her family; perhaps this happens often enough that she cannot afford to feed all the stranded hikers who don't pay afterwards. These are the sorts of decisions that only right-holders are in a position to make knowledgeably. Rights allocations are not made from the godly perspective of a person who knows the correct answers to all these questions.

In sum, sometimes the perception of a gap between justice and interest may be unfounded because the calculation of interest is inaccurate and other times because precepts of justice have become immaterial. Yet even if, as some people advocate, emergency conditions can sometimes release decisions about one's interest from the normal constraints of justice, there remains the potential for a gap between justice and interest when persons finding themselves in an emergency situation require assistance from others who do not share the same predicament and for whom the normal precepts of justice still apply. If, under this or any other circumstance, it is just to constrain a person who finds himself in an emergency situation, then this person may face a genuine gap between justice and interest. We may say that the source of this gap between justice and interest is *emergency conditions*.

Second, and far more commonly, acting unjustly may sometimes present opportunities for substantial material gains, particularly in the short run. Some people who have entered into contracts in good faith, for example, may perceive that performance is no longer in their interest when the time comes for them to perform their part of the bargain. This is particularly likely when they have already received the performance due them from the other party. Other persons who are interested solely in material gain are likely to commit such crimes as burglary, auto theft, and various kinds of fraud. These criminals are rarely armed and sometimes go to elaborate lengths to avoid confronting the victims of their acts. In these circumstances, we may say that the source of this gap between justice and interest is *pecuniary gain*.

Third, persons will perceive a genuine conflict between justice and interest when they gain great subjective satisfaction from committing an act that has been ruled out-of-bounds by principles of justice. Unfortunately, it is not as rare as we would like for a person to subjectively enjoy the sheer wrongfulness of an act. This phenomenon is typically associated with the commission of violent crimes, such as murder, rape, and armed robbery, but this sort of interest can also motivate persons to commit fraud against others. With violent

---

[2] If punishment for committing a crime is normally thought warranted, the absence of a moral duty of obedience might mitigate the severity of punishment or completely obviate any punishment of the hiker, though the continued existence of the owner's rights would still justify compelling payment of restitution.

crimes, the subjugation of the victim to the criminal's will rather than any material gain is often what motivates and gives satisfaction to the criminal. With crimes of fraud, outwitting the victim or "mark" is often what satisfies the criminal. We may say that the source of this gap between justice and interest is *psychological gain*.

To better understand how these factors create conflicts between justice and interest requires that we take into account the varying "time horizons"[3] of different people. Each person adopts a mix between present and future consumption. The mix depends upon one's psychological time horizon. When a person's time horizon is very short—referred to as a "high time preference"—he heavily discounts the value of any benefits to be received in the future. High time preferences are not necessarily bad or "irrational." For example, in wartime or in places where one's property rights are very insecure, a person may well be irrational to defer consumption of a good to the future since, when the future arrives, either the person or the good will no longer be around.

However, because many of the benefits gained from adhering to justice are future benefits, a very high time preference is quite likely to create a perceived gap between justice and interest. Because the benefits accruing from justice are often long term in nature, a high time preference exacerbates the gap between justice and interest that stems from the desire for either pecuniary or psychological gain. Persons who strongly prefer present to future values are far more likely than others to value immediate pecuniary or psychological gain over the more long-range benefits (which may also be pecuniary and psychological) of adhering to the requirements of justice. In sum, to the extent that future benefits have little subjective value to a person with a high time preference, the constraints imposed by justice may not have enough appeal to outweigh the benefits to be gained by acting unjustly.

Related to this is another situation in which a gap between justice and interest is likely to arise: when, for whatever reason, people have lived their lives in such a way as to no longer be in a position to obtain gains from cooperation with others. Someone who has dropped out of school and pursued a life on the streets or in a gang may not have much by way of marketable skills—and by skills I include the habits of honesty, punctuality, and reliability that full-time employment requires. At this point in his life, the benefits to be gained by cooperative activity that respects the rights of others may be substantially outweighed by those to be gained by acting unjustly, for example, by stealing cars or burglarizing houses.

To deal with genuine gaps between justice and interest and achieve just conduct in practice, some way is needed to align the perception of interest with the requirements of justice. Perhaps the most pervasive and effective means of achieving compliance with justice is *socialization*. Socialization is particularly

---

[3] This term was introduced in Chapter 8.

effective because it prevents gaps from arising in the first instance by affecting people's subjective perception of their interest. In cultures that best handle the knowledge and partiality problems, people are able to imbue in others a respect for basic principles of justice so that these values become a part of the subjective preferences of most individuals. Parents imbue this attitude in their children, teachers in their students, clergy in their congregations, etc. This strategy is particularly effective when the benefits of adhering to principles of justice are well-understood.

Of course, socialization can be a powerful mechanism for bad as well as for good. People can and often are socialized to accept as in their interest both immoral and unjust actions. For example, some may be socialized to accept or practice invidious discrimination against others; some engaged in business may be socialized to accept or lobby for subsidies or trade protection that violate others' rights of several property or freedom of contract. Nevertheless, when socialization is put in the service of justice and subjective perceptions of interest are suitably altered, the perceived conflict between principles of justice and interest is usually eliminated and compliance is achieved. When, however, this process fails and the conflict between interest and justice remains, those who are motivated by interest will still be inclined to act contrary to the dictates of justice.

A special compliance problem arises when a gap exists between the formal requirements of the rule of law and the interest of one who is charged with administering justice. We need somehow to close the gap between the fair conduct that the rule of law requires of the legal system itself and the partiality that can affect the behavior of those who participate in the legal system. Securing compliance with the rule of law shares much in common with the problem of securing compliance with justice and this aspect of the partiality problem may be viewed as a special case of the compliance problem. Yet it deserves special attention because it peculiarly applies to those charged with administering justice. While we can deal with the general problem of compliance with justice by appealing to institutions whose job it is to develop and apply principles of justice, to whom do we appeal to get these institutions to adhere, not only to precepts of justice, but also to the fair procedures required by the rule of law? Acknowledging the problem of compliance with the rule of law forces us to consider the generally neglected question, "Who guards the guardians?" I shall return to this issue in Chapter 13.

2. Using Force to Achieve Compliance

In previous chapters we discussed some ways of closing the gaps that may arise between desirable conduct and the interest of the actor. Requiring the consent of right-holders before transferring rights, for example, helps provide incentives for making knowledgeable decisions about resource use. Requiring that judges adhere to the rule of law makes it more apparent when they decide to exercise partiality. In the previous section, I suggested that socialization encourages persons to incorporate a concern for justice into their assessment of subjective interest. Yet even with these and other techniques in place, people will sometimes consider it in their interest to disregard their knowledge in making decisions and to act contrary to the requirements of justice and the rule of law. What further means are available to close these residual gaps?

I now turn my attention to the most obvious alternative that has until this point been conspicuously absent from my discussion of justice and the rule of law: the use or threatened use of forcible coercion or *power*. A secondary mechanism, and a distant second at that, for achieving compliance with justice is to use or threaten to use forcible coercion or power (I shall use the terms "force" and "power" interchangeably). The compliance problem refers to situations in which "bad" persons are willing for reasons of interest to act unjustly or illegally. For such persons, force can be a potent way of rendering harmonious both justice and interest, provided that the practice of using force to defend against and rectify rights violations is effectively communicated to them.

Notice that *no use of force is needed to solve the problem of knowledge*. Taken in isolation, the knowledge problem assumes that persons are willing to act justly toward each other provided only that they know what justice requires of them. The knowledge problem refers to the fundamental problems for which justice and the rule of law are needed that arise even for "good" persons. Once the appropriate principles of justice are known and followed, the knowledge problem is resolved. The use of force or power is only needed when we take into account the problem of interest—in particular, when there exists a perceived gap between interest and the requirements of justice or the rule of law.

In short, while communicating the requirements of justice can alone handle the problem of knowledge, the compliance problem sometimes requires the credible threat of force or power to handle the gap between justice and interest that socialization alone cannot close. A credible threat consists of the willingness to use force and an effective means of communicating this willingness to others. There are several different ways it can be used to affect the calculation of interest so as to bring the calculation in line with tenets of justice.

First, force may be used in advance of unjust conduct (*ex ante*) to prevent such conduct from occurring. Preventive detention of criminals and court "injunctions" in civil cases ordering that some action either be halted or be performed to avoid future harm are two examples of *ex ante* force. Another example is the advance "regulation" of individual activity by government agencies. Second, force may be used during the commission of an unjust act to resist or repel its commission. Traditional self-defense is an example of this type of force. Third, force can be used after (*ex post*) the commission of an unjust act to impose a penalty upon or exact compensation from a person who has acted unjustly. Imprisonment of criminals and the awarding of money damages to injured persons are two examples of the *ex post* use of force. To the extent that these practices are well-known in a given society, they can substantially raise the expected costs to a person contemplating acting unjustly. In this way, these exercises of force or power or their threat can potentially alter the calculation of interest made by persons contemplating acting unjustly and narrow or eliminate the gap between justice and interest.

Using Force to Collect Restitution

In theory, victims of crime have always had a right to restitution from the person who victimized them. Tort law gives victims the right to sue criminals for the damages caused by their crimes. Moreover, after a period of agitation on behalf of victims' rights beginning in the 1970s, most states in the US have passed victim restitution legislation that permits judges to order criminals to make restitution to their victims (though usually these statutes do not make restitution an enforceable right).[4] In practice, however, comparatively few victims receive restitution because criminals cannot now be forced to pay, and the more serious the offense the less likely is restitution even to be ordered. One supporter of restitution programs who is critical of their implementation to date criticizes, among other things the "too rigid selection criteria" of most programs: "Almost all such programs serve only property or first-time offenders. . . . Participants in restitution and mediation programs are usually low-risk offenders; come from white, middle-class backgrounds; and are better educated. Minority offenders are the exception."[5] The reason for this is apparent:

---

[4] The literature on various restitution proposals and programs is enormous. See e.g. Charles F. Abel and Frank F. Marsh, *Punishment and Restitution: A Restitutionary Approach to Crime and the Criminal* (Westport, Conn.: Greenwood Press, 1984); Stephen Schafer, *Compensation and Restitution to Victims of Crime* (Montclair, NJ: Patterson Smith, 1970); Martin Wright, *Justice for Victims and Offenders: A Restorative Response to Crime* (Philadelphia, Pa.: Open University Press, 1991). A cross-section of perspectives on restitution programs can be found in a series of anthologies edited by Professors Burt Galaway and Joe Hudson. See Burt Galaway and Joe Hudson (eds.), *Criminal Justice, Restitution, and Reconciliation* (Monsay, NY: Criminal Justice Press, 1991); Burt Galaway and Joe Hudson, (eds.), *Perspectives on Crime Victims* (St. Louis, Mo.: C.V. Mosby, 1981); Joe Hudson and Burt Galaway (eds.), *Victims, Offenders, and Alternative Sanctions* (Lexington, Mass.: Lexington Books, 1980); Joe Hudson and Burt Galaway (eds.), *Restitution in Criminal Sanctions* (Lexington, Mass.: Lexington Books, 1975); Joe Hudson and Burt Galaway (eds.), *Considering the Victim* (Springfield, Ill.: Charles C. Thomas, 1975).

[5] Elmar Weitekamp, "Can Restitution Serve as a Reasonable Alternative to Imprisonment? An Assessment of the Situation in the USA," in H. Messmer and H.-U. Otto (eds.), *Restorative Justice in Trial* (The Netherlands: Kluwer Academic Publishers, 1992). See also Elmar Weitekamp, "Recent Developments on Restitution and Victim-Offender Reconciliation in the USA and Canada," in Gunther Kaiser, Helmut Kury, and Hans-Jorg Albrecht, *Victims and Criminal Justice: Legal Protection, Restitution, and Support* (Freiburg: Max Planck Institute, 1991).

many criminals, but by no means all, have little money and no regular earnings from which to make court-ordered restitution, and judges know it. Those who do have money often deny it and are routinely believed. As important, when the normal response to crime is to punish criminals by imprisonment, criminals who are incarcerated have no means by which to make restitution.

While existing restitution programs are certainly a step in the right direction, a more thorough adherence to the liberal conception of justice promises to make the collection of restitution from most criminals a real, rather than a merely theoretical possibility. Because victims would have an *enforceable* right to restitution, unlike today, agencies acting on the victim's behalf would be justified in using force to incarcerate criminals who could not be entrusted to make restitution on their own. Any agency that confined convicted criminals for this purpose would be legally obliged to provide them with productive work at market wages reflecting their productivity in a secure environment. Their wages would be used to pay for their living costs and to make reparations to their victims. And they would be released only when full restitution had been made or when it was adjudged that reparations could more quickly be made by unconfined employment.[6] Prisoners in such a system might even engage in collective bargaining and would be entitled to take legal action to ensure that their rights are respected.

Contrary to popular prejudice, confinement need not be synonymous with nonproductivity. And productivity is not synonymous with chain gangs. Recent years have witnessed a boom in prison employment. For example, experimental projects in the United States have used prison labor to build low-cost houses,[7] restore automobiles and make limousines,[8] and manufacture such goods as computer disk drives, blue jeans[9] and other types of clothing.[10] "Inmates staff phone lines and book reservations for Trans World Airlines and Best Western International. They have been employed as telemarketers by AT&T, and they staff State-tourism toll-free telephone lines in at least one dozen states."[11] Among women inmates employed in prison industry:

---

[6] See Kathleen D. Smith, "Implementing Restitution Within a Penal Setting: The Case for the Self-Determinate Sentence," in Hudson and Galaway (eds.), *Restitution in Criminal Justice*, pp. 131–46.

[7] See Stephen Buckley, "From Destroying Lives to Building Dreams—Housing Project is Foundation for Inmates," *Washington Post*, Aug. 10 1992, at D1 (reporting on Maryland program); Keith A. Harrison, "Rebuilding Futures Inmates Work on Houses and their Lives," *Washington Post*, Mar. 26 1994, at B1 (reporting on Washington, DC program).

[8] See "Restoring Autos and People," *Washington Post*, Oct. 28 1993, at T5.

[9] Steven Mardon, "Inmate Jeans Catch on in Oregon," *Corrections Today*, July 1992, p. 29.

[10] See William Kissel, "Behind Bars for Rape and Murder, Convicts Vie for the Chance to Cut and Sew for Sportswear Labels," *Los Angeles Times*, Jan. 16 1992, at E1.

[11] Jonathan M. Cowen, "One Nation's 'Gulag' is Another Nation's 'Factory Within a Fence': Prison-Labor in the People's Republic of China and the United States of America," *UCLA Pacific Basin Law Journal*, vol. 12 (1993), p. 211.

The most common programs are sewing (in 25 states), data entry/data processing (in 16 states), reupholstering furniture (in seven states), microfilming (in six states) and telemarketing (in six states). Women are also involved in farming, printing and manufacturing items such as glasses, decals, sewn products and circuit boards.[12]

Prisoners have also manufactured goods for state governments:

In New York, for example, prison inmates make office furniture, metal cabinets, and cleaning supplies that can be used by the state government. In Minnesota, inmates manufacture road signs and prison clothing. In other parts of the country, inmates manufacture military helmets, electrical cables, and wooden furniture.[13]

It is no accident that present programs are new, rudimentary, and experimental. The Ashurst–Sumner Act of 1935 completely banned the interstate commerce of "any goods, wares, and merchandise manufactured, produced, or mined wholly or in part by convicts or prisoners"[14] in any prison in the United States and its territories. In 1979 the statute was amended to create an exception to this prohibition for "not more that seven pilot projects."[15] The motivation for restricting the number of such projects was also made explicit by Congress:

The provisions of this section creating exemptions to Federal restrictions on the marketability of prison made goods shall not apply unless—

(1) representatives of local union central bodies or similar labor union organizations have been consulted prior to the initiation of any project qualifying of any exemption created by this section; and

(2) such paid inmate employment will not result in the displacement of employed workers, or be applied in skills, crafts, or trades in which there is a surplus of available gainful labor in the locality, or impair existing contracts for services.[16]

Only in 1990 was this statute again amended to permit "not more than 50 non-Federal prison work pilot projects."[17] And both these state pilot programs and comparable Federal projects are hobbled, not only because they are administered by government agencies, but by numerous restrictions imposed upon them by Congress at the behest of both business and labor interests,[18] and at the expense of the interests of crime victims.

---

[12] Donna Duncan, "ACA Survey Examines Industry Programs for Women Offenders," *Corrections Today*, Feb. 1992, p. 114.

[13] Jeff Potts, "American Penal Institutions and Two Alternative Proposals for Punishment," *South Texas Law Review*, vol. 34 (1993), p. 500.

[14] Ashurst–Sumner Act, ch. 412, § 1, 49 Stat. 494 (1935) (current version at 18 U.S.C. § 1761 (*a*)).

[15] 18 U.S.C. § 1761 (*a*) (as it appears prior to 1990 amendment).

[16] Pub.L. 90–351, Title I, § 827(c), as added Pub.L. 96–157, § 2, Dec, 27, 1979, 93 Stat. 1215. See also Gail S. Funke, Billy L. Wayson, and Neal Miller, *Assets and Liabilities of Correctional Industries* (Lexington, Mass.: Lexington Books, 1982), p. 2 (The original depression-era prohibition "was enacted mainly because of pressures from garment workers.").

[17] 18 U.S.C. 1761 (*c*) (1).

[18] See e.g. 18 U.S.C. § 1722(*b*)(2) ("Federal Prison Industries shall conduct its operations so as to produce products on an economic basis, but shall avoid capturing more

The past experience with prison labor suggests that, although there are obvious difficulties in supplanting completely the current system of imprisonment with a system of prison employment, the idea of productive prison labor cannot be dismissed as impractical until it is fully permitted. We may reasonably assume that the demand for such labor is sufficiently great to motivate competitors to lobby for legislation prohibiting the freedom to contract of producers and consumers of prison-made goods. History may also be a guide: "In 1885, 90 percent of the inmate population were employed in state-prison industries. Nearly a hundred years later, 10 percent or about 30,000 prisoners were so employed."[19]

Wholly apart from employing prisoners, private companies have also been building conventional prisons under contract with local and federal authorities for some time now. Such companies as Corrections Corporation of America, Behavioral Systems Southwest, Palo Duro Private Detention Services and the security firm, Wackenhut, have built and operated corrections facilities in Arizona, California, Florida, Kentucky, Pennsylvania, Tennessee, and Texas.[20] Moreover, as Bruce Benson notes, "almost every aspect of corrections, including food services, counseling, industrial program[s], maintenance, security, education, and vocational training, is under contract with private firms on a piecemeal basis."[21] In his comprehensive study of current private prisons operating under contracts with governments, Charles Logan concludes:

I have examined here every known criticism of private prisons and jails, and I do not dismiss any of them lightly. However, I have been unable to find any criticism of private facilities that cannot be matched by equally serious and analogous criticism of noncontracted facilities. Virtually all potential problems facing private prisons have close counterparts among the problems troubling prisons run directly by government. All prisons, both public and private, face challenges in the areas of authority, legitimacy, procedural justice, accountability, liability, cost, security, safety, corruptibility, and so on. They face these challenges primarily because of the nature of their mission, not because of their incorporation as public or private entities.[22]

than a reasonable share of the market among Federal departments, agencies, and institutions for any specific product."); ibid. § 1722 (*b*)(4)(A–C) ("The corporation shall prepare a detailed written analysis of the probable impact on industry and free labor of the plans for new production or expanded production. . . . The corporation shall announce in a publication designed to most effectively provide notice to potentially affected private vendors the plans to produce any new product or to significantly expand production of an existing product. . . . The corporation shall directly advise those affected trade associations that the corporation can reasonably identify the plans for new production or expanded production, and the corporation shall invite such trade associations to submit comments on those plans."); 18 U.S.C. § 4123 ("Any industry established under this chapter shall be so operated as not to curtail the production of any existing arsenal, navy yard, or other Government workshop.").

[19] Funke, Wayson, and Miller, *Assets and Liabilities*, p. 5.
[20] See Benson, *Enterprise of Law*, pp. 182–3.   [21] Ibid. 182.
[22] Charles Logan, *Private Prisons* (Oxford: Oxford University Press, 1990), p. 237.

As a "faint approximation" of the potential for private prisons coupled with prison labor, Logan cites the experience of the Maine State Prison. For 40 years inmates at this maximum security had produced wooden craft items and novelties which were sold through a prison-run store.

In 1976, a new warden was hired who instituted changes that allowed the inmates greater economic liberty. As a result, Maine's novelty sales program blossomed rapidly into what was undoubtedly the most economically successful inmate craft program in the country. What the new warden did was to appoint a supervisory novelty committee, composed primarily of inmates, and to significantly raise the upper limits on value, variety, and volume of output allowed per inmate. The revenue cap, for example, went from $5,000 a year in 1976 to $15,000 in 1978. To circumvent even these limits, more enterprising businessmen took on partners, buying their quotas in exchange for a share in the profits.

In contrast to most prison industry programs, which employ only a small fraction of the population, the crafts industry at MSP, at its peak, involved from half to three-quarters of the inmates. In 1979, the prison store had gross sales of over half a million dollars. To keep the store open longer hours, inmates themselves paid the overtime salaries of the state-employed store managers. Some inmates were said to earn over $38,000 per year, with claims as high as $100,000 for the most successful "novelty kings."

An unusual aspect of the MSP program was that it allowed inmates to form businesses and employ other inmates. This promoted labor specialization, managerial skills, and productivity. The inmate economy was also allowed to have a legal and transferable currency, in the form of canteen coupons. This currency allowed the development of a secondary economy within the prison, offering such services as a barbershop, laundry, and television rentals.

The novelty committee . . . issued patents for new product patterns designed by inmates. Although inmates were restricted in the number of patents that they could own personally, these were effectively transferable property rights. When patent holders left prison, they would sell their patents to others. One inmate controlled 50 patterns, only 10 of which could be in his own name.[23]

Logan concludes that "what developed at the Maine State prison was not just an inmate work program, but an environment that allowed prisoners to become entrepreneurs."[24]

We may summarize all this as follows: In light of the right to use force to collect restitution, the formulation of justice should be modified:

---

[23] Ibid. 251–2. I have visited the prison store and witnessed the amazing variety and quality of the items sold there.

[24] Ibid. 252. The enterprise largely ended when the Director of Corrections, advised by outside corrections experts that the staff had lost control of the institution, confined all prisoners to their cells for two and a half months and, following the lock-down, imposed new restrictions on the crafts industry. "The cap on gross income was cut from $15,000 to $8,000, canteen coupons were declared nontransferable, and procedural restrictions were placed on inter-inmate employment." Ibid. While Logan concurs in the judgment that the staff had lost too much control, he questions whether this was properly blamed "on having a strong and relatively unrestricted inmate economy." Ibid.

FORMULATION 5. *Justice is respect for the rights of individuals and associations.*

(1) The *right of several property* specifies a right to acquire, possess, use, and dispose of scarce physical resources—including their own bodies. Resources may be used in any way that does not physically interfere with other persons' use and enjoyment of their resources. While most property rights are freely alienable, the right to one's person is inalienable.

(2) The *right of first possession* specifies that property rights to unowned resources are acquired by being the first to establish control over them and to stake a claim

(3) The *right of freedom of contract* specifies that a rightholder's consent is both necessary (freedom *from* contract) and sufficient (freedom *to* contract) to transfer alienable property rights—both during one's life and, by using a "will," upon one's death. A manifestation of assent is ordinarily necessary unless one party somehow has access to the other's subjective intent.

(4) Violating these rights by *force or fraud* is unjust.

(5) The *right of restitution* requires that one who violates the rights that define justice must compensate the victim of the rights violation for the harm caused by the injustice, **and such compensation may be collected by force, if necessary.**

Implementing this proposal requires a merger of three now-separate reform movements that have been growing since the 1970s: the victims' rights movement (which begat restitution statutes nationwide), the prison labor movement (which brought industries into prisons and prisoners into industries), and the private prison movement (which has built and operated prisons under contract with governments). Prior experience with restitution programs, prison industry, and private prisons does not prove that the proposal made here will work, but suggests that further reforms in this direction are worth pursuing.

While these reforms would likely pose many problems (as does our present system), two objections immediately come to the minds of most when first confronted with the idea. What about restitution awards that in many cases would exceed the ability of prison employees to repay? And what about wealthy criminals who could easily make restitution and go free?

The fact that full compensation might be impossible to collect in some cases would provide a powerful incentive to buy crime insurance and the comparative efficiency of restitution employment projects to obtain payments from criminals would be reflected in insurance premiums. Insurance companies who made full payments to victims could reserve a right of subrogation in their insurance contracts giving them the right to collect payments from criminals in place of the already compensated victim. Most importantly, when the damages caused by a criminal are so extensive than he would never be able to earn enough to make full restitution, an insurance company or victim would have a powerful incentive to reduce the amount to a level that could be repaid.

Otherwise, the offender would have no incentive to make any payments at all.

While it is unlikely that indigent criminals would be asked to make more restitution than they can reasonably be expected to earn, there would be no need to compromise with wealthy criminals. They would certainly have to make full restitution, which could be very substantial. Those who accept the justice of punishing criminal offenders need only slightly modify the proposal presented here to require that all intentional rights violators be confined to an employment facility until a specified level of restitution had been earned there.

While some are concerned with the justice of letting wealthy criminals escape punishment by making full restitution, others worry that the wealthy will have little incentive to refrain from committing crimes in a system of pure restitution. Such concerns, though not entirely unwarranted, are usually wildly exaggerated and often border on the fanciful. The subjective costs to the wealthy of being convicted of committing a serious crime are much greater than the cost of making reparations. The wealthy tend to place a very high subjective premium on their social standing and other sorts of reputational effects that would be severely damaged by a successful prosecution. Many would suffer heavy business losses if the potential for such criminal conduct became known. Indeed, these sorts of subjective costs account, far more than punishment, for why the wealthy do not and have never posed the same magnitude of a crime threat as those who are less well off. Does anyone seriously believe that it is the threat of punishment that makes the streets of Beverly Hills, Brentwood, or Palm Springs safer than those in the inner city?

Another deterrent to wealthy offenders was discovered by the early Icelanders whose system of justice was based largely on restitution. As related in *Njal's Saga*,[25] Hallgert, an evil woman, ordered her overseer, an "utter scoundrel" named Kol, to murder Svart, the beloved servant of Njal and his wife, Bergthora. Gunnar, Hallgert's wealthy husband, informed Njal of the killing,[26] and the two of them met to settle the matter. Gunnar told Njal to "name the terms of compensation."[27] Njal accepted this offer and said: "I am not going to make an issue out of this. You are to pay twelve ounces of silver. But I want to add this condition: that you should be no less lenient with us if you ever have to assess compensation for something that we are responsible for."[28] One day when Njal produced the purse with the silver he had been paid

[25] Magnus Magnusson and Herman Pálsson, trans., *Njal's Saga* (London: Penguin Books, 1960).
[26] In this system, "[a]ccording to the law, it was necessary to announce the killing promptly; otherwise, the killer was guilty of the much more serious crime of 'secret murder'" Ibid. 105 n.*. Whereas an unconcealed homicide was sanctioned exclusively by restitution, a secret murder could result in the death of the offender. As will be seen in the next section discussing the right of extended self-defense, this distinction might well be consistent with the conception of justice described here.
[27] Ibid. 100.   [28] Ibid.

by Gunnar, his son asked, "What is that, father?" Njal answered, "This is the money that Gunnar paid me last summer for our servant." His son grinned and replied, "That will come in handy."[29]

Sometime after this, Bergthora hired Atli as her servant on the condition that he be prepared to do whatever she asked, even to kill someone. He agreed and, while Njal was away, she ordered him to find and kill Kol, which he did. When Njal was informed of the slaying, he took the purse he had saved and went to see Gunnar. "This is bad," he said, "that my wife should have broken our settlement and had your servant killed." He then told Gunnar to name his compensation. "Very well," said Gunnar. "I put an equal price on the two men, Svart and Kol; and you are to pay me 12 ounces of silver." Njal then handed the purse to Gunnar, who recognized it as being the money that he himself had given Njal.[30] The story concludes: "Gunnar and Njal took care that nothing else happened that year."[31]

This story illustrates the potential for reprisals that wealthy offenders, above all others, would have to fear in a system of restitution. For the amount previously paid in restitution could, if the victim or the victims' friends and family so wished, be used to make complete restitution for the commission of a like offense against the wealthy offender. While this may not seem an entirely attractive aspect of a system of restitution,[32] it would nevertheless serve as a potential deterrent to wealthy offenders. Indeed, it might well provide a more effective deterrent than the likelihood that our current system will catch, successfully prosecute, and punish a wealthy offender—particularly if a successful reprisal is well-publicized as it was among Icelanders by *Njal's Saga*. The potential for reprisals was simply one feature of Iceland's decentralized legal order, an order which, either despite or because of its lack of centralized public law enforcement, appears to have been relatively peaceful.[33]

On the other hand, the fact that they would have to give up the restitution they had received as reparations would cause victims to consider long and hard whether they really want a reprisal. Not only would a reprisal truly cost

[29] Ibid. 101.　　　　[30] Ibid. 103.　　　　[31] Ibid. 104.
[32] For those who are bothered by the "private" nature of such reprisals, it could be institutionalized by allowing victims to choose between receiving restitution or inflicting punishment. One problem with this option is that it legitimates reprisals in a way that the approach described here does not. Because an act of reprisal against an offender by a victim who is willing to pay restitution is not rightful, the offender retains his right of self defense and cannot be sanctioned for exercising it. This is a risk that victims must run when seeking reprisals.
[33] See Jesse L. Byock, *Medieval Iceland: Society, Sagas, and Power* (Berkeley: University of California Press, 1988), p. 36 ("Because the rules of feuding . . . regulated conflict and limited breakdowns of order, violence was kept within acceptable bounds throughout most of the history of the Free State."); William Ian Miller, *Bloodtaking and Peacemaking: Feud, Law, and Society in Saga Iceland* (Chicago: University of Chicago Press, 1990), p 304 ("The sagas do not show people *continually* living with the anticipation of violence, rape, or expropriation that many American urban dwellers must live with daily.") Moreover, as an aside, "[j]urally and actually, [women] were less disabled than their continental counterparts of equivalent social ranges." Ibid. 305.

them something, but they would have to take full responsibility for it. This stands in sharp contrast with our system today which effectively offers victims only punishment, and a punishment they must neither pay for nor be responsible for executing. I suggest that a less retributivist state of mind would likely result from a system in which victims and their families had to choose between accepting complete restitution or arranging for a reprisal as compared to a system in which government-authored punishment is the victim's only option. That the right of restitution—or composition—largely supplanted the blood feud in medieval Europe tends to support this suggestion.[34]

For these reasons, I do not expect that requiring the wealthy to make full restitution will greatly expand their criminality. Were this to occur, however, the liberal conception of justice does sanction *additional* actions against such persons. I now turn to the principle of justice which permits preventive action to be taken to defend against any person, including a wealthy one, who has proven by his or her conduct to be a threat to the rights of others.

Using Force to Prevent Crime

For the past several centuries, crimes and torts have been considered distinct types of legal causes of action. Whereas the commission of a tort justifies compensation to the injured victim, the commission of a crime is thought to justify the imposition of punishment. In an analysis in which, to this point, all rights violation are rectified by exacting compensation from the rights violator, there seems little reason to distinguish torts from crimes. In this section, I will argue that the principle of restitution requires supplementation and, when supplemented, the crime–tort distinction reemerges.

Let me begin by clarifying my earlier claims about restitution.[35] I have claimed that:

(1) injustice arises when one person violates the rights of another;
(2) justice requires the rectification of this rights violation;
(3) rectification should consist of forcing the offender to raise the victim up (restitution) rather than an effort to lower the criminal to the level of his victim (punishment).

---

[34] See Berman, *Law and Revolution*, pp. 52–6. It was not until the rise of the nation state in Europe that truly awful grisly punishments—via what we now think of as criminal law—were superimposed upon and eventually supplanted composition—what we now think of as tort law—as the principal means of dealing with offenses against others.

[35] See Randy E. Barnett and John Hagel III, "Assessing the Criminal: Restitution, Retribution, and the Legal Process," in Barnett and Hagel, *Assessing the Criminal*, p. 1; Randy E. Barnett, "Restitution: A New Paradigm of Criminal Justice," *Ethics*, vol. 87 (1977), p. 279; Randy E. Barnett, "The Justice of Restitution," *American Journal of Jurisprudence*, vol. 25 (1980), p. 117; Randy E. Barnett, "Pursuing Justice in a Free Society: Part Two—Crime Prevention and the Legal Order," *Criminal Justice Ethics*, Winter/Spring 1986, p. 30; see also Randy E. Barnett, "Resolving the Dilemma of the Exclusionary Rule: An Application of Restitutive Principles of Justice," *Emory Law Journal*, vol. 32 (1983), p. 937 (assessing the deterrent effects of a restitutive alternative to the exclusionary rule).

By removing punishment from the focus of criminal justice, so too is removed an inquiry into the desert or blameworthiness of the offender of the kind that is needed to justify the imposition of punishment. In the liberal conception of justice, of which the principle of restitution is simply a part, restitution describes, in my view, the appropriate response to a rights violation. Doing justice requires restoration of the victim, not punishment of the offender.[36]

The problem of crime *prevention* is not, however, the same as the problem of rectifying rights violations. And the liberal conception of justice does not require that we wait for injury to occur before we deem a right to have been violated. The liberal conception of justice prohibits not only the unjustified use of force against another, but the unjustified *threat* of force as well. For example, the crime of assault occurs when one person "engages in conduct which places another in reasonable apprehension of receiving a battery."[37] Still, the prohibition of threats to use force does not suggest that such threats be rectified by punishment or incarceration rather than by restitution.

There is, however, another principle of justice that bears on the question of preventing future crimes. It is the right of self-defense that permits persons to use force to repel a threat of wrongful harm before the harm occurs. In the words of the Illinois statute providing for the use of force in defense of a person, "[a] person is justified in the use of force against another when and to the extent that he reasonably believes that such conduct is necessary to defend himself or another against the imminent use of unlawful force."[38] Similarly, the Illinois statute for the use of force in defense of a dwelling states that "[a] person is justified in the use of force against another when and to the extent that he reasonably believes that such conduct is necessary to prevent or terminate such other's unlawful entry into or attack upon a dwelling."[39] Finally, the Illinois statute for use of force in defense of other property states that:

A person is justified in the use of force against another when and to the extent that he reasonably believes that such conduct is necessary to prevent or terminate such other's trespass on or other tortious or criminal interference with either real property (other than a dwelling) or personal property, lawfully in his possession or in the possession of another who is a member of his immediate family or household or of a person whose property he has a legal duty to protect.[40]

Of course, each of these statutory embodiments of the traditional right of self-defense is limited to *imminent* attacks, or attacks and trespasses already in progress.[41] This limitation is well-founded, I think, because of the enormous knowledge problem that would be confronted if we were to permit self-defense

---

[36] I do not claim to have completely demonstrated this proposition either in my earlier writings, or in this book. However, I do offer additional arguments on behalf of this position in Part III, where I discuss the problems of enforcement error and abuse, and in Chapter 15, where I discuss problems with retributive theories of punishment.

[37] See e.g. Illinois Annotated Statutes, ch. 720, sect. 5/12–1 (Smith-Hurd 1993).

[38] Ibid. sect. 5/7–1.   [39] Ibid. sect. 5/7–2.   [40] Ibid. sect. 5/7–3.

[41] Though advocates of a battered woman's defense would extend the right of self-defense much further.

actions prior to a threat becoming imminent. Moreover, serious problems of interest would arise as well when those who are not facing threats falsely assert a right of self-defense to escape responsibility for their own rights violations against others.

Still, the right of self-defense is intriguing and revealing for three reasons. First, it sanctions the use of force *prior* to the infliction of harm in order to prevent its infliction instead of simply permitting the collection of restitution *ex post* for any harm that may have been inflicted.[42] Second, it does not legitimate the use of force to *punish* a prospective injurer for a harmful action he has yet to commit, but rather to *prevent* that person from committing an injurious act. Third, to determine whether or not a threat exists we require a showing that an unlawful threat is imminent, and to show this, we inquire into conduct that reveals the manifested intent of the aggressor. For example, the brandishing of a weapon in such a manner as to suggest an intention to fire it at another would justify the use of self-defense by the intended victim or by another going to her defense. Thus, while the right of self-defense is preventative, not punitive, the intention of the person against whom force is being used is highly relevant to determining the reasonableness of a self-defense action.

The question then arises, what theory best accounts for the right of self-defense and would this same theory also account for some other forms of preventative uses of force against prospective criminals, such as preventive detention? Let me begin by posing a series of hypotheticals. Suppose Ben takes out a gun and moves towards Ann stating, "I'm going to kill you!" Would she or anyone else in the room be justified in using force to restrain him or even possibly to kill him as a means of protecting Ann from harm? Of course, the answer is yes. She need not wait until after Ben has shot her to use force to collect restitution (or to punish him). In addition to any right of rectification she may have should he succeed in harming her, she and others may also use force to prevent him from succeeding.[43]

---

[42] The continued existence of a right of self-defense enables us to distinguish "property rules" for which violation restitution is owed from "liability rules" which permit certain actions provided compensation is made. See Guido Calabresi and Douglas Melamed, "Property Rules, Liability Rules, and Inalienability: One View of the Cathedral," *Harvard Law Review*, vol. 85 (1972), p. 1089. When a property rule is violated the property right-holder may use self-defense, but there is no right to defend oneself against violations of liability rules.

[43] Third parties sometimes stand in a different relationship to victims in asserting the right to use force in defense of others. For example, whereas a person who has previously committed a criminal act may know that the person afterwards confronting him is acting in self-defense, bystanders may reasonably assume that the victim is actually an aggressor. Those engaging in self-defense assume the risk that their actions will manifest an intention to violate the rights of another, even though this is not actually the case. As George Smith writes: "[T]he user of unidentified violence, innocent or not, sends the message of 'Invader' to the public in general. A Third Party, therefore, acting on the signal generated by the apparent Invader, is justified in exercising his primary right of defensive violence. Again, it is not just the reasonableness of the Third Party that exonerates him, but the fact that his belief is triggered by the violent actions of the apparent

What is it about Ben's actions that create in Ann and others a right of self-defense? I suggest that self-defense is justified because his conduct objectively manifests or *communicates* his intention to violate Ann's rights. We are accustomed to the claim that criminal laws be used to "send a message" *to* potential criminals. I suggest that self-defense is a justifiable response to a message communicated *by* a potential criminal.

Now, suppose we modify the hypothetical a bit by eliminating the statement "I'm going to kill you!" What result? In the absence of any explicit statement, the meaning of Ben's conduct—taking out a gun and moving towards Ann—is somewhat less clear, but surely clear enough to find that he is communicating the very same message and that self-defense would still be justified.

Suppose now that Ben is no longer brandishing a gun and makes no statement. When he step towards Anne, his subjective or inner intention may be the same, and he may have a weapon concealed beneath his jacket. The message being communicated is far from clear, however, and probably is not a clear enough threat to justify Ann using self-defense. But notice how contextual this judgment is. Consider the following additional fact. Suppose that yesterday, Ben sent Ann a letter stating that he would kill her sometime within the next forty-eight hours. Now a sudden movement in her direction, even absent a gun or an explicit statement of intention, might seem to communicate a threat.

The point of these hypotheticals is to reveal that a threat is a form of communication, the message of which is, "I intend to violate the rights of another." When the message is sufficiently unambiguous, we may conclude that preventative actions in the form of self-defense are warranted. When an individual sends such a message, we are justified to act—not to punish or to compensate—but to prevent a communicated threat from being carried out. And the more irreparable the threatened act, the more we may be entitled to do to prevent its commission. To understand what bearing this theory might have on crime prevention, let us consider some further variations on our hypothetical threat.

Suppose now that Ben takes out a full page ad in the *New York Times* in which he declares his intention to kill Ann within the next week. Suppose further that there is reason to believe that this threat is serious, not a parody or joke, and that Ben has the means to carry it out. When Ben approaches Ann on the street, does she have to wait until he produces a weapon of some kind before she or another may use force to restrain him? Indeed, need she wait passively until Ben chooses the time and place for his attack? Or would Ann be

Invader". George H. Smith, "A Reply to Critics," *Journal of Libertarian Studies*, vol. 3, (1979), pp. 453, 458. This notion is akin to the objective theory of assent in contract law and to apparent authority in agency law. See Barnett, *Sound of Silence*, pp. 855–9 (discussing the basis of the objective theory); Randy E. Barnett, "Squaring Undisclosed Agency Law with Contract Theory," *California Law Review*, vol. 75 (1987), pp. 1969, 1994–7 (discussing apparent authority in agency law).

justified in seeking him out in order to protect herself from Ben's threat? I am not now asking what current doctrine involving self-defense would permit, nor what "rule of law" constraints we might wish to place on such behavior,[44] but whether any preventive actions by Ann would be rightful or just. Would she be acting justly or rightfully if she took steps to protect herself from Ben? Had Ben threatened Ann, would she be acting unjustly if she sought him out to use force to prevent his announced attack?

Finally, suppose that Ben's ad does not specify Ann as his victim and, instead, he asserts that within the next week he will kill another human being. Would not every potential victim be entitled without acting unjustly to take steps to prevent his attack? Would not others be entitled to use force in the aid of whoever the victim might turn out to be? If the answers to these questions are all yes, it is because Ben has credibly communicated to the victim or to the world his intention to violate the rights of another, in which case the principle of self-defense seems applicable. According to this analysis, while intentions are not relevant to the *rectification* of a prior injustice, the communication of an intention to violate rights is one circumstance that justifies the use of self-defense to *prevent* the act from occurring in the first place.

According to Aristotelians, while all persons share a common "nature," some persons can acquire by engaging in habitual behavior something like a "second nature" that is as much a determinant of their actions as is their "first" nature.[45] Could we not conclude that, though human beings are not by nature

[44] The problem of enforcement error—one of the two problems of power discussed in Part III—argues for restrictions being placed on all uses of force, even uses of force that are justified by the rights of restitution and self-defense. The problem of enforcement error and the appropriate restrictions needed to handle it will be considered in Chapter 10.

[45] See, e.g., Harold H. Joachim, *Aristotle: The Nicomachean Ethics* (Oxford: Clarendon Press, 1951), p. 85 ("If you attribute to a man, for example, knowledge or bravery, you are qualifying him under that type of quality which Aristotle calls [*hexis*]. For to be learned, or to be brave, implies that certain natural capacities . . . have become established conditions—a second nature, or habit, of the soul."); see also Martin Ostwald, "Glossary of Technical Terms," in Aristotle, *Nicomachean Ethics* (trans. Martin Ostwald) pp. 308–9 (Indianapolis, Ind.: Bobbs-Merrill, 1962): "*hexis*[]: CHARACTERISTIC, ALSO TRAINED ABILITY, CHARACTERISTIC CONDITION, CHARACTERISTIC ATTITUDE. A noun . . . designating a firmly fixed possession of the mind, established by repeated and habitual action. Once attained, it is ever present, at least in a potential form. . . . '[H]abit' has often been used as an English equivalent".

The idea of a "second" nature that some persons acquire by habitual action, in contrast with a "first" nature that is common to all human beings by virtue of their being human, derives from Aristotle's analysis of virtue and vice in the *Nicomachean Ethics*. According to Aristotle, virtues—and their opposites, vices—are not part of our natures. "[T]he virtues are implanted in us neither by nature nor contrary to nature: we are by nature equipped with the ability to receive them, and habit brings this ability to completion and fulfillment." Ibid. 33. These virtuous or vicious habits are a type of skill or characteristic that can be acquired only by action. "[I]t is from playing the lyre that both good and bad lyre-players are produced. And the corresponding statement is true of builders and of all the rest; men will be good or bad builders as a result of building well or badly. . . . This, then, is the case with the virtues also; by doing the acts that we do in our transactions with other men we become just or unjust, and by doing the acts that

cannibalistic or vampirish, Jeffery Dahmer, who kidnapped and murdered seventeen victims and then ate their corpses, had by his own habitual actions become a cannibalistic threat to others? Could we not be as certain that, should he have been released from confinement, John Gacy, who tortured and murdered thirty-three young men and then buried their bodies beneath his suburban home, was also a genuine threat to some as yet unknown young men, as we would if he had taken out an ad to that effect in the *Chicago Tribune*?

Of course, we might be wrong about Jeffrey Dahmer or John Gacy, but if we reach the wrong conclusion, whose fault is it? Is it not reasonable to say that a person who has been convicted of repeatedly violating the rights of others has assumed the risk that, when this becomes known, others will reasonably take him to be communicating a threat to them? This is not to claim that they waive the moral right to proportionate criminal punishment. In a retributivist theory based on moral desert, punishment, like restitution, is a matter of rectifying, not preventing injustice. I am merely claiming that when some people have communicated a message that they will violate the rights of others, they have assumed the risk that others might take their communication seriously and may rightfully act upon it in self defense to prevent irreparable harm.

But what about the mentally ill person who refuses to take his medication? Can we say that such a person communicates his intention to violate rights in the future? Can we say that he too has assumed the risk of such a communication? In thinking about this question, consider whether the mental state of the aggressor negates one's right of self-defense.[46] Must you desist from self-defense if your attacker is mentally incompetent? Hardly. Indeed, if a person is so incompetent as to be unable to control his conduct, he becomes a greater threat, not a lesser threat, and therefore, by the approach I am suggesting, even more the appropriate object of criminal law.

So there may be not one, but two circumstances that give rise to threats sufficient to justify some form of individual and collective self-defense: (1) the communication of an intention to violate rights by persons who are otherwise

we do in the presence of danger, and being habituated to feel fear or confidence, we become brave or cowardly. The same is true of appetites and feelings of anger; some men become temperate and good-tempered, others self-indulgent and irascible, by behaving in one way or the other in the appropriate circumstances. Thus, in one word, states of character [*hexis*] arise out of like activities. This is why the activities we exhibit must be of a certain kind; it is because the states of character correspond to the differences between these." Aristotle, *Nicomachean Ethics* (trans. W. D. Ross), in Richard McKeon (ed.), *The Basic Works of Aristotle* (New York: Random House, 1941), pp. 952–3. The idea that action begets virtue is perhaps clearer in Ostwald's translation of the last two sentences: "In a word, characteristics [*hexis*] develop from corresponding activities. For that reason, we must see to it that our activities are of a certain kind, since any variations in them will be reflected in our characteristics." Ostwald, *Nichomachean Ethics*, p. 34.

[46] Recall that "[a] person is justified in the use of force against another when and to the extent that he reasonably believes that such conduct is necessary to defend himself or another against [the] imminent use of unlawful force." *Illinois Annotated Statutes*, ch. 720, sect. 5/7–1 (Smith-Hurd 1993).

mentally normal; and (2) a mental abnormality that would make it highly likely that a person will violate the rights of another. With this analysis in mind, let me offer the following distinction between crime and tort, though I would not necessarily use those terms.

The principle of rectification by which victims or their heirs may claim a right to restitution for a past rights violation conforms to what we now think of as the civil law category of "tort," though, prior to the development of criminal law, these were simply conceived of as offenses. In contrast, "criminal law" deals with what we might call *the right of extended self-defense*. Whereas tort law involves using force to obtain justice for victims, criminal law involves using force to respond to threats of future rights violations; criminal law only incidentally concerns the use of punishment to deter others from committing crimes in the future. Its primary concern is the use of force to protect against those who have communicated a threat to harm others. Like the traditional right of self-defense that requires that a threat be imminent, the right of extended self-defense requires a sufficiently unambiguous communication of a threat. We are not permitted to guess at a person's intentions; we are permitted only to react to *reasonable interpretations of their words and deeds*.

We may supplement the formulation of justice accordingly:

FORMULATION 6. *Justice is respect for the rights of individuals and associations.*
(1) The *right of several property* specifies a right to acquire, possess, use, and dispose of scarce physical resources—including their own bodies. Resources may be used in any way that does not physically interfere with other persons' use and enjoyment of their resources. While most property rights are freely alienable, the right to one's person is inalienable.
(2) The *right of first possession* specifies that property rights to unowned resources are acquired by being the first to establish control over them and to stake a claim.
(3) The *right of freedom of contract* specifies that a rightholder's consent is both necessary (freedom *from* contract) and sufficient (freedom *to* contract) to transfer alienable property rights—both during one's life and, by using a "will," upon one's death. A manifestation of assent is ordinarily necessary unless one party somehow has access to the other's subjective intent.
(4) Violating these rights by *force or fraud* is unjust.
(5) The *right of restitution* requires that one who violates the rights that define justice must compensate the victim of the rights violation for the harm caused by the injustice, and such compensation may be collected by force, if necessary.
(6) **The *right of self-defense* permits the use of force against those who communicate a credible threat to violate the rights of another.**

Having identified criminal law with prevention and with the right of extended self-defense, I must emphasize the need for substantive and procedural limitations on both this right and on the right to restitution. As I explain at some length in Chapter 10, these are needed to address the serious problems of power that are the subject of Part III. All that I have argued for to this point is the justice of using force to collect restitution and to prevent the commission of a crime by a person who has communicated a threat to the rights of others.

Finally, I should note a potential tension between the right of restitution and the right of extended self-defense. The principle of extended self-defense might well be used to justify life imprisonment for some violent offenders who have communicated by their past actions the intent to commit violence again. However, criminals who are incarcerated in employment facilities where they may earn money to pay for their keep as well as for their debt to their victims would have little incentive to do so should they be sentenced for life. Therefore, some "out date" is needed if we hope, as a practical matter, to obtain restitution for victims. To the extent that we prevent future misconduct by lifetime incarceration, we will not only incur the costs of incarceration, but the victims of past crimes will likely lose their compensation as well. This tension may require some radical changes to the structure of our criminal justice system so that crime victims themselves are involved in making such trade-offs.

Punishment and Insanity

According to the distinction just drawn, a tort is an action for restitution, whereas a crime is an action to prevent future rights violations. The prevailing understanding of the crime–tort distinction is quite different. Today, while tort law is thought to be based on compensation for injuries, criminal law is thought to be based on the punishment of those who deserve to be punished. Stephen Morse offers the following summary of what he calls the "standard account" of criminal law: "[T]he moral legitimacy of the criminal law requires that offenders receive punishments that are proportionate to their culpability. If punishments are too harsh or excuses too restrictive, harmdoers may be punished more than they deserve, thus undermining the criminal law's legitimacy. The criminal sanction should apply only to those who are blameworthy, and then strictly in proportion to the offender's desert."[47]

Yet if punishment is based on "desert" or "blameworthiness," then a criminal who is shown to be unable to appreciate the criminality of his acts does not "deserve" punishment and should be freed. This is the theoretical origin of the highly unpopular insanity defense to crime. Moreover, according to the prevailing theory of criminal law, any preventive detention is in conflict with the standard account because it appears to justify the punishment of persons who have committed no crime, and who are therefore blameless, on the strength of a prediction that they will commit a crime in the future, thus

[47] Stephen J. Morse, "Blame and Danger: An Essay on Preventive Detention," *Boston University Law Review*, vol. 76 (1996), p. 121.

undermining the legitimating conditions of the criminal law. The same objection can be made against imprisoning an offender longer than he "deserves" to be imprisoned on the basis of his "culpability" for the offense, solely on the ground that he may commit another offense in the future.

A significant advantage of the account presented here is that, by rejecting punishment as the rationale either for restitution or for incarceration, it leaves no room for an insanity defense. A person who by his prior conduct has proven himself incapabable of distinguishing right from wrong is often *more* dangerous, not less, than a criminal who can tell the difference and is capable of avoiding acting unjustly towards others. And only dangerousness that constitutes a threat to the rights of others that is communicated by words or deeds, not blameworthiness or desert, need be shown to protect the community from people who would violate the rights of others.

Summary

(1) The *compliance problem* concerns conduct that conflicts with the rights that define justice or the requirements of the rule of law; it is the need to close the gap between the conduct that justice and the rule of law requires and what people perceive to be in their interest to do.

(2) Some perceptions of conflict between justice and interest are illusory and can be resolved by a better appreciation of one's true interest or the limits of justice.

(3) Genuine gaps between justice and interest can, however, be caused by emergency conditions or by the desire for pecuniary gain or psychological gain.

(4) Because the benefits of adhering to the requirements of justice tend to accrue over the long term, persons who heavily discount the future are far more likely to perceive a gap between justice and interest than persons with lower time preferences.

(5) Usually, the gap between justice and interest is closed by the processes of socialization.

(6) Residual gaps between justice and interest can be ameliorated by the use or threatened use of force or power in advance of, during, or after a rights violation.

(7) Rights violaters may permissibly be forced to make restitution to the victim of a rights violation.

(8) The right to receive restitution in such a system would justify the creation of institutions responsible for collecting such payments.

(9) The problem of collecting restitution from indigent offenders would be handled by institutions who would employ such persons at market wages. Any difference between the amount owed and that which could be earned would be covered by insurance contracts.

(10) The problem of wealthy criminals committing more crimes is highly exaggerated; even so, effective measures are possible if a problem with wealthy criminals did arise.

(11) Force may also be used to prevent rights violators who have demonstrated their dangerousness by their past conduct from committing further crimes whether or not these persons are "blameworthy" or "deserve" to be punished.

(12) The use of force to collect restitution or engage in self-defense should be limited in ways and for reasons that will be discussed in Chapter 10.

Using force to close the gap between justice and interest is both obvious and very popular. Still, such a strategy has substantial costs that are often minimized or ignored entirely. Using power to address the problems of interest raises new problems of its own. These problems are particularly virulent problems of knowledge and interest that attach to the use of force. In Part III, I shall refer to them as the *problems of power*.

PART THREE

The Problems of Power

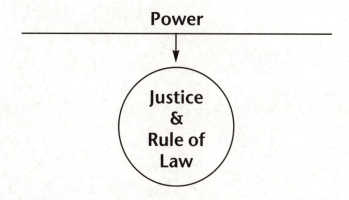

Power

Justice
&
Rule of
Law

TEN

The Problem of Enforcement Error

POWER—the use or threat of force—addresses the compliance problem by closing the gap that can arise between interest and the requirements of justice and the rule of law. At times it may be the only measure that can close this gap. Yet using power to address the compliance problem creates its own quite serious set of difficulties—difficulties that may be viewed as particularly acute problems of knowledge and interest. In this chapter, I shall explain how using power creates serious problems of knowledge. Innocent errors of judgment are possible, indeed inevitable, whenever fallible human beings are called upon to use force justly.

Apart from the problem of innocent errors, using force to address the compliance problem gives rise to serious problems of interest in which those authorized to use force to ensure justice use it instead to aggrandize themselves and their allies. In Chapters 12, 13, and 14, I discuss this problem and how it argues for a structure of law enforcement that constrains abuse. In this part, we shall see not only that these twin problems of power reinforce the need for the liberal conception of justice and the rule of law, but also that we may do better to tolerate some compliance problems than to suffer the full brunt of the problems of power.

1. The Cost of Error

To appreciate the knowledge problem associated with the use of power we must begin by considering the *cost of error*. I touched upon this notion briefly in Chapter 5 when I observed that even an unjust decision in favor of Ann did far less harm to Ben if it was made before he had incurred the substantial costs of building a house on the disputed land rather than after. The cost unjustly imposed on one party to a dispute by an erroneous reallocation of rights *before* that party acts in reliance on a prior allocation is often less severe than would be imposed by the very same erroneous decision made after the party had acted. In this way, the guidance provided by *ex ante* precepts can be preferable to *ex post* decision making even though *ex ante* precepts may not reflect the details of a particular dispute as accurately. In short, *ex ante* precepts help reduce the cost of error.

Similarly, using power to prevent or rectify rights violations also affects the cost of error that may result from adjudicating disputes, creating what I shall refer to here as the *problem of enforcement error*:

> The *problem of enforcement error* arises when using power to achieve compliance with justice and the rule of law increases the costs imposed by erroneous judgments on the innocent.

The *problem of* enforcement error—as I use the term—runs only in one direction: it is the erroneous *use* of force against the innocent. It does not include the erroneous *failure* to use force against the guilty, which I shall refer to below as the problem of *non*enforcement error.

Ironically, the very reason why power closes the gap between interest and justice accounts as well for why power increases the cost of enforcement error. The imposition of force is thought to be valuable to solve the compliance problem precisely because it is subjectively perceived as onerous or "costly" by the persons on whom it is being imposed. The threatened imposition of a subjective harm brings a person's *ex ante* perception of interest in line with the requirements of justice and the rule of law. (Imagine if we tried to solve the compliance problem by promising to give a soothing massage to anyone who acted unjustly or illegally. The gap between interest and justice would increase rather than decrease.) Yet *the distinctive ability of forcible measures to raise the* ex ante *cost of unjust or illegal actions also unavoidably raises the* ex post *cost of whatever enforcement error may occur.*

What is the link between the cost imposed *ex ante* on potential wrongdoers and the cost imposed *ex post* on the wrongfully accused? Notice that the *threat* of force does not impose enforcement costs on the innocent; the cost of enforcement error is only incurred if force is actually *used* either in self-defense or in an attempt to rectify injustice.[1] If the strategy of threatening to use force always succeeded in closing the gap between interest and justice there would never be occasion actually to use force *ex post* and enforcement errors with their accompanying costs would never occur. However, given that a threat to use force is not credible *ex ante* unless persons believe it would be forthcoming *ex post*, the willingness to use force must continually be demonstrated by its actual imposition. Consequently, any attempt to increase the *ex ante* cost of acting unjustly by threatening to use force against the guilty unavoidably increases the costs imposed *ex post* on innocent defendants by enforcement error. This,

---

[1] Although a threat to use force can sometimes deter the cautious from rightful conduct—imposing a genuine error cost to the innocent—this only occurs if there is an *ex ante* prospect that force will be imposed erroneously *ex post*; thus this error cost too can be attributed, not to the threat, but to the erroneous use of force.

in turn, will also increase the risk *ex ante* to everyone of being victimized by an unjust imposition of power and can deter rightful as well as wrongful conduct depending upon the cautiousness of the actor. In this way, addressing the compliance problem of interest by using force (to make the threat of force credible) unavoidably creates a serious problem of enforcement error.

The extent of the cost imposed by enforcement error is a function of two factors: the *severity* of the erroneous enforcement and the *rate* of such error. The more severe the consequences of an enforcement error the higher the cost such error will impose unjustly on one of the parties. The higher the rate of error, the more likely it will be that a cost of error will be unjustly imposed. How then do we reduce the cost of enforcement error? We do so in at least two ways. First, we place substantive limits on the use of force—limits associated with justice—that tend to reduce the severity of enforcement error. Second, we place procedural limits on the use of force—limits associated with the rule of law—that tend to reduce the rate of enforcement error.

Before examining the first of these two methods of reducing the cost of enforcement error, I must add an important caveat. In what follows, despite the rhetorical similarity, I am *not* offering an efficiency analysis of enforcement. That is, I am not claiming that restitutive justice "optimally" reduces or minimizes error cost or does so better than other strategies. A complete optimality assessment would require knowledge of those innocent victims who are victimized by undeterred criminals, some way of quantifying the subjective costs of this loss, and some way to aggregate these costs and compare them with the costs of enforcement error which are avoided by placing limits on the sanctions that can be forcibly imposed on the accused. Any attempt to determine a theoretically optimal strategy would be hopelessly swamped in practice by intractable knowledge problems.

I believe that the information required is unavailable in principle, and even were this not so, would nonetheless be unavailable in practice. Absent this information, any formal optimality model is a game unconnected to actual policy and, however intrinsically interesting, is immaterial to considerations of real justice that are my concern here. Instead, I explain here how a proper conception of the background right of restitution and of the rule of law helps address these problems by reducing (as opposed to minimizing) both the rate and the severity of enforcement error.

2. Justice and the Severity of Enforcement Error

Rights as a Necessary Evil

Since I have placed so much emphasis on background rights as the means by which we define justice and handle the problems of knowledge and interest, I may have given the impression that background rights are an unmitigated good. Many people seem to adopt this stance when they assert the existence of background rights to food, clothing, shelter, safety, education, transportation, health care, parks, and far less compelling claims as well.[2] To some, it would seem that any problem that exists, especially any social problem that is deemed to be serious, can and should be addressed by creating a right. Otherwise we do not mean business.

The problem of enforcement error (and abuse) should, however, cause us to temper our enthusiasm for recognizing rights. For the background rights that define justice serve also to legitimate the use of force or violence to secure compliance. *The more rights we recognize the more violence we legitimate.* And every exercise of violence imposes serious enforcement costs on the innocent. Moreover, every erroneous and unjust use of violence threatens to induce resentment, bitterness and the desire on the part of those against whom violence is used to rectify this injustice by responding violently, thereby setting off a cascade of violence. Indeed, even *just* uses of force can have this effect.

Therefore, far from being unmitigated goods, *rights are a necessary evil.* Because each right legitimates violence, the fewer we can manage with the better. I have contended here that the background rights of several property, freedom of contract, first possession, and restitution are rights that we cannot do without if we are to address the problems of knowledge, interest, and power, problems we must address somehow. We should strive to limit the number and types of background rights that are legally enforced by violent means to those which handle pervasive social problems that cannot be handled any other way. Thus we arrive at a natural rights version of Ockham's razor:[3] To reduce the legitimated use of power in society that enforceable rights engender, any social problems, no matter how serious, that can be handled adequately by other means should be.

Remedies and the Severity of Enforcement Error

Not only do the number of recognized rights affect the cost imposed by enforcement errors (and abuse), so too does the remedy we choose to rectify

---

[2] I have noticed in popular discourse that many who would disparage the rights to several property and freedom of contract as unjustified or unsupported, advocate other rights by mere assertion without any effort to justify them or show how they fit together with other rights.

[3] See Ernest A. Moody, "William of Ockham," in Paul Edwards (ed.), *The Encyclopedia of Philosophy*, viii (New York: Macmillan and Free Press, 1967), p. 307: "The principle of parsimony, whose frequent use by Ockham gained it the name 'Ockham's razor,' was employed as a methodological principle of economy in explanation. He invoked it most frequently under such forms as 'Plurality is not to be assumed without necessity' and 'What can be done with fewer [assumptions] is done in vain with more'. . . . The principal use made by Ockham of the principle of parsimony was in the elimination of pseudo-explanatory entities . . . in accounting for any fact, unless it is established by evident experience or evident reasoning, or is required by articles of faith".

rights violations. To appreciate how certain remedies can reduce the severity of enforcement error, we must first appreciate how using power to prevent or rectify rights violations affects the severity of such error. Consider a few very simple examples. Suppose that the sanction for theft—the wrongful taking of the property of another—was to apologize. The cost unjustly imposed on a innocent person who was erroneously adjudged to be guilty of theft would be the subjective cost of making an apology. Suppose instead that thefts were punished literally by a slap on the wrist. Should a person be wrongly judged to be guilty of theft, she would have to suffer unjustly the subjective cost of having her wrist slapped. Now suppose that theft was punished with death. With this sanction, the subjective cost imposed unjustly on an innocent person is greatly increased.

Of course, we cannot be sure that the cost imposed by enforcement error with one sanction is greater than another unless we know the subjective preferences of the victim of the error. So, for example, some people may perceive a slap on the wrist to be less onerous (because less demeaning) than an apology. However, to address both the compliance problem and the problem of enforcement error it is necessary to make certain rough generalizations about most people's preferences. For example, most everyone would prefer either of these sanctions to death.[4] Although such generalizations are necessary, we must never forget that not every person will react the way our generalizations suggest.

Any attempt to increase the cost imposed *ex ante* upon potential rights violators by increasing the severity of sanctions imposed *ex post* on the guilty will raise the cost of enforcement error imposed on the innocent. To see this, suppose that the full subjective cost imposed on a particular victim of an auto theft, whose car is worth $10,000, is $20,000. The full cost of the theft includes not only the price of a comparable replacement car ($10,000), but also compensation for its loss of use, for the trauma of having someone take one's property, as well as for the costs incurred to catch, prosecute, and collect compensation from the thief (this will become significant in Chapter 11). The following chart illustrates how different measures of restitution impose different costs on the victim and thief respectively.

One can see that, according to this chart, viewed at the point from which they started (*ex ante*), a sanction of $20,000 reduces the cost imposed on the victim to $0, while imposing a net cost of $10,000 on the thief.[5] The victim is fully compensated for the theft and the criminal disgorges the benefit conferred upon him by the theft plus an amount equal to the extra costs imposed

---

[4] The problem of objectifying subjective value here, while serious, is no more so than that facing deterrence theories of punishment that need to assess the subjective onerousness of varying degrees of punishment.

[5] I am assuming either that the car was sold to another person, in which case the thief pays the full amount, or that it is returned to the victim, in which case the thief pays the difference between the value of the car (including damages) and $20,000.

Sanction for theft of $10,000 Car[6]	Cost of crime to victim	Cost of crime to thief
+$40,000	+$20,000	– $30,000
+$30,000	+$10,000	–$20,000
+$20,000	$0	–$10,000[7]
+$10,000	–$10,000	$0
$0	–$20,000[8]	+$10,000

upon the victim by the theft. As the amount of the fine is increased the criminal suffers an added cost and the victim enjoys a benefit in excess of the cost inflicted by the theft. As the fine is decreased below $20,000, the victim suffers a cost and the criminal benefits in excess of the cost of making restitution.

Now let us add to the chart a column recording the cost of enforcement error imposed on an innocent accused by forcibly imposing a sanction for the auto theft.

Sanction for theft of $10,000 car	Cost of crime to victim	Cost of crime to thief	**Cost of error to innocent accused**
+$40,000	+$20,000	–$30,000	–$40,000
+$30,000	+$10,000	–$20,000	–$30,000
+$20,000	$0	–$10,000	–$20,000
+$10,000	–$10,000	$0	–$10,000
$0	–$20,000	+$10,000	$0

One can see that the first and last columns are mirror images. As the cost of the sanction increases, so too does the cost of error imposed unjustly on the innocent. The only way to completely avoid any unjust imposition on the innocent would be to reduce the amount of the restitution to nothing.

6 In addition to the value of the stolen car ($10,000), this sanction assumes that the victim has also incurred costs of $10,000 for, e.g., loss of use, emotional trauma, and enforcement costs.

7 This figure assumes that $10,000 of the cost of paying the victim $20,000 is offset by the value to the criminal of the car. If the criminal values the car less than the victim, as is likely the case, the offset declines and the cost to the criminal increases.

8 This figure assumes that the victim incurs costs in trying but failing to collect restitution. If there was no right to restitution, then presumably the victim would avoid the costs of obtaining restitution and the resulting loss would be reduced to $10,000 plus compensation for loss of use and any emotional loss.

However, addressing enforcement error in this way would undermine the ability of justice and the rule of law to address three of the problems identified in earlier chapters.

First, eliminating any sanction for such a theft would guarantee that in *every* case, the victim would bear unjustly the full cost of the theft. In this example, every victim of such a theft would have to bear the entire replacement cost of $10,000 plus any costs incurred due to loss of use or emotional suffering (with no incentive to seek enforcement, presumably the victim would incur no enforcement costs). This cost is imposed on the victim by the thief, not by enforcement, and is unjust according the liberal principles of justice identified in Chapter 4, which handles the first-order problem of knowledge. Contrast this with a sanction of $20,000 which merely runs a risk that it will be imposed unjustly on the innocent. Surely a rule—"no restitution for injustice"—resulting in the *certainty* of injustice to every innocent victim is inferior to a rule creating only a *chance* of an injustice an innocent accused. (Bear in mind also that, as will be discussed in the next section, the extent of this risk can be addressed to some degree by the rule of law.)

Second, as the amount of restitution drops below the subjective costs imposed upon the victim, the incentive problem discussed in Chapter 8 will be exacerbated. Finally, as the amount of restitution drops below the subjective value to the thief of what was taken, we fail to address the compliance problem discussed in Chapter 9. These considerations suggest that to avoid running afoul of such problems, the lower limit on the amount of restitution should be the full cost caused by the theft or $20,000.

While this analysis argues for placing a lower limit on the amount of restitution, it does not suggest that we ignore entirely the problem of enforcement error. Instead, the problem of enforcement costs can be addressed by placing some upper limit on the amount of restitution imposed on offenders. In particular, in our example, it would seem that restitution of $20,000 (the full cost caused by the theft) is an appropriate limit. At any higher level of compensation, the harm imposed on the innocent accused is increased while the benefits gained by innocent victims exceeds their loss.

This analysis is not intended to establish that full compensation is the efficient level of sanctions for violation of the requirements of justice. Rather it is intended to reveal that the problem of enforcement error creates an unavoidable *conflict of interests* between innocent victims and innocent persons who are wrongfully accused of violating rights. If, to reduce the cost imposed on the innocent accused, we lower forcible sanctions in all cases (including those in which the guilty party has been correctly identified) below what it takes to compensate victims fully, innocent victims of rights violations will invariably incur some or all of the loss that had been unjustly inflicted by the rights violator. By requiring less than full compensation to the victim, we guarantee that every innocent victim of a crime will absorb at least some and perhaps all of the cost of the rights violation.

On the other hand, if we increase the amount of restitution above zero, the costs coercively imposed on the innocent accused will increase. A requirement of full compensation trades a risk of imposing the costs of enforcement error on any given innocent accused in favor of a certainty of injustice against every victim. Conversely, a strategy of increasing the amount of restitution beyond that which would fully compensate the victim confers benefits on innocent victims at the expense of increasing the costs erroneously imposed on the innocent accused.

This analysis of the problem of enforcement error provides another refinement of the principles of justice first identified in Part I in the context of the problems of knowledge. In Part II, we saw both that the incentive problem can be addressed by awarding restitution to the victims of rights violations (Chapter 8) and that force or power may be needed to ensure that such restitution is forthcoming (Chapter 9). The analysis of the problem of enforcement error in this chapter suggests the adoption of a *principle of strict proportionality*:

> A proportionality principle stipulates that restitution for the commission of a rights violation should be proportionate to the harm suffered by the victim. The *principle of strict proportionality* requires that the amount of the sanction be limited to what is necessary to fully compensate without overcompensating the victim.

Because the phrase "restitution governed by the principle of strict proportionality" is unwieldy I shall refer to this as *pure restitution*:

> *Pure restitution* is compensation made by the rights violator to the victim that is limited to what is necessary to fully compensate for the harm caused to the victim by the rights violation.

In contrast with pure restitution, we can distinguish two other types of legal sanction: punitive restitution and pure punishment.

> *Punitive restitution* is compensation made by the offender to the victim that is calculated to inflict a harm upon the offender in addition to the harm incidental to the obligation to make full compensation.

and:

> *Pure punishment* is the deliberate and forcible infliction of a sanction that is calculated to inflict harm upon the offender without a requirement that the offender compensate the victim.

I must hasten to acknowledge that a system of justice limited to exacting pure restitution is vulnerable to an obvious and powerful criticism: pure restitution is insufficient to adequately deal with the compliance problem. Apart from retributivist theories based on moral desert, a subject to which I return in Chapter 15, the principal reason for favoring punitive restitution or pure punishment over pure restitution is that adherence to these principles will better secure compliance with the requirements of justice. We shall take up this important and widely perceived difficulty with pure restitution and the alleged advantages of punishment in Chapter 11. There I shall explain (1) how adopting the liberal conception of justice described here would remove serious obstacles now in the path of effective crime prevention, and (2) how increasing the severity of legal sanctions via either punitive restitution or pure punishment is not at all certain to increase compliance.

Assuming that the problem of crime prevention is adequately handled by other means, the problem of enforcement error discussed here suggests that the use of power should be limited to imposing a remedy of pure restitution. *For any gains obtained by increasing sanctions beyond what is required to compensate innocent victims will inevitably increase the suffering of those innocent persons who have been wrongfully accused of crimes.* This produces the following revised formulation of justice:

FORMULATION 7. *Justice is respect for the rights of individuals and associations.*
(1) The *right of several property* specifies a right to acquire, possess, use, and dispose of scarce physical resources—including their own bodies. Resources may be used in any way that does not physically interfere with other persons' use and enjoyment of their resources. While most property rights are freely alienable, the right to one's person is inalienable.
(2) The *right of first possession* specifies that property rights to unowned resources are acquired by being the first to establish control over them and to stake a claim
(3) The *right of freedom of contract* specifies that a rightholder's consent is both necessary (freedom *from* contract) and sufficient (freedom *to* contract) to transfer alienable property rights—both during one's life and, by using a "will," upon one's death. A manifestation of assent is ordinarily necessary unless one party somehow has access to the other's subjective intent.
(4) Violating these rights by *force or fraud* is unjust.
(5) The *right of restitution* requires that one who violates the rights that define justice must compensate the victim of the rights violation for the harm caused by the injustice, and such compensation may be collected by force, if necessary. **The *principle of strict proportionality* limits the amount of restitution to that which is necessary to fully compensate, but not overcompensate, the victim.**
(6) The *right of self-defense* permits the use of force against those who threaten to violate the rights of another.

Before turning to the compliance problem potentially caused by adherence to the principle of strict proportionality, we must first consider how the rule of law also helps address the problem of enforcement error. For as we shall see in Chapter 11, respecting the rule of law will severely reduce the ability of punitive restitution or pure punishment to address the compliance problem.

3. The Rule of Law and the Rate of Enforcement Error

We have now to consider the other factor that determines the seriousness of the problem of enforcement error: the *rate* of such errors. By what means can we reduce the incidents of enforcement error? One common method of handling a problem of uncertain or imperfect knowledge is to adopt an operative presumption, like the *presumption of competence* discussed in Chapter 3. A presumption assumes that a particular conclusion is warranted unless sufficient evidence exists to show that it is not. If we know nothing at all about a particular matter, then a prevailing presumption provides a conclusion to be accepted unless enough contrary information is presented.[9]

Enforcement Error and the Burden of Proof

Presumptions can run in two directions. In a legal system, for example, we could adopt either a "presumption of innocence" that presumes persons to be innocent of committing a rights violation until sufficient evidence of their guilt is presented or a "presumption of guilt" that presumes persons to be guilty of violating rights until sufficient evidence of their innocence is presented. By adopting a presumption of innocence we necessarily accept a greater risk that guilty people will escape a legal sanction than with a presumption of guilt. Conversely, with a presumption of guilt we accept a greater risk that innocent persons will suffer the imposition of a legal sanction than with a presumption of innocence. In either case, however, the value of the presumptive approach is that it provides a "default" answer to the question of guilt or innocence *in the absence of evidence to the contrary*.

When sufficient evidence exists to draw a conclusion that conflicts with the presumption, we say that the presumption is "rebutted" and we decide the case the other way. So, for example, when evidence exists to show beyond a reasonable doubt that Ben has stolen from Ann, we find Ben guilty of theft, despite the existence of a presumption of innocence in Ben's favor. Whenever insufficient evidence of guilt exists and the presumption of innocence causes us to find in Ben's favor, we cannot by assumption be sure whether Ben is innocent or guilty. A failure to find a person "guilty" is not the same as a finding of "innocence." When a presumption of innocence has not been overcome by sufficient evidence of guilt, all we know is that there is inadequate evidence to conclude that he is guilty. A presumption of guilt would work the same way. When insufficient evidence of innocence is presented and conse-

---

[9]   For a discussion of the pervasive use of presumptions in legal and philosophical discourse, see Richard H. Gaskins, *Burdens of Proof in Modern Discourse* (New Haven, Conn.: Yale University Press, 1992).

quently we find a person guilty according to the presumption, we cannot know for sure that the person is truly guilty, but only that there is inadequate evidence to conclude that he is innocent.

A set of presumptions can tell us what to do when we are ignorant of the facts of a particular case, but which presumption should we choose? If we had nothing but the knowledge problem to worry about we would be influenced by two considerations. First, we must be concerned with the comparative rate of error produced by one presumption or the other. Second, we must be concerned with the comparative severity of the error produced by one presumption or the other. In assessing the rate of error permitted by a presumption, we cannot, of course, appeal to the facts of the very cases to be decided by the presumption. For presumptions operate precisely when we are ignorant of the facts. Therefore, if we are to assess the comparative rate of error incurred by these presumptions, we must do so in a far more general fashion than case-by-case.

At least initially we might make some gross assessment of what is normally the case and what is abnormal. If, on the basis of experience or other empirical information, we conclude that most people do not violate the rights of others then—knowing nothing more about any particular case—a presumption of innocence will be right more often than it is wrong. Conversely, if we conclude that persons normally do violate the rights of others then—knowing nothing more about any particular case—a presumption of guilt is going to lead to a lower rate of error. My own view, and I suspect most would agree, is that people normally respect the rights of others and this norm argues in favor of a presumption of innocence.

Perhaps, though, I have focussed on the wrong group of persons. Are we not really concerned with persons who have been *accused* of violating rights and are brought before courts? What is the norm here? Are most persons charged with violating rights guilty or innocent? Perhaps, "where there is smoke there is fire." Perhaps, unlike the general population, those persons who have been singled out for accusation are more likely to be guilty than innocent. In fact, I believe strongly that most of the persons I prosecuted were guilty—indeed I believed each one to be guilty, though I surely could have been mistaken. (Certainly had I a good reason to believe a defendant to be innocent I had an ethical obligation to refrain from prosecution.) Yet, assuming that my assessment is correct, we must ask why it was that most defendants I prosecuted were guilty.

My belief that every defendant I prosecuted was guilty was based almost entirely on my evaluation of the evidence at my disposal. After all I did not myself witness any of the crimes that I prosecuted. How is it that such evidence came to exist? To me there is little doubt that persons charged with crimes are generally guilty because the prosecution knows in advance that it has to overcome the presumption of innocence in every case. This means that there was little point in charging a person against whom evidence of guilt did not exist. This incentive, in turn, reduces the incidence of wrongful prosecutions.

Many people who are accused of crimes are released without charging due to insufficient evidence. When I was assigned to the Felony Review Unit, my job was to review the evidence of guilt whenever a felony charge was sought by the police. Even though the police knew that evidence of guilt was necessary before charges would be lodged against an accused, in my capacity as a member of felony review, I rejected about 40 per cent of all the charges requested—about par for the unit as a whole. Given the fact that the police routinely refuse to act on accusations they viewed to be "unfounded" upon the evidence, this screening process accounts for why evidence existed to support my judgment as a trial prosecutor that most defendants I prosecuted were guilty. Absent this evidence, how would I know?

So the fact that the overwhelming majority of persons I prosecuted were guilty, if it is a fact, is largely if not entirely a consequence of having first adopted a presumption of innocence. The incentive to prosecute only those persons against whom evidence of guilt existed was *created* by the presumption of innocence. Much of the evidence at my disposal as a prosecutor and which I made available to the judge or jury would likely never have existed had it not been for incentives provided by the presumption of innocence. Without this evidence we would have been quite ignorant about the guilt or innocence of the accused.

By providing an incentive to produce evidence of guilt, a presumption of innocence can be viewed as addressing a problem of interest facing law enforcement. There is no such thing as free evidence. Evidence is costly to produce. Preventing persons from being convicted in the absence of evidence creates an incentive to produce the sort of evidence that we need to determine guilt or innocence, and this incentive in turn helps address the problem of enforcement error. Therefore, the fact that the overwhelming proportion of persons charged and prosecuted for crimes are guilty in a system in which there is a presumption of innocence cannot be used to justify adopting a presumption of guilt.

In considering whether to adopt a presumption of innocence or guilt, we cannot consider in isolation our current system that incorporates a presumption of innocence. We must compare such a system to the rate of error in a system that lacked incentives to produce evidence of guilt and that consequently lacked such evidence.

Nonenforcement Error and the Standard of Proof

To this point in the analysis, what I have been calling the problem of enforcement error has referred exclusively to wrongfully imposing sanctions on the innocent. This kind of error is sometimes referred to a "type one" errors or "false positives." What about errors in the other direction—that is, the wrongful release of a guilty person? This kind of error is sometimes called "type two" or false negatives. I shall call it the problem of *non*enforcement error.

Recall that according to the fifth formulation of justice, "The *right of restitution* requires that one who violates the rights that define justice must compensate the victim of the rights violation for the harm caused by the injustice." In this scheme, injustice necessarily involves two parties: the party whose rights are violated and the party who violated the rights. With enforcement errors we erroneously find an innocent defendant guilty and unjustly impose a cost on him; with nonenforcement errors we erroneously find a guilty person innocent and unjustly impose a cost on the victim of the rights violation. In this respect, at least, the problem of power in a liberal scheme appears to be symmetrical: the use of power to rectify rights violations creates a risk that this power will be used against an innocent person; this risk is directly opposed by the risk that the failure to use power will leave a prior injustice (whether by force or fraud) unrectified. Any effort to reduce enforcement error will have the effect of increasing nonenforcement error.

When we deem an error in one direction to be more serious than an error in the other we can compensate for this by our choice of presumption. For example, we put the burden of proving liability on the victim because it is widely believed that it is worse for an innocent person to be punished than for a victim to go uncompensated. One source of this lack of symmetry is the fact that, though an uncompensated victim is not stigmatized by nonenforcement, enforcement does serve, and intentionally so, to stigmatize the wrongfully accused. "An erroneous decision for the defendant, whose breach of duty is at issue" Dale Nance has observed,

does not necessarily attribute fault to the plaintiff; it only attributes the absence of fault to the defendant. Thus, the placing of the burden on the plaintiff reflects the greater weight to be attributed to the risk of error in one direction than to the corresponding risk of error in the other.[10]

The asymmetry caused by the stigma attaching to finding that one has breached a serious duty results in what Professor Nance has called the "principle of civility."

One ought to presume, until sufficient evidence is adduced to show otherwise, that any given person has acted in accordance with serious social obligations. As a corollary, how much evidence is "sufficient" depends upon the nature and severity of the alleged breach, as well as the nature and severity of the contemplated consequences of a determination of breach.[11]

This principle is easiest to appreciate in a system of pure punishment without any obligation to make restitution. With pure punishment, there is a

---

[10] Dale A. Nance, "Civility and the Burden of Proof," *Harvard Journal of Law and Public Policy*, vol. 17 (1994), pp. 647, 661.
[11] Ibid. 648.

pronounced asymmetry between enforcement and nonenforcement error. When Ben is wrongfully prosecuted for violating Ann's rights, this only serves to add his suffering to hers. This can be represented as follows:

$$H = I_a + I_b$$

H represents the harm caused both by the crime and by enforcement error; *I* represents the respective injuries to Ann and Ben. I_a represents the injury to Ann caused by the rights violation; I_b represents the added injury done to Ben by the wrongful prosecution. Here and elsewhere in this discussion when I use the "+" symbol, I am not suggesting that the extent of these two harms can literally be summed to reach some aggregate total, but only that the harm suffered by Ben, however serious, is in addition to that suffered by Ann. In a regime of punishment, by reducing the likelihood of punishing the innocent we can lower the extent of harm unjustly imposed upon Ben without aggravating the tangible harm done to Ann.

In a regime limited to the remedy of pure restitution, however, a comparison of harm caused by enforcement error with the harm caused by nonenforcement error is more complex. In such a system, the unjust imposition on Ben of a duty to make restitution tangibly benefits Ann; and Ben is himself entitled to compensation for the wrongful prosecution. In which case, the harm caused by nonenforcement error (H_n) is simply that Ann must bear the injury caused by the crime uncompensated (I_a) or:

$$H_n = I_a$$

The harm caused by enforcement error (H_e), in contrast, must include both the harm caused to Ben by wrongful enforcement in excess of the value he places on the compensation to which he is entitled and also the extent to which the harm imposed upon Ann by the crime is reduced by the restitution Ben makes or:

$$H_e = (I_a - C_a) + (I_b - C_b)$$

C_a represents the subjective value Ann attaches to the compensation she receives from Ben and C_b represents the value that Ben attaches to the compensation he receives from the authorities who wrongfully prosecuted him.

As a practical matter, however, it is quite unrealistic to assume that Ben will receive compensation for his wrongful conviction. Although he is entitled to restitution, given the deficiency of knowledge that led to the wrongful prosecution, the chance that he will ever receive compensation is exceedingly remote. In which case the harm caused by enforcement is more likely to be:

$$H_e = (I_a - C_a) + I_b$$

If compensation completely negates the injury caused by the crime (I = C) as we assumed (perhaps unrealistically) above, then compensation received by Ann completely negates the injury she sustained due to the crime or:

$$I_a - C_a = 0$$

in which case the harm of enforcement error is limited to the harm imposed on Ben:

$$H_e = 0 + I_b$$

or simply:

$$H_e = I_b$$

In sum, unlike the regime of pure punishment in which the harm caused by enforcement error can simply be added to the injury suffered by the victim of the crime, in a regime of pure restitution, the harm caused by enforcement error is equal solely to the harm imposed upon Ben ($H_e = I_b$), whereas the harm caused by nonenforcement equals solely the harm to Ann caused by the crime ($H_n = I_a$). Consequently, whether the harm of nonenforcement exceeds the harm of enforcement error involves a direct comparison of the subjective injury to Ann (I_a) with the subjective injury incurred by Ben (I_b). Since these harms cannot be measured objectively, such interpersonal comparisons of subjective harms is impractical. Because our knowledge of the respective harms will always be lacking, there is simply no way to know whether the harm caused by enforcement error in a regime of pure restitution is more or less serious than the harm caused by nonenforcement.

This analysis is not changed even if we adopt a more realistic assumption that enforcing sanctions against the guilty does not completely "erase" or eliminate the original injustice, but assume instead that compensation merely mitigates the effects of an injustice as much as is possible but not completely. Assuming that the subjective harm caused by the rights violation (I) is always greater than the subjective benefit attached by the victim compensation (C)— or

$$I > C$$

then:

$$I_a - C_a > 0$$

On this assumption, even after compensating both Ann and Ben as best we can, some harm will still remain from the combination of the initial rights violation and the enforcement error.

However, because we cannot measure and then compare the subjective values that Ann and Ben attach to their respective injuries and compensation there still is no way to know whether the harm done to Anne by the crime (I_a) is greater than the net harm done to Anne after compensation coupled with the harm to Ben of enforcement [($I_a - C_a$) + I_b]. Consequently, although we can assume that both H_n and H_e are positive, we still cannot know whether H_n is greater or less than H_e.

Yet the very inability to determine whether harm caused by enforcement error is worse than the harm caused by nonenforcement suggests another principle to be incorporated in the liberal conception of the rule of law. This principle concerns the degree of certainty we require before considering the presumption of innocence to have been rebutted. In our current criminal justice system there is not only a *burden of proof* placed on accusers; there is also a *standard of proof.* Whereas a burden of proof dictates which party will lose if it fails to rebut the operative presumption, the standard of proof dictates how much evidence must be presented to rebut the operative presumption.

In "criminal" cases, we require that the party bearing the burden of proof, the prosecution, prove the defendant's guilt *beyond a reasonable doubt.* In contrast, in a "civil" trial for damages, while placing the burden of proving that the defendant is liable on the plaintiff, we adopt a standard of proof *beyond a preponderance of the evidence.* One way of appreciating the difference between these two standards of proof is by imagining that proof beyond a preponderance of the evidence requires a finding that the probability of the defendant being liable is 51 per cent, while proof beyond a reasonable doubt requires a much higher likelihood of guilt, say 90 per cent. Though a helpful heuristic, probability analysis is not really appropriate here since the guilt or innocence of defendants are not reproducible events, like coin flips, to which genuine probabilities may attach. The percentages 51 per cent and 90 per cent should, therefore, be interpreted more as degrees of certainty, from somewhat certain ("preponderance of the evidence") to highly certain ("proof beyond a reasonable doubt").

The analysis of burdens of proof presented earlier is also useful to understand the difference between the standards of proof in civil and criminal cases. When dealing with a system of pure punishment in which the harm suffered by the criminal is over and above any benefits received by the victim, we are in a situation in which the subjective harm to Ann caused by the rights violation is added to the harm caused to Ben by an enforcement error or:

$$H = I_a + I_b$$

Putting the burden on the prosecution not only to prove guilt, but to do so beyond a reasonable doubt simply operates to lower the likelihood of injury to Ben (I_b) without affecting the magnitude of injury to Ann (I_a). (Although this benefit surely comes at the cost of acquitting more guilty defendants and this nonenforcement error undermines our ability to deal with the compliance problem.)

If, however, we are operating in a system that adheres to the principle of pure restitution as the civil justice system does in the main,[12] the effort to reduce the injury to Ben (I_b) comes at the direct expense of increasing the likelihood of injury to Ann (I_a). Since we have no reason to prefer one sort of injury to the other, adopting a standard of proof beyond a reasonable doubt in a system of pure restitution yields no benefits comparable to that achieved in a system of pure punishment.

Consequently, in a regime of pure restitution, although we have good reason for adopting the presumption of innocence because (as was discussed above) such a presumption greatly reduces the rate of enforcement error and

---

[12] Sometimes punitive damages are awarded in civil suits, in which case many of the protections we associate with criminal law ought to be, but often are not, introduced. But punitive damages awards are exceptional.

reflects the principle of civility, we cannot be sure that raising the standard of proof beyond proof by a preponderance of the evidence will yield any additional benefits that will not come entirely at the expense of the innocent victims of rights violations. We therefore have reason to conclude that:

> In a system of pure restitution, the standard of proof should be *proof beyond a preponderance of the evidence*. In a system of pure punishment the standard of proof should be *proof beyond a reasonable doubt*.

What does this analysis suggest for the type of "criminal" cases (as I used the term in Chapter 9) in which dangerous persons are forcibly confined, not to punish them, but to prevent their future criminality? It is to this issue I now turn.

Limitations on Extended Self-Defense

Taken as a principle, extended self-defense would seem to justify restricting the liberty of any person who we conclude constitutes a threat to the rights of others in the future. I think here, as elsewhere, justice needs to be tempered by the requirements of the rule of law. These are not ad hoc limitations. The formal and procedural constraints provided by the rule of law represent an essential partner of the liberal conception of justice in the effort to combat enforcement error and abuse.

The most important reason why the principle of self-defense must be tempered by rule of law constraints concerns the overenforcement that arises from the pervasive problems of knowledge and interest. As was just discussed, the problem of knowledge reflects our inability to predict future behavior, which leads to "false positives"—that is, finding that someone constitutes a threat to others who really is not. The problem of interest stems from the willingness of some to exploit this uncertainty to incarcerate persons who they dislike or wish to persecute or oppress. Then there is the *principle of civility* discussed above that applies with even greater force to predictions of future, as opposed to condemnation of past, conduct.

What rule of law constraints are appropriately applied to an extended right of self-defense embodied in what some would call a criminal law? First and foremost, I would limit the use of preventive detention to those persons who have communicated a threat to others by their *past criminal behavior*—that is, to those who have been convicted, perhaps more than once, of a crime. I would wager that the odds of a crime being committed by someone who has already committed a crime greatly exceed the odds of a crime being committed by who has never committed a crime. This is, I think, the impetus behind the so-called "three strikes and you're out" statutes now being advocated.[13] Second, I would limit its application to those who have been proved

---

[13] See e.g. People v. Superior Court, 53 Cal.Rptr. 2d 789, 13 Cal. 4th 497, 917 P.2d 628 (1996) (Supreme Court of California opinion holding unconstitutional a "three strikes and you're out" statute).

to have committed a crime by a heightened standard of proof, such as proof beyond a reasonable doubt. The uncertainty associated with making such judgments of future dangerousness as well as the increased cost of error presented by preventive detention provides, I think, the impetus for requiring this standard in all criminal cases. Third, the means taken to prevent future criminal conduct should be proportionate to the threat communicated by prior conduct. At the extremes, we would be justified in taking stronger preventive measures against a repeat violent criminal than, for example, against a career auto thief.

In light of these limitations, I would qualify the right of self defense in the following manner:

FORMULATION 8. *Justice is respect for the rights of individuals and associations.*

(1) The *right of several property* specifies a right to acquire, possess, use, and dispose of scarce physical resources—including their own bodies. Resources may be used in any way that does not physically interfere with other persons' use and enjoyment of their resources. While most property rights are freely alienable, the right to one's person is inalienable.

(2) The *right of first possession* specifies that property rights to unowned resources are acquired by being the first to establish control over them and to stake a claim

(3) The *right of freedom of contract* specifies that a rightholder's consent is both necessary (freedom *from* contract) and sufficient (freedom *to* contract) to transfer alienable property rights—both during one's life and, by using a "will," upon one's death. A manifestation of assent is ordinarily necessary unless one party somehow has access to the other's subjective intent.

(4) Violating these rights by *force or fraud* is unjust.

(5) The *right of restitution* requires that one who violates the rights that define justice must compensate the victim of the rights violation for the harm caused by the injustice, and such compensation may be collected by force, if necessary. The *principle of strict proportionality* limits the amount of restitution to that which is necessary to fully compensate, but not overcompensate, the victim.

(6) The *right of self-defense* permits the use of force against those who threaten to violate the rights of another. **Normal self-defense is permissible when the commission of a rights violation is imminent. Extended self-defense is permissible when a person has communicated, by prior rights violations or some other prior conduct proven to a high degree of certainty, a threat to violate rights in the future. Self-defense should be proportionate to the risk posed by the threat.**

Summary

We can summarize the conclusions reached in this chapter as follows:

(1) The *problem of enforcement error* arises when using power to achieve compliance with justice and the rule of law increases the costs imposed by erroneous judgments on the innocent.

(2) Because the use of power imposes costs on the innocent, and rights legitimate the use of power, we need to limit the number and kind of rights we recognize to those which address pervasive social problems that cannot be dealt with adequately by any other means.

(3) The need to address the problem of enforcement error supports further refinement of our principles of justice and the rule of law:

   (*a*) with regard to justice, we need to limit the enforceable remedy to pure restitution;

   (*b*) with regard to the rule of law, we need to adopt a presumption of innocence and a standard of proof that increases with the severity of the sanction to be imposed coercively.

(4) So, too, the use of force to prevent previous offenders from committing further crimes should be limited to those who have demonstrated by their past criminality or other conduct their intention to violate rights in the future. This showing should be subjected to a standard of proof beyond a reasonable doubt.

ELEVEN

Fighting Crime Without Punishment

T HE most obvious objection to relying on self-defense—both traditional and extended—and restitution to prevent and rectify rights violations, is that these measures will be inadequate to deter criminals. And, while it must be conceded that these measures will not deter every criminal, the seriousness of this objection depends on comparing a society governed by the entire liberal conception of justice, of which rights of self-defense and restitution are but a part, with one governed by the types of institutions we presently have. While punishment may be viewed by retributivists as an end in itself,[1] deterring criminals by threatening them with punishment is only a means to prevent crime. But deterrence is neither the only, nor the most effective, means to prevent crime, though sometimes we seem to forget this. Crime *prevention* means taking measures so that a crime not take place. In this chapter, I provide reason to believe that crime prevention, in its fullest sense, can be greatly increased by adhering to the complete package of rights specified by the liberal conception of justice with its rights of several property and freedom of contract.

Most people fail to appreciate the fundamental obstacles placed in the path of crime prevention by the perverse logic of *public* property, *public* law enforcement, and *public* imprisonment. Step one: start with public streets, sidewalks, and parks where every citizen must be permitted unless proved guilty of a crime. Step two: rely on an inherently inefficient public bureaucracy to catch, prosecute, and try those criminals against whom enough evidence of guilt exists. Step three: should they be convicted, subject criminals to the dangerous, unproductive, and sometimes uncontrollable setting of public prisons to prevent them from engaging in further misconduct. Step four: periodically release most prisoners back into the community and then return to step one and repeat the cycle. Each step follows from the preceding step, and each step unavoidably leaves considerable room for criminal conduct to thrive.

---

[1] A position I discuss in chapter 15.

If we set out deliberately to design a system that encouraged criminal conduct and nurtured hardened career criminals, we could hardly do a better job. And I have omitted any discussion of the bizarre legal system which attempts to deal with those criminals who are defined as "juveniles." In this chapter, I examine each of these steps in some detail and show how a fuller respect for the rights of several property, freedom of contract, restitution, and self-defense combine to break this vicious circle and permit more effective law enforcement than is possible at present. Then I challenge the common belief that, with such rights in place, increased punishment beyond making full restitution to crime victims is necessary to achieve "deterrence" of criminals.

Far from being utopian, the following discussion attempts to answer the "practical" objection to restitution by providing a more realistic appraisal of crime prevention than usually accompanies discussions of deterrence. If any stance is utopian and unrealistic, it is the widely-held belief that the best or only way to prevent more crime is by increasing punishment.

1. Crime Prevention as a Commons Problem

No one believes that any legal system will eliminate all crime. Moreover, we know that we might have far less crime today, except for the value we place on the liberal features of a free society that would be lost in the unbridled pursuit of lower crime rates. So the appropriate standard against which to hold any system of justice is somewhere less than perfection. Still, a greater adherence to the liberal fusion of justice and the rule of law than we enjoy at present would permit more effective crime prevention.

When several property rights are ill-defined, misallocations of resources will occur. If a particular resource is thought to be held in common—that is, if all are thought to have an equal right to exploit the use of this property—then no person has the right to exclude others from using the resource. Without the right to exclude, it is unlikely that the benefits accruing to persons who privately invest in the care or improvement of a resource will exceed the costs of their efforts. Indeed, the overriding incentive for resource users lacking a right to exclude others is to maximize their own consumption lest others consume the resource first.

For this reason, commonly held resources are typically overused and undermaintained. This has been called the "tragedy of the commons."[2] While this analysis of the use and consumption of farmland and other physical resources is well known, it has seldom been applied to the problem of crime prevention. If the traditional economic assessment of the commons problem is valid, it is

[2] See H. S. Gordon, "The Economic Theory of a Common Property Resource: The Fishery," *Journal of Political Economy*, vol. 62 (1954), p. 124; Garrett Hardin, "The Tragedy of the Commons," *Science*, vol. 162 (1968), pp. 1243–8.

reasonable to suggest that at least part of the problem of "crime in the streets" may stem from the belief that the streets (and parks, sidewalks, and alleyways) must be owned in common. The fact that public parks and streets are held in common adversely affects crime prevention in three important ways.

First, little incentive exists for individuals to commit their private resources to prevent rights-violating conduct on so-called "public"[3] or government-held property. There then appears no choice but to create an inherently inefficient coercive monopoly to provide "public" police protection. Second, when property is owned and administered by a central government, constitutional constraints on the government's power to exclude citizens from using public property are needed to minimize abuses of power. For this reason, dangerous persons cannot be excluded from public property *before* they prey on victims. Finally, in absence of a right to exclude from public property, great reliance is placed upon public imprisonment of criminals. Let us consider each of these factors in more detail.

The Inefficacy of Public Law Enforcement

Just as a parent will not invest in playground equipment to be put in a public park for the use of his or her children, neither will individuals voluntarily pay for private security patrols to protect themselves or their children while they use the public parks and streets unless, as is sometimes the case, the provision of this service can be limited to those who are paying for it. Security guards may be hired to patrol a government-owned street if conditions become so dangerous that most residents of that street are induced to contribute. Or guards may be employed to escort a sufficiently valuable shipment of property that is being conveyed on public streets if the risk of loss is great enough to justify the costs. And where conditions are particularly dangerous, wealthy people can and do hire private bodyguards.

Normally, however, because private investors in protective services on public property cannot adequately benefit from their investment, such services are unlikely to be privately provided. As a result, all responsibility for such protection must fall upon whatever governmental agency has assumed jurisdiction over the property in question. Taxes must be raised and government employees hired to protect the users of the property. Here, as elsewhere, defining a package of goods and services—in this case protective services—as a "public good" and then attempting to provide that good by government agencies is inherently less responsive to the needs and demands of consumers than defining property rights in such a manner as to allow both private investment and consumption.

---

[3] I put "public" in quotes because it is a euphemism for government administered property. Apart from the fact that government owns the streets and sidewalks (and the implications that follow from this fact discussed here), a downtown shopping district is no more public than a "private" shopping center.

The practical accountability of government law enforcement agencies to the consumer are indirect at best and nonexistent at worst. Government police agencies, especially those in large cities, are beholden first to the political establishment that dictates their funding and second, if at all, to individual members of the general public. Tax-financed government agencies are protected from competition and need not obtain the actual consent of their "customers." Unlike market institutions, which must rely on consensual agreements and payments, government police agencies lack both the motivation and the ability to discover and respond to shifting and diverse consumer preferences. In the absence of the freedom to contract for such services and the freedom from having a "contract" imposed by a coercive monopoly, government police agencies are hopelessly plagued by the first-order problem of knowledge. Ever inefficient, often counterproductive, and occasionally abusive police services are among the more easily anticipated results of relying on government-provided monopolistic police agencies.

The Inefficacy of Public Property

The problem of government ownership of public spaces extends beyond the need this creates for government police forces. One of the essential characteristics of several property is the right of an owner to control its use. You need not let into your home any person who knocks on your door; nor must you wait for a guest on your property to commit an aggressive act before you may ask that person to leave. Being a property owner gives you the right to consent to its use by others, and such a right is meaningless unless you have the right to withhold consent as well.

When governments assume control over streets, parks, and other common resources, they are acting in the capacity of property owners. For good reason, however, governments in a free society are denied many of the rights accorded private individuals and institutions. Republican theory specifies that government exists at the pleasure and for the benefit of the general public. Public property is said to belong to all the people and is merely "held in trust" by the government. A governmental right to limit the access of citizens to public property without some acceptable reason would be inconsistent with this theoretical premise. As a practical matter, a free society would not remain free for long if a government, which coercively maintained control over all streets, sidewalks, and parks, were accorded the same rights and discretion enjoyed by private property owners.

For these reasons, governments must be prevented by constitutional constraints from denying access to public property, which (in theory) is held for the use and benefit of all citizens, unless good cause can be shown. But restricting the right of governments to control public property unavoidably creates intractable problems of social control. Requiring only a mere suspicion or reasonable belief that someone might commit a crime to justify governmental exclusion would not adequately protect citizens from government abuses. Such a standard would be too easy for the government to meet and too hard for the citizen to contest. But requiring probable cause before government can arrest a suspect, and proof beyond a reasonable doubt before it can use incarceration to deny access to public areas by those who have already committed crimes, leaves considerable opportunity for criminal profit.

A society that includes extensive public property holdings is therefore faced with what might be called a *dilemma of vulnerability*. Since governments enjoy privileges denied their citizens and are subject to few of the economic constraints of private institutions, their citizens are forever vulnerable to governmental tyranny. Therefore, freedom can only be preserved by denying government police agencies the right to regulate public property with the same discretion accorded private property owners. Yet steps taken to protect society from the government also serve to make citizens more vulnerable to criminally-inclined persons by providing such persons with a greater opportunity for a safe haven on the public streets and sidewalks and in the public parks.

The dilemma of vulnerability created by public property leads to an ever-present temptation to trade liberty for security—that is, to compensate for the inefficiency of government-provided law enforcement by unjustly restricting individual rights, for example, by prior restraints on conduct that "leads to crime," such as books and music, by implementing random searches, or by increasing the punishment of those few criminals who are caught in the hopes of deterring the many whom the government police cannot catch or the government courts cannot convict. In this manner, pursuing the goal of crime prevention constrained by the institution of public property creates a serious social instability that is always threatening a free society from within. And, as we shall see later in this chapter, the last strategy of increasing punishment has a tendency to reduce the certainty of its imposition.

The Inefficacy of Public Imprisonment

When people cannot be excluded from public property unless they have been convicted of a crime, great pressure is created to build public prisons to keep those who have been convicted away from others. Imprisonment can at best be viewed as a crude approximation of how a regime of several property could respond to criminal conduct. Just as private citizens may individually or collectively bar others from their property, the government uses the penitentiary system to keep dangerous individuals out of public (and private) property. But public imprisonment has several significant drawbacks.

First, and foremost, public prisons as they now exist are unjust to victims of crime. The practice of incarcerating criminals in public prisons effectively deprives victims of their right to restitution in those cases where the greatest rights violations have occurred. Victims of the most serious crimes and their families are thereby twice victimized: once by the rights violator and again by the enforcement agencies that require victims to participate at some considerable risk and cost while denying to them any effective ability to obtain reparations from the offender.

Second, because a complete deprivation of liberty is such a severe sanction, the cost of error is greatly increased. Consequently, one must be proved guilty beyond a reasonable doubt of a most serious crime before imprisonment is permitted and many guilty persons escape the sanction and remain free. Third, imprisonment is a blunt instrument. Although sentence lengths can vary, you are either in prison or you are out. As a result criminal sanctions for many offenders admit of only two degrees of severity: onerous or virtually nonexistent. Fourth, imprisonment is expensive. While scarce resources are expended to confine, prisoners are prevented from producing anything of value to others.

Finally, because only the worst offenders are incarcerated, prisons become very dangerous places. Dangerousness is thereby added to the deprivation of liberty to heighten still further the severity of imprisonment and the cost of error. As a result, judges become even more reluctant to sentence a person to prison for fear of a very real risk of overpunishment. When they have discretion, judges become increasingly inclined to give even serious felons the benefit of the doubt by sentencing them to a period of probation until they have established a sufficiently serious criminal record. Thus, the certainty of punishment is further eroded.

As was discussed in Chapter 10, were we to fully implement a right of restitution, a majority of offenders would face, not imprisonment as we currently know it, but confinement in an employment project in which they can work at productive jobs to make restitution to their victims. There is no reason why these facilities need be government owned or managed. Indeed, as was discussed in Chapter 9, such private companies as Corrections Corporation of America and Wackenhut are today building and managing prisons.[4]

Comparing Public with Several Property

A more thorough commitment to the rights that define the liberal conception of justice promises a way to break free of the vicious cycle of public property, public police, and public prisons. Private social control and genuine crime prevention become feasible as the institution of public property is supplanted by a more extensive recognition of several property rights. Where several property rights are well defined (or where government officials can act more like private owners) crime prevention is more easily accomplished.

In relatively well-to-do areas, where large shopping centers and office complexes are the most common forms of commercial activity, roads, parking lots, sidewalks, and security patrols are all privately provided. As a result, "[t]here

---

[4] See text accompanying ch. 9, n. 20.

are now more private security personnel than public law enforcement personnel in the United States, and during the past fifteen to twenty years, the growth rate of the private [security] industry has substantially outpaced that of public law enforcement."[5] Summarizing the studies that monitored this growth, Bruce Benson has noted:

Private police perform many functions beyond patrolling or guarding residential buildings, neighborhoods, and corporate headquarters. They also provide security for airports, sports arenas, hospitals, colleges, state and municipal government buildings, banks, manufacturing plants, hotels, and retail stores. They provide armored-car services and central-alarm systems. Private security employees range from minimum-wage contract guards or watchmen in retail establishments where skill requirements are minimal, to guard positions in corporate headquarters that required college educations and substantial additional training, to highly trained body-guards and security consultants. The industry has developed a high level of specialization over the last 25 years.[6]

Moreover, in contrast to shopping districts in big cities, the owners of private developments can control access to the common areas between stores and offices. Any failure to effectively curtail criminal conduct will carry with it serious economic costs since increased crime causes rent receipts to decline. By the same token, discourtesy and overly restrictive crime control efforts can also cause lost business and bad will. These consumer-oriented incentives exist as well for owners of larger private residential developments. Such incentives impel law enforcement efforts that are more responsive than government bureaus to the needs of both the property owner and the consumer to whom the property owner is attempting to appeal.

Similarly, in smaller communities where values are relatively homogeneous, informal social pressure is more effective in inhibiting disapproved behavior and government officials can more easily exert control over governmental police agencies and public property akin to the control of private property owners. Consequently, the problem of crime control will be diminished in these places for much the same reason that it is with a regime of several property. However, minorities and strangers are likely to suffer in such settings far more than they would in a regime of extensive several property regulated by the liberal conception of justice and the rule of law. (Jim Crow laws restricting the activities of African-Americans in the south, apartheid restrictions on blacks in South Africa, and employment restrictions imposed upon Jews throughout most of history would have been impossible without extensive public property and coercive interferences with freedom of contract.[7])

[5] Benson, *Enterprise of Law*, p. 201 (citing Truet A. Ricks, Bill G. Tillet, and Clifford W. Van Meter, *Principles of Security* (Cincinnati: Criminal Justice Studies, Anderson, 1981), p. 11).

[6] Benson, *Enterprise of Law*, p. 213.

[7] See e.g. Jennifer Roback, "The Political Economy of Segregation: The Case of Segregated Streetcars," *Journal of Economic History*, vol. 46 (Dec. 1986), pp. 893–918 (describing how legal coercion was needed to compel private streetcar companies to segregate whites and blacks).

When some people think of private security, they imagine conditions in some Latin American countries where wealthy persons live behind walls and machine-gun toting guards stand by the gates. They do not think about the many vast residential communities in the United States where both streets and police patrols are privately provided, because such communities are so similar in appearance to government-protected areas. In these developments, streets and police protection can be "collectively," though still privately, provided by and to all the property owners more effectively than it can be to individual owners who are not part of the development. Some of these developments restrict entry more or less strictly; others do not. All are free, however, to remove potential offenders before they can harm others—a means of crime prevention that public police operating on public streets are unable to provide. The result is far safer homes and streets.

The problem is to provide the same protection to those persons, particularly poor persons, who now must rely exclusively on the protection of public police in areas where true prevention is inhibited because access cannot be controlled. The brunt of today's crime problem occurs in older, predominantly poorer areas, where commercial, residential, and recreational activity must depend most heavily on traditional forms of public property management (not to mention large-scale government housing projects), and in those places where the diversity of the population prevents a monocentric system from mimicking a system of several property, as might be possible in smaller, more insular, and more homogeneous communities. If this reliance on public property and public law enforcement is reduced, the benefits that only several property and efficient law enforcement can provide will be made more readily available to less affluent communities.[8]

A more extensive adherence to the liberal fusion of justice and the rule of law also promises significantly more effective law enforcement efforts. First, in contrast to the public response, which must await the commission of a crime before taking action, private owners who will directly suffer from a crime can directly benefit from truly *preventative* measures. Their interest is in seeing that the crime not take place at all. Ask yourself whether a *smart* public policeman who saw a suspected burglar in a public alley behind your house would stop him *before* he entered the house—that is, before a crime had been committed—

---

[8] One place where this has been tried on a limited scale is St. Louis, Missouri. Oscar Newman has written that "the decline of St. Louis, Missouri, has come to epitomize the impotence of federal, state, and local resources in coping with the consequences of large scale population change. Yet buried within those very areas of St. Louis which have been experiencing the most radical turnover of population are a series of streets where residents have adopted a program to stabilize their communities to deter crime, and to guarantee the necessities of a middle-class life-style. These residents have been able to create and maintain for themselves what their city was no longer able to provide: low crime rates, stable property values and a sense of community. . . . *The distinguishing characteristic of these streets is that they have been deeded back from the city to the residents and are now legally owned and maintained by the residents themselves*". Oscar Newman, *Community of Interest* (Garden City, NY: Anchor Press, 1980), p. 124 (emphasis added).

or would he stand by instead until after the burglary was in progress? If he acted before a crime was committed he would have to release the offender, or charge him with only a minor offense. Is it not perverse that public law enforcement makes waiting until a crime is being committed the smart way to "prevent" crime?

Second, as was discussed above, ownership rights and free contracts both enable and compel private law enforcement agencies to allocate their resources more efficiently than public police departments do. Law enforcement agencies that must obtain the consent of their clients are more truly accountable than those who are supposed to protect a captive market of voters. The opportunity for profit made possible by freedom of contract provides powerful incentives for competitors, and providers of substitute goods and services, to exploit deficiencies in the existing services. They also are free to innovate without the constraints now imposed by organized political groups demanding the continuation of services for which they are unwilling to pay. Such a competitive system could be very far from perfect and still vastly outperform government-provided law enforcement.

Third, in contrast to a penitentiary system, where one is either in prison or out, exclusion from private property is a far more decentralized process of individual decisions. Suspicious persons can be excluded from some "public" places and not others, resulting in a far more graduated response to the threat of crime than imprisonment. Communication networks can make possible the exclusion from most public places of persons repeatedly convicted of crimes who are thought to pose a danger to society without the complete banishment of such persons to the four walls of a brutal penitentiary. (Although it is not difficult to imagine that the most dangerous persons would be free to enter only those limited areas that cater to them, past experience with penal colonies suggests that such areas may evolve into increasingly less dangerous places.[9])

Other Factors Influencing Criminal Conduct

Of course, other factors contribute to the problem of crime besides those discussed here. For example, governmentally-enforced restrictions on the labor market and on entrepreneurial activity have prevented "classes" of people from escaping their dependence on government assistance or on criminal conduct. To the extent that persons are principally motivated to commit crimes (usually property crimes) by genuine financial need, a freer and more prosperous society where more economic opportunities are available to those who are willing to work should significantly reduce this incentive.

---

[9] For a history of the English "transportation" of criminals to penal colonies, see Leonard P. Liggio, "The Transportation of Criminals: A Brief Political-Economic History," in Barnett and Hegel, *Assessing the Criminal*, pp. 273–94.

Moreover, statutes against victimless activities of all kinds have created lucrative black markets which provide enormous profits to those persons who are willing to break these "laws."[10] Criminalizing such activity will inevitably undermine whatever respect for law a person engaged in such conduct may once have had. In such a setting, it is unrealistic to expect most black market-eers, whose livelihood is earned by providing goods and services that are deemed to be illegal, to observe the fine line between violating such statutes and violating the genuine rights of others—particularly when their black-market activities are denied the protection of recognized legal institutions and they must routinely resort to self help.[11]

Victimless crime laws not only breed violations of victim's rights, the huge premiums that result from making certain highly desired transactions illicit create powerful financial incentives for criminals to organize into groups which in effect purchase the "right" or privilege to engage in criminal conduct by corrupting law enforcement agents at all levels. Where legal constraints on exchanges between consenting adults are eliminated, the source of the artificially inflated profits earned by those who are willing to accept the substantial risks of doing business on the black market would also be eliminated. Without these profits, the other sordid criminogenic side effects of these statutes would rapidly and markedly diminish.

2. The Fallacy of Punitive Deterrence

To compensate for the inefficiencies of the regime of public property, public police, and public prisons, all attention has typically been fixed upon increasing punishment to deter criminals from committing crimes. A few people have advocated a system of punitive restitution in which deterrence is sought by increasing the amount of compensation owed to the victim beyond that which is required by strict proportionality.[12] Historically more common,

[10] See Randy E. Barnett, "Bad Trip: Drug Prohibition and the Weakness of Public Policy," *Yale Law Journal*, vol. 103 (1994), p. 2593; and Randy E. Barnett, "Curing the Drug Law Addition: The Harmful Side Effects of Legal Prohibition," in Ronald Hamowy (ed.), *Dealing with Drugs: Consequences of Government Control* (San Francisco: Pacific Research Institute, 1987), pp. 73–102.

[11] See Stergios Skaperdas and Constantine Syropoulos, "Gangs as Primitive States," in Sam Pelzman (ed.), *The Economics of Organized Crime* (Cambridge: Cambridge University Press, 1995), p. 64: "Laws prohibiting the production and distribution of certain commodities (drugs, alcohol, prostitution, gambling) also imply that the state effectively abrogates the enforcement of its other laws in the affected illegal market; private parties can no longer use the ordinary channels for the adjudication of disputes and the enforcement of contracts".

[12] See e.g. Stephen Schafer, *Restitution to Victims of Crime* (Chicago: Quadrangle Books, 1960); *id.*, "Restitution to Victims of Crime—An Old Correctional Aim Modernized," *Minnesota Law Review*, vol. 50 (1965), p. 246; Murray N. Rothbard, "Punishment and Proportionality," in Barnett and Hagel, *Assessing the Criminal*, pp. 259–70.

however, is a system that imposes upon offenders some physical unpleasant-ness—from torture, to incarceration, to death—that is unrelated to the obligation to compensate victims. Stanley Benn has offered the following definition of punishment:

Characteristically, punishment is unpleasant. It is inflicted on an offender because of an offense he has committed; it is deliberately imposed, not just the natural con-sequence of a person's action (like a hang-over), and the unpleasantness is essen-tial to it, not an accidental accompaniment to some other treatment (like the pain of the dentist's drill.)[13]

Thus according to the traditional definition of punishment, the exercise of the rights of restitution and self-defense are not punishments, strictly speaking, because any unpleasantness this may inflict upon an offender is incidental to the purpose of collecting restitution and incapacitating the dangerous.

In this section, I want to contest the commonplace assumption that impos-ing a punishment in addition to forcing criminals to make complete restitu-tion will "logically" and therefore inevitably lead to increased deterrence. By deterrence I mean the idea that a threat of punishment will induce persons to refrain from criminal activity. Deterrence is to be distinguished from disable-ment or incapacitation in which people are physically prevented from com-mitting crimes.[14] While I cannot prove and do not contend that punishment over and above restitution never increases deterrence, I will show why the confidence of some that it *must and invariably will* do so is misplaced. In sum, I show here that the strategy of punitive deterrence, as it is widely held, is a fallacy.

Proponents of the strategy of punitive deterrence who criticize pure restitu-tion purport to be realists. So in the discussion that follows, I will examine just how realistic are their assumptions and the conclusions they draw from them.

---

[13] Stanley I. Benn, "Punishment," *The Encyclopedia of Philosophy*, vol. vii, (New York: Macmillan and Free Press, 1967), p. 29.

[14] There is a further distinction, irrelevant here, between "special" and "general" deterrence. As explained by Jeffrie Murphy and Jules Coleman, punishment of Jones for a crime: "might prevent *other* crimes in one or more of the following ways: (1) the expe-rience of being punished might affect Jones in such a way that the fear of future pun-ishment will deter him from committing more crimes in the future. This is called *special* deterrence. (2) When others know that Jones has been punished (when he has been used as an example), they might take the threat of state punishment more seriously and thus might be less inclined because of their increased fear to engage in criminal conduct." Jeffrie Murphy and Jules Coleman, *The Philosophy of Law* (Totowa, NJ: Rowman & Allanheld, 1984), pp. 123–4. Of relevance, however, is that Murphy and Coleman dis-tinguish both forms of deterrence from disablement or incapacitation: "(3) Even if Jones and others will not be deterred by Jones' punishment, certain methods of punishment (e.g. incarceration) will *incapacitate* Jones and keep him out of circulation so that he will not be free to prey on others again. This justification may strike us as particularly per-suasive for highly violent offenders". Ibid. 124 (emphasis added). While they refer to incarceration as "punishment," it need not be conceived as a deliberate infliction of unpleasantness on an offender—the traditional conception of punishment. Instead it can be viewed as a means by which the innocent may defend themselves against the dangerous.

Assumptions Underlying the Strategy of Punitive Deterrence

However implemented, advocates of the strategy of punitive deterrence quite reasonably assume that there will always be a less than perfect rate of catching criminals. If so, when calculating whether to commit a crime, the criminal will discount the subjective value to him of paying the restitution that will be owed by the chance of being caught and punished. So, for example, if the chance of catching and successfully prosecuting an auto thief is 50 per cent, then in calculating his expected return for the theft, the auto thief will discount the chance of paying full compensation of $20,000 by 50 per cent or $10,000. If the stolen car is worth $20,000 to the thief, he will receive an expected profit of $10,000 from the theft and the threat of having to make full restitution will not induce him to comply with the requirements of justice. According to this theory, with an apprehension rate of 50 per cent, achieving compliance by the strategy of punitive deterrence requires that the amount of restitution be set at $40,000.

We can summarize this assumption underlying the deterrence strategy as follows: the *ex ante* cost imposed on a criminal by a legal sanction equals the rate of apprehension times the severity of the sanction imposed or:

$$\text{COST OF PUNISHMENT} = \text{RATE OF CAPTURE} \times \text{SEVERITY OF PUNISHMENT}$$

This means that, to deter a criminal from committing a crime, the subjective cost of punishment should equal (and thereby negate) the subjective benefit of the crime. Therefore, the severity of sanction should be determined as follows:

$$\text{SEVERITY OF SANCTION} = \frac{\text{BENEFIT OF CRIME}}{\text{RATE OF CAPTURE}}$$

In the example of the auto theft, if the subjective benefit to the criminal of an auto theft is $20,000 and the rate of apprehension is 50 per cent, to achieve deterrence the severity of the sanction must be $40,000 or

$$\$40,000 = \frac{\$20,000}{.5}$$

Of course, if this formula is meant to be applied to actual persons, we must take account of the fact that each of these variables is highly subjective. To achieve deterrence, for example, it matters not what the actual rate of apprehension may be, but what the particular offender perceives his chance of apprehension to be. The relative optimism and pessimism of a particular offender, though related perhaps to actual rates of apprehension, is entirely subjective and likely to vary widely. Indeed we might expect people with deviantly high optimism about their chances of evading capture to be attracted to criminal activity. And the chances of capture for any particular offender might well depend on the nature of the crime or the manner in which it is carried out.[15] So too with the subjective perception of severity of punishment or benefit to be gained from a crime. The subjectivity of each of these variables undercuts the illusory inevitability of results promised by this formula. Moreover, the analysis presented in Chapter 10 suggests a serious problem with the strategy of punitive deterrence: it typically ignores the cost of enforcement error.

The Immorality of Punitive Deterrence

Utilitarians have long been accused of adhering to a theory that would justify, in some circumstances, the punishment of the innocent to deter others from committing crimes.[16] And they have long and loudly denied the accusation. Yet the analysis of enforcement error presented here reveals that the strategy of punitive deterrence, which utilitarians commonly favor, involves precisely this sacrifice.

Any attempt to compensate for the inefficiency of mechanisms to catch criminals and bring them to justice by increasing the severity of sanctions must come at the expense of persons who are wrongfully accused. Every increase in the *level* of punishment to enhance deterrence of the guilty increases the harm inflicted upon the wrongfully accused. That is, once we assume—as we must if we want to be realistic—the inevitability of enforcement error, a *rule* requiring punishment in addition to full compensation comes at the direct expense of the innocent. In sum, absent perfect information, a strategy of punitive deterrence requires that some people who are wrongfully accused be sacrificed to deter more crime.

The infliction of harm on the innocent should provide a powerful reason to hesitate before embracing a strategy of punitive deterrence. The fact that many utilitarians embrace this strategy without even considering this consequence gives support to those who criticize utilitarian theory as immoral, though it might mean only that advocates of punitive deterrence are not as realistic as they think. True, adhering to the principle of pure restitution also risks imposing costs on innocent defendants. But, as I argued above, the only alternative to imposing this risk, is to guaranty that *every* innocent victim of crime will suffer an injustice.

[15] When I was a prosecutor it was commonly said that the justice system would grind to a halt if criminals just wore masks and gloves and did not talk to the police when they are caught. They would also benefit by leaving their immediate neighborhood where they were easily recognized. Of course, this suggests that those criminals who did travel outside their neighborhoods and who did wear gloves and masks and who did not make statements to the police have a much reduced chance of being punished.

[16] See e.g. J. J. C. Smart, "Utilitarianism," in *The Encyclopedia of Philosophy*, vol. viii, (New York: Macmillan and Free Press, 1967), p. 208: "For example, a riot involving hundreds of deaths may be averted only by punishing some innocent scapegoat and calling it punishment. Given certain empirical assumptions, which may perhaps not in fact be true, but which in a certain sort of society might be true, it is hard to see how a rule utilitarian could object to such a practice of punishing the innocent in these circumstances."

The Mirage of Punitive Deterrence

While the moral difficulty with punitive deterrence deserves wider recognition than it receives, it does not lead to a conclusion that a strategy of punitive deterrence is a fallacy. When enforcement error is incorporated into the analysis of deterrence, however, another more subtle but equally serious problem with enhanced penalties can be revealed: it is not at all clear that increasing the amount of the legal sanction will have the desired effect on criminals' calculation of interest. That is, when the problem of enforcement error is taken into account, it is highly uncertain that a strategy of punitive deterrence will actually work as the theory suggests. When (a chance of) deterrence is offered as a justification for going beyond restitution and imposing increased suffering on the innocent accused, the uncertainty of achieving this objective with a strategy of punitive deterrence should count heavily against it.

The strategy of punitive deterrence purports to compensate for the less than perfect rate of imposing sanctions by increasing the severity of sanctions. Crucially, a strategy of punitive deterrence *assumes that the rate and severity of sanctions are independent variables*—that is, it assumes that increases in the variable of severity will not be offset by reductions in the variable of certainty. But there are at least three factors that render the rate of imposing a sanction highly dependent upon its severity.

First, once we acknowledge that increasing the severity of sanctions will increase the severity of enforcement error, we ought to adopt more weighty presumptions of innocence to protect more effectively the wrongfully accused. For example, as was discussed in Chapter 10, instead of requiring proof beyond a preponderance of the evidence—the "civil" standard applicable to pure restitution—we may require proof beyond a reasonable doubt—the "criminal" standard applicable to pure punishment. Yet, by requiring more persuasive evidence to rebut the presumption of innocence, we are making convictions more difficult and acquittals of the guilty more likely. In other words, given a justified concern with protecting the innocent from unjust punishment, increases in the severity of sanctions are likely to lead to reductions in the rate of imposition. It is far from clear, therefore, that such a strategy of increasing severity will have the actual effect of increasing the *ex ante* incentives facing criminals.

Second, increasing the severity of sanctions increases the incentives for any accused, whether guilty or innocent, to resist capture and prosecution. That is, as the cost of conviction increases so too does the incentive to invest in acquittal. This will mean, for example, hiring better lawyers, insisting on full trials rather than pleas of guilty, etc. These actions will have the effect of making convictions more difficult to obtain and the rate of acquittals to rise. Once again, therefore, the incentives created by increasing the severity of sanctions will tend to reduce the rate of successful imposition and thereby reduce its certainty. True, any "avoidance costs" incurred by a criminal will have some *ex ante* deterrent effect (assuming, as explained below, that these costs fall within the subjective "time horizon" of the criminal).[17] Nonetheless, because we must assume that a criminal would not invest in avoidance if he did not subjectively prefer incurring these costs to punishment, it is doubtful that these avoidance costs will equal the subjective cost of punishment.

Third, it is not at all certain that increasing the *stated* severity of sanctions will increase their *actual* severity. The formula usually assumed by those advocating a strategy of punitive deterrence (COST OF PUNISHMENT = RATE × SEVERITY) leaves out the crucial variable of *proximity*. If, however, proximity of imposition is also taken into account so that:

$$\text{COST OF PUNISHMENT} = \text{RATE} \times \text{SEVERITY} \times \text{PROXIMITY}$$

then the longer the delay in imposing a sanction, the more it will be discounted and the less impact it will have on criminal calculation. So, if increasing the severity of a sanction also increases the procedural protections afforded criminal defendants, as well as the incentives of criminals to invest in legal (and illegal) resistance, this will decrease the proximity of the imposition. However, as the imposition of the sanctions are postponed to the future, because of the natural tendency to discount the future, their ability to affect the *ex ante* interest of criminals declines. This is yet another reason to doubt that increasing the stated sanction for a rights violation will actually increase the *ex ante* cost imposed on a criminal.

Finally, there is a potentially decisive reason why increasing punishment does not invariably or logically increase deterrence. Different persons discount future costs and benefits at substantially different rates. As was discussed in Chapter 9, each person has his or her own subjective time horizon. Those with a high time preference place comparatively greater value on present consumption than someone with a low time preference. A great many factors influence our time horizon or rate of discounting the future.[18] These need not concern us here.

Of relevance is the fact that we all discount the future differently and, by and large, those who intentionally violate the rights of others are disproportionately persons with extremely high time preferences. That is, such persons so greatly prefer present consumption over a benefit or cost in the future that the future impedes on *ex ante* calculation little if at all. As was discussed in Chapter 9, this is one reason they perceive a conflict between their interests and the requirements of justice. Because such persons discount the variable of proximity to zero or nearly zero, the *ex ante* costs of a sanction is approximately zero regardless of the severity of the sanction.

Even if the severity of sanction is doubled or trebled to compensate for a reduced rate of capture, the potential offender is still likely to perceive a

---

[17] My thanks to David Friedman for pointing this out to me.
[18] See Edward C. Banfield, "Present-orientedness and Crime," in Barnett and Hagel, *Assessing the Criminal*, pp. 133–9.

benefit from committing the offense. For example, if the (subjective) probability of imposition is 50 per cent, the (subjective) severity of the sanction is doubled, and the subjective proximity of the imposition is discounted to zero, then for the theft of the car worth $20,000, the *ex ante* cost imposed by punishment is zero:

$$\text{COST OF PUNISHMENT} = 50\% \times \$40,000 \times 0 = 0$$

In this way, for the worst criminals, the subjectivity of proximity completely defeats the strategy of punitive deterrence.

Adherents to the strategy of punitive deterrence typically will advocate compensating for the subjectivity of severity, certainty, and proximity by still further increases in severity. By now it should be apparent why this is both a losing and immoral game. The interdependence of these variables will doom this response either to ineffectiveness, or hopelessly random deterrence—at the same time as it raises the cost of enforcement error imposed unjustly on the innocent.

The Conflict Between Punitive Deterrence and the Rule of Law

The strategy of punitive deterrence must come to grips with another problem that is distinct from the dependent relationship among the variables of severity, certainty, and proximity of coercive sanctions. The strategy of punitive deterrence is likely to clash with the rule of law requirement of generality.[19] If it were announced, for example, that any person committing a rights violation in a system with a 50 per cent rate of capture would owe 200 per cent restitution, this principle of double compensation would satisfy the formal requirement of generality. But the problem for punitive deterrence is that it would be entirely coincidental if the real *ex ante* cost imposed on the offender corresponded to the *ex ante* benefit to be gained from the offense. That is, it would be mere happenstance that the deterrent affect of the punishment will match the gain from the crime. The reason for this is that, as mentioned above, each of these variables is highly subjective.

First, and most obviously, one confronts the *subjectivity of severity*. The cost any particular criminal attaches to a sanction is thoroughly subjective. Each person is likely to value the threat of a particular sanction differently—or at a minimum, there is no way to know just how great a cost any particular sanction will impose on any given person. For some the humiliation of a criminal conviction would be a massive punishment; for others even extended incarceration is not perceived as onerous. To adjust the sanction to approximate the subjective perception of the individual would require different custom-tailored sentences for each offender.

Any effort to do this runs afoul of both the problems of knowledge and interest. Because the knowledge of the cost of a sanction is intensely personal

---

[19] See Chapter 5.

knowledge, it is virtually impossible for outsiders to have any idea what this cost may be. It would be mere chance if the legal system imposed the correct sanction. Prospective offenders would fail to calculate accurately the severity of the sentence they will eventually receive if caught. Moreover, by permitting the legal system to vary the punishment according to the offender rather than the offense, a tremendous opportunity for abuse by law enforcement and the judiciary is created.[20] For both these reasons our experience with so-called "indeterminate sentences" has not been happy.

The same holds true with the *subjectivity of certainty*. While there may be an objective rate of capture for a legal system as a whole, the rate of certainty that counts when a given criminal makes his calculation is the certainty he subjectively attaches to his own capture. However, as I mentioned earlier, the chances of any given criminal being caught are both highly dependent on the circumstances of the particular crime and highly uncertain. For this reason, different criminals are likely to make substantially different assessments of the likelihood of their capture. Once more, to accomplish deterrence, the extent of *ex post* punishment would have to be varied to reflect the subjectivity of certainty and—even if this could be done, which is doubtful—this would violate the rule of law.

Finally, there is the *subjectivity of proximity* discussed above. The severity of a sanction would, once again, have to be individually tailored to the subjective time horizon of each individual if the strategy of punitive deterrence is to work. And, once again, this would require us to violate the formal requirements of the rule of law with the attendant difficulties of knowledge and interest that such a violation would engender.[21]

In sum, the strategy of punitive deterrence is deeply flawed. The fallacy of punitive deterrence is not that coercive sanctions, including those that are punitive, fail to address the compliance problem (they do). The fallacy is that by *increasing* the severity of any given sanction beyond that required to fully compensate the victim we are certain to increase our ability to address the compliance problem by providing a greater deterrent to misconduct. This is akin to the fallacy that increasing marginal income tax rates will necessarily and invariably increase tax revenues. The source of both fallacies is the failure to realize that human behavior will adjust to and attempt to avoid increasingly onerous penalties in highly unpredictable ways.

Although increasing punishments, as the strategy of punitive deterrence requires, will unavoidably increase the cost of error imposed on the innocent, there is no assurance that it handles the compliance problem better than pure restitution when coupled with other preventative measures discussed at the

---

[20] Thus the principle of strict proportionality also addresses the problem of enforcement abuse, a problem I shall discuss in Chapter 12.

[21] Though it is true that subjectivity also effects the remedy of restitution, it is limited to one variable: the subjective valuation that the victim of crime places on compensation for her loss.

start of this chapter that are made possible by increasing adherence to the rights of several property, freedom of contract, and self-defense. Although I have not claimed that restitution deters better than punishment, the analysis presented does undermine the belief, widely-held among both economists and lay persons, that punishment inevitably—or even logically—deters better than pure restitution.

True, the calculation of restitution damages also must objectify the subjective harm imposed upon the victim, but some compensation is better than none and more is better than less. More importantly, the *tragedy of justice* is that this is the best we can do for victims. In contrast, punitive deterrence is far from the best way of preventing crime. We rely on it so heavily because the vicious circle of public property, public law enforcement, and public prisons effectively stymies crime prevention.

3. Improving Deterrence Without Punishment

The previous discussion was not meant to suggest that the use of force can never deter some from committing crimes. Rather, it simply was intended to undermine the widespread confidence that adding punishment to the duty to make full restitution would logically increase deterrence. The strategy of punitive deterrence is an attempt to address the compliance problem that arises when criminals will perceive that the risk of capture is outweighed by the potential gain of committing the crime because the rate of successfully imposing a sanction is less than 100 per cent. The strategy of punitive deterrence attempts to handle the fact that the variable of certainty is less than 100 per cent by raising the variable of severity. We have seen how this is problematic. When it comes to deterring criminals, what alternative is there?

The Advantages of Pure Restitution

There is some reason to think that a legal system which enforced the rights of pure restitution and self-defense would deter criminals to some significant extent. First, like punishment, self-defense actions, both normal and extended, permitted by the liberal conception of justice also raise the *ex ante* costs of violating rights. Every criminal will need to take the risk of forcible resistance by the victim into account in assessing the benefits to be gained from the offense. But unlike a punishment that is postponed into the distant future, because normal self-defense is immediate, it is more likely to be taken into account by an offender with a high time preference. Indeed, in a survey of state prisoners conducted under the auspices of the National Institute of Justice, 57 per cent of surveyed felons agreed that "[m]ost criminals are more worried about meeting an armed victim than they are about running into the police."[22] As has already been discussed, a regime of decentralized jurisdiction makes self-defense and other preventative efforts far more effective than at present.[23]

Second, full compensation requires far more than the subjective value of the violated right; it also includes paying for the costs of enforcement. Full compensation includes compensation for the costs of detection, apprehension, and prosecution. This is why in Chapter 10, I assumed that full compensation for theft of a car worth $10,000 was $20,000. In such a case it is likely that the subjective cost of making restitution will often exceed the subjective benefit gained from the crime. A criminal may value a stolen car worth $10,000 (to the victim) at $5,000 (or less) and be liable for $20,000 worth of restitution.[24]

Pure restitution can also increase the certainty of sanctions and their proximity to the offense. Restitution increases incentives for victims to report offenses and to cooperate with law-enforcement authorities. Given that their expenses are paid for by successful prosecutions, law-enforcement agencies have an increased incentive actually to solve crimes. Moreover, since the cost of making restitution increases as time passes, even offenders will have an incentive to avoid prolonging the proceedings. The longer the delay, the more restitution will be owed.[25]

In the final analysis, however, it is an all too common mistake to think that the compliance problem must be handled exclusively or even primarily by the sanctions imposed after an offense (*ex post*). Because of the variables of certainty and proximity as well as the high time preference of most criminals, the most powerful disincentives to rights violations are those that are brought to bear before the offense (*ex ante*) or during the offense. Effective crime preven-

[22] James Wright and Peter Rossi, *Armed and Considered Dangerous: A Survey of Felons and their Firearms* (New York: Aldine de Gruyter, 1986), p. 145 and table 7.2. The study also found that 34% of the convicts "said they had been scared off, shot at, wounded or captured by an armed victim, and about two-thirds (69%) had at least one acquaintance who had this experience." Ibid. 154. 34% of the felons said that in contemplating a crime they either "often" or "regularly" worried that they "[m]ight get shot at by the victim." Ibid. at 145.

[23] Of course advocates of punishment may claim that they can gain the advantages of *both* punitive deterrence and these reforms. As has already been explained, however, punishment creates certain public goods problems that restitution does not. More importantly, however, since punishment never delivers perfect deterrence, the salient issue is whether pure restitution plus institutional reforms will adequately, not perfectly, address the compliance problem.

[24] But is not the increased amount of restitution also being imposed unjustly on the innocent and therefore immoral? No. What is morally suspect is raising the sanction imposed on the innocent (and the guilty) defendants not to compensate victims but solely to deter persons from committing crimes. This is a significantly different principle than one of collecting full compensation from defendants. For, as was argued above, to eliminate all restitution would be to guarantee that injustice will be done in every criminal case.

[25] Indeed, the incentives for increased certainty and proximity created by a complete system of restitution may be so powerful that they create new and different problems of enforcement error and these problems may require some additional protections of the innocent.

tion does not wait until *after* the crime has occurred but affects the criminal's incentives by making commission of the offense more difficult and capture more certain.

In the beginning of this chapter I discussed many *ex ante* law-enforcement measures that are consistent with the background rights that define the liberal conception of justice. Indeed, I suggest that our fixation on punishment is a consequence of our having accepted a woefully inefficient mechanism of crime prevention. Remember, the whole discussion of the compliance problem began with the assumption that the rate of capture is less than 100 per cent. A great deal turns on whether this rate is 25 per cent or 85 per cent. *The social problem of crime is best addressed, not by increasing the severity of the sanction, but rather by increasing the rate of apprehension.* Unlike the variable of severity, the rate of apprehension can be increased without deleterious effects on the other variables.

The Feasibility of a Dual System

The analysis presented thus far compares the strategy of punitive deterrence with the rights of restitution and self-defense. Why cannot both systems be combined into a dual system with the advantages of each? So, for example, a victim of a rights violation may need only prove the defendant's liability beyond a preponderance of the evidence to collect strictly proportionate compensation. Over and above this, we address the compliance problem by punishment after proving the defendant's guilt beyond a reasonable doubt. Since proportionate compensation is governed by the lower burden, it will be as certain as in a system of pure restitution. Even if punishment occurs only infrequently and randomly, to some degree it will still close the gap between interest and justice and reduce the extent of the compliance problem.

From the standpoint of the compliance problem, this dual strategy sounds completely plausible. Indeed, it describes the underlying theory of our legal system that distinguishes compensation from punishment, the "civil" from the "criminal," "torts" from "crimes," and, in theory, permits both types of legal actions. Even apart from the fact that such a dual system raises the costs of error imposed on the innocent, however, there are serious problems with such a theory.

Given that this is the theory on which our current system is based, the most obvious question, of course, is why we do not see an enforceable right to restitution combined with punishment in practice today? A realistic assessment of combining restitution with punishment must begin with the observation that, in all but the rarest of cases, our legal system does not even remotely conform to this theory. Most criminals, particularly those who use violence, never make any restitution; nonviolent criminals are rarely punished; civil courts routinely award punitive damages upon a showing of only proof beyond a preponderance of the evidence. All this is no accident. Punishment and compensation simply do not mix. Rather than peacefully coexist, punishment tends to drive out compensation, but why? I think both systemic and psychological factors are at work.

Systemically, the safeguards implemented to protect the innocent from unjust punishment effectively prevent a civil lawsuit from proceeding until the criminal prosecution is concluded. For example, the constitutional right against self-incrimination prevents the normal discovery procedures associated with the common law from operating effectively. However, after a successful criminal prosecution, the offender is rarely in a position to make restitution, even if a subsequent suit was successful. Imprisonment (as we know it) or capital punishment does not provide any opportunity to earn the money needed for restitution. With those who have committed financial crimes, vast sums of money are spent resisting the imposition of onerous punishment. By the time a prosecution is over, there may be little, if any, of the wrongfully acquired property left from which to make restitution. When punishment and compensation are combined, as they now are in civil actions, the safeguards adopted to protect against wrongful punishment are largely absent.

Severing punishment from compensation creates a genuine public goods problem.[26] It is hardly in the victim's interest to invest in punishing the offender over and above the amount the victim will collect in restitution.[27] To address this problem, institutions of public law enforcement are created that effectively drive a wedge between the interests of victims and of the enforcer. Public law enforcement agencies consider victims to be "complaining witnesses" to crimes committed against "the people" or "the state"—crimes which take priority over whatever interest the victim has in restitution. Indeed, unlike plaintiffs in civil actions who choose whether or not to pursue the tortfeasor, victims have no choice (in theory) but to cooperate in a prosecution or face sanctions for contempt of court. Should a victim accept restitution in lieu of punishment, he or she could be criminally charged with "compounding a crime."[28] In the quest to punish criminals, whether for retributivist motivations or to protect the public, crime victims become mere means to the ends of the institutions created to punish.

Perhaps more importantly, where the impulse to punish is permitted free rein, compensation seems to pale by comparison. When the infliction of harm upon the offender comes to be the approved and expected consequence of wrongdoing, compensation is usually disparaged as merely "putting a price on crime" or some such thing. The mind set of punishment seems to be incompatible with that of compensation—particularly when it is a "free good" pro-

---

[26] See Benson, *Enterprise of Law*, pp. 62–76, 97–101, 271–86.

[27] This problem does not, obviously, attach to punitive damages payable to the victim.

[28] See e.g. Illinois Revised Statutes, ch. 720, sect. 5/32–1: "Compounding a Crime. . . . A person compounds a crime when he receives or offers to another any consideration for a promise not to prosecute or aid in the prosecution of an offender."

vided by government. Like Gresham's law of currencies ("bad money drives good money out of circulation"), punishment drives out restitution.

Yet, this analysis cannot conclusively prove that no combination of compensation or punishment can ever address effectively the compliance problem. If punishment takes the form of payments to victims in excess of full compensation—what I call *punitive restitution*—then many of the disincentives of pure punishment are ameliorated. Punitive damages awards are quite likely to induce significant private investment in law enforcement provided that a mechanism exists for extracting payment from indigent defendants. The more serious problem with punitive restitution is actually the converse of inadequate incentives to prosecute. We would have to be very worried about the incentives that such a practice would create for enforcement abuse (the subject of Chapter 11) by persons wrongfully accusing others of crimes. This would, in turn, create the need for further procedural safeguards that would diminish both the certainty and proximity of punishment.

Perhaps, despite all these difficulties, a dual system of compensation could be devised in which pure restitution can be obtained by victims more easily than any premium imposed punitively. In any event, from the standpoint of compliance, the only plausible alternative to pure restitution is a separate system of punitive restitution also payable to victims, but subject to increased safeguards for the innocent.

Summary

(1) The ability of pure restitution and self-defense to address the compliance problem must be analyzed in the context of a more extensive reliance upon several property and freedom of contract.
(2) In such a regime, the ability to effectively prevent crime rather than deter its commission by *ex post* punishment is greatly enhanced.
(3) Unlike public property, several property creates incentives to invest in crime prevention and the ability to exclude dangerous persons before they can act.
(4) Freedom of contract makes possible far more responsive law-enforcement agencies than can be provided by a coercive monopoly.
(5) While pure restitution will not "deter" all criminal behavior, it is a fallacy to believe that increased deterrence invariably or logically follows increasing the severity of punishment.
(6) Moreover, adding a right to punish to the right of restitution increases the costs of enforcement error imposed on the wrongfully accused.
(7) Restitution increases the incentives to catch and prosecute defendants, thus increasing the rate at which legal sanctions are imposed.

TWELVE

The Problem of Enforcement Abuse

IN Chapter 10, we saw how using power to address the compliance problem raises the costs of errors. As with the general discussion of the knowledge problem in Part I, the analysis of enforcement error in Chapter 10 assumed the good faith of those charged with enforcement. In this chapter, like the discussion of the problem of interest in Part II, I now relax this assumption and consider the grave problems that are presented when the power of enforcement is made to serve the interests of the enforcers rather than of justice. We are then faced with the age-old question of "who guards the guardians?" This is the problem of enforcement abuse:

> The *problem of enforcement abuse* arises when persons responsible for using power impartially to address the compliance problem use it instead to serve their own interests or the partial interests of others.

The problem of enforcement abuse is so obvious and well-recognized that there is little reason to dwell on its description. We all know that power can be abused so that it is made to serve the interests of those who wield it and their favorites, rather then serve the purpose for which such power was initially granted: to serve impartially the ends of justice. The way the liberal conception of justice and the rule of law ameliorate this problem was laid out in my discussion of the partiality problem in Chapter 7.

The very existence of discernible principles of justice communicated by the rule of law make it more difficult to serve one's interest at the expense of others. Violating these publically accessible precepts provides a warning sensor that enforcement abuse may be taking place, a prerequisite to taking action against offending authorities. The right of several property compartmentalizes partiality and, to the extent several property rights are respected, law-enforcement agencies who abuse their power will be faced with consumers who have resources that may be used to resist this abuse.

A similar sentiment motivated the drafting of the Second Amendment to the United States Constitution protecting "the right of the people to keep and bear arms."[1] Such a right was thought necessary to enable people to exercise their right of self-defense against both individuals and governments that abuse their power. This amendment was not thought to create a right of resistance—such a right was considered a natural one and needed no such recognition. Rather, the provision was thought necessary to help preserve the means of resistance to oppression should resistance ever become necessary.[2] By the same token, a people in rightful control of resources are in a position to resist the use of power when violations of the rule of law reveal it to have been abused.

Perhaps of greatest importance is that the rights that define the liberal conception of justice be recognized as *rights* and not mere goals or interests. We have already seen how the failure to recognize a right to restitution has condemned restitution schemes to marginality. When the "interest" of a victim to receive restitution is "balanced" against the "interest" of the public to punish, it is the victim's interests that are inevitably sacrificed. Reducing rights to mere "interests" which must then be balanced against other "competing" social goals, enables those wielding power to conceal their partiality with the veneer of the highly indeterminate "greater" good. Similarly, considering several property, freedom of contract, the right of first possession, or the right of self-defense to be anything less than rights, opens them up to infringement by persons to whom the power of enforcement has been delegated. These persons may then much more easily abuse their powers to pursue their own interests or those of some partial "interest group," at the expense of the interests of those whose rights are violated. These are all reasons why the concept of natural rights was formulated in the first place.

Yet while recognizing the *rights* provided by the liberal conception of justice and the principles of *legality* provided by the rule of law may be necessary to cabin the abuse of power, this is not sufficient to handle the problem of enforcement abuse. In practice, these rights and principles, even when formally recognized, can be and have been overwhelmed by the institutional structure in which they are applied. It is the institutional dimension of the problem that I consider in the balance of this chapter. Then, in Chapter 13, I explain how the rights of several property and freedom of contract yield two *constitutional* principles that should be recognized and respected if we are to constrain effectively enforcement abuse.

---

[1] *Constitution of the United States*, amend. II. The amendment reads in its entirety: "A well regulated Militia, being necessary to the security of a free State, the right of the people to keep and bear Arms, shall not be infringed."

[2] That this and not some intention to protect state militias was the purpose of the Second Amendment has been established beyond peradventure by numerous constitutional scholars of all ideological stripes. This body of research is summarized in Randy E. Barnett and Don B. Kates, *Under Fire: The New Consensus on the Second Amendment*, vol. 45 (1996), pp. 1139–59.

1. The Centralized Control of Power

In Chapter 3, I discussed two methods of achieving social order: centralized and decentralized. We saw how the liberal fusion of justice and the rule of law permits centralized organizations or firms to arise within a decentralized order, but rejects the centralized control of an entire society. Ironically then, although liberalism arose out of the largely decentralized political setting of Europe,[3] today nearly everyone agrees that power must be centrally con-trolled. Most otherwise competing political philosophies share a common tenet that somewhere in society there must exist a "coercive monopoly of power."

As my grandfather put the matter: "Randy," he said, "there's got to be a boss." Of course, depending on how it is taken, there is much truth in this assertion. But in political and legal theory this view is rather concrete and con-stitutes what I shall call the *Single Power Principle*:

> The *Single Power Principle* specifies that there must exist somewhere in soci-ety (a) a single institution per unit of geography (a "monopoly"), (b) that is charged with authorizing the use of force ("power"), and that (c) the monopoly itself must be preserved by force ("coercively"). In sum, the Single Power Principle involves a belief in the need for a *coercive monopoly of power*.[4]

A good case could be made that this definition is redundant. In a technical sense, a sole provider of services that does not protect its market share by force (coercively) is not a true "monopoly." Still, the definition offered in the text is intended to avoid misunderstanding among the many persons who do not conceive of "monopoly" in this limited fashion.

The Appeal of the Single Power Principle

The Single Power Principle attempts to confine the legitimate use of power to a single central institution. Its appeal extends well beyond the need to control enforcement abuse. The Right believes that a coercive monopoly of power is needed to preserve "civilization" and prevent social chaos; that without a coer-cive monopoly of power, people will give in to their animalistic side and engage in a Hobbesian social "war of all against all."

---

[3] See Berman, *Law and Revolution* (describing the pluralistic origins of the Western legal tradition).

[4] Cf. Max Weber, *The Theory of Social and Economic Organization* (New York: Free Press, 1964), p. 154: "A compulsory political organization with a continuous organization (*politischer Anstaltsbetrieb*) will be called a 'state' if and insofar as its administrative staff successfully upholds a claim to the *monopoly* of the *legitimate* use of physical force in the enforcement of its order."

Thus, it is argued that, to avoid such social degeneration, a central authority must outlaw certain kinds of conduct: the forcible interference with person and possessions should be prohibited, to be sure, but also included should be sexual conduct, such as prostitution, pornography, homosexuality, and extramarital sexual relations; or conduct that encourages "antisocial" beliefs, such as religious "cults," unacceptable books and music, manners of dress, Internet communication, and public assembly; or behavior that is "destructive of values," such as drug and alcohol consumption, gambling, pool rooms, video arcades, and rock and roll. (The list changes as new "degenerate" activities are discovered.)

The image that best describes the world the Right sees as ultimately resulting from the absence of a coercive monopoly of power is one in which people are fornicating in public places with heroin needles hanging from their arms. To prevent this there must be a boss: a President, a Congress, a Supreme Court, or a Moral Majority.

The Left believes in the Single Power Principle to ensure some positive conception of "social" justice. According to this view, resources must be distributed among individuals in society according to some formula or, to use Robert Nozick's term, a "pattern."[5] Resources must be held, for example, according to some criterion of need, desert, or desires, or all holdings must be "equal" or "efficient"—that is, distributed to their highest valued use. It is argued that without a coercive monopoly of power, actual distributions of resources will not be in accordance with the mandated pattern or principle.

Thus, in addition to prohibiting the forcible interference by some with the person and possessions of others, a central authority is needed to "regulate" (usually a euphemism for prohibit) economic transfers between individuals by such measures as labor regulations, antitrust regulations, price or rent controls, and licensing schemes in various occupations; to regulate other social interactions by such measures as quotas and preferences; and to regulate consumptive activity, by such measures as food and drug regulation and the regulation of automobile design. Above all, we must redistribute income by tax and "welfare" laws.

The image that best describes the world that the Left sees as resulting from the absence of a coercive monopoly of power is one in which unreconstructed Scrooge-like characters enslave or exploit helpless Cratchets and Tiny Tims at below subsistence wages in small, cold (or hot, depending on the imagery), dark rooms. To prevent this from happening, there must be a boss: a President, a Congress, a Supreme Court, or The People.

I have deliberately drawn each of these views as broadly as possible. While ideologues exist on the Left and the Right, most people are "in the middle" in that they hold some mixture of these two general views. None of this is to say that all of the policies described above are unjustified or wrong or that these

---

[5] See Nozick, *Anarchy and Utopia*, pp. 155–60.

categories are inviolable. Notice that the positive concern for efficient allocation of wealth is now associated with some on the Right. And something
amounting to a new wave of puritanism on the Left can be observed emanat-
ing from the radical feminist movement.

Rather, the point is (*a*) that the belief in the correctness of these policies usually results from subscribing to one of these world views or some mixture of
each; (*b*) that both positions view the natural result of individual choice to be
bad; and (*c*) that both views arrive at essentially the same centralized *means*—
a coercive monopoly of power—to pursue their fundamentally different *ends*.
While it sometimes seems impossible to define precisely Left and Right, these
two visions of what would happen in the absence of a coercive monopoly of
power come closer than any formal distinction to capturing these mindsets.

Both of these visions of society are illiberal. Classical liberals do not assume
that, if left to themselves, human beings will be reduced to base animalism or
cruel exploitation. Still, many classical liberals have also accepted the Single
Power Principle because they believe that a coercive monopoly of power is
necessary to handle the problem of enforcement abuse. Though John Locke
argued strongly "that *in the State of Nature every one has the Executive Power* of
the law of nature"[6] to enforce their natural rights, he acknowledged the objection that

> it is unreasonable for Men to be Judges in their own Cases, that Self-love will make
> Men partial to themselves and their Friends. And on the other side, that Ill Nature,
> Passion and Revenge will carry them too far in punishing others. And hence noth-
> ing but Confusion and Disorder will follow.[7]

To this he responded

> I easily grant that *Civil Government* is the proper Remedy for the Inconveniences of
> the State of Nature, which must certainly be Great, where Men may be Judges in
> their own Case, since 'tis easily to be imagined, that he who is so unjust as to do
> his Brother an Injury, will scarce be so just as to condemn himself for it.[8]

In sum, according to Locke and other classical liberals we need a coercive
monopoly of power to handle the problem of enforcement abuse. Unless a single *impartial* centralized and hierarchical institution sets the rules for all and
polices abuses, eventually the enforcement of justice will be corrupted and
genuine exploitation will occur through the very institutions of coercion that
are supposed to enforce justice neutrally.

Unlike Left and Right, however, classical liberals have been more realistic in
readily acknowledging that the coercive monopoly of power is itself the source
of danger, even tyranny. As Locke himself observed in a passage immediately
following the one I just quoted:

> But I shall desire those who make this Objection, to remember that *Absolute
> Monarchs* are but Men, and if Government is to be the Remedy of those Evils, which

---

[6] John Locke, *Two Treatises*, vol. ii, para. 13, p. 316.   [7] Ibid.   [8] Ibid.

necessarily follow from Mens being Judges in their own Cases, and the State of Nature is therefore not to be endured, I desire to know what kind of Government that is, and how much better it is than the State of Nature, where one Man commanding a multitude, has the Liberty to be Judge in his own Case, and may do to all his Subjects whatever he pleases, without the least liberty to any one to question or controle those who Execute his Pleasure? And in whatsoever he doth, whether led by Reason, Mistake or Passion, must be submitted to? Much better it is in the State of Nature wherein Men are not bound to submit to the unjust will of another: And if he that judges, judges amiss in his own, or any other Case, he is answerable for it to the rest of mankind.[9]

For this reason, classical liberals have long advocated shackling the coercive monopoly of power in a variety of ways. I shall consider some of these methods and their drawbacks shortly.

The almost irresistible nature of the Single Power Principle may stem not only from explicitly held ideological beliefs, but from a more deep-seated need for security and imposed order. Indeed ideologies of Left and Right may themselves be a product of such needs. For some, the Single Power Principle functions as a kind of religion in which people "believed in" a coercive monopoly of power as an earthly way to prevent bad things from happening and to right every wrong. For these persons, faith in the institutions of power becomes a nontheistic substitute for faith in God in an age where theism is thought by many to be unscientific and irrational, or when God is thought to be insufficiently interventionist in human affairs. For others, the Single Power Principle serves as a throwback to the security of childhood where father and mother provided an assurance that all would be taken care of. For these persons institutions of power perform a paternalistic role.

Whatever the functions it is believed necessary to perform, the Single Power Principle leads to a serious problem of enforcement abuse that, while not unknown, is normally ignored. Perhaps these problems are almost never discussed because a coercive monopoly of power is so widely thought to be necessary that any difficulties it creates—even those of the most fundamental and serious nature—must simply be accepted as inevitable problems of social life, like "death and taxes" as the saying goes.

The Single Power Principle and the Problem of Enforcement Abuse

Although the Single Power Principle is believed to be necessary for a variety of purposes besides the control of enforcement abuse, regardless of the particular reason for favoring a coercive monopoly of power, the *problem* with the Single Power Principle ultimately devolves into a problem of enforcement abuse. For adherents to the Single Power Principle always invoke it for *some* purposes, but not for all purposes. They invariably claim that only *certain* purposes and not others can and should be effectively pursued by means of a coercive

---

[9] Ibid. 316–17.

244 Problems of Power

monopoly of force. (Only a committed totalitarian would maintain that such a monopoly should be used for *any* purpose whatsoever.) In the United States Constitution, for example, Congress does not have the power to pass any laws it wishes, but only those "laws *which shall be necessary and proper* for carrying into execution the forgoing Powers."[10]

For this reason, whatever their rationale for a coercive monopoly of power, all those who adhere to the Single Power Principle must come to grips with the problem of enforcement abuse. Enforcement abuse occurs whenever power is used for an inappropriate or, to borrow the term used in the US Constitution, an *improper* purpose—whether these are defined as improper by the agenda of the Left, the Right, or the classical liberal. The primary problem for adherents to the Single Power Principle is to ensure that the monopoly, once it is created for a presumably good reason, will be used to achieve only the proper ends and not improper ones. Not only has no society that has resorted to the Single Power Principle ever been successful at so limiting its use, there are good reasons why no society could ever be successful in the long run.

To understand why the Single Power Principle has a difficult time with the problem of enforcement abuse we must recall that its adherents, who are nearly everyone, base their belief on some combination of the following factual assumptions:

> Human beings are either essentially corrupt or corruptible (the Right), or they will, if given a chance, try to gain unfair advantage over each other (the Left), or if given the opportunity, human beings will abuse the "executive power" of enforcing rights (classical liberals).

They conclude from their respective assumptions that there must be a coercive monopoly of force to prevent this attribute of human behavior from leading to serious social problems.

The Single Power Principle engenders a serious problem of enforcement abuse, however, not because these assumptions about human conduct are necessarily false, but precisely because they are to some extent a quite plausible account of one tendency of human behavior. It is precisely because human beings *are* corruptible, that some *will* try to take unfair advantage over others, and that they should *not* be trusted to be the judge in their own cases, that a coercive monopoly of power is so dangerous. If we take the assumptions made by its proponents as true, to avoid the problem of enforcement abuse, the Single Power Principle must somehow solve four subsidiary problems: the selection problem, the capture problem, the corruption problem, and the legitimacy problem. In addition, a commitment to the Single Power Principle

---

[10] *Constitution of the United States*, Art. I, sect. 8 (emphasis added). See Randy E. Barnett, "Necessary and Proper," *UCLA Law Review*, vol. 44 (1997), pp. 745–93; Gary Lawson and Patricia Granger, "The 'Proper' Scope of Federal Power: A Jurisdictional Interpretation of the Sweeping Clause," *Duke Law Journal*, vol. 43 (1993), pp. 267–336.

poses a serious rule of law problem of internal consistency. I shall consider each of these problems in turn.

The Selection Problem. Let us assume that it is true that human beings are either essentially corrupt or corruptible or that they will, if given a chance, try to gain unfair advantage over each other. Advocates of the Single Power Principle are immediately faced with a difficulty we may call the *selection problem*: who is to get the power? Whoever is chosen, it must be a human being, so whoever is put in charge will be (by assumption) "essentially corrupt or corruptible or will try to take unfair advantage over others."

Therefore, the proposed solution to the assumed problem seems to be nothing short of folly and dangerous folly at that. For the human beings who are put in control of the monopoly would have a far greater capability for corruption and advantage-taking than they would have as ordinary citizens. Whatever corruption or advantage-taking these people engage in is likely to greatly exceed that which they would be able to engage in if deprived of their power. And by granting some a capability for greater gains from corruption and advantage-taking, the incentives for such conduct are enhanced, thereby increasing both its frequency and its severity. In other words, given their capacity for corruption and advantage-taking, *bad human beings are more dangerous with power than without it.* The Single Power Principle, then, appears to aggravate the very problem it was devised to solve.

At this point, adherents of the Single Power Principle will usually soften the starting assumption so that it now specifies that only *some* human beings are essentially or potentially corrupt (though they usually fail to acknowledge that softening the initial assumption also weakens the claim that a coercive monopoly of power is necessary). They then posit that only the good human beings will be put in charge of the monopoly. This strategy, however, gives rise to a serious knowledge problem. We need a practical way to distinguish the good people from the bad people. We have to specify those people who are to decide who gets the power and how to obtain and disseminate the information needed for these decision makers to distinguish the good from the bad. Some might argue that electing rulers for fixed terms is the best way to make such decisions. Even assuming that this method produces the correct initial allocation of power, however, the Single Power Principle runs afoul of several further problems.

The Capture Problem. Let us assume that the selection problem is somehow solved; that a way is found to select only (or mostly) the good people to hold power. Perhaps an election is held and the electorate makes the correct choice among potential rulers. Another problem now arises that we may call the *capture problem*: how do we keep the people who will abuse their power from eventually wresting control of the monopoly from the good? Remember we started with the assumption that all or perhaps many people are corrupt or will try to take unfair advantage over others, for which reason we need a coercive monopoly of force. However, the solution provided by the Single Power Principle creates an enormously attractive target of opportunity for those people in society who wish to take advantage of others.

Maybe some of the bad people excluded from power will be content to try to privately exploit their fellow human beings. Inevitably, however, at least some of the more enterprising of them will recognize the enormous gain that would be derived from controlling the monopoly and using it to exploit others. All that is required to reap these gains is a strategy for capturing positions of power from those who currently possess them. Such strategies are numerous. One that has been employed often—especially in societies where rulers rule for indefinite periods—is simply to take over the monopoly by force. This strategy, however, entails considerable risks for those who would employ it. A much safer approach would be to assume the posture of a good person and get into power in a legitimate way (assuming that some such option exists). Or, alternatively, they might simply corrupt the good people who are in power to serve their interests. This last possibility suggests the next hurdle that adherents to the Single Power Principle must overcome.

The Corruption Problem. That bad people outside the monopoly may bribe and corrupt (formerly) good people who hold power reveals yet another very serious flaw in the Single Power Principle that we may call the *corruption problem*. Liberals have long realized that power itself has a corrupting influence. The nineteenth-century liberal Lord Acton famously declared that: "Power tends to corrupt and absolute power corrupts absolutely."[11] People who start out as good can become advantage-takers simply because, as monopoly holders, the temptations to do so are great and the risks of being caught are small. But this "rational calculation" conception of corruption understates the insidious corrupting effects of power. For the mere possession of power itself—with its privileged status and ability to control and seduce others—is addictive. The satisfaction or pleasure it gives can permanently alter one's character. As Acton observed in his day: "Great men are almost always bad men."[12]

So, even assuming power has initially been allocated to good people, these people will probably not remain good for long. This problem of corruption is consistently underestimated by adherents to the Single Power Principle on both the Left and Right, though less so by classical liberals. The inherent instability of a coercive monopoly of power can be analogized to that of the old nuclear weapons policy of "mutual assured destruction." Once a sufficiently serious mistake is made, the game is up. With nuclear weapons we risk the destruction of the human race. With the Single Power Principle we risk the

[11] John E. Dalberg-Acton, "Letter to Bishop Mandell Creighton" (5 Apr. 1887) in *Essays on Freedom and Power* (Boston: Beacon Press and Glencoe, Ill.: Free Press, 1948), p. 364.
[12] Ibid. There is irony in the fact that politicians who so fervently seek to control the consumption of intoxicating drugs by others are quite silent about the "high" that causes them to cling so tenaciously to their offices.

institutionalized abuse of power. Given the perquisites of power, bad rulers can be locked in place requiring nothing short of a revolution to remove them. What is the likelihood of forever making the correct choices in this winner-take-all game of picking rulers?

The Legitimacy Problem. The Single Power Principle is by itself not only ineffective in addressing the problem of corruption and advantage-taking, it exacerbates these problems still further by creating a "halo effect." A coercive monopoly of power would not be (peacefully) established unless most people in society were convinced that its establishment is the right or expedient thing to do. Recall the quote from H. L. A. Hart in Chapter 1:

> Rules are conceived and spoken of as obligatory when the general demand for conformity is insistent and the social pressure brought to bear upon those who deviate or threaten to deviate is great. . . . The rules supported by this serious social pressure are thought important because they are believed to be necessary to the maintenance of social life or some highly prized feature of it.[13]

The same may be said of the coercive monopoly of power. It too is believed by those on the Left and Right, as well as by many classical liberals "to be necessary to the maintenance of social life or some highly prized feature of it"—a necessary evil, perhaps, but necessary nonetheless. Therefore, those who wield this power will possess not only power but something that may be more helpful to their pursuit of advantage-taking than power alone could ever be: they will be perceived to have *legitimacy*. That is, their use of power will be perceived by most people to be at least presumptively justified.[14] This is the *legitimacy problem.*

Because many good people will hesitate to oppose the legitimate or "duly constituted authority," the halo effect created by the perception of legitimacy severely exacerbates the problem of enforcement abuse. Perhaps they do not know the facts of the situation and therefore presume that those in power are correct, or perhaps they can see some personal advantage to a particular use of power against another, or perhaps they fear the disruptive consequences of "civil disobedience." Whatever their motives may be, this natural conservatism greatly increases the potential for corruption and advantage-taking. And those wielding power know it.

The Single Power Principle cannot by itself solve the selection, capture, corruption, and legitimacy problems without setting up a kind of infinite regress of power. Although the weakness of human beings is exacerbated by a centralized monopoly of power, there is no other species that can be put in control of the monopoly. Therefore, one must forever propose "higher" authorities to correct the ills of "lower" authorities and ensure that subordinate authorities remain honest. (One could, of course, posit that God or a

---

[13] Hart, *Concept of Law*, pp. 84–5.
[14] Lord Acton argued against this benefit of the doubt: "If there is any presumption it is the other way against holders of power, increasing as the power increases." Acton, "Letter to Bishop," p. 364.

group of gods would divinely rule the human rulers. I shall not here consider the practical problems with this approach.) Trying to control the abuse of a centralized monopoly of power hierarchically or vertically is futile, though this is not to deny that some schemes are better than others. No matter how high you build your hierarchy of power, there is simply no one to put on top who will not himself be potentially corrupt. The answer to human corruption and advantage-taking must, therefore, lie elsewhere.

The Conceptual Problem with the Single Power Principle

Before turning to the various ways we might control the problem of enforcement abuse, it is revealing to observe that the Single Power Principle also presents a serious "internal" conceptual problem for those who otherwise accept a liberal fusion of justice and the rule of law. The rule of law stipulates that precepts specifying the requirements of justice should be of general application and should apply equally to the persons who make and enforce the law. Yet by virtue of their monopoly status, at the very least those who are given a monopoly of power have the power to put competitors out of business, a power that would be a wrongful violation of rights if exercised by so-called "private" citizens.

The Single Power Principle thus posits a fundamental *inequality* of human beings; rulers have the power to violate rights, a power that subjects may never possess. This is what James Madison had in mind when, as a member of Congress, he criticized the formation of the first national bank because "[i]t involves a monopoly, which affects the equal rights of every citizen."[15] A coercive grant of monopoly power always infringes the right of freedom to contract of those who would do business but are coercively prohibited from doing so by the privileged monopoly. In this respect, if no other, those in charge of the monopoly of power are thought to have certain powers (or rights) that violate the background rights specified by the liberal conception of justice.

Moreover, most schemes accord those who hold the coercive monopoly of power the further power to collect taxes to fund their activity—that is, to seize the property of others by force without the prior consent or wrongdoing of the property owner—another violation of rights if exercised by anyone else. Many schemes also grant the rulers the power to obtain conscript or semi-slave labor for certain purposes—such as war-making or jury duty. If done by any other institutions or persons this would be flagrantly unjust. Indeed, the Thirteenth

---

[15] *Annals of Congress*, vol. i, p. 1900. This speech is reproduced in its entirety as an appendix to Barnett, *Rights Retained*, pp. 417–26. Nor was Madison alone among the founding generation in his antipathy towards monopolies. Three states accompanied their ratification of the Constitution with a proposed amendment prohibiting Congress from granting monopolies to particular businesses. See Donald S. Lutz, "The Bill of Rights in the States," *Southern Illinois University Law Journal*, vol. 16 (1992), p. 256. These and the other amendments proposed by the states are reproduced as an appendix to Barnett *Rights Retained*, vol. i, pp. 353–85.

Amendment to the Constitution prohibits the practice when it states: "Neither slavery nor involuntary servitude, except as punishment for crime whereof the party shall have been duly convicted, shall exist within the United States, or any place subject to their jurisdiction."[16] Yet the government of the United States claims the power (nowhere enumerated in the Constitution[17]) to draft men to involuntary servitude in the armed forces.

Some monopoly schemes even legitimate such arcane powers as the power to compel people to accept monopoly script in return for their labor or property—known as "legal tender" laws[18]—and the sole power to run certain businesses, such as the delivery of writings and packages,[19] the driving of buses, or the picking up of garbage. Other schemes accord to privileged rulers the power to grant monopoly "franchises" to sell grain or "licenses" to provide television or telephone services. Some give them the power to restrict access to certain occupations. Anyone who becomes a taxi driver, lawyer, or hairdresser without the approval of those who hold the monopoly may be fined or imprisoned. The list goes on and on. The potential that these powers have to induce the corruption and advantage-taking described above is quite obvious.[20] And each of these powers would ordinarily be a violation of rights if exercised by anyone else.

Advocates of the Single Power Principle respond to this conceptual problem by denying that such powers violate rights when they are exercised by the persons who control the monopoly of power. They simply define the rights of individuals and associations in such a way as to exempt these privileged exercises of power. The usual justification of these exceptions to the normal strictures of justice is their necessity. Without a coercive monopoly of power, it is said, bad consequences will occur. Therefore, individual rights cannot stand in the way of such power.

A mere definitional response to this conceptual problem is dubious. Conceptual structures such as that provided by background rights serve important social functions, as we have repeatedly seen. Defining these rights

[16] *United States Constitution*, Amend. XIII. Notice that this amendment does not preclude prison labor as "punishment for crime." So work facilities in which prisoners earned wages to make restitution would not be unconstitutional under this amendment.

[17] In Article 1, sect. 8, the Constitution grants Congress the power "To raise and support Armies." It says nothing about conscription, a power first claimed during the Civil War.

[18] Once again not enumerated in the United States Constitution, which in Article 1, sect. 8, empowers the Congress "[t]o coin money, regulate the Value thereof, and of foreign Coin. . . ." It is silent on any power to compel persons to accept paper money as legal tender in settlement of any debt.

[19] Although Article 1, sect. 8 of the Constitution gives Congress the power "[t]o establish Post Offices and post Roads," it says nothing about granting its post office monopoly powers to deliver first class mail—a power that had been explicitly claimed by Congress under the Articles of Confederation that preceded the Constitution.

[20] See e.g. Clint Bolick, *Grassroots Tyranny: The Limits of Federalism* (Washington DC: Cato Institute, 1993) (describing instances of abuses by local governments of the power to regulate economic activity).

away when they seem to be inconvenient is like cutting the wires to a fire alarm when the noise proves to be annoying. At the very least, the conceptual double standard implicit in the Single Power Principle should serve as a warning to be skeptical of its legitimacy. The liberal conception of justice was itself seen as necessary to solve the twin problems of knowledge and interest. The problems of enforcement error and abuse are merely special and often extreme instances of these two pervasive problems. Any strategy that overrides the normal solution to these problems must include some adequate substitute for justice and the rule of law. Those who advocate a coercive monopoly of power to solve the problem of corruption and advantage-taking bear a heavy burden to prove that they can handle the problems of enforcement abuse in some manner other than by forcing law enforcement to respect the very same rights as everyone else. This burden is hardly met merely by defining rights to include an exception for a privileged monopoly allegedly on grounds of necessity. Once the exercise of power is legitimated to address the compliance problem, handling the problem of enforcement abuse also becomes a matter of necessity.

2. Constraining Centralized Power

Whether or not classical liberals have understood the problem of enforcement abuse better than those on the Left and Right, they have certainly taken it more seriously. To combat the selection, capture, corruption, and legitimacy problems, they innovated certain centralized institutional arrangements with nonhierarchical or horizontal dimensions. What I mean by "nonhierarchical" or "horizontal" should become clearer as I describe these arrangements. Many of these institutional arrangements were sufficiently effective in curbing enforcement abuse that they, rather than the liberal conception of justice and the rule of law I have described here, were given the lion's share of the credit for the relative freedom and prosperity that arose in the West. Some, think these arrangements constitute the structure of liberty.

Yet each of these institutional arrangements has serious shortcomings that become more apparent in societies that rely upon them without also adhering robustly to the liberal fusion of justice and the rule of law. Though I shall discuss their shortcomings in the balance of this chapter, I shall not attempt a systematic or definitive critique of these arrangements here. For I consider each of these measures to embody an important insight concerning how power can be constrained. Their shortcomings stem primarily from failing to take them seriously enough. I identify and critique them here as a means to showing, in Chapter 13, how they may better be put into effect.

Reciprocity: Decision Making by Ballot

The democratic or popular election of rulers is the most commonly favored method of handling the problem of enforcement abuse. The essence of this familiar idea was summarized by Lon Fuller:

Elections present themselves in many forms, varying from the town meeting to the "ja–nein" plebescite. Voting can be organized in many ways: simple majority vote, PR [proportional representation], STV [single transferable voting], and various complicated mixed forms. At the same time all of these expressions of political democracy have in common that they afford the person affected by the decision which emerges a peculiar form of participation in that decision, namely, some form of voting.[21]

The core of this idea is a good one: establish *reciprocity* between rulers and subjects. The central problem with the coercive monopoly of power is its non-reciprocal nature. Rulers have powers that mere "subjects" are denied and are themselves subject to no restraints in the exercise of these privileged powers. Establishing elections of rulers begins to provide some reciprocal power on the part of the subject to remove those with power and consequently a reciprocal duty on the part of lawmakers to be accountable to the rights and interests of their subjects. Still there are any number of difficulties with the electoral approach. I shall only briefly mention a few.

First, an electoral system faces a serious knowledge problem. Such a system assumes that voters can be sufficiently informed about matters of enforcement to have knowledgeable opinions about how these powers should be used; it assumes that they can know enough about candidates to make an intelligent choice; and that they can monitor the performance of their rulers closely enough to hold them accountable for any enforcement abuse. Experience provides no reason for confidence that any of these knowledge problems are adequately handled in an electoral system.

Second, an electoral system creates a serious incentive problem. A system of periodic elections tends to give rulers a very short-run perspective. Rulers, especially those who rule for fixed terms, have no way of capturing the long-run benefits of their policies. If the system works as designed, good rulers will not survive to see the long run unless their policies appear to be working in the short run. Bad rulers must plunder while the plundering is good. In light of this problem, it is ironic that private individuals and organizations are so often accused of taking a short-run view of profits and resource use (as compared with rulers), since private owners of companies and resources do have a ready ability to profit from the long-run value of their policies. In the absence of confiscatory takings, they can also anticipate passing these gains to their children. In a democracy, rulers are quite rightly supposed to lack these incentives since the people, not they, are said to "own" the country. Yet without

---

[21] Fuller, "Forms and Limits," p. 364.

these incentives, representative democracies are forced to rely almost exclusively on the altruism of politicians to adopt measures for the common good that do not redound to their interest in reelection, a somewhat unrealistic, if not utopian, expectation.

Finally, the balloting solution to the problem of who gets to control the monopoly creates another serious problem of partiality. According to the principal justification for the Single Power Principle, human beings are essentially corrupt or corruptible. Yet only human beings vote. A unanimous vote is a practical impossibility but, if anything less than unanimity is required to elect a ruler, the majority can be expected (sooner or later) to vote out of corrupt or advantage-taking motives. The same point can be made less stridently: Because the decisions that result from the electoral process will be imposed monopolistically on everyone in a polity, a decision made by some fraction of the whole may not adequately take into account the interests of the rest.

As was noted in Chapter 7, James Madison, one of the principal framers of the United States Constitution and, especially, of the Bill of Rights, famously referred to this problem of interest attaching to majority (or minority) rule as the "problem of faction":

By a faction I understand a number of citizens, whether amounting to a majority or minority of the whole, who are united and actuated by some common impulse of passion, or *of interest*, adverse to *the rights* of other citizens, or to the permanent and aggregate interests of the community.[22]

In a letter to Thomas Jefferson he wrote, "the invasion of private rights is chiefly to be apprehended, not from acts of Government contrary to the sense of its constituents, but from acts in which the Government is a mere instrument of the major number of the Constituents."[23]

Under Jefferson's influence, Madison came to think that review of legislation by judges who were not accountable to electoral politics would help keep legislative majorities within constitutional constraints and would protect individual rights to some extent:

If they are incorporated into the constitution, independent tribunals of justice will consider themselves in a peculiar manner the guardians of those rights; they will be an impenetrable bulwark against every assumption of power in the legislative or executive; they will naturally be led to resist every encroachment upon rights expressly stipulated for in the constitution by the declaration of rights.[24]

Judicially enforced constitutional restraints on majoritarian sentiments have proved to be less than reliable. Judges must interpret and enforce a constitution and judges are also human beings. Quite often they have supported

---

[22] *Federalist* No. 10 (Madison), p. 54 (emphases added).
[23] Letter from James Madison to Thomas Jefferson (17 Oct. 1788), rep. in Bernard Schwartz, *The Bill of Rights: A Documentary History*, vol. i (New York: Chelsea House, 1971), p. 616.
[24] *Annals of Congress*, vol. i, p. 457 (statement of Rep. Madison).

majoritarian abuses and by their support they have legitimated them. Indeed, Charles Black has contended that legitimating the acts of government has been the judiciary's principal function:

> The role of the [Supreme] Court has usually been conceived as that of *invalidating* "hasty" or "unwise" legislation, of acting as a "check" in the other departments. It has played such a role on occasion, and may play it again in the future.
>
> But a case can be made for believing that the prime and most necessary function of the Court has been that of *validation*, not that of invalidation. What a government of limited powers needs, at the beginning and forever, is some means of satisfying the people that it has taken all steps humanly possible to stay within its powers. That is the condition of its legitimacy, and its legitimacy, in the long run, is the condition of its life. And the Court, through its history, has acted as the legitimator of the government. In a very real sense, the Government of the United States is based on the opinions of the Supreme Court.[25]

While judicial review has in some instances been crucial to preserving some measure of liberty, when put in service of partial legislation, this power can serve to insulate enforcement abuse from criticism. And, of course, judges who are part of the coercive monopoly are more than capable of abusing power themselves.

Checks and Balances: Federalism and Separation of Powers

For James Madison and the other framers of the United States Constitution, judicial review was not the principal remedy for the ills of balloting or enforcement abuse more generally. Madison and his colleagues were more concerned that government be structured in such a way as to balance interests against each other so none would come to dominate. These balancing structures have come to be referred to as federalism and separation of powers.

The essence of this strategy is to create an oligopoly or a "shared" monopoly of power. This scheme preserves a monopoly of power but purports to divide this power among a number of groups, each having limited jurisdiction over the others. So, for example, there might be a division of powers between groups of people known as "state officials" and others called "federal officials." Or there might be a separation of powers between some people called "legislators" and others called "judges" or "executives." The object of such schemes is to create *checks and balances*.

Like balloting, a scheme of checks and balances is a good idea. The problem with the Single Power Principle is not the recognition of the legitimate use of force or power itself. Those who reject the Single Power Principle are not necessarily pacifists—that is, they do not reject every right to use force under any circumstances. Rather, the root of the problem with the Single Power Principle is its adherence to a *monopoly* allocation of power with all the

---

[25] Charles L. Black, Jr., *The People and the Court: Judicial Review in a Democracy* (New York: Macmillan, 1960), p. 52.

254 *Problems of Power*

attendant problems discussed above. It is this that the federalism and the separation of powers strategies attempt to address.

A formal separation of powers is unquestionably an improvement over
other versions of the Single Power Principle—witness the experience of the
United States—but eventually similar results are reached (though these results
may neither develop as quickly nor be quite as severe.) For all its advantages,
this scheme still preserves the unearned legitimacy of power and coercive barriers to entry. However many power centers are created, they remain in control indefinitely, short of a revolution.

Even in the beginning of such a regime, since each has the other by the
throat, no one is willing to squeeze too hard. Eventually, entrepreneurs of
power—master politicians, judges, executives, or outsiders called "special
interest groups"—figure out ways to teach those who share the monopoly that
each has an interest in cooperating with the others in using force against those
who are outside the monopoly. This process may take some time, but gradu-
ally what is originally conceived of as "checks and balances" eventually
becomes a scheme more aptly described as "you don't step on my toes and I
won't step on yours" or "you scratch my back, I'll scratch yours." When this
result is reached, the Single Power Principle continues to provide these rulers
with the legitimacy that makes corruption and advantage-taking all the easier.

In a democracy, even the people, not merely those persons who are formally
part of the government, may be corrupted by the temptation to gain benefits
at the expense of others, while they resist, often unsuccessfully, being
exploited by others. At the point when nearly everyone is exploiting everyone
else, no group is willing to give up its benefits so long as it is being forced to
confer benefits on others. Far from being conducive to harmonious and
beneficial social interaction, this institutional arrangement comes to resemble
the "war of all against all" for which the coercive monopoly of power was supposed to be a solution.

The Power of Exit: Free Emigration and Secession

Another way to constrain power is to permit persons to leave the jurisdiction.
In the United States, for example, citizens of one state are free to move to
another state and establish residence and citizenship there. Companies may
incorporate in any state regardless of where they do business. Citizens are also
free to renounce their United States citizenship and emigrate to another country. This is sometimes referred to as "voting with one's feet." The idea of free
emigration reflects a more basic strategy for constraining power: the *power of
exit.*

Implementing the power of exit by permitting free emigration, though
important, is quite limited. In the United States, for example, the freedom of
individuals and companies to change states has led to many governmental ini-
tiatives being removed to the federal government. Moreover, having to move

to another state or to another country imposes huge costs on those exercising this power. Just to change states of residence, one must usually leave one's job, abandon one's friends and extended family, as well as one's community. To change nationalities is even more onerous, often requiring one to confront and adapt to a different culture and language. The abuse of power must be particularly egregious before even the brave-hearted are willing to make these sacrifices. Witness the millions of Jews who remained in Nazi Germany and surrounding countries when they still had the opportunity to escape.

For these reasons, the power of exit is most efficaciously exercised when persons, associations, and geographical areas have a *right to secede* from the jurisdiction of the coercive monopoly of power.[26] In this way, those in charge of the monopoly are aware that there are limits to their effective exercise of power and if they exceed those limits their jurisdiction will shrink. Unfortunately, perhaps because of its potential effectiveness, a right of secession has only been weakly incorporated into modern schemes. In 1991 Allen Buchanan wrote, "[a]t present only the Soviet Constitution contains such a right."[27] With the collapse of that empire, expedited in no small part by the constitutional legitimacy accorded the Baltic states' right to secede, this leaves none.

Although a right of geographical regions to secede would dramatically reduce the cost of exit, such a right is largely nonexistent in the United States and elsewhere. In the United States this right was tainted severely by its association with the slave states of the American South who tried to exercise it to preserve their unjust dominion over African-Americans. (Of course, those who wished to preserve their power within the larger unit will be quick to brand *any* secessionist movement as motivated by unjust or immoral concerns whether or not it is.) Yet despite the fact that a right of secession was once used to protect a license to enslave other persons, the experience of the Baltic states in their successful secession from the former Soviet Union in the late 1980s suggests that a right by individuals, associations, and regions to secede would be an important potential constraint on the abuse of power if it were more effectively available than it is today.

Summary

Adherents to the Single Power Principle have devised a rather peculiar way of dealing with the problem of enforcement abuse caused by human corruption and advantage-taking. They advocate giving some human beings a monopoly on the use of force, thereby elevating some human beings to a higher moral and legal status than others.

[26] The best, and only comprehensive, descriptive and normative treatment of the right of secession is Buchanan, *Secession*.

[27] Ibid. 3.

But no one can be sure to whom to give this monopoly. And, assuming that the initial allocation is made correctly, the alleged solution creates an irresistible target of opportunity for anyone in society who wishes to exploit another and who is clever or ruthless enough to devise a way of capturing the monopoly that has been created. The monopoly also poses grave temptations to the good to become less than good—in short, the alleged solution to the problem of corruption is itself a most potent corrupting influence. Finally, in this scheme those who possess the monopoly, as a practical matter, are presumed to employ it properly, thus enhancing their ability to use the monopoly to take advantage of others.

Various institutional features to deal with the problem of enforcement abuse by a coercive monopoly of power have been tried. I have discussed the three most well-known: elections, federalism, and free emigration. Each has attempted to combat the "top-down" or hierarchical relationship between ruler and subject that is inherent in a coercive monopoly of power by establishing a more "bottom-up" or horizontal relationship. Though these three practices have largely failed in keeping a coercive monopoly of power within the constraints defined by the liberal conception of justice and the rule of law, each reflects a more fundamental principle that needs to be more robustly incorporated into institutional arrangements: *reciprocity, checks and balances,* and the *power of exit.*

Each of these principles is an integral part of an authentic constitutional solution to the problem of corruption and advantage-taking: a decentralized or horizontal system of enforcement which could provide genuine reciprocity, real checks and balances, and effective exit powers, but of a far more sophisticated variety than can be provided by any constitutional constraints on a coercive monopoly of power. And the conceptual problem of inequality inherent in the Single Power Principle points the way to another facet of an authentic constitutional solution: an effort to craft a decentralized enforcement mechanism that conforms to the same liberal conception of justice that applies to everyone else.

THIRTEEN

Constitutional Constraints on Power

IF power is to be used to address the compliance problem, some effective means must be found to constrain enforcement abuse. Adopting the liberal fusion of justice and the rule of law helps to constrain abuse to a degree by providing persons with some means to resist tyranny and a publicly-accessible conceptual limitation on power that serves as a warning that power is being abused. Standing alone, however, the concepts of justice and the rule of law are not sufficient to handle the problem of enforcement abuse because they are not self-enforcing. We also need an *institutional structure* that is able to ensure that justice and the rule of law will be respected.

The approach I shall suggest tracks the tripartite scheme embodied in the United States Constitution by considering the legislative, executive, and judicial functions of a legal order as distinct. As was seen in Chapter 6, a common-law system of adjudication provides a decentralized method of discovering precepts of law that serve the interests of justice and provides an alternative to legislation. I shall now turn my attention to the judicial power—that is, the power to *adjudicate* disputes—and the executive power—that is, the power to execute or *enforce* the laws.

The discussion at the end of Chapter 12 described three devices that classical liberals long have favored to constrain abuses of a coercive monopoly of power: elections, federalism or separations of power, and free emigration. These mechanisms reflect three complementary constitutional strategies for constraining power generally: reciprocity, checks and balances, and exit. In this chapter, I discuss ways that these principles may be more thoroughly realized in a "polycentric"[1] constitutional order that avoids a coercive monopoly

---

[1] See Michael Polanyi, *Logic of Liberty*, (Chicago: University of Chicago Press, 1951), pp. 170–84 (defining and explaining the concept of polycentricity). This concept was then imported into jurisprudence by F. A. Hayek and Lon Fuller. See Hayek, *Law and Liberty*, vol. ii, p. 15; Fuller, "Forms and Limits," pp. 394–404. Both Hayek and Fuller were heavily influenced by Polanyi's treatment of polycentricity, tacit knowledge, and spontaneous order and this intellectual commonality helps account for the similarities in their approaches.

of power. The term polycentric refers not just to a system with multiple nodes or "centers of decision,"[2] but to one in which each of the centers of decision needs to and is able to adjust to the decisions of the others.[3] Order is thereby achieved "spontaneously"—that is, by a decentralized process of mutual adjustment—rather than by centralized command.

In a polycentric constitutional order, as distinct from a monocentric one, multiple legal systems exercise the judicial function and multiple law-enforcement agencies exercise the executive function. These multiple decision makers operate within constitutional constraints that permit them to co-exist and adjust to each other. The phrase legal or constitutional *order* is used here when speaking of the entire legal structure, and the phrase legal or court *system* when speaking of one court or other dispute resolution system within the larger constitutional order. Just as the liberal conception of justice requires "several property" to handle the problems of knowledge and interest, a decentralized or polycentric constitutional order consisting of several legal systems and several law-enforcement agencies provides an institutional framework to address the problem of enforcement abuse.

Although a polycentric constitutional order will initially appear to be a radical departure from our current arrangements, such an order will arise naturally if just two constitutional principles that depart from our current approach to law enforcement and adjudication are adopted—principles that are commonplace features of social arrangements outside the context of law enforcement and adjudication. These are the *Nonconfiscation Principle* and the *Competition Principle*. I define these constitutional principles as follows:

> (1) *The Nonconfiscation Principle*: Law-enforcement and adjudicative agencies should not be able to confiscate their income by force, but should have to contract with the persons they serve.
> (2) *The Competition Principle*. Law-enforcement and adjudicative agencies should not be able to put their competitors out of business by force.

There are two questions facing anyone proposing fundamental reforms of the sort I have described in this book: *how do we get there and, once there, how do we stay there?* The Nonconfiscation Principle tells us how we arrive at a polycentric regime, while the Competition Principle tells us how we stay there. If citizens who are dissatisfied with existing agencies have the power to withhold their patronage from them and contract with new ones, then a polycentric

---

[2] See Hayek, *Law and Liberty*, vol. ii, p. 15 ("The multiplicity of independent ends implies also a multiplicity of independent *centres of decision*, and different types of society are accordingly sometimes distinguished as monocentric and polycentric.") (emphasis added).

[3] See Polanyi, *Logic of Liberty*, p. 191 (a polycentric task is one that "requires the balancing of a large number of variable items against all others."); Fuller, "Forms and Limits," pp. 397 ("[T]he more interacting centers there are, the more the likelihood that one of them will be affected by a change in circumstances, and, if the situation is polycentric, this change will communicate itself after a complex pattern to other centers.").

order will eventually evolve. And having evolved, it will remain in place if the currently prevailing agencies cannot put their new competitors out of business by force.[4]

Even if these two principles were implemented immediately, however, no changes in the current array of law enforcement and adjudicative agencies need be made. Though every existing agency would have to obtain revenue in a different manner than at present, each could continue to perform the same services that it currently does. Indeed, if current institutions are "natural monopolies"[5] as some allege, then no structural changes will occur. If, however, current arrangements are less than satisfactory to many consumers of their services, then effectuating these two principles will permit the evolution of a polycentric regime of law enforcement and adjudication with genuine reciprocity, checks and balances, and exit powers. I know on which of these eventualities I would bet.

Let us now consider the implications of each of these constitutional principles in turn.

1. The Nonconfiscation Principle

The Nonconfiscation Principle is really just an application of the first aspect of the liberal principle of freedom of contract—freedom *from* contract.

---

[4] Only because he granted the "dominant protection agency" a power to put competitors out of business by force, was Robert Nozick able to argue that a minimal (monopoly) state could evolve from a polycentric legal order without violating rights. See Robert Nozick, *Anarchy and Utopia*, p. 88: "An independent might be prohibited from privately exacting justice because his procedure is known to be too risky and dangerous—that is, it involves a higher risk (than another procedure) of punishing an innocent person or overpunishing a guilty one—or because his procedure isn't known not to be risky". For responses to this argument see Roy A. Childs, "The Invisible Hand Strikes Back," *Journal of Libertarian Studies*, vol. 1 (1977), pp. 23–33, and Murray N. Rothbard, "Robert Nozick and the Immaculate Conception of the State," *Journal of Libertarian Studies*, vol. 1 (1977), pp. 45–57.

[5] The term "natural monopoly" has come to have a specialized meaning to economists. See e.g. *The New Palgrave* (London: Macmillan Press, 1987), p. 603 (defining natural monopoly as an industry in which "the total costs of production are lower when a single firm produces the entire industry output than when any collection of two or more firms divide the total among themselves."). I am using the term, however, in its popular sense of a monopoly that, for whatever reason, arises naturally in a free market without aid of coercion. See e.g. *The McGraw-Hill Dictionary of Modern Economics* (New York: McGraw-Hill, 1983), pp. 315–16. Natural monopoly is defined there as: "A natural condition that makes the optimum size of the firm so large in relation to the market that there is room for only one firm. The crucial criterion for the existence of a natural monopoly is that the market must be sufficiently small so that it can be satisfied by a single firm which is operating in an area of decreasing costs. It is not feasible for a second firm to enter the industry because one firm alone could produce the potential output of both firms at a lower total cost then the two firms would incur. Therefore, an entering firm must seek to capture the entire market through price-cutting techniques, and thus only one of the two firms would survive". Ibid.

Consumers of law enforcement and adjudication services should not be compelled to transfer resources to another—including those engaged in enforcing laws and adjudicating disputes—without their having manifested consent to the transfer. The fact that law-enforcement and adjudicative agencies are exempt from this normal requirement of justice suggests a serious difficulty with the Single Power Principle.

As I discussed in Chapters 3 and 4, freedom from contract helps to solve the knowledge problem by enabling (and forcing) everyone to take into account the personal and local knowledge that others possess. A coercive monopoly of power is deprived of this vital information by its ability to foist its services upon consumers. Such a monopoly need not—and does not—incorporate into its operation the knowledge of consumers of legal services—including the knowledge of their local circumstances and preferences. For this reason monocentric law-enforcement and adjudication agencies are hopelessly unresponsive to consumer needs and desires.

Freedom from contract also helps address the problem of interest. As a practical matter—and despite the accountability supposedly provided by elections—law-enforcement agencies and courts give priority to their own partial interests before the interests of others. Having the power to confiscate their revenue from others deprives law-enforcement and adjudicative agencies of a powerful incentive to be responsive to the requirements of justice and the rule of law. As the framers of the US Constitution believed, the "power of the purse" is the most important constraint on any institution. Without such financial constraints, institutions are free to pursue their own interests rather than the interests of the persons they are supposed to serve.

The right to withhold one's patronage is the most effective means of disciplining law enforcement and is essential to creating a relationship of genuine reciprocity between the provider and the individual consumer of legal services. Deprived of the power to collect revenues and to coercively impose their services upon consumers, law-enforcement and adjudicative agencies dependent upon contracts rather than taxation for revenue would have to be comparatively more responsive to the needs and desires of their consumers than agencies with the right to confiscate their revenues. This hypothesis may be tested by comparing the treatment one receives from government police with how one is treated by the police who work for private residential communities, many of whom are former government police officers. The fact that individuals and firms respond to the incentives provided by competition is acknowledged to be true in every other area of human endeavor. Human nature does not suddenly change when one gets a job providing law enforcement or adjudicative services.

How, then, will law enforcement and adjudication be paid for in the absence of a power to confiscate revenue from the public? There is no inherent reason why either a law-enforcement agency or a court system cannot charge for its services, in much the same way as do such other essential "public" institutions as water departments, gas and electric companies, hospitals, banks, and schools. Each of these institutions requires expertise and integrity, and those engaged in such activities must earn the trust of the consumer. Unlike courts and law-enforcement agencies, however, water departments, gas and electric companies, hospitals, banks, and schools rely primarily on fees charged to their customers, though payment of these charges can be made in a variety of different ways.[6]

The very large and largely unanticipated expenditures for emergency hospital care are normally financed by insurance arrangements, by conventional credit and, of course, by cash payments. Banks raise the bulk of their revenue from the difference between the interest they charge borrowers and the interest they pay depositors, and where this differential is narrow, service charges may be imposed as well. Those schools that do not receive tax receipts rely largely on tuition payments made by parents and students out of savings or from the proceeds of long-term loans. A significant portion of both educational and health services is subsidized by private charitable contributions. Water, gas, and electric bills are mailed to consumers who usually pay them by check, though sometimes they are permitted to pay a prorated monthly portion of their estimated annual expenditure to even out the payments.

It takes no great imagination to envision law-enforcement agencies providing police protection to paying subscribers—especially in a regime of extensive several property in which streets, sidewalks, and parks are privately owned. Park and road owners could, for example, "bundle" the provision of protective services with their other transportation and recreational services. Just as some motor clubs today offer reimbursement for the expense of road repairs that were needed when club-provided services were unavailable, law-enforcement agencies could enhance the value of their services to the consumer by agreeing to reimburse each other if they provide services in an emergency to another firm's client.

Court systems could utilize many of the same techniques as hospitals to fund their services: insurance, credit, cash, and charitable donations. Prepaid legal service plans or other forms of legal insurance are also possible and, where permitted, sometimes are available even today.[7] Such insurance plans

[6] I have deliberately included both goods and services provided by enterprises where fees are solely a product of market forces and those currently provided by legal monopolies in which fees are regulated by government agencies. Of relevance at this juncture is that the costs of providing these authentically vital public services (including a profit to the shareholders of the providing firms) are recouped from fees paid by those who use them.

[7] See Gregory E. Maggs and Michael D. Weiss, "Progress on Attorney's Fees: Expanding the 'Loser Pays' Rule in Texas," *Houston Law Review*, vol. 30 (1994), p. 1929 and n. 66 (citing companies offering legal benefits to their employees, such as Hardee's Food Systems, General Motors, Ford, AT&T, Chrysler, American Express, Proctor & Gamble, Prudential, Pepsico, and its Pizza Hut, Kentucky Fried Chicken, and Taco Bell subsidiaries.) They also note that "[o]ver twenty million Americans are already covered by [legal expense] insurance," (ibid. 1930) provided by such companies as Pre-Paid Legal Services, Inc. and Midwest Legal Services, Inc. Further today "some credit card companies offer certain prepaid legal insurance services to their patrons." Ibid. 1931.

would help victims retain lawyers in cases where criminals are indigent and may have to spend considerable time in an employment center to make restitution. In a sense, the current system of public prosecution is a form of insurance in which people pay taxes to support a system that they hope they will never use. Yet there is a world of difference in the responsiveness to consumers between a system of voluntary insurance and one in which a noncompetitive "insurance" company obtains its "premiums," like the Mafia, by coercion.

In addition, court systems could profit by selling the written opinions of their judges to the various data retrieval services on which lawyers rely. Such opinions would have a market value to lawyers only to the extent that they are truly useful to predict the future actions of these judges. So to fully profit from such publications, each court system would have to monitor and provide internal incentives to encourage its judges both to write and to follow precedential decisions. Unlike today, where there is little besides peer pressure to induce government judges to adhere to precedent, the ability of adjudicative agencies to profit from predictability would render more harmonious the interests of the judges and the requirements of the rule of law.

At present, attorneys bill clients by the hour or collect a percentage of the damage awards they succeed in obtaining. They also work *pro bono*—that is, they donate their services in the interests of justice. Except in unusual cases, however, those who successfully bring or defend lawsuits in the United States today cannot recover their legal fees from those persons who either violated their rights or who wrongfully brought suit against them. In contrast, the liberal conception of justice elaborated in Chapters 9 and 12 requires restitution to compensate as completely as possible for *all* the determinable expenses which result from a rights violation. Therefore, the loser of a lawsuit must be liable (at least presumptively) for the full legal costs of the prevailing party. In the absence of such a "loser pays" rule—the so-called "English rule"—the innocent party would be made to absorb some of the costs of the other party's wrongdoing. And a loser pays rule would also serve both to protect innocent persons from the expense and injustice of baseless lawsuits by increasing the costs of losing weak cases, and to help pay for meritorious winning lawsuits brought by people who could not otherwise afford the legal costs.

Once again, these are smaller changes than first appear. Consumers using such institutions as hospitals, schools, and banks must now pay not only for the services of doctors, bankers, and teachers but also for the overhead of the facility (the hospital, the bank, or the school) where these professionals practice. With the legal profession, however, we are accustomed to paying privately for lawyers, while providing the capital and labor used by lawyers— courts and court personnel—by tax receipts. This "public good" arrangement encourages overuse by some until court backlogs and overcrowding create queues that substitute for prices or fees to clear the market.

Such queues have led many commercial firms to opt out of the government system in favor of "private courts" or what is called Alternative Dispute

Resolution (ADR). Thousands of contracts contain something like the following provision sponsored by the American Arbitration Association:

Any controversy or claim arising out of or relating to this contract, or breach thereof, shall be settled by arbitration in accordance with the Rules of the American Arbitration Association, and judgment upon the award rendering by the arbitrators may be entered in any court having jurisdiction thereof.[8]

The fact that this provision refers to a "judgment . . . entered in any court" does not undermine the potency of this example. For the actual adjudication is provided by the private arbitration mechanism, is paid for by the parties, and is normally not reviewable by government courts. An arbitrator's award is the functional equivalent of a trial court verdict. This clause merely reflects the fact that where an award is not paid voluntarily, in our system, enforcement still requires a formal "judgment" by a government court. Bear in mind, adjudication and enforcement are fundamentally different services and I am only speaking now of the former.

While ADR at present retains ultimate appellate and enforcement jurisdiction in the monocentric system,[9] it does permit fee-for-service adjudication that many disputants find preferable to the "free" government courts that they pay for with their taxes. Such for-profit firms as "Civicourt in Phoenix and Judicate in Philadelphia have offered quick inexpensive dispute resolution since 1983"[10] as have Washington Arbitration Services, Inc. in the state of Washington, Judicial Mediation, Inc. of Santa Ana, California, Resolution, Inc., of Connecticut, and EnDispute, Inc. which has offices in Washington DC, Los Angeles, Chicago, Cambridge, Massachusetts, and Santa Ana, California.[11] Bruce Benson describes the operation of two of these firms:

As of March 1987, Judicate employed 308 judges in 45 states and has been called the "national private court." A typical hearing at Judicate takes one or two days. Charges for simple cases are $600 per court session, while more complex suits involving multiple parties cost $1,000 a session. Half the money is paid to the judge. Judicate's procedures are streamlined adaptations of government court procedures, allowing pretrial conferences, discovery process, settlement conferences, and so on. At Civicourt, three hours of judge time costs each litigant $250; thereafter, each additional hour costs $75. Most trials are completed quickly, with no

---

[8] Tai Schneider Denenberg and R. V. Denenberg, *Dispute Resolution: Settling Conflicts without Legal Action*, Public Affairs Pamphlet No. 597 (New York: Public Affairs Committee, 1981), p. 5. For a fascinating description of how ADR works in the diamond industry, see Lisa Bernstein, "Opting out of the Legal System: Extralegal Contractual Relations in the Diamond Industry," *Journal of Legal Studies*, vol. 21 (1992), p. 115.

[9] Government courts were initially quite resistant to honoring the judgments of their competitors, but such competition was eventually protected by legislation, especially the Federal Arbitration Act of 1947. According to Jerold Auerbach, by the 1950s nearly 75% of all commercial disputes were being adjudicated by arbitrators, rather than government courts. See Jerold S. Auerbach, *Justice without Law?* (New York: Oxford University Press, 1983), p. 113.

[10] Benson, *Enterprise of Law*, p. 223.   [11] See ibid. 223–4.

juries to contend with, and the trials are held at the convenience of the parties to the dispute.[12]

Fee-for-service legal systems are then quite possible. Imagine the potential growth of such systems if government courts could no longer confiscate their income via taxation and had to cover *their* costs through fees charged to litigants. Before turning to the issues that might arise with a constitutional order comprised of many such legal systems, let me consider two types of objections to legal systems that charge for their services.

A Polycentric Constitutional Order and "The Rich"

Some people worry that allocating court resources by means of a market price mechanism will unfairly reward "the rich."[13] Of course, in any society where some people have more wealth than others—which is to say every society[14]—those with more wealth will be able to buy better things and services than those with less. After all, the ability to buy better things and services is a major incentive to engage in productive activities that often lead to the acquisition of more wealth. As my grandfather used to say, "rich or poor, it's nice to have money." Wealthier people get better health care, better schools, better food, better clothing, and better shelter. And even the poorest of those who live in wealthy countries get better goods and services than those who live in much poorer countries.

That the consequences of disparate wealth are pervasive in all other aspects of social life should at least raise a tiny suspicion that the Single Power Principle may be hopelessly ineffective in preventing disparate treatment of the wealthy in the legal arena. Indeed, although the existing monocentric system is supposed to provide "equal" and "free" access to both law enforcement and the courts, such access is largely hypothetical. Like "free" government schools, "free" law enforcement in the poorest communities is far inferior to that provided in more affluent areas. And the court system as it now exists rewards those litigants who are better able to wait out the imposed delays and penalizes those who for any reason require a fast decision. Who is more likely to be in each group, the wealthy or the poor, a company or an injured consumer, the guilty or the innocent? As former West Virginia supreme court justice Richard Neely observed:

Since courts are available free of charge, they are overused, and the result is justice defying delays. . . . Our egalitarian tradition forbids any explicit price system to

[12] Benson, *Enterprise of Law*, p. 223.
[13] "The rich" is a construct with no objective referent, except that it typically refers to someone who has more wealth than the speaker who employs it.
[14] Even the most ostensibly egalitarian society has a class of rulers with material privileges that their subjects lack. Indeed, because rulers are needed to use force to preserve an equality of resources, egalitarian societies need a ruling class far more than do liberal societies.

ration court services; however, since demand for free court services exceeds supply, rationing must occur, and it is accomplished by standing in line. Unfortunately, the people who can afford to stand in line the longest are not necessarily the people who have the most urgent need to litigate, yet egalitarian tradition prohibits the sale of one's place in line to someone with more pressing need for court services.[15]

Moreover, the current system requires that winners—those who have proven the justice of their claims or defense—must absorb all their own legal costs.

But would not a fee-based system only exacerbate the problem of unequal justice? While it is true that such a system will not eliminate differential quality of services—no system can—this is no more required here than with any other good or service. A perfectly adequate spoon need not be made out of silver, and the fact that some have access to silver spoons does not detract in any way from the adequacy of spoons made of steel. What is needed is some assurance that legal services available to those who are not wealthy are above a threshold of quality that assures justice. I am not confident that the current monocentric legal system animated by the Single Power Principle can provide this assurance today. Because the reciprocity created by a fee-based system provides a far stronger constraint on enforcement abuse than a monocentric system, to show the superiority of a polycentric legal order we need only show that the services such a system would provide to those who are not wealthy would surely be no worse and are likely to be much better than what they consistently receive from the current monopolistic system.

In assessing this issue, we must always be careful to distinguish the truly indigent from those who have some resources, but less than others. For all but a handful of persons, "free" law enforcement does not really mean no *cost*; it means no *prices*. Unlike the indigent, those with some resources (including most poor persons and all those in the middle-class) currently do pay for the current system through myriad sales, income and property taxes, the taxes of their landlords that are recouped from their rent, and the taxes of the companies they buy goods from that are recouped from the prices of the goods.

The idea that these persons are currently getting something for nothing is a pernicious hoax. Those who are not wealthy simply receive very shoddy services for their money and then cannot afford to pay the *additional* amount necessary to opt out of the monocentric system. The real question then is whether everyone could receive better services for the amount they *currently* pay if they were free to choose their service provider than if they must take what the political system foists upon them in return for the money it confiscates. The quality of enforcement and judicial services now provided is so low that it would be difficult for a suitably reformed polycentric regime to do no better.

In Chapter 12, I discussed how the decentralized provision of law enforcement services eliminates the current "commons problem" that afflicts poorer

---

[15] Richard Neely, *Why Courts Don't Work* (New York: McGraw-Hill, 1983), pp. 164–5.

communities far worse than any others. Such an approach has clear advantages for a court system as well. Current experience with ADR suggests that the most likely result of adopting a polycentric legal order with market-based pricing is that lawsuits would be expedited, thereby greatly reducing all legal costs from their present level, enabling successful litigants to keep a higher proportion of whatever damages awards they recovered. Remember also that, according to the right of restitution, the loser would have to reimburse the prevailing party for court costs, including all costs caused by delaying tactics.

The idea that "justice should not be bought" suggests another quite different concern. Would not disparities of wealth in a fee-based legal system lead to different problems of enforcement abuse? Would not judges in such a system favor those who can pay them the most to decide a case? While superficially plausible, this objection reveals a fundamental misunderstanding of the service actually provided by courts. Unlike agencies that enforce the law, the only "good" a court produces is a piece of paper called a "judgment." A judgment authorizes or "warrants" an enforcement agency, such as a sheriff's office, to use force against someone's property or person. Acting without such a warrant or judgment would expose a law-enforcement agency to liability for its acts.[16] So would acting on the basis of a judgment issued by an agency known to be partial or otherwise unreliable.

Just as pieces of paper called "money" or "travelers' checks"—or pieces of plastic called "credit cards"—are only worth obtaining from an issuing bank because of a widespread perception that they will be accepted in exchange for goods and services,[17] pieces of paper called "judgments" are worth paying for only because of a widespread perception that they were the product of a fair procedure and therefore provide a warrant for the use of force. People accept paper money, traveler's checks, or credit cards in exchange for goods for the same reason enforcement agencies "accept" paper judgments: confidence about the reliability of the issuer. To pay for a piece of paper called a judgment that lacks this perception of legitimacy would be a complete waste of money. Perhaps for this reason, under current ADR arrangements, judges are paid an hourly rate set by their firm irrespective of who they rule for.

Consider that an efficient judicial system not only must accumulate and organize the historical information and legal analysis needed to do justice between contending parties, it must also demonstrate to the relevant social

[16] Before the idea of sovereign immunity extended to enforcement officials, judicial warrants served the function of shielding them from liability and provided a strong incentive to seek judicial approval of arrests and searches beforehand.

[17] For a discussion of how maintaining public confidence in redeemability was needed in a system of "free" or competitive note issuance by banks, see Lawrence H. White, *Free Banking in Britain* (Cambridge: Cambridge University Press, 1984), at p. 84: "An important determinant of the ability of a claim to circulate as a medium of exchange . . . was the reputation of its issuer. Rival banks of issue were correspondingly obliged to compete in cultivating public confidence in the redeemability of their notes. The creation and maintenance of that confidence was the production of a scarce good, subject like any other to limited economies of scale."

group that justice is being done. To have something that people would be willing to pay for, then, a successful court system must fulfill at least two distinct functions: the *justice function* and the *fairness function*. The justice function consists of devising and implementing reliable means of accurately determining facts and law. This function concerns the *actual* legitimacy of a legal process.

The concept of legitimacy that I am employing refers to whether the process by which a law is determined to be valid is such as to warrant that the law is just. That is, was a particular law made in such a manner as to provide some assurance that it is just? A law produced by such justice-assuring procedures is legitimate. Thus, according to my usage, a valid law could be illegitimate; and a legitimate law could be unjust. A law may be "valid" because produced in accordance to all procedures required by a particular lawmaking system, but be "illegitimate" because these procedures are inadequate to provide assurances that a law is just. A law might be "legitimate" because produced according to procedures that assure that it is just, and yet be "unjust" because in this case the procedures (which can never be perfect) have failed. Nonetheless, the concept of legitimacy that I employ here links the process that determines legal validity in a particular legal system to the issue of justice. Although the process by which legal validity is determined need not (as a conceptual matter) take justice into account, legitimacy suggests that (as a normative matter) it ought to do so.[18]

The fairness function, in contrast, concerns the *perception* of legitimacy— that is, public perception that justice is being done. No system will be perceived as legitimate unless it convinces (*a*) the practicing bar who must recommend to clients where to initiate lawsuits, (*b*) the litigants who must suffer the consequences of this choice, and (*c*) the general public who must acquiesce to the enforcement of legal judgments in their midst, that the procedures it has employed have produced justice. In sum, whereas the justice function concerns the actual legitimacy of a legal process, the fairness function consists of creating a perception of legitimacy. A legal system will not provide a service *worth paying for* if it fails to fulfill either function. In contrast, a coercive monopoly of power can let slide both the justice and fairness functions and still command obedience.

Suppose that I get in a dispute with my neighbor over the ownership of the tree that stands between our houses. I appeal to *Randy's Mother's Court* and receive from this court (my mom) a very handsome piece of parchment that says *Judgment* on the top and is dripping with ribbons and fancy wax seals. The parchment says that the tree is mine. But of what value is it? None at all. Of course, knowing it was issued by my mom, my neighbor will be less than impressed with its binding force. More importantly, it will not assist me in

[18] I elaborate this concept of legitimacy and apply it to constitutional adjudication in Randy E. Barnett, "Getting Normative: The Role of Natural Rights in Constitutional Adjudication," *Constitutional Commentary*, vol. 12 (1995), pp. 98–105.

obtaining legal enforcement because, in a liberal regime, law-enforcement agencies will be liable for their actions like everyone else. Unless they can defend as warranted any action they take against my neighbor, they will be liable to him for restitution if my claim is unjustified. Consequently, because it is not a judgment issued by a legal system that has a perception of legitimacy attaching to it, a judgment from *Randy's Mother's Court* will provide a law-enforcement agency with no reason or "warrant" whatsoever to help me rather than my neighbor. They would no sooner accept a judgment from *Randy's Mother's Court* than they would accept paper money issued by *Randy's Mother's Bank*. My mother's efforts notwithstanding, I would simply be back where I began.

The primary difference in this regard between a legal system in a polycentric constitutional order versus a legal system in an order based on the Single Power Principle is that a court system in a polycentric order would have to *earn* its perceived legitimacy by building a reputation for fairness. The current monocentric legal system gets what perceived legitimacy it has automatically from being the only game in town. Its perceived legitimacy ultimately derives not from a perception of fairness, but from the widespread acceptance of the Single Power Principle. Because there is thought to be no alternative to the Single Power Principle, a monocentric system retains this perception of legitimacy even when knowledge exists of widespread enforcement abuse.

While no system will eliminate all opportunity for enforcement abuse, a court system in a polycentric constitutional order that must continually earn its legitimacy by providing genuinely fair procedures promises clear advantages over one that gains its legitimacy from the Single Power Principle. A rich person who bought a favorable judgment from a legal system known to favor the rich would have accomplished nothing but to diminish his wealth. And a legal system that in fact routinely favored the wealthy would gain such a reputation in short order and have nothing of value to sell.

A Polycentric Constitutional Order and "The Poor"

What about those who are truly indigent? How are they to receive law enforcement and adjudicative services in a fee-based system? Part of the answer has already been suggested. To satisfy both the fairness and justice functions so their judgments could be relied upon by law-enforcement agencies, legal systems would have to appoint lawyers to represent criminal defendants. Consider the actual and perceived reliability of a judgment obtained by one party against another too poor to be represented by counsel. This sets legal systems apart from providers of other vital goods and services. And both those who are sued and those who bring suit are entitled, if they win, to recover their legal fees from the losing party.

Whatever problems may remain in providing indigents with law enforcement and judicial services exist as well with hospitals and schools. But the existence of persons who cannot afford essential services does not justify taxation to provide such services to *everyone* without fees, *whether indigent or not*. Nor, as I shall explain, does it justify providing these services to indigents *in kind*, as opposed to providing a voucher in which they can buy the same services as everyone else.

Whoever remains unable to pay for law enforcement and adjudicative services may receive them either through voluntary or coercive means. Such services might be voluntarily provided to poor persons without charge (*pro bono*) by law-enforcement agencies and court systems; or people concerned about the well-being of others can voluntarily give to charitable agencies who will pay agencies they trust to provide services for the poor. Conversely, law-enforcement and adjudicative agencies can be forced to provide service to those who cannot afford to pay their fees, or some people can be forced to contribute their money to those agencies who serve the poor.

Whether one favors or opposes forced redistribution to the poor has no bearing on whether law enforcement and adjudication can or should be provided in a decentralized and fee-based manner. Supposing (as most people do) that some degree of forced redistribution of wealth to the poor is justified, this provides no reason for creating or preserving an inferior monocentric system of "public" law enforcement and adjudication just to service those who are not wealthy enough to pay for competitive "private" law enforcement. In a redistributive scheme, either direct cash payments or "vouchers" (which are money payments with use restrictions attached) can be provided to the poor to pay for those competitively provided services that are now monopolistically provided.[19]

Providing the poor with law enforcement and judicial services "in kind" makes as much sense as creating a coercive monopoly in food production and distribution *for everyone* to ensure that the poor have food. Instead, vouchers—called "food stamps"—are given so that the poor can buy food from private competitive sources. Had the competitive food production and distribution system been supplanted by a monocentric system at some distant point in our history (as it was in the former Soviet Union), exactly the same criticisms would undoubtedly be made of a proposal to decentralize food production as are made of proposals to decentralize areas of social life where our history has been less fortunate and the Single Power Principle has prevailed.

The public schools and the post office demonstrate the ineffectiveness of providing vital services in kind. Many families opt out of the public school system, even though this means that they will have to pay for two school systems

---

[19] It is true, however, that a scheme of taxation would require a coercive mechanism, to collect taxes—perhaps even a monopoly. To my mind the increased costs of enforcement error and abuse created by such a scheme, not to mention the inevitable invasions of privacy, provide powerful arguments against it. Once created, a system designed to "legitimately" confiscate the wealth of some to give it to others is an irresistible source of factionalized struggle. I shall return to this subject in Chapter 15.

at the same time. Others cannot afford to pay twice and are stuck in the public system.[20] The premiums charged by the burgeoning express package delivery industry indicate a similar failure of government-provided postal services. With legal services, in contrast, most people do not have the option of (lawfully) paying a premium for better service. Where the stakes are high enough and the parties knowledgeable enough, however, many large companies insist on private arbitration clauses in their commercial contracts.[21]

With each of these examples, when legal monopolies are created to produce and distribute a good or service, only those with considerable wealth may exercise any choice because the monocentric system must be paid for coercively in any event. The only way to provide poor and middle-income persons with choice is to free them from the coercive monopoly of power so that they need pay for only the system of their choice. So a polycentric constitutional order may be viewed as advantageous, whether one believes that practices satisfying the justice and fairness functions, supplemented by the loser pays rule and voluntary charity are sufficient to provide services to the poor or one believes that forced redistribution is needed for this purpose.

Some may respond that the provision of force is different from that of even such vital goods and services as food, shelter, and schooling. But even if the provision of law enforcement ought to be subject to different constraints than are imposed on these other activities, this objection does not apply to the service of providing judgments. Law enforcement and adjudication are two distinct types of services; services that are provided even today by very different kinds of institutions. Moreover, there is nothing peculiar about law enforcement that suggests it must be paid for by confiscating the wealth of its consumers. (Bear in mind that I am now only addressing the merits of the Nonconfiscation Principle.) To the contrary, it would seem particularly foolish to empower agencies charged with protecting person's rights to forcibly confiscate their income.

Nevertheless, it is true that both law enforcement and adjudication need to be constrained if we are to mitigate the problem of enforcement abuse. This does not mean, however, that those who provide this service be given privileged monopolies. To the contrary, it suggests the need for the robust checks and balances provided by competition, and it is to this constitutional principle I now turn.

---

[20] For the record, though my wife and I can afford to pay twice for our children's education, we also can afford to live in a town with a public school system good enough to send our children to, and that is what we do.

[21] See Benson, *Enterprise of Law*, pp. 217–20.

2. The Competition Principle

The second principle of a polycentric constitutional order is that enforcement agencies and courts should not be able to put their competitors out of business by force. Whereas the Nonconfiscation Principle was an application of freedom *from* contract, the Competition Principle is an application of the other dimension of freedom of contract: freedom *to* contract. According to the liberal conception of justice, all persons have an equal right to make enforceable contracts. This means that third parties are acting unjustly when they intervene to prevent such contracts from operating. This precept of justice is violated when law-enforcement agencies or court systems (or any other firm) are empowered to put potential competitors out of business by force. To put competitors out of business by force is simply to interfere with the freedom to contract of their rivals and those consumers who would do business with them.

Some think that law enforcement and adjudication are so important that we must make an exception to the background right of freedom of contract and permit a coercive monopoly to provide such services. Yet this argument is odd. If one had to identify a service that is the most central to social well-being, it would be the provision of food. Yet no one today, at least no one in the United States, seriously suggests that this service is "too important" to be left to a decentralized arrangement of private firms subject to the market competition. On the contrary, both theory and history demonstrate that food production is simply too important to be left to a coercive monopoly.

The more vital a good or service is, the *more* dangerous it is to let it be produced by a coercive monopoly. A monopoly post office does far less harm than monopoly law-enforcement and court systems. And a coercive monopoly might go largely unnoticed if it were limited to making paper clips—that is, the inferior and costly paper clips inevitably produced by such a monopoly might not bother us too much. We face the most serious problems when something really important is left to a coercive monopoly.

Of course, adjudication and law enforcement might be so different in kind from these other vital goods and services that they must, for some reason, be delivered by a privileged monopoly. Yet one suspects the tendency to treat these services as unique results more from a failure of imagination than from any essential difference in kind. It may also result from unfamiliarity with our legal history. For the seemingly radical proposal to end the geographical monopoly of legal systems is actually a rather short step from the competitive spirit in the provision of legal services to which we have been, and to some lesser extent still are, accustomed. Defending what he called a "horizontal" conception of law, Lon Fuller wrote: "A possible . . . objection to the view [of law] taken here is that it permits the existence of more than one legal system governing the same population. The answer is, of course, that such multiple legal systems do exist and have in history been more common than unitary systems."[22]

Until comparatively recently, the Western legal tradition was largely polycentric and competitive in nature. As legal historian Harold Berman has extensively chronicled:

Legal pluralism originated in the differentiation of the ecclesiastical polity from the secular polities. . . . Laymen, though governed generally by secular law, were subject to ecclesiastical law, and to the jurisdiction of the ecclesiastical courts, in matters of marriage and family relations, inheritance, spiritual crimes, contract relations where faith was pledged, and a number of other matters as well. Conversely, the clergy, though governed by canon law, were subject to secular law, and to the jurisdiction of secular courts, with respect to certain types of crimes, certain types of property disputes, and the like. Secular law itself was divided into various competing types, including royal law, feudal law, manorial law, urban law, and mercantile law. The same person might be subject to the ecclesiastical courts in one type of case, the king's courts in another, his lord's courts in a third, the manorial courts in a fourth, a town court in a fifth, a merchant's court in a sixth.[23]

As Berman makes clear, the multiplicity of jurisdictions had a clear effect on the potential for enforcement abuse.

The pluralism of Western law . . . has been, or once was, a source of freedom. A serf might run to the town court for protection against his master. A vassal might run to the king's court for protection against his lord. A cleric might run to the ecclesiastical court for protection against the king.[24]

Even today the federal system in the United States preserves a degree of competition between state and federal courts. As was discussed in Chapter 12, we are accustomed to the idea of "checks and balances" among governmental power centers that is said to be embodied in the constitutional framework. And as has already been discussed in the previous section, private adjudication and arbitration organizations routinely compete with government courts for commercial business at an ever-increasing rate.

As with our consideration of the Nonconfiscation Principle, when evaluating the merits of a polycentric constitutional order we must be careful always to take a comparative approach. It is tempting but ultimately misleading to compare any proposal for change to an ideal that no other possible legal order could more closely achieve or could achieve only at an unacceptable cost. When comparing the realistic prospects of a polycentric constitutional order made up of diverse legal systems with the reality of a monocentric legal system, the advantages are readily apparent.

In contrast with a coercive monopoly, actual or potential competition provides genuine checks and balances that can effectively constrain enforcement abuse. As was noted by Berman, in a competitive legal order, an individual excluded from or oppressed by one legal system can appeal to another. An

---

[22] Lon L. Fuller, *Morality and Law*, p. 123. [23] Berman, *Law and Revolution*, p. 10.
[24] Ibid.

individual shut out of a monocentric legal system cannot, though such appeals do occasionally take place now when citizens of one state or country flee to another and then contest, with occasional success, their extradition.

With a polycentric constitutional order, it is far more practical to exercise a power of exit.[25] People are extremely reluctant to "vote with their feet" by leaving a country because doing so means abandoning one's friends, family, culture, and career. And yet people do leave if things get bad enough. By having the choice to shift one's legal affiliation without having to incur the substantial costs of expatriation means that things do not have to get nearly so bad before people are willing to switch. The increased threat of potential secession or exit that results from lowering its cost, can greatly constrain the potential for enforcement abuse.

Each legal system would be influenced by the knowledge that alternative systems exist, in much the same way that individual states in a federal system are constrained in how they make corporation law by the knowledge that it is always possible for companies to reincorporate in another state without moving their assets.[26] There would also exist an ever-present threat of *potential* competition. Where opportunities for better service and increased profits are perceived by entrepreneurs, free capital markets permit enormous amounts of money to be raised in a short period of time, either to purchase existing firms which are mismanaged, to start a new firm, or to diversify from one area of law enforcement into another.

Moreover, given the availability of alternative firms, even a rumor of unreliability can be expected to shake the biggest of companies. Witness what

[25] In his examination of secession, Allen Buchanan deliberately confines his attention to the right of a *group* occupying a subterritory to withdraw from the jurisdiction of a polity controlling a larger territory. See e.g. Buchanan, "Secession," pp. 13–14 (confining his attention to group secession); and ibid. 24 n.18 (confining his attention to "taking control of territory"). Such a group right gives rise to the many perplexing problems he examines in his book: for example, what sort of injustices justify secession, how is the extent of the subterritory to be determined, when a minority ethnic or racial group secedes from the majority, what happens to those members of the majority who now become a new minority in the seceded territory? All these complexities result from recognizing a group right of territorial secession. In contrast, I am referring here to a *power* (not a right) of exit that results from the exercise of the individual and association's right of freedom of contract and the jurisdiction that each person or association has over its own property. This sort of shift of jurisdictional allegiance promises many of the benefits of a group right of secession with many fewer of the conceptual and practical difficulties.

[26] Federal Appeals Court Judge Ralph Winter, a former corporations professor at Yale Law School, favors a limited expansion of the law-making competition that presently exists among the several states in the corporate law area into other areas such as secured transactions, sales, and landlord–tenant law. See Ralph Winter, "Private Goals and Competition among State Legal Systems," *Harvard Journal of Law and Public Policy*, vol. 6 (1982), pp. 128–9: "With Delaware leading this race, you no longer have to worry about what the right law is. As long as Delaware is competing, there will be a race to the top. There will be a race to establish the optimal corporation code. . . . The system I am talking about is peculiar because it is one area of the law in which *the contracting parties can choose among the law of fifty states*" (emphasis added).

happens to an airline when customers begin to lose "faith" in the economic viability of the company. People will stop buying its tickets for fear that they won't be honored, but this constraint would not exist if alternative airlines were illegal. It is no accident that owners of banks, another institution that relies heavily on a reputation for integrity, traditionally built impressive and very permanent looking buildings to house their operations. While dependent on voluntary deposits, banks do not retain their assets in a form that can be readily seen by the public, so (before government deposit insurance) their architecture was chosen to provide the appearance of being substantial and tangible.

Of course, adherence to the Competition Principle does not ensure a perfect market. A polycentric constitutional order in which legal systems compete with one another for the patronage of consumers would be far from perfect, just as banks, insurance companies, and airlines are far from perfect. But neither does a monocentric legal system guarantee either perfection or justice. We must always strive to compare the real with the real. When we do, there is good reason to conclude that a polycentric constitutional order with competing legal systems would be far more responsive to the needs and interests of consumers than a coercive monopoly.

Dealing with Jurisdictional Conflicts

When one seriously compares the potential features of each system, one might well concede the responsiveness of a competing legal system and offer the opposite objection: competing legal systems would most likely be *too* responsive to *their* customers, and this would inevitably lead to injustice and serious conflicts among agencies, creating serious social disruption. What is to prevent one judicial organization from fighting with or ignoring the rulings of another? Why should any organization heed the call of another? These are serious questions deserving of serious answers, but first some perspective is needed.

There are fifty state court systems in the United States, each with its own hierarchical structure, plus twelve Federal Circuit Courts of Appeals. There is no general right to appeal from the decision of any one of them to the Supreme Court of the United States. With minor exceptions, the Supreme Court of the United States must choose to accept a petition for review and it accepts very few each year. And the situation is, in fact, still more diverse. For *within* each state, there are usually numerous appellate court jurisdictions from whose judgment one has no general right to appeal to the supreme court of that state. Again, with few exceptions, the supreme courts of each state must choose to accept a petition for review.

Moreover, the federal as well as many state appellate court districts are divided into "panels" of judges, who are randomly assigned to hear cases arising from the same jurisdiction. Add to this diversity the many municipal court systems and courts of limited jurisdiction—such as bankruptcy and admiralty courts—and the image of a monolithic hierarchical court system begins to blur. Although some element of hierarchy certainly does exist, much of the cooperation between these diverse systems is "voluntary" in the sense that no system anticipates it would gain by initiating conflicts with other systems.

Given the current multiplicity of "centers of decision," the abolition of geography-based jurisdictional monopolies would mean only that jurisdictional conflicts would arise between persons who had chosen different court systems *by contract*, rather than as now between persons who have decided to live in different places. Where two disputants have chosen the same court system, no jurisdictional conflict is presented. Where individuals have chosen different court systems, conflicts between the two disputants would be governed by the same type of preexisting agreements between the court systems that presently exist between the court systems of states and nations. As I discussed in Chapter 8 with respect to lawyers, legal systems are repeat players and have a much greater incentive to cooperate with one another than do individual disputants.

Of course, the reality of a polycentric constitutional order is likely to be considerably less open-ended than this sketch suggests. To minimize the costs of transacting in such a legal order, many kinds of property will undoubtedly be sold with jurisdictions over at least some legal issues specified in advance, as condominiums are sold today. When you buy a condominium, you buy the rules, procedures, and jurisdiction of the condominium association along with it. These packages of contractual rights and procedures are sometimes what makes some condominiums more or less attractive than others. Specifying the relevant rules and procedures in advance does not guarantee that jurisdictional problems will not arise. It just minimizes their occurrence and severity.

Moreover, we are accustomed to thinking about a single agency with a geographical monopoly providing *both* the judicial system and the police agency to enforce its orders—such as is typically provided in the United States by the executive and judicial "branches" of county governments. In a polycentric constitutional order no such combination of executive and judicial powers is either likely or desirable. Wholly different skills and resources are needed to efficiently render just decisions than are needed to efficiently enforce such decisions as are rendered by a court.

For example, efficient law enforcement (as opposed to adjudication) involves the use of coercion (*a*) to protect people from harm—a function now performed by local police departments; (*b*) to seize and sell property in satisfaction of judgments by a "recognized" court—a function now performed privately or by county sheriffs' offices; and (*c*) to administer a system of productive enterprises where persons who are either unable or unwilling to make payments from regular earnings can be employed under controlled conditions and paid market wages from which reparations are deducted until their debt to the victim is satisfied—a function now performed by no one.

The fact that a particular institution performs one of these functions well would seem to be unrelated to its ability to effectively perform any of the others. It is implausible that a single agency would perform any two of these many different enforcement services more efficiently than more specialized institutions. It is even more implausible that a firm that successfully provided these law enforcement services could also most efficiently supply adjudicative services.

As was emphasized above, an efficient judicial system must perform both a *justice function* and a *fairness function*. While the "good" or service produced by law-enforcement agencies is the threat of coercion, the "good" produced by judicial agencies are pieces of paper called "judgments." Although judgments are recognized warrants or justifications for law-enforcement agencies to use coercion, the ability to produce one sort of good has nothing to do with the ability to produce the other. There is every reason to doubt that efficient providers of enforcement services will also be efficient providers of the judgments that warrant such coercion.

Extended conflicts between different court systems in a polycentric constitutional order are also quite unlikely. It is simply not in the interest of repeat players (and most of their clients) to attempt to obtain short-run gains at the cost of long-run conflict. As was noted in Chapter 8, where they have the opportunity to cooperate, participants in even the most intense conflicts—warfare, for example—tend to evolve a "live and let live" philosophy.[27] There I discussed the reason why most successful lawyers do not today go to any lengths to pursue a given client's interests: they must live to fight another day and to preserve their ability to effectively defend *other* clients.

Likewise, it is not in the interest of any judge or court system to use or threaten force to resolve a legal or jurisdictional conflict in any but the most serious of circumstances. Indeed, like lawyers, a legal system that was "feuding" with all others would have no service to sell to those who find themselves in conflict with members of another legal system. Imagine a phone company that could not connect you with customers of any other company; or a credit card that was only accepted by depositors of the issuing bank.[28]

---

[27] See Axelrod, *Evolution of Cooperation*, p. 3 (presenting a theory of cooperation that can be used to discover what is necessary for cooperation to emerge "in a world of egoists without central authority"); and Sugden, *Economics of Rights* (same).

[28] This is how Visa and Mastercard began. "Bank cards" were initially honored only by local merchants with a direct agreement with the issuing bank. Eventually, reciprocal agreements between issuing banks evolved into the associations known as Visa (originally BankAmericard) and Mastercard. Though each credit card is issued by a particular bank (look on the back of your bank card), each member bank has entered into a pre-existing agreement with all the other members of the system, enabling their card holders to receive credit from merchants and services dealing with other member banks around the world. Thus by cooperating with their rivals, banks were able to offer a much more valuable service to their customers, just as they do by joining associations of automatic teller machines such as NYCE, Maestro, and Cirrus. Competition now takes place among credit card associations and between bank cards and other credit cards such as Discover, American Express, and Diner's Club, a list that is sure to be dated very soon.

For these reasons, in the Western legal tradition dominated by multiple court systems each with limited jurisdiction, judges have peacefully developed rules of law to resolve the two questions most likely to lead to conflict when multiple legal jurisdictions exist: *Which court system* is to hear the case when more than one might do so? And *which substantive law* is to be applied when more than one law might be applied? Much of the judicially-developed law of "civil procedure" addresses the first question, and an entire body of judicially-developed law—called the "conflict of laws"—has evolved to provide a means of resolving the second of these two questions.

Before elaborating on these two bodies of law, it is important to note that while a legal system that did not provide a *final* decision of a particular case or controversy would be unsatisfactory, it is a widespread misconception that a final decision requires there to be a *single* final decision maker. As was noted above, for most practical purposes, there are hundreds of final decision makers in the United States at the level of federal and state courts of appeals. The United States Supreme Court and the supreme courts of the fifty states for the most part decide only the cases they choose to decide. In all but a small number of cases, there is no right of appeal to these courts; instead one must "petition" to be heard by them at their discretion.

But how do parties to a dispute know to which of the hundreds of courts that can reach the initial decision they may later appeal to receive a final decision? This question has long been handled by a body of legal precepts known as *civil procedure* that determine which court among the many has jurisdiction. A typical jurisdictional problem facing the *present* legal system is described by a leading American civil procedure casebook as follows:

If the defendant does not want to submit to the jurisdiction [of a court], he plainly would not enter, or authorize his attorney to enter, a general appearance. If he is confident that jurisdiction over his person is lacking, he may, in theory at least, simply ignore the lawsuit entirely. To illustrate: P commences an action against D in State X for an alleged tort committed by D in State Y, seeking money damages. D resides in State Y and has never set foot in nor had any other connection with State X. P delivers process to D in State Y. State X has not acquired jurisdiction over D's person. If judgment on D's default is entered against him, and an attempt made to enforce the judgment in State Y or elsewhere, he can set up the voidness of the judgment in a collateral attack.

But D may wish to contest State X's jurisdiction over his person in the original action. He may be in genuine doubt whether State X has acquired jurisdiction over him, or he may not relish the prospect of an overhanging judgment against him even though he is convinced it is void . . . [in which case] the defendant would file a notice that he was appearing solely for the purpose of challenging the jurisdiction [of the court] and not submitting generally to the jurisdiction.[29]

Assuming one decides which court is to hear the case and make a final decision, which body of law is the court to follow? Once again, given the

[29] Richard H. Field, Benjamin Kaplan, and Kevin M. Clermont, *Civil Procedure*, 4th edn. (Mineola, Minn.: Foundation Press, 1978), pp. 729–30.

278 **Problems of Power**

multiplicity of legal systems in the West, this problem has long been handled by an elaborate set of legal precepts known as *conflict of laws*. According to the American Law Institute, "[t]he world is composed of territorial states having separate and differing systems of law. Events and transactions occur, and issues arise, that may have a significant relationship to more than one state, making necessary a special body of rules and methods for their ordering and resolution."[30] The conflict of laws is then defined as "that part of the law of each state which determines what effect is given to the fact that the case may have a significant relationship to more than one state."[31] Quite commonly, courts in one state decide a dispute using only the law of another state. In the famous multi-billion dollar lawsuit between Texaco and Pennzoil over the purchase of Getty Oil, for example, the Texas state courts applied New York state law to determine whether a contract to buy Getty had existed with which Texaco had allegedly interfered.[32]

Although these elaborate sets of rules, principles, and theories are generally unknown to nonlawyers, the impetus for their development was simply to resolve the inevitable conflicts that arose over the centuries between competing legal jurisdictions. As Harold Berman has emphasized: "The very complexity of a common legal *order* containing diverse legal *systems* contributed to legal sophistication. Which court has jurisdiction? Which law is applicable? How are legal differences to be reconciled?"[33] The principles developed over centuries to answer these questions would apply as well to competitive legal systems whose jurisdiction was based on contract, rather than on residence and geography.

Finally, suppose an individual refuses to contract with a reputable legal system having agreements with other legal systems. In the absence of such consent, would a competitive legal system be powerless to enforce its judgments? No. The justice of using force against such a person is based on the fact that he or she violated the rights of the victim, not that he or she consented to the jurisdiction of a court. As with the right to be represented by an attorney, fairness is accomplished if all persons have the *right to choose* a reputable legal system to protect them[34] and a *right to participate* freely in any legal proceedings

---

[30] American Law Institute, *Restatement of the Law of Conflicts 2d*, vol. i (St. Paul, Minn., 1971), § 1.

[31] Ibid. at § 2. See also Russell J. Weintraub, *Commentary on the Conflicts of Laws* (Mineola, NY: Foundation Press, 1971), p. 1 ("[T]he conflict of laws is the study of whether or not and, if so, in what way, the answer to a legal problem will be affected because the elements of the problem have contacts with more than one jurisdiction."); and Elliott E. Cheatham and Willis L. M. Reese, *Columbia Law Review*, vol. 52 (1952), p. 959 (discussing the various policies to be weighed in deciding choice of law problems).

[32] See Texaco v. Pennzoil, 729 S.W.2d 768 (1987).

[33] Berman, *Law and Revolution*, p. 10 (emphasis in original).

[34] Of course, if the initial legal system is perceived to be just, there is no reason founded on fairness to incur the costs of appealing to a rival legal system rather than participating in the first. A major incentive for legal systems to fulfill the fairness function by being widely perceived as just is to induce litigants to choose to participate rather than appeal to another system.

brought against them, not by the fact that they exercise these rights wisely in every instance. By the same token, fairness is not undermined when a person refuses to exercise his or her rights to choose and participate.

Although everyone would have a strong interest in gaining the support of a reputable legal system, we can imagine criminals who simply ignore the process entirely. Enforcing judgments and compelling participation are two different things. Today, although government court systems will not compel a person to participate in a trial,[35] they will issue judgments against persons who refuse to do so. The prosecution of mass murderer Charles Manson, who was removed from the court after he repeatedly disrupted the proceedings, is one notable example.[36] Further, numerous defendants are tried and convicted *in absentia* when, while on bond, they flee the jurisdiction of the court during a trial.

We would expect a fair system to take pains to ensure the reliability of its judgment even in the absence of the defendant's participation or consent to jurisdiction. Ultimately, though, the use of force against a rights violator is justified to rectify an injustice. The use of force by law-enforcement agencies is proper when a person's culpability for an injustice is determined by a court system that is known to be fair and that has jurisdiction according to the rules of civil procedure.

Dealing with Conflicting Law-Enforcement Agencies

What about the problem of law-enforcement agencies in a polycentric constitutional order fighting with each other? Any such scenario is highly unrealistic. Competing law-enforcement agencies' incentive to cooperate with each other would be greatly affected by their lack of access to a steady stream of coercively obtained revenue—that is, taxation. Those contemplating a conflict would know that the resources available to fight would not exceed those on hand and those which people were freely willing to contribute to the fight. And, unlike national governments, they could not obtain by coercion—that is by draft—personnel to enforce their judgment.

A "renegade" law-enforcement firm, no matter how financially well endowed it might be as compared with any single rival, would undoubtedly be dwarfed by the capital market as a whole. Imagine the Cook County Sheriff's Office, whose jurisdiction includes all of Chicago and surrounding suburbs, fighting all the other sheriffs' offices and police departments in the region, state, or country with only the resources it had on hand. (Actually, the polycentricity of such a constitutional order makes McDonald's declaring war on Wendy's and Burger King a far more apt analogy.)

[35] They may, however, appoint legal counsel who will test the sufficiency of the evidence against a recalcitrant defendant.
[36] See Vincent Bugliosi, *Helter Skelter* (New York: W.W. Norton, 1974) (describing the Manson trial).

Here is a thought experiment for those who do not immediately appreciate the arguments in favor of a polycentric constitutional order. Posit the creation of a monocentric international or "one-world" court system and police force to supplant the several governments, legal systems, police forces, and armies of today. Would you favor or oppose such a change and why? Very few would favor such a system largely because of their quite reasonable fear of enforcement abuse and their inability to flee to competing jurisdictions should abuses occur. Most everyone can well imagine the awful consequences of such a monocentric system erring or abusing its powers. These same fears should apply to national monopolies in law enforcement or adjudication—albeit with somewhat diminished force since some people have the ability to flee if a single country becomes too tyrannical. The abolition of national geographical monopolies would simply strengthen the constraints on enforcement abuse by making alternative legal systems available without leaving home.

Moreover, the arguments typically made on behalf of the Single Power Principle cannot be confined to the borders of our current array of nation-states. Any argument that a coercive monopoly of power is necessary also suggests the need for a single world court system with one super-supreme court to decide international disputes and a single super-police force to enforce its decisions. After all, the logic of the arguments against a competitive polycentric constitutional order applies with equal force to autonomous nations. As John Locke noted,

"all *Princes* and Rulers of *Independent* governments are in a state of Nature . . . whether they are, or are not, in League with others: For 'tis not every Compact that puts an end to the State of Nature between Men, but only this one of agreeing together mutually to enter into one Community, and make one Body politick; other Promises and Compacts, Man may make with another, and yet still be in the State of Nature."[37]

So the reason why people would leave the "state of nature" to establish a coercive monopoly of power would presumably apply to independent governments as well. It is far from clear why these arguments, like arguments for redistributing wealth, end at the current borders of nation states.

And as for the danger of violent conflict, monopolistic *governments* do regularly go to war against one another. With their singular powers to tax their populations, draft soldiers, and put their domestic competitors out of business by force, they are far better able to wage war than agencies adhering to the Nonconfiscation and Competition principles. Yet notwithstanding this genuine threat to the pursuit of happiness, peace, and prosperity, few people favor addressing the serious problem of war between monopoly governments by invoking the Single Power Principle on behalf of a one-world monocentric legal system and police force. Instead most favor the use of treaties or agreements—contracts, if you will—between nations to settle their conflicts. That

---

[37] Locke, *Two Treatises*, §14, p. 317.

is, they favor the very same device that a polycentric constitutional order would use to prevent and resolve conflicts between competing legal systems.

When put in proper historical, comparative, and theoretical perspective, then, conflicts between court systems whose jurisdictions geographically overlap or between competing law-enforcement agencies present no insurmountable practical problem. As with any other decentralized regime, it is more reasonable to expect a never-ending series of "little" problems around the edges. Information must be shared; duplicated efforts avoided; minor conflicts settled amicably; and profit margins preserved. As with any other organization, the normal problems confronting business and political rivals—who must constantly strike a balance between competition and cooperation—would have to be managed. How these edges would be smoothed would sometimes require ingenuity. Such problems provide no good reason, however, to refrain from addressing the serious problem of enforcement abuse by adopting the Nonconfiscation and Competition principles.

Will a Polycentric Constitutional Order be Liberal?

Can we expect that the substantive rights and remedies of the liberal fusion of justice and the rule of law I have defended here will be the law adopted by legal systems operating within a polycentric constitutional order?[38] After all, these rights go far beyond the simple abolition of the coercive monopoly of power. Moreover, it surely is possible to imagine an illiberal "decentralized" regime—witness Lebanon in the 1980s. My view is that whether or not a polycentric regime would be liberal depends on how it comes about.

If decentralization comes about as a result of a violent conflict between ethnic, religious, or national *groups* fighting to control a coercive monopoly of power in which no side prevails, then the stalemate that results is likely to be an illiberal Hobbesian war of group against group—at least for a time. If the combatants remain unable to defeat each other, eventually we can expect a cooperative solution to the conflict to be adopted, though this process may take a very long time to occur and many thousands may die in the process.

On the other hand, if decentralization comes about as a relatively peaceful reform movement in which the Nonconfiscation and Competition principles are adopted and a polycentric constitutional order evolves spontaneously, then we can expect the resulting order to be more or less liberal. For it is difficult to imagine a society that did not adhere to some version of a liberal conception of justice ever accepting a polycentric constitutional order in the

---

[38] Cf. David Friedman, *The Machinery of Freedom* (New York: Harper Colophon Books, 1973), p. 173: "I have described how a private system of courts and police might function, but not the laws it would produce and enforce; I have discussed institutions, not results. . . . Whether these institutions will produce a libertarian society—a society in which each person is free to do as he likes with himself and his property as long as he does not use either to initiate force against others—remains to be proven."

first instance. A societal consensus supporting these rights and remedies would seem to be a precondition for ever peacefully ending adherence to the Single Power Principle. And, once adopted, the inherent stability of the robust "checks and balances" provided by a competitive system is likely to preserve this initial consensus.

In the last analysis, where no consensus about liberty and individual rights exists, it is unlikely that even a coercive monopoly of power will do much to prevent violations of these rights from occurring. This is the sad but important lesson of the forcible internment and confiscation of the homes, businesses, and land of Americans of Japanese descent by the government of the United States during the Second World War.[39] Far from preventing such enforcement abuse, adherence to the Single Power Principle made it possible.

Summary

We are now in a position to summarize how a polycentric constitutional order that adheres to the Nonconfiscation and Competition principles can deal with the four problems of power that were discussed in Chapter 12.

(1) *The Selection Problem.* Who gets the power? Those court systems whose jurisdiction people agree to accept and those law-enforcement agencies to which people are willing to subscribe.

(2) *The Corruption and Capture Problems.* How do you keep power in the hands of the good? By permitting people to withdraw their consent and their financial support from those who are perceived to be corrupt or advantage-takers and letting them shift their support to others who are perceived to be better. The power of consumers to swing resources rapidly away from those agencies perceived as corrupt towards those who are seen as better, coupled with the ability of rival law-abiding organizations to organize their resistance to aggression would help assure that swift preventative measures will be forcefully and smoothly implemented.

(3) *The Legitimacy Problem.* How do you prevent holders of power from receiving undue legitimacy? No enforcement agency or court system in a polycentric constitutional order would be entitled to any special legal privileges. Each would be legally responsible to make restitution for its

---

[39] See Korematsu v. United States, 323 US 214 (1944). In this case the Supreme Court upheld as constitutional this internment and confiscation "because we are at war with the Japanese empire, because the properly constituted military authorities feared an invasion of our West Coast and felt constrained to take proper security measures, because they decided that the military urgency of the situation demanded that all citizens of Japanese ancestry be segregated from the West Coast temporarily, and finally, because Congress, reposing its confidence in this time of war in our military leaders—as inevitably it must—determined that they should have the power to do just this." Ibid. 223.

mistakes. Stripped of the legitimacy traditionally accorded rulers, enforcement agencies and court systems would be constantly scrutinized by competitors, consumers, consumer protection groups, and the press to detect any self-serving behavior. Their perceived legitimacy would depend solely on their individual reputations. While a track record of integrity heavily shapes reputations, an effective court system would need constantly to scrutinize its current practices and policies to ensure that they do not jeopardize its reputation in any way.

Let us now try to imagine what a polycentric constitutional order might look like.

FOURTEEN

Imagining a Polycentric Constitutional Order: A Short Fable

ASSUMING the Nonconfiscation and Competition principles were adopted, it is no easier to predict the formal organization and division of labor of the polycentric constitutional order that will result than it is to predict the formal organization of the personal computer market twenty years from now. (Of course, twenty years ago the challenge would have been to predict the very *existence* of a personal computer market.) Difficulties of prediction notwithstanding, some speculation is needed, for without some image of a polycentric constitutional order in mind, few will be inspired to move to adopt these principles. Rather than attempt the impossible task of comprehensively assessing the limitless alternatives that such freedom would make possible, let us instead imagine that somewhere there exists the constitutional order that I shall now describe.

1. Paying for Law Enforcement and Legal Services

In this hypothetical constitutional order, the vast majority of people who work or who have spouses or parents who work are covered by health insurance arrangements (like those provided in our world by such companies as Blue Cross/Blue Shield). In return for a monthly fee, if they are ever sick they receive medical attention by presenting their membership card to an approved doctor or hospital. In this hypothetical legal order, many people also carry a Blue Coif/Blue Gavel card ("You won't leave jail without it!") as well. If they ever need legal services, they present their card to an approved lawyer and court system. Of course, as with medical insurance, not all kinds of legal actions are covered and there may be limits to some kinds of coverage; and not everyone makes use of this type of system.

Others belong to a "Rights Maintenance Organization" (or "RMO"). These firms keep lawyers on staff as salaried employees (rather than as partners) providing "preventative" legal services. RMOs claim that they more tightly control costs created by needless or hopeless litigation than is possible with conventional legal insurance arrangements, and this permits them to offer more coverage for a lower premium. Legal disputes between members of the same RMO are very expeditiously and informally handled internally. And when it is necessary to go to an outside court, the RMO will pay the court fee (having arranged group discounts for its members in advance). On the other hand, the freedom to pick your own lawyer within an RMO is necessarily quite limited, and this feature does not satisfy everyone. Another drawback is the fact that the client is more dependent on the RMOs determination that a lawsuit is cost-justified than is a client who has coverage by Blue Coif/Blue Gavel.

Legal service provider franchises dot the landscape with well-lit (some think garish) "Golden Scales of Justice" signs prominently displayed at street side; many are located adjacent to "urgent care" walk-up medical facilities. Located in shopping malls and along busy streets, these firms advertise nationally and specialize in high volume (some say homogenized) practices, handling routine legal matters at standardized fees. (They accept Blue Coif/Blue Gavel and major credit cards.) Large retailers who sell insurance, investment, or real estate services also sell legal services, as do an increasing number of bank, trust, and even brokerage companies. Some offer in-house revolving charge accounts as an alternative to insurance and other kinds of credit arrangements.

Such mass merchandising is not for everyone. Many clients still prefer the personal touch and custom-tailored work of solo practitioners who thrive by providing a more individualized approach. Some of these independent lawyers offer more specialized expertise than the chains; others try to be "generalists" and claim that they can spot interrelated legal problems that the lawyers who only handle certain kinds of less complicated legal matters often miss. Most large companies with commercial legal problems prefer the elegance, prestige, and economies of scale of large, traditionally organized high-rise law firms. (Some things never change.)

Besides insurance, other means of financing lawsuits are also available. A few credit card companies offer extended payment plans when used for legal services. Contingency-fee-based entrepreneurs (who, like everyone else, can and do advertise widely) serve many who cannot or choose not to advance the money for legal services. True, to help minimize the number of improvident lawsuits, a few court systems have established rules restricting contingent payment arrangements in a manner similar to the rules established in our world by private stock and mercantile exchanges. But traditional contingent fee arrangements by which lawyers are paid out of damages awarded their clients are not as necessary in this world because "loser pays" damage awards include compensation for reasonable attorney's costs. Therefore, unlike in our world, attorneys fees are generally paid *in addition to* full compensation for the client's injuries. And, unlike our world where contingent fees are criticized for leading to irresponsible lawsuits by entrepreneurial lawyers, contingency fee lawyers are held financially responsible for the legal costs of the other party if a contingent fee suit is unsuccessful.

Finally, in cases where commitment to a restitution center is a possible sanction (more on this shortly), all judicial firms provide defendants who cannot afford them an attorney. If convicted, this cost is added to the amount of restitution that need be paid. Judicial firms have no financial incentives to convict, however, because when defendants are acquitted, the complainant is liable for these costs. Although most people have insurance or RMO policies that cover this contingency, to be eligible for payment most insurance companies and all RMOs require complaints and evidence be reviewed by approved "prosecution" attorneys prior to being filed in order to prevent unsupported charges being brought. In this way, there has evolved a decentralized screening system for bringing complaints.[1]

2. The Judicial System

The judicial system mirrors the diversity of the legal profession as a whole. Judges work for "judicial firms," the way lawyers in our world work for law firms. There are well-known and well-advertised national judicial centers, with regional and local offices, that handle the bulk of routine commercial practice. In addition to judges, these firms sometimes attempt to satisfy the fairness function by hiring lay jurors to decide simple factual issues, particularly those that involve "criminal" matters. In this world, the conscription of jurors is considered unjust involuntary servitude.

There are intermediate-sized firms that handle specialized legal matters like maritime cases and patent or mineral disputes. These firms almost never use lay jurors, but rely instead on panels of professional experts who receive long-term publicly-disclosed retainers from the company regardless of the nature of the opinions they render. And there are thousands of individual judges who hang out a shingle in neighborhoods after registering with the *National Registry of Judges and Justices of the Peace*, which requires of its members a minimum (some say minimal) level of legal education and experience. Many of these judges share the ethnic heritage of the communities where their offices are located. And many are multilingual, unlike most judges for major judicial firms who must rely on interpreters.

Individuals and businesses tend to avoid judges and judicial systems that lack some significant certification of quality due to the difficulty of enforcing

---

[1] This resembles the felony review unit I worked in as a prosecutor which reviewed and had to approve all felony charges and search warrants.

judgments from such firms. Numerous rating agencies exist and judicial firms often advertise the names of agencies from whom they have received a favorable rating. The *Harvard Law School Guide to the American Judiciary*, for example, is one useful source of information (but it is often accused of being elitist). *Who's Who in the American Judiciary*, published by a nonacademic publishing firm is another (though it is considerably less selective). Many prefer the annual guide *Judicial Reports* published by the Consumers Union (it accepts no advertising). Still others consult the *Whole Earth Catalog of Judges* (though its listings are often considerably out of date). The *Michelin Guide to International Law Judges* uses a five-star rating system. Even with all of these publications providing information about the legal system that is unavailable to us in our world, newspapers and television "news magazines" never seem to tire of running stories about what they claim are judicial mistakes. Such exposés sometimes lead to reforms by the various judicial firms and rating agencies.

To attract business, most judges guarantee enforcement of their judgments by affiliating with specified law-enforcement agencies. Otherwise only the moral authority of their rulings would induce compliance. Since all law-enforcement agencies are legally liable to those who can prove to the satisfaction of an impartial legal system that an erroneous judgment had been imposed upon them, no enforcement company will long maintain an affiliation with an unreliable judicial agency or an unregistered judge. Some judges advertise to law-enforcement firms and the general public: "Judgment affirmed or your money back!" Until a few years ago, several large judicial agencies even owned their own police company (more on this development later).

Surprisingly, however, not every judge is affiliated with an enforcement agency. The *American Association of Adjudicators* (AAA) does not promise enforcement but only a fair and just decision. Like arbitration agreements in our world, all parties must contractually agree to binding adjudication in a form recognized as enforceable by law-enforcement agencies or by *other* courts who do have enforcement affiliations and who will only on rare occasions fail to summarily honor an AAA adjudicator's decision. Other judges don't rely even indirectly on law-enforcement agencies. In a significant number of discrete communities—like the diamond trading community in our world whose private judges apply a variant of Jewish law[2]—social sanctions are all that are required to effectively enforce judgments.

The Appellate Process

In some respects, though "horizontal" not "vertical," the appellate process that has evolved is similar to federal court review of state court decisions in the United States. The judgment of any legal system can be appealed to any other, but legal systems are generally reluctant to reverse the decision of another

[2] See Bernstein, 'Opting out'.

system unless given good reason to do so. They know that in the future their cases can also be appealed to the legal systems whose decisions they are evaluating. On the other hand, were they to fail to reverse decisions when they have reason to do so, they would lose out on lucrative appellate business. (Appellate business is profitable because the costs of deciding appeals is quite low, as compared with trials, and can be done very quickly.) Moreover, their trial judges learn a great deal from hearing appeals of the decisions of trial judges for other legal systems. They are, however, a good deal more empathetic with problems confronting a trial judge than are appellate court judges in our world who themselves may never have been trial judges or even trial lawyers.

When a conflict exists between two legal systems (the original system and the "appellate" system) that cannot be resolved, all legal systems have agreed to abide by the decision of a third "supreme" court system. Any court system can be a supreme court in case of a dispute between two other legal systems. One difference between the U.S. federal system and external appeals to another system in this constitutional order is that, in this order, the decision of *any* court can be appealed to any other. Contrast this with the U.S. system, where state court decisions can sometimes be reviewed by federal courts, but federal decisions are never reviewed by any outside court system.[3]

In another respect, the system of appeals in this legal order resembles the "hierarchical" appellate structure within both the federal and state court systems of the United States. External appeals of the sort just described are more costly than appeals handled "internally" or within a judicial firm. Judicial firms guarantee a free internal appeal from any legal decision, whether a decision of fact or of law. This gives them a substantial market advantage over solo judges and justices of the peace practitioners, though the reputations of solo practitioners are often well known in their communities.

As was mentioned above, enforcement agencies are not immune from being held responsible for their wrongful uses of force and, as a result, some judicial firms enhance the enforceability of their judgments by guaranteeing to reimburse enforcement agencies for any liability they incur as a result of relying on an erroneous judgment. Since either party may claim that an error was made, this provides an added incentive for judges to make every effort to reach the right result or at least a result that is unimpeachable. And this, in turn, increases the attractiveness of these firms to prospective litigants. Moreover, one of the principal selling points of any legal system (and a major factor that influences rating agencies) is the legal consistency and internal discipline of judges.

---

[3] In cases involving statutory interpretation, however, a Supreme Court decision is sometimes, though rarely, reviewed and altered by Congress.

Law and Legislation

To maintain the legitimacy of their legal rulings, judges usually justify their decisions by adhering to the precedential opinions of other judges in their and other firms. These opinions are readily available via subscriptions to one of two computer on-line services that pay judicial firms a royalty for electronically publishing their opinions. In addition to offsetting judges' cost of on-line access, they are a small profit center for judicial agencies. The on-line services' profits come mainly from subscribing attorneys. In addition, while some judicial firms maintain their own internal guidelines to govern some types of disputes, to enhance both consistency and the perception of justice (the fairness function), most subscribe to a variety of on-line expert services that survey and summarize trends among judicial opinions.

Still, judicial opinions are commonly supplemented by reference to "codes" or legislation written by authoritative outside institutions. The American Law Institute (ALI) is one such institution in this legal order. (Coincidentally, this prestigious group exists in our world too.) As in our world, the ALI is a private organization comprised of a select group of lawyers, judges, and law professors which meets annually to periodically issue detailed "Restatements of the Law"® that judges of different court systems have made in a wide variety of different fields. These Restatements systematize and sometimes refine the precepts that have evolved in countless cases from different legal systems. Many contracts stipulate that, if litigated, the parties have agreed to be governed by the relevant Restatement of the Law.

While the ALI dominates the production of codified law in this legal order, other legal experts who have written massive multi-volume works on particular areas of law are routinely consulted and cited as "authorities" by judges in every legal system to legitimate their decisions. The influence of all these standard authorities has greatly minimized radical disparities among legal systems—though, as in our world, some differences of opinion still exist. Such differences of opinion that inevitably arise form the basis for legal change as the authorities study each deviation and assess its wisdom.

Any rule that varies quite substantially from the norms considered just will not usually be applied by judges in rival legal systems unless the parties had so stipulated in a contract. Thus has developed a core set of "common law" principles that are shared by nearly all legal systems, despite their differences. Rules that vary from this common law would still apply, however, to two subscribers to the same legal system. Nonetheless, sometimes novel rules attract sufficient numbers of new clients that rival legal systems begin to emulate them—as happened in our world when the English royal courts changed their rules of contract law to reclaim lucrative business they had lost to ecclesiastical courts who had been more liberally enforcing informal promises.[4]

---

[4] See R. H. Helmholz, "Assumpsit and *Fidei Laesio*," *Law Quarterly Review*, vol. 91 (1975), p. 406.

Judicial Discipline

To ensure the appearance of impartiality or fairness, most legal systems grant their judges "lifetime tenure" after a probationary period; essentially, this is an employment contract, like tenured professors have in our world, that cannot be terminated except for good cause. Still, judges who persistently disregard the codes adopted by the firm or the precedent of other judges are dismissed, since the costs incurred by the firm when their decisions are reversed both internally and externally can be substantial. To insulate judges from undue influence, most judicial employment contracts specify that such dismissals may be adjudicated, often by an outside firm, at the firm's expense.

As was mentioned above, because any judicial firm handling an appeal from another legal system could one day have its own decisions reviewed by the system whose judgment is under review, a certain level of deference towards the judgments of others has evolved. Nonetheless, because there is substantial money to be made from appellate work (remember, the losing party must pay the cost), no legal system can afford simply to rubber stamp the judgments of another.

3. Law Enforcement

In this legal order (as in ours), the distinct functions of enforcing legal judgments and of preventing and responding to crimes are handled by different law-enforcement agencies.

Enforcing Judgments

The agencies that enforce the judgments of the legal system tend to specialize in what we call criminal and civil cases. This distinction turns on the differing enforcement problems that necessitate a division of labor. The "civil" agencies must be adept at sorting through paper arrangements to locate assets that can be legitimately seized and sold to satisfy judgments. Occasionally, when a civil agency is done with a convicted defendant, the case must be turned over to a criminal agency to collect the balance.

Some of those law-enforcement agencies specializing in "criminal" matters catch criminals while others provide work to those who may not be able to earn enough to satisfy the judgment against them if left on their own. Those incarcerated in restitution centers to make restitution are offered a variety of jobs to perform depending on their prior skills and training. Most, but not all, restitution centers specialize in one particular kind of industry. Some incarcerated laborers are also "contracted out" to private firms. Often firms that hire incarcerated workers under contract will retain those they have trained after their restitution obligation is met and they are released.

Like prison workers in our world, it is difficult to enumerate all the types of jobs that restitution workers perform. As in our world, many work in manufacturing facilities making clothing and other goods; some build low-cost prefabricated homes that are shipped in flat-bed trucks to distant cities; others restore old automobiles that are then sold at auction; and some answer calls to toll reservation lines or do data processing for the service industry. (Unlike our world, none make license plates.) Consumers often deal with services provided by restitution workers without even being aware of it, though there is no bias against such goods. Indeed, the overwhelming public sentiment is that criminals *should* work at productive activities rather than be supported by law-abiding folks.

Those convicts who refuse to work are incarcerated indefinitely. No firm could afford to release anyone who had refused to work. If they did, no one would work. Thus, the potential consequence of a refusal to work is lifetime incarceration (as I shall describe in the next section). While abuses of restitution workers is not unknown, every worker is entitled to legal representation and specialized law firms have arisen to handle these matters. Such firms are paid contingently on their success.

To be sure, conflicts between enforcement agencies have arisen. Most have been quickly resolved by the agencies themselves. Some conflicts have required the intervention of other agencies. These have been resolved with the help of judicial systems acting as mediators. Of course, minor though persistent friction persists between a few enforcement agencies.

Crime Prevention

Crime prevention takes a variety of forms. Police protection is normally retained and paid for by the property owner—whether residential or commercial—as it is on private property in our world. All law-enforcement agencies subscribe to one or more of several competing computer networks that gather and store information about individuals who have been convicted of offenses in much the same manner as government police departments and private credit rating agencies share information in our world. Such electronic data services provide their clients with near instantaneous information about individuals and firms with whom they might be contemplating doing business—something like the information that local Better Business Bureaus in our world claim to provide— or persons whom they might consider excluding from their property.

Repeat offenders who have demonstrated themselves by their past conduct to be dangerous are handled in one of two ways. Those who have made restitution but appear to pose a continuing threat to others can publicly be declared "outlaws." This means that, should they ever be attacked or victimized by anyone—including crime victims seeking retribution—all law-enforcement agencies agree to refrain from rendering them any assistance, and no judicial firm will issue a judgment on their behalf. Once their outlaw status becomes known, they are then fair game for other criminals and their very lives become precarious. In this manner, outlawry provides a virtual cost-free "punishment" that does not require any force to be used against the offender. Further, after living as fugitives from other criminals and disgruntled victims for a time, some outlaws who survive seek to escape the danger by voluntarily applying for readmission to a restitution center where they are protected in return for working to pay for their maintenance.

Other outlaws seek safety (and freedom) by gathering in remote privately-owned "havens" populated largely by other outlaws. Unlike our prisons, owners of these havens are themselves entrepreneurs who exact a heavy rent from outlaws and operate farms and sometimes hazardous factories in which they can earn their keep. Havens are governed by very rough rules of justice and some even have legal systems of their own to adjudicate disputes. Death penalties for offenses committed in such areas are said not to be uncommon. Some report that these areas are actually surprisingly peaceful (no "official" crime statistics are available of course), though any "citizen," as outsiders are called, who happens to enter would be in great danger. Over time, people expect at least some of these areas to evolve into law-abiding communities, as did such eighteenth- and nineteenth-century English penal colonies of Georgia (now the state of Georgia), Botany Bay (now Australia), and Van Diemen's Land (now Tasmania).[5] In the meantime, haven owners can and have been held vicariously responsible for making restitution if one of their outlaws commits an offense against a person outside a haven.

Those comparatively few offenders who refuse to make restitution, who commit an offense while incarcerated, who are considered too dangerous to be treated as outlaws, or who as outlaws continue to prey on non-outlaws, can be confined to maximum-security detention facilities for life. Their maintenance is paid for by associations of crime insurance companies and enforcement agencies. As these offenders are confined under extremely spartan conditions, the cost of their confinement is really quite low. Those who wish to enjoy more amenities may do so if they agree to work to pay for their entire maintenance, but since most restitution centers will not emperil their workers by exposing them to such dangerous offenders, small specialized firms have arisen to employ at least some of the hardened offenders who wish to work.

Though crime has certainly not been eliminated, most citizens seem satisfied that offenders are treated more justly and in some cases more severely than they were under their previous (and our current) system of probation and tax-payer funded government imprisonment. Recidivism has been reduced since it is likely to result either in outlawry or life imprisonment. And victims of crime are generally pleased to receive partial or complete restitution as com-

---

[5] See Liggio, "*Transportation of Criminals*," 273–94.

pensation for having their rights violated. Finally, because dangerous persons have largely been removed from civil society, either by housing them in restitution centers, detention facilities, or havens, most locales have experienced a substantial drop in crime and a corresponding increase in personal security.

4. Other Matters

While it does not directly concern the delivery of adjudication and enforcement services, some may be interested to learn that most common areas in this world are as accessible as private shopping centers and other commercial and residential developments are in ours. Some parks are free, provided by community associations or philanthropists—often these parks are their former dwellings and grounds and are supported by foundations funded by their estates. However, most large parks, even many of the not-for-profit parks operated by community associations, charge admission fees and usually offer many organized activities, such as sports leagues of all kinds, concerts, arts and food festivals, etc. to attract patrons. They issue single admission tickets, group tickets for such things as picnics and softball leagues, and season passes. Those owned by community associations often offer free admission passes to those who cannot afford to pay. Most smaller parks tend to be for the exclusive use of those neighborhood residents, who pay annual fees, and their guests. Of course, people who do not use the parks at all are free to spend their money on other types of goods and services.

All intercity highways charge tolls. Some intra-urban commuter highways issue license plates that vary in price (and color) depending on whether or not they can be used during "rush hours." Visiting tourists can obtain temporary permits at outlying toll booths. As is starting to happen in our world as well, an increasing number use electronic monitors attached to cars to send monthly bills based on actual usage—with rates that can more precisely reflect such factors as distance, time, and day. Price rationing has eliminated regular traffic jams. For example, as with some long distance phone services, usage between 8.00 pm and 6.00 am is heavily discounted. Many employers offer flex-hours to take advantage of these lower commuting costs, which helps even out traffic patterns. Finally, with road use subject to market pricing, competing private train and bus firms seem to do far better financially in this world than in ours where they must compete with toll-free roads whose use is rationed only by gas prices, gas taxes, and traffic jams.

All new commercial and residential developments must build their own streets, and all leases and land titles include both contractual rights of access and stipulated maintenance fees. Ownership of formerly government-owned streets was deeded to shareholding street companies. Voting stock in these companies was assigned to owners of commercial or residential property adjacent to the streets, and these property owners also receive contractual rights of access and egress. These street companies have continued to merge with one another and break up until their sizes and configurations approximate those of newly constructed commercial or residential developments.

5. The Problem with TopCops and Justice, Inc.: A Worst-Case Scenario

Although this legal order is not without its problems, none has amounted to a crisis—with the exception of a quite serious problem that developed about five years after the old monocentric system had ended. TopCops, one of the country's largest law-enforcement agencies (commanding about one-third of the national market in protective services) merged with Justice, Inc., one of the largest court systems. Many observers were quite disturbed by this development, and the other judicial companies and law-enforcement agencies also became concerned. Since the merger violated no one's rights, no legal action against this new institution could be taken. The fears, however, turned out to be well founded.

Initially, the operation of this organization seemed unobjectionable but, after a time, rumors began to circulate that when subscribers to TopCops came into conflict with subscribers to other agencies, Justice, Inc. sided with TopCops in some highly questionable decisions. In response to these widespread rumors, both the Chief Judge of Justice, Inc. and the corporate president of TopCops issued a public statement denying that any lack of fairness existed. They condemned the "rumor-mongers" as jealous business rivals who were just trying to destroy their competition, but they also promised a thorough internal investigation.

Still, the rumors persisted and took a new turn. Officers of TopCops were discovered to have been accused of committing crimes, but Justice, Inc. rarely if ever found for their accusers. Unbeknownst to the general public, in response to these rumors a secret task force was formed by a consortium of major rival enforcement agencies and court systems to devise a strategy to deal with the problem. (It was thought at the time that secrecy was important so as not to shake the faith of the general public in the relatively new polycentric constitutional order as a whole.) The following policies were quietly adopted and implemented by the rival companies:

> *First, no subscriber of a court system belonging to the consortium would submit to the sole jurisdiction of Justice, Inc. This had not been the usual practice because avoiding duplicate legal actions saved costs for both sides.*
>
> *Second, all decisions of Justice, Inc. that were in conflict with a decision of a court belonging to the consortium were to be automatically appealed to an*

outside court system according to the appellate structure established by the
Cambridge Convention (of which Justice, Inc. was a member).

Finally, no decision of Justice, Inc. that conflicted with that of a member court
would be recognized and enforced by a member law-enforcement agency.

Smaller court systems and law-enforcement agencies quickly got wind of the
new policy and began emulating it. The immediate consequence of these
actions was a drastic increase in the adjudication and enforcement costs
incurred by Justice, Inc. and TopCops. A backlog of cases began to develop,
and prices charged by both companies eventually had to be raised. As a result,
subscribers began switching to alternative services. A major faction of
TopCops' board of directors resigned when the board refused to adopt any
significant reforms. Instead, those who remained on the board voted to sever
their affiliation with the Cambridge Convention and began to search for
alliances with other companies. (The true reason for this apparently irrational
behavior was discovered only later.)

Several small enforcement companies and even one medium sized company
were induced to affiliate with TopCops, forming the Confederation of
Enforcement Agencies. Rumors flew that some had been intimidated to
affiliate. These alliances, however, did little more than make up for the steady
drop in both subscribers and revenues. At its zenith, the entire Confederation
controlled about a quarter of the enforcement market—somewhat less than
the one-third share of the market that TopCops alone had previously controlled.

In response, the Cambridge Convention formally severed relations with the
members of the Confederation and went public with its factual findings.
Notwithstanding the Confederation's public protests, its already jittery subscribers began to repudiate their contracts in large numbers. The
Confederation first announced that it would no longer give *pro rata* refunds for
subscription fees. When resignations nonetheless persisted, the Confederation
announced that because they were a result of "unfounded panic," it would not
recognize them as valid until the "rumor mongering" of what it now called the
"Cambridge Cartel" ceased.

Then a new and frightening story broke. It was learned that the board members of TopCops who had pioneered these developments were secretly
affiliated with members of the remnants of the old "organized crime syndicate." Since all victimless crimes—crimes involving drugs, gambling, prostitution, pornography, and so on—had long ago been abolished, the syndicate's
power and income had drastically declined. It obtained what income it
received primarily from organizing and attempting to monopolize fraud, burglary, auto theft, and extortion activities. Of course, even these activities were
not as profitable as they had once been because preventative law-enforcement
efforts had greatly increased, and the corruption of law-enforcement officers
had become much more difficult. Hence the scheme to infiltrate TopCops was

hatched both as a source of income from those who would pay to have their cases "fixed" and as a way of protecting its own members from successful prosecution.

A search by independent investigative journalists of the court records made available by the Consortium revealed that the syndicate-affiliated criminals had received unjustifiably favorable treatment by Justice, Inc. With this news, the Cambridge Convention communicated the following extraordinary order to all law-enforcement agencies and to the general public:

> *No order of Justice, Inc. is to be recognized or obeyed. Free protection is to be extended to any subscriber of TopCops who is threatened in any way. Any victim of a burglary or auto theft whose case had been adversely decided by Justice, Inc. since the merger is entitled to a free rehearing, and all previously acquitted defendants in such cases are subject to immediate rearrest and retrial. All TopCops employees are to be placed under immediate surveillance.*

With this action, Justice, Inc. was forced to close its operations because of lack of business. The remainder of TopCops' honest subscribers repudiated their affiliation, and scores of burglars and auto thieves were placed under arrest. Several of TopCops' employees turned out to have been acquitted burglary and auto theft defendants. Without a cash flow, and with the risk of personal liability now present, TopCops' honest employees began quitting the company in very large numbers. Since TopCops had been a national organization, it did not have a single location that was strategically defensible, so there was little armed resistance to the law-enforcement actions of the Consortium members. In most instances, TopCops facilities were within a few blocks of other agencies. Within a matter of weeks, the TopCops organization had been disbanded and its assets auctioned off to provide funds to partially reimburse persons whose rights it had violated—all without a shot being fired. Soon, offices formerly operated by TopCops were reopened for business as new branches of other established companies.

The Moral

The entire unhappy episode had taken not quite six months to unfold, but some important lessons were learned. First, the initial euphoria surrounding the abolition of the archaic monocentric legal system was tempered. People realized that a polycentric constitutional order, though an improvement over a monocentric system animated by the Single Power Principle, was no panacea for the problems of law enforcement and adjudication. Diligence was still required to prevent injustice and tyranny from recurring. Second, the Cambridge Convention announced that, in the future, it would not recognize the judgments of any court system created or purchased by a law-enforcement agency. Court systems were still able to administer or contract for a small enforcement contingent for internal security, but strict guidelines were formulated for such arrangements. Third, organized burglary, auto theft, and extortion rings had been dealt a serious financial blow (though they still persist).

Finally, after all the turmoil, talk of "crisis," and news magazine cover stories had subsided, most people came to realize that their new constitutional order was even more stable and self-correcting than many had expected it to be. The entire unhappy incident had unfolded in a matter of months and had been successfully and largely peacefully resolved. And this realization extended to members of the law-enforcement and judicial communities as well, making any future forays into illicit and aggressive activities much less likely than ever before.

Conclusion

Any effort to describe a legal order that departs substantially from people's settled image of the current order risks sounding utopian (and even dystopian to some). But, while it may be idealistic, I have tried hard to tell a story that is not utopian. This fable incorporates many aspects of our legal tradition, though these elements are largely unknown and may conflict with the unrealistic image most people have constructed of our legal past and present. Nothing in this story would require a basic change in the nature of human beings or the principles that order society. I assumed neither an optimistic, nor pessimistic view of human nature.

And I make no claim to prescience. If the two principles of a polycentric constitutional order were adopted, the resulting legal world would likely look far different than the world I imagined, with problems (and solutions) we cannot possibly anticipate. Yet without an idea of where we want ultimately to go, we have no interest in taking even a single step in the right direction. Nothing is more frightening for some than the unknown. If this account helps make more concrete the somewhat abstract discussion, in Chapter 13, of a polycentric constitutional order, then it has served its intended purpose.

PART FOUR

Responses to Objections

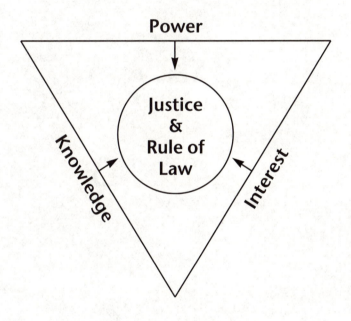

FIFTEEN

Beyond Justice and the Rule of Law?

THE liberal fusion of justice and the rule of law of the sort defended here has not been without its critics. Some criticize it for erecting a barrier to the realization of certain desired forms of social life. Others criticize it for being inadequate to ensure the sort of social life or "community" we need or desire, or a just distribution of resources, or the retributive punishment of criminals. According to the first of these criticisms, the liberal fusion of justice and the rule of law prevents the achievement of some visions of the good and is therefore "too much"; according to the second it is "too little" to guarantee the achievement of some vision of the good or a different conception of justice. While the analysis presented in the previous chapters does not address every particular of these charges, it does cast some new light on these perennial controversies.

Liberalism distinguishes between "the just" and "the good." The just is defined by the liberal fusion of justice and the rule of law and is enforceable. The good—whether good conduct or a good society—is defined by other kinds of moral analysis and is unenforceable. The distinction between the just and the good also corresponds to the distinction described in Chapter 1 between natural rights which define justice and injustice, and the natural law which defines virtue or good conduct and vice or bad conduct.

To distinguish the just from the good, natural rights theorists sometimes separated "perfect" rights and duties that are enforceable from "imperfect" rights and duties which are not.

[S]ome things are due us by a perfect, others by a imperfect right. When what is due us in the former score is not voluntarily given, it is the right of those in enjoyment of natural liberty to resort to violence and war in forcing another to furnish it, or, if we live within the same state, an action against him at law is allowed; but what is due on the latter score cannot be claimed by war or extorted by the threat of the law . . . But the reason why some things are due us perfectly and others imperfectly, is because among those who live in a state of mutual natural law there is a diversity of the rules of this law, *some of which conduce to the mere existence of society, others to an improved existence*. And since it is less necessary that the latter be observed towards another than the former, it is, therefore reasonable that the former be exacted more rigorously than the latter, for *it is foolish to prescribe a medicine far more troublesome and dangerous than the disease.*[1]

To appreciate Pufendorf's claim that the "medicine" of enforcement is "far more troublesome and dangerous than the disease," recall the discussion in Chapter 10 of rights as a "necessary evil." There I emphasized that because rights legitimate the use of force, *the more rights we recognize the more violence we legitimate.* Every exercise of violence imposes serious enforcement costs on the innocent and every erroneous and unjust use of violence threatens to induce resentment, bitterness, and the desire on the part of those against whom violence is used to rectify this injustice by responding violently, thereby setting off a cascade of violence. In considering whether liberalism does too much or too little in pursuing the good, as opposed to the just, or whether the concept of justice should be expanded beyond the rights needed to handle the problems of knowledge, interest, or power, it is important to keep this in mind.

1. Is the Liberal Fusion of Justice and the Rule of Law Too Much?

In the classical liberal approach described here, force can only be used to vindicate the "perfect" rights that define justice, not to mandate or prohibit other types of conduct that may be considered morally good or bad. Because it neither mandates nor prohibits good or bad conduct, but only just or unjust conduct, it is commonly said that liberalism is "neutral" with respect to different theories of the good.

Some critics argue, however, that although a liberal fusion of justice and the rule of law professes to be neutral with respect to the good, it inevitably precludes certain visions of the good and leads to others. In particular, it tends to undermine homogeneous visions of "community" and encourages a heterogeneous or pluralist vision of society that is quite disturbing to many. Cultures that require for their maintenance a certain amount of coercion to perpetuate themselves are eventually obliterated by the aggregate of free choice. These aggregate results are thought by some to be less than satisfactory, even to those who exercised the choices that brought them about.

There is considerable truth to this charge. A society that adheres to a liberal conception of justice and the rule of law could not prohibit ways of living that some or even many find bothersome or offensive and, consequently, those ways of living may persist and possibly may even come to dominate social life. Some may detest the "blight" of fast-food restaurants, the leveling influence of the mass media, an alleged loss of cultural diversity, etc. A world in which free

---

[1] Pufendorf, *De Jure Naturae*, p. 118 (emphases added).

choices are allowed will surely look quite different and, to some, quite inferior to a world in which people are compelled to act in socially approved ways. For better or worse, regulating choice so as to ensure "good" choices will result in a substantially different world than one in which free choices are permitted.

Furthermore, despite the assertion by some liberals and their critics that a liberal conception of justice does not specify a particular theory of the good and permits the pursuit of differing conceptions of the good life, this conception of justice admittedly permits the use of force to protect the rights of several property and freedom of contract. This use of force will prevent, at least indirectly, certain conceptions of the good from being achieved. The liberal conception of justice solves the problems of knowledge, interest, and power by placing certain restrictions on the means one may use to pursue happiness. As was seen in Chapter 3, it mandates that individual discretion be "bounded." Consequently and unavoidably, there is a systemic bias against those who believe that their pursuit of happiness requires them to use the very means that are proscribed and who will be prevented from doing so. And there is a systemic bias in favor of the types of society that arise when people have the liberty that the liberal conception of justice defines and serves to protect.

So for all these reasons, perhaps liberalism is not so neutral as between visions of the good as some pretend. Of course, the liberal conception of justice and the rule of law can be said to be neutral towards the resulting shape of society in the significant sense that one who favors it need not *intend* that society take one particular form or another. Nor is the liberal conception of justice and the rule of law *justified* on the ground that it facilitates or inhibits particular visions of the good. Whether a musical culture dominated by symphonies, rock, or Muzak (I leave it to the reader to judge which is good and which is bad) results from the free choices of individuals and associations is something about which liberalism has nothing to say. (That this degree of neutrality is itself objectionable is a criticism I shall consider in the next section.) If neutrality is the willingness to accept any society that results from the free choices of each of its members constrained by the boundaries established by rights, whether or not one morally approves of them, then liberalism can be said to be genuinely neutral.

Moreover, the restrictions that the liberal conception of justice places on the means by which the good may be pursued operate "neutrally" to restrict both the pursuit of some ends that may be morally reprehensible along with some that may be morally praiseworthy. Those who believe that the good life requires them to have sexual intercourse with unwilling partners are prohibited from doing so, just as are those who believe the good life requires that they take from the rich to give to the poor. In this sense, even the restrictions that the liberal conception of justice places on the pursuit of the good are neutral as to ends. It restricts any and all activities that require for their exercise means that violate justice, regardless of the virtue of the ends.

These responses will scarcely satisfy the critic who will merely reply that although liberalism may appear neutral in its form, some ends—whether aggregate or individual—are effectively prevented by the constraints justice and the rule of law place on means by which ends may be achieved. Because this restriction on means may effectively preclude the achievement of certain ends, liberalism in its substance is not *truly* neutral as to ends.

Yet I am not aware of any critic who makes this argument because he or she favors *greater* neutrality than is possible within a liberal conception of justice. To the contrary, this objection is invariably made to reveal the alleged hypocrisy of the liberal claim of neutrality and, thereby, to legitimate *less* neutrality than the liberal fusion of justice and the rule of law would permit. In other words, this argument is used by those who wish to strip away liberalism's allegedly false veneer of neutrality so as to permit the pursuit of a particular vision of the good that is barred by liberalism. The aim is to permit the forcible imposition of some particular and decidedly nonneutral vision of either personal or social life.

The charge of hypocrisy does not, therefore, take us very far. Given that those who criticize the genuine neutrality of liberalism favor less rather than more neutrality, their objection fails to challenge the precise *degree* of neutrality entailed by the liberal conception of justice. That is, since the critic offers no argument in favor of a more perfect neutrality (something the critic rejects), it must be shown that something is wrong with the degree of neutrality actually required by liberalism. The criticism that liberalism is not perfectly neutral, or neutral in every sense of the word, in no way assists this inquiry.

Perhaps most importantly, any criticism of the precise degree of neutrality entailed by liberalism is particularly difficult in light of the analysis presented in the previous chapters. Nowhere was neutrality presented as a desired *end* of the liberal conception of justice and the rule of law. Neutrality has played no role in the analysis whatsoever. Rather, some degree of neutrality towards visions of the good is an unavoidable *consequence* of adopting a conception of justice and the rule of law that is needed to solve the pervasive problems of knowledge, interest, and power. These problems require a conception of justice and the rule of law that places restrictions on the use of certain means—for example, on force and fraud—but *otherwise* places no restrictions on ends. To this degree then—no more, no less—the liberal conception is neutral as to the ends that can justly be pursued.

Those who claim that liberalism is "too much" because it excludes certain social or personal visions of the good must show how these problems are to be addressed by any system that requires either more or less neutrality than does the liberal fusion of justice and the rule of law. Assuming the social problems of knowledge, interest and, especially, the problems of power must somehow be solved, the burden falls to the critic to show exactly how a more or less neutral system can accomplish this. Perhaps it can be done. At least it would be an interesting debate. My only point here is that simply accusing liberalism of being incompletely neutral does not satisfy this burden.

2. Is the Liberal Fusion of Justice and the Rule of Law Too Little?

Justice and the Good

The criticism of liberalism for being insufficiently neutral or "too much" is invariably an attempt to undermine the value of neutrality itself. The objective is to permit less, rather than more, neutrality. The real objection is that, however biased liberalism may be for or against certain visions of the good, it is *too* neutral and consequently is "too little" to ensure the achievement of the critic's conception of the good at the level of the individual, the group, or of society as a whole. Somewhat oddly, the strategy is to displace liberalism first by offering a criticism *internal* to liberalism ("inadequate neutrality"), in order to clear a path for an *external* criticism of liberalism ("too much neutrality").

Yet even those sympathetic to the analysis I have presented may retain a lingering sense that the liberal fusion of justice and the rule of law—even if it operated as advertised—may somehow not be *enough*; that to achieve the kind of society to which we aspire requires more than the rights, duties, and legal order specified by this approach. In an important respect, I think that this concern is justified. Mere adherence to justice and the rule of law *is* too little to ensure that a good society will be achieved—a world with culture, with learning, with wisdom, with generosity, with manners, with respect for others, with integrity, with tolerance, with a sense of humor, and much more. The liberal conception of justice and the rule of law neither includes such values in its prescriptions nor seems to *ensure* that by adhering to its prescriptions such a world will be attained.

So what does the liberal fusion of justice and the rule of law have to offer to those who share these values? The real issue is not whether the liberal fusion of justice and the rule of law is *sufficient* to achieve the kind of world many want to live in (it isn't), but whether it is functionally *necessary* to do so. Lon Fuller once distinguished between two moralities—the morality of aspiration and the morality of duty—that closely resembles the distinction drawn by classical natural rights theorists between perfect and imperfect rights and duties. The morality of aspiration, he said,

is the morality of the Good Life, of excellence, of the fullest realization of human powers. . . . [A] man might fail to realize his full capabilities. As a citizen or as an official, he might be found wanting. But in such a case he . . . [is] condemned for failure, not for being recreant to duty; for shortcoming, not for wrongdoing. . . .

Where the morality of aspiration starts at the top of human achievement, the morality of duty starts at the bottom. It lays down the basic rules without which an ordered society is impossible, or without which an ordered society directed toward certain specific goals must fail of its mark. . . . It does not condemn men for failing to embrace opportunities for the fullest realization of their powers.

Instead, it condemns them for failing to respect the basic requirements of social living.[2]

The rights specified by the liberal conception of justice and the requirements of the rule of law, if correct, constitute a morality of duty. They purport to specify what justice is and how it may best be pursued. They do not comprise an entire ethical system for achieving a good society. Adherents to the liberal fusion of justice and the rule of law seek to identify, in Fuller's words, "the basic rules without which an *ordered society is impossible."* They do not deny that more than justice is important. Nor do they deny that the pursuit of justice will be influenced by the extent to which people adhere to a morality of aspiration. But they maintain no less firmly that the liberal fusion of justice and the rule of law offers humankind the best opportunity to pursue both virtue and justice.

Indeed, without the liberal conception of justice the pursuit of a good society is hopeless. A well-functioning society is a necessary precondition for achieving a good society; and adherence to the liberal fusion of justice and the rule of law is a price that simply must be paid if we are to have a well-functioning society. Therefore, like it or not, adherence to the liberal fusion of justice and the rule of law is the price that must be paid to achieve a good society as well.

Let us be frank. The only alternative to pursuing virtue voluntarily within the framework provided by justice and the rule of law is to enforce a morality of aspiration as we enforce a morality of duty. The analysis presented in this book strongly suggests that any such attempt will ultimately undermine *both* projects—the medicine will be worse than the disease. Those who favor imposing a morality of aspiration face intractable problems of knowledge, interest, and power. They must somehow settle on the one right conception of "the good" to be enforced on all. They must gather the information necessary to assess who is acting "well" and who is acting "badly." They must solve the problem of communicating knowledge of the good in advance of persons acting. The system they develop to make these assessments must somehow avoid the problems of partiality and incentives. Perhaps most importantly, such a system must also take seriously and somehow come to grips with the problems of enforcement error and abuse. Hand waving won't do. We have seen how the twin problems of power are sufficiently grave to warrant some limits on using power even to assure compliance with the liberal conception of justice that constitutes the morality of duty. The problem of enforcement error is much greater with the far more situation-dependent judgment required by a morality of aspiration.

Moreover, since people so often fail to live up to the demands of a morality of aspiration, the opportunity for making erroneous judgments is greatly increased. Further, punishing bad behavior or coercively mandating good

---

[2] Fuller, *Morality and Law*, pp. 5–6.

behavior substantially raises the cost of enforcement error—witness the ghastly effects of alcohol or drug prohibition on those whom these policies are purporting to help.[3] Finally, the incompatibility of a morality of aspiration with either the formal requirements of the rule of law or a decentralized legal order makes the risk of enforcement abuse simply intolerable.

If we have learned nothing else from the millions of killings we have witnessed in the twentieth century we have learned that the problems of power are only magnified when force is used to assure compliance with a vision of "the good." One purpose for recognizing and respecting rights is to avoid the occurrence of such devastations without resorting to social experimentation. In this regard, the most important contribution of this book is the identification of the social problems that are addressed by the liberal fusion of justice and the rule of law.

Those who reject this conception in favor of enforcing a morality of aspiration must take these pervasive social problems seriously if they expect us to take seriously their proposed alternative. This is a task that few critics of liberalism have been willing even to attempt. Critics of liberalism either ignore these problems altogether or describe how they would deal with them in far too cursory a fashion. Yet neither theory nor historical experience gives us any reason to suspect that a system that attempted to impose coercively a morality of aspiration upon everyone could possibly handle the problems of knowledge, interest, and power.

If a morality of aspiration ought not be enforced by a coercive monopoly, then what kinds of institutions can promote it voluntarily? In a society that rigorously adhered to the liberal conception of justice, the most important institution for inculcating a morality of aspiration is the family. Given the knowledge that immediate family members have of the facts of time and place, they seem uniquely qualified to handle this responsibility and also uniquely interested as well. Although families may sometimes fail miserably at this task, we are speaking now of comparative competence based on the knowledge that such a task requires. And when families fail, their failure is compartmentalized—its breadth far more limited then when coercive regimes fail.

In addition, so-called "intermediate" institutions that have traditionally bridged the gap between individuals, their families, and the larger community—schools, theaters, publishers, clubs, neighborhood groups, charities, religious and fraternal groups, and other voluntary associations—all serve a vital function of developing and inculcating values. As a practical matter, our values come not from coercion but from the exhortations and examples set by countless individuals and groups. In a completely free society, all these institutions could pursue a morality of aspiration unburdened by the forcible interference of third parties that is now made possible by the Single Power Principle.

---

[3] See sources cited in Ch. 11 n. 10.

To some this all may sound a bit trite, even hackneyed. But it is no coincidence that totalitarian regimes invariably strive to regulate, co-opt, subvert, and ultimately annihilate these institutions at every turn. And is it not exceedingly odd that the same critics of liberalism who view the impact of "economic" choices in a market as powerful enough to invariably obliterate any conception of a good society that stands in the way, at the same time so seriously underestimate and deprecate the social institutions created by the free "moral" choices that liberalism also makes possible? Perhaps there is an element of the expedient in such arguments.

Of course, there is no enforceable guarantee that such voluntary institutions will be "enough" to ensure that a morality of aspiration will be achieved. But, as by now should be apparent, a system that uses a Single Power Principle to impose a morality of aspiration offers no such guarantees either, or cannot honor any guarantees its proponents may issue. Even an ideally wielded coercive monopoly of power is only as "good" as the persons wielding the power. But power to coercively impose morality invariably corrupts those who wield it, and virtue is its first victim.

Then there is the perennial question of *which* conception of the good will turn out to be mandated? What are the chances that the "correct" one will be "guaranteed" by the coercive monopoly of power? Despite their denials, advocates of imposing a particular morality of aspiration invariably assume that theirs will win out or that the struggle will continue indefinitely, but what if the wrong morality is coercively imposed upon them instead? True, if given a choice, most of us would want to see our moral vision prevail. But if they cannot get their own way, which would most people prefer: the *amorality* of the liberal conception of justice or the *immorality* of their rivals? Given the risks that, in a conflict among competing moralities, we will be subjected to someone else's morality, *the liberal conception of justice becomes nearly everyone's second-best outcome*. And this turns out to be its greatest strength.

Justice and Distribution

Some, perhaps even most, who condemn the particular conception of justice and the rule of law presented here as "too little" do not mean by this that it fails to ensure the achievement of some particular conception of the good. Rather, they think the rights of several property, freedom of contract, first possession, restitution, and self-defense provide an inadequate or impoverished conception of *justice* itself. In particular, by barring forced takings, these rights are imcompossible with an enforceable right to certain basic or primary goods, or the "rights and liberties, powers and opportunities, income and wealth,"[4] that are the prerequisites of the pursuit of happiness. In the words of John Rawls, "these goods normally have a use whatever a person's rational plan of

---

[4] John Rawls, *A Theory of Justice* (Cambridge, Mass.: Harvard University Press, 1971), p. 62.

life."[5] By barring forced takings, the objection goes, the rights discussed here provide inadequate, indeed no, assurance that these primary goods will be provided to anyone and certainly not to everyone. There must be some means of assuring that people have enough of the primary goods that enable them to pursue happiness. At minimum, it is argued, justice requires forced takings sufficient to achieve an appropriate *distribution* of physical resources.

Of those contemporary political theorists who believe in justice, there is a remarkable consensus that it should include some forced redistribution of primary goods. There is also a remarkable lack of consensus about the exact position being advocated.[6] Does distributive justice require a complete *equality* of primary goods, or only a *fair* distribution? Is it the equality or fairness of an *initial* distribution of primary goods that matters, or a *continual* lifetime access to an equal or fair supply of such goods? If absolute equality is not required, does a "fair" distribution mean a minimum quantity or something more than that? If only a minimum level of such goods are to be mandated, is the standard by which "minimum" is to be determined absolute or relative? That is, does it require some standard level of primary goods or is the minimum amount to which one is entitled relative to the amount others may have? Does the level of goods depend on "need" and do we employ an objective or a subjective conception of "need"? Does a person having much *more* than others or much more than they "need," perhaps from inheriting wealth from one's parents, violate distributive justice? Is the just distribution of primary goods to be assessed within the boundaries of existing nation-states, or is it a global standard? And which exactly are the primary goods that must be supplied? Are they material goods and, if so, which ones? Does distributive justice also include a right to "equal respect and concern"?

To define the core of the position being advanced under the label "distributive justice," each of these questions must be answered. Without a definition, we can neither evaluate the challenge that claims based on distributive justice pose to the conception of justice presented here, nor formulate a complete response. But the questions that need to be answered do not end there. Once we understand which conception of distribution is being advocated, we need to ask what justifies considering it a requirement of justice. Is the justification based on some maximization of social welfare or minimization of risk? Is it based on the need to achieve some measure of social stability? Is it based on

---

[5] Ibid.

[6] Two strong proponents of redistribution have chronicled some of the many variations of the concept while defending their own. See Amartya Sen, "Equality of What?" in Stephen Darwall (ed.), *Equal Freedom* (Ann Arbor, Mich.: University of Michigan Press, 1995), pp. 307–30 (identifying "three particular types of equality, viz., (i) utilitarian equality, (ii) total utility equality, and (iii) Rawlsian equality," and favoring a fourth: "basic capability equality."); G. A. Cohen, "On the Currency of Egalitarian Justice," *Ethics*, vol. 99 (July 1989), pp. 906–44 (distinguishing "qualified" and "unqualified" equality of welfare—whether hedonic welfare, preference satisfaction welfare, or inoffensive welfare—equality of resources, capability equality, equal opportunity for welfare, and favoring "equal access for advantage").

what all "rational" persons would agree to and, if so, would these rational persons be aware of their own particular circumstances or would they have to choose behind a "veil of ignorance." Is it based on the "intrinsic" value of human life? Under any of these rationales, can the claims of distributive justice be cabined by national boundaries or limited to human beings?

I am not suggesting that those who advocate forced takings to achieve some conception of distributive justice must first reach agreement among themselves on a particular conception of distribution and a rationale for calling it justice before they indict the classical liberal conception of justice for failing to measure up. Such matters ought to be determined by the merits of each and every argument, not by consensus—neither the widespread consensus among classical liberals in favor of the rights of several property, freedom of contract, self-defense, and restitution,[7] nor the widespread consensus of contemporary political theorists in favor of some conception of distributive justice. The lack of consensus does mean, however, that any criticism of the conception of justice defended here on the grounds that it fails to adequately take "distributive justice" into account lacks specificity until the particular conception of distributive justice and its rationale is provided. It is chimerical to allude to a single concept, the concept of distributive justice, that must either be accepted or rejected without specifying which among the many incompatible conceptions of distributive justice is the appropriate one.

Nor am I suggesting that contemporary theorists have no answers to these questions. To the contrary, they have *many* answers to *each* of them. Yet the diversity of interesting and respectable conceptions and justifications of distributive justice makes it difficult to respond in a manner that is likely to satisfy any given advocate of distributive justice. A response to a pure egalitarian might not apply to a fairness theorist; a response to a social contractarian might not satisfy a classical Aristotelian. There are simply so many variations of views of distributive justice that the charitable reader will, perhaps, forgive me if I confine myself to some general remarks about claims of distributive justice.

Though there are many different kinds of objections to distributive justice that may be raised, it is appropriate, I think, to limit my focus to some of the

---

[7] Despite the widespread consensus among classical liberals about these rights which comprise their core conception of justice, important differences emerge when discussing such matters as inalienability, punishment, and the role, if any, for the government in administering justice or providing public goods. And while there is no consensus among classical liberals on the justification for the rights they advocate in common, the rationales that have been offered are not mutually exclusive. Such rights might be defended as necessary to solve the problems of knowledge, interest, and power, as inherent to human beings, and also as instrumental to maximizing social welfare. See Barnett, "Chickens and Eggs," pp. 611–35. Indeed, one of the purposes of this book is to provide a framework which organizes many of the different, but still compatible, arguments that have been advanced by others on behalf of the liberal conception of justice and the rule of law.

challenges posed for *any* theory of distributive justice by the problems of knowledge, interest, and power I have elaborated here. From the perspective of these problems, there are two general categories of difficulties facing proponents of distributive justice. The first are the problems of knowledge, interest, and power that confront those who would implement this conception of justice. The second is how implementing distributive justice by means of forced takings impedes the ability of the liberal conception of justice to address these problems.

Any quest to implement distributive justice faces serious problems of knowledge, interest, and power. Let's assume we settle on a particular conception of distributive justice. We are now faced with the task of determining who will have their resources taken away and who will be the beneficiary of the taking. Whatever conception of distributive justice one adopts, the circumstances of every person in the community, or state, or nation, or world will have to be examined to see if they meet the posited standard. Does each person have "enough" of the primary goods? Which person has a surplus that may be taken from her to give to another. This is every bit as daunting a knowledge problem as the one I identified in Chapter 2. An advocate of distributive justice cannot advocate a particular conception without also telling us how the knowledge his conception requires is systematically to be acquired.

Problems of partiality, incentives, and compliance also must be handled. When people clamor for their "fair share" of the pie, their claims are likely to be highly partial and unlikely to take into account the partial interests of those who are remote to them We can expect dehumanizing constructs and labels such as "the rich" (or "filthy rich" or "capitalist pig" or "dirty Jew") to be employed in pursuit of one's partial interest. Some authorized person or group must determine the appropriate standard of distributive justice and their decision is likely to be a partial one. It is not enough for the theorist to insist that of all the competing conceptions of distributive justice, *his and his alone* will be adopted. Once redistribution is legitimated, different conceptions of distributive justice will be advocated and some choice among them must be made. The partiality of the decision makers, whether they be autocrats or democrats, will surely influence the outcome. What is the likelihood that the one "correct" conception of distributive justice will be impartially adopted? Some assurance on this score is required.

Incentive problems created by any conception of distributive justice are acute. In any system in which money is taken from Ann to give to Ben, the intangible benefits gained from engaging in intrinsically rewarding activity are not taken away. Only monetary or other tangible benefits can be taken. Thus, a policy of redistributing material wealth would have a disparate impact on those whose highest value choices depend on receiving material wealth in return. And it will adversely impact upon *all* entrepreneurs for whom entrepreneurial profit is their sole incentive to discover previously unknown information about the use of scarce resources.

When redistribution is implemented, then, people engaged in less intrinsically rewarding activity are treated worse than those for whom their conduct is its own reward. Only the incentives of those doing tasks they find too onerous to perform unless they receive money in return are adversely affected by a policy of redistribution. Robert Nozick noticed this curiously perverse implication of redistribution when he observed:

Why should the man who prefers seeing a movie (and who has to earn money for a ticket) be open to the required call to aid the needy, while the person who prefers looking at a sunset (and hence need earn no extra money) is not? Indeed isn't it surprising that redistributionists choose to ignore the man whose pleasures are so easily attainable without extra labor, while adding yet another burden to the poor unfortunate who must work for his pleasures? If anything, one would have expected the reverse. Why is the person with the nonmaterial or nonconsumptive desire allowed to proceed unimpeded to his most favored feasible alternative, whereas the man whose pleasures or desires involve material things and who must work for extra money (thereby serving whomever considers his activities valuable enough to pay him) is constrained in what he can realize?[8]

A policy of systemic redistribution therefore undermines the incentives for people to engage in activities that are not intrinsically rewarding to them. Perhaps most activities that are primarily of service to *others* fall into this category. Other-regarding activity that is not intrinsically rewarding requires more monetary compensation in return than does self-regarding activity. Entrepreneurship is one example, but there are innumerable others, including manufacturing clothing, growing food, repairing electric lines, picking up and recycling garbage, and working as an attorney to facilitate parties engaged in economic transactions. The list is endless. Expropriating a share of the gains to be realized from such valuable activities undermines the incentive to perform them.

Sometimes the incentive effects of redistributing the benefits of one's action depend upon the identity of the recipient. More precisely, the nature of the incentives created by redistribution depends on the affection a person has for the recipient. If a person from whom the benefits are taken cares about the recipient, then he or she may incorporate the recipient's interest into her own. For example, the subjective interest of parents will almost always incorporate their perception of their children's interests. The fact that the benefits produced by a parent will inure to his or her children may increase, rather than diminish, the incentive for continuing these actions.

Still, a person's natural interest in recipients of redistribution will tend to diminish as the recipients become more remote. We may picture this diminishing range of interest as the ripples produced by throwing a stone in a pond. Just as the circles become increasingly diffused as they get farther from the point of entry until at some point they completely disappear, the interest that

---

[8] Nozick, *Anarchy and Utopia*, p. 170.

a person has in others tends to diminish as these other persons become increasingly remote from and unknown to them.

Adam Smith imagined the typical reaction of the most humane of Europeans to the deaths of millions of Chinese by an earthquake. Of course, he would express his sorrow and horror and "make many melancholy reflections on the precariousness of human life,"[9] as well as speculate on the effects of this disaster on the commerce of Europe and the world.

> And when all this fine philosophy was over, when all these humane sentiments had been once fairly expressed, he would pursue his business and his pleasure, take his repose or his diversion, with the same ease and tranquillity, as if no such accident had happened. The most frivolous disaster which could befal himself would occasion a more real disturbance. If he was to lose his little finger to-morrow, he would not sleep to-night; but, provided he never saw them, he will snore with the most profound security over the ruin of a hundred millions of his brethren, and the destruction of that immense multitude seems plainly an object less interesting to him, than this paltry misfortune of his own.[10]

Smith, of course, was not praising this aspect of human nature, only describing it. But to understand the incentive effects of any regime of distribution, we must take this partiality into account.

The incentive effects created by redistribution will change as the range of recipients extends increasingly far from the person from whom the benefits are taken. Redistribution to others who stand very near psychologically to one may create positive incentives, but at some point, as the range of redistribution increases and includes more persons, redistribution will create disincentives to provide benefits to these other persons. Imposing a duty to support others will have a negative incentive effect when the beneficiaries are strangers and a neutral or even a positive effect when the duty is to loved ones.

Of course, where affection exists there is a natural incentive that greatly reduces the need for any artificially imposed duty. Disregarding the positive effects that would largely exist in the absence of an imposed duty, we are then left with the adverse incentive effects of imposing any duty that would sever benefits from the actions that produce them. This suggests that, just as the distribution of control over resources should correspond to the distribution of knowledge in society, to handle the incentive problem, the distribution of benefits should correspond to the distribution of control.

True, redistribution would not create an incentive problem if persons generally viewed their own interests as subordinate to those of others in society who may receive their redistributed rights. But the problem of interest in general, and the partiality problem in particular, reflects the fact that, barring some change in the basic constitution of human beings, persons generally do not equate their own interest with the interests of complete strangers. Were this characteristic of human beings to change, we would not have to worry about this (or any other) problem of interest.

<hr>

[9] Smith, *Moral Sentiments*, p. 136.   [10] Ibid. 136–7.

Then there is the problem of compliance. Redistribution exacerbates the potential conflict between justice and interest. Whole classes of persons from whom resources are taken will experience a gap between their subjective interests and the requirements of justice. Advocates of redistribution realize this, of course, which is why they argue so hard for defining redistribution as a theory of justice. By doing so they can justify using violence or force to coerce the takings that are required to meet the chosen distributive standard. But as was seen above, employing force to implement a scheme of rights raises the costs of enforcement error and leads to enforcement abuse. Distributive justice gives rise to enforcement error in at least two ways. First, the costs of error imposed on the innocent are increased when an incorrect conception of distributive justice is chosen. Second, whatever conception of distributive justice is chosen will be incorrectly applied on occasion. When either error is made, innocent people will be jailed, their incomes attached, their homes and businesses confiscated. Lives will be ruined. No theorist of distributive justice can assume perfect information if their theories are to be implemented in a world of imperfect information and fallible human decision makers. They must explain both how their theories will handle the problems of power and how the inevitable sacrifice of the innocent is to be justified.

Even more serious, however, is the problem of enforcement abuse. Those given the power to forcibly confiscate resources can be expected to abuse this power in innumerable ways. For example, the massive amounts of personal information to implement any scheme of redistribution will inevitably be misused. Worse yet, the potential either to benefit from redistribution or be harmed by it creates factions of persons who will, depending on how the conception of distributive justice is chosen, lobby for favorable treatment or attempt to corrupt those who are charged with choosing who will benefit and by how much. Vast amounts of wealth will be expended seeking the "rents" that redistribution can provide or avoiding its imposition.

Were this a book on distributive justice, the treatment of each of these problems could be greatly expanded and supported by historical and empirical evidence. I raise them in this cursory fashion only to illustrate the problems with distributive justice that are revealed when we begin to appreciate the problems of knowledge, interest, and power. I am not claiming that no proponent of distributive justice has ever made the attempt to grapple with any of these problems. But unless an attempt is made, and made persuasively, to comprehensively deal with all of these problems, it is not clear what challenge to the conception of justice I have presented here is actually posed by the concept of distributive justice.

The thesis of this book was how certain rights and procedures that define the liberal conception of justice and the rule of law address the serious and pervasive problems of knowledge, interest, and power. Using coercive takings to implement a scheme of redistribution impedes the ability of these rights to perform their task. This is not always fully appreciated by advocates of distributive justice. For example, John Rawls has written that

among the basic liberties of the person is the right to hold and to have the exclusive use of personal property. The role of this liberty is to allow a sufficient material basis for a sense of personal independence and self-respect, both of which are essential for the development and exercise of the moral powers.[11]

With so limited a recognition of the functions of several property, Rawls predictably adopts an impoverished view of the right itself. Rawls excludes from the set of basic liberties the "certain rights of acquisition and bequest, as well as the right to own the means of production and natural resources" on the ground that these property rights "cannot, I think, be accounted for as necessary for the development and exercise of the moral powers."[12] Perhaps they cannot, though I strongly suspect otherwise.[13] But when Rawls limits his basic liberties to those that "are essential for the adequate development and full exercise of . . . moral personality over a complete life,"[14] his conclusions cannot help but be affected by his failure to take into account how property handles the problems of knowledge, interest, and power.[15]

What about Rawls's well-known claim that because, "[n]o one deserves his greater natural capacity nor merits a more favorable starting place in society,"[16] physical resources should be distributed in a manner so that "no one gains or loses from his arbitrary place in the natural distribution of assets or his initial position in society without giving or receiving compensating advantages in return."[17] Would this not apply to one's own knowledge as well as to one's natural endowments? If people do not "deserve" the personal and local knowledge they possess, how does the mere "arbitrary" fact of their possessing personal and local knowledge justify any particular distribution of physical resources?

Before answering this challenge directly, it is interesting to notice that Rawls's argument concerning desert resembles the objection, discussed above, that liberalism is insufficiently impartial. For Rawls would not himself distribute all resources on the basis of desert. "There is a tendency," he writes, "for

---

[11] John Rawls, *Political Liberalism*, rev. edn. (New York: Columbia University Press, 1996), p. 298.

[12] Ibid.

[13] See Lomasky, *Persons, Rights*, pp. 111–51 (describing the need for extensive property rights to facilitate the pursuit of personal projects).

[14] Rawls, *Political Liberalism*, p. 293.

[15] Rawls might be read as merely shifting the treatment of problems like these to "other stages when more information about a society's circumstances" (ibid. 298) is available. But this would be to miss the fact that these social problems are pervasive and must be confronted by every person in every society, and that the rights of several property, freedom of contract, first possession, restitution, and self defense, are available to every society as solutions regardless of its particular circumstances. Particular circumstances will, however, influence greatly how these abstract rights are implemented in conventional rules and practices.

[16] Rawls, *Theory of Justice*, p. 102.   [17] Ibid.

common sense to suppose that income and wealth, and the good things in life generally, should be distributed according to moral desert. . . . Now justice as fairness rejects this conception."[18] Why? Because "[t]he idea of rewarding desert is impracticable. And certainly to the extent that the precept of need is emphasized, moral worth is ignored."[19] In this manner, like those critics who condemn liberalism's insufficient neutrality in pursuit of even less neutrality, Rawls uses the concept of desert to undermine the legitimacy of holdings allocated by the rights of several property, first possession, and freedom of contract. At the same time, however, the theory of justice he advocates does not promise to do any better on this score. In his words, "none of the precepts of justice aim at rewarding virtue."[20]

Rawls's use of desert to challenge the holdings allocated by the rights of several property acquisition, use, and transfer identified here looks considerably less substantial once one acknowledges the myriad social problems that these rights address. Given that the distribution of knowledge throughout society cannot be redistributed, a jurisdiction to exercise bounded individual and personal discretion over physical resources enables persons and associations to put their knowledge to work. Although physical resources differ from personal and local knowledge in that it is possible to redistribute them, if adhering to the liberal conception justice described here is the best or only way to handle the first-order problem of knowledge, as well as the problems of interest and of power, then the fact that personal and local knowledge cannot be redistributed places serious limits on the wisdom or justice of redistributing physical resources in some other manner. Doing so would be, in Rawls's term, "impracticable."

Moreover, even if it is true that persons do not deserve the knowledge they have—a claim that appears less compelling than the claim that natural endowments are undeserved since much knowledge acquisition is a product of effort—recognizing that the concepts of several property and freedom of contract function, in part, to handle the first-order problem of knowledge suggests that the notion of "moral desert" is irrelevant and even pernicious in this context. The dispersion of personal and local knowledge to which individuals and associations have limited access is one of the pervasive and intractable social problems addressed by the concept of justice being examined here. *The idea that the possession of resources or endowments or knowledge must be deserved has no place in solving this problem.* (Nor will it assist us in solving the problems of interest or power.) The knowledge problem exists and must somehow be dealt with whether or not individuals and associations deserve the knowledge in their possession. To the extent that persons are deprived of their ability to act

---

[18] Rawls, *Theory of Justice*, p. 310.   [19] Ibid. 312.
[20] Ibid. 311. In one respect, the argument concerning neutrality is stronger because it is based on the alleged failure of liberalism to live up to its own ideals. Yet classical liberals rarely, if ever, defend the justice of the rights they favor on the ground that everyone "deserves" the holdings they have.

on the basis of their knowledge and the information needed to take the knowledge of others into account, distributing physical resources according to principles that ignore all "undeserved" personal characteristics exacerbates the problem.

Arguments for and against distributive justice are not the subject of this book. Yet objections to the conclusions I reach are likely to come from those who favor some conception of distributive justice. While I do not pretend to have treated all claims for distributive justice comprehensively, I hope I have shown how a focus on the pervasive social problems caused by the radical dispersal and relative inaccessibility of personal and local knowledge, as well as by the problems of partiality, incentives, compliance, and enforcement error and abuse, casts this perennial debate in a new light. Moreover, using the concept of desert to drive a wedge between ownership and justice is a mistake because it prevents the concept of ownership based on several property and freedom of contract from performing its essential functions.

Justice and Retribution

Others argue that the liberal conception of justice formulated here is "too little" because it fails to provide *retribution* against criminals. The rights that distinguish liberty from license define a regime in which people may prevent crime by excluding potentially dangerous persons from their property and by exercising their right of self-defense. Persons who violate rights must make restitution to their victims and, if they cannot be trusted to do so, may be confined to a work facility where they are paid market-level wages from which restitution will be made. Criminals—people whose past rights-violating conduct communicates their intention to violate rights in the future—may be declared outside the protection of the justice system or, in rare cases, preventively confined. All this is not enough, it is said. Retribution against criminals should also be imposed.

I have already discussed, in Chapter 11, how imposing punishment impedes the ability of victims to obtain restitution, reduces their incentives to cooperate with law enforcement, and turns law enforcement into a public good engendering the inefficiencies associated with public police, public courts, and public prisons. I have also spoken of how punishment, when institutionalized and legitimated, supplants restitution rather then supplements it. Let me now turn to the special problems that attach to theories that attempt to justify additional punishment as retribution for crime.

Like distributive justice, retributivism does not represent a single position but rather a constellation of views depending upon how the retributivist answers the following sorts of questions. Is retribution appropriate because of the nature of the wrong, or the because of the bad intentions of the wrongdoer? Is retribution limited to rights violations, or can it be extended to other types of immoral or "vicious" conduct? Need retribution be limited to conduct, or could it be exercised against people with morally objectionable beliefs or intentions? Who should be the author of retribution? Is retribution a right belonging to victims or a right belonging to "society"? If it is a victim's right, is the amount of retribution whatever it would take to subjectively satisfy the victim, or is it to be limited somehow? If it is a right belonging to society, what is the nature of the wrong that warrants retribution? Is it an offense against an individual or an offense against "society"? What is appropriate retribution? Should it approximate the harm inflicted on victims, or somehow respond to the evil of the offender? Should retribution be proportionate? If so, proportionate to what, and what is the appropriate proportion (1 : 1, 2 : 1, 3 : 1, etc.)? Should or may retribution take the form of the harm the offender inflicted on the victim ("an eye for an eye") or are other forms of retribution (torture, mutilation, disembowelling, drawing and quartering, branding, execution, imprisonment, etc.[21]) appropriate and when?

Just as one can sympathize with people getting the rewards in life they deserve, so too does one wish that evil people get the punishment they deserve. Notwithstanding my views on the justice of coercively imposed punishment, I confess to harboring retributivist feelings when, as a prosecutor, I confronted suffering crime victims and heartless criminals.[22] Yet much of the previous discussion of desert applies as well to those retributivists who seek to inflict suffering on criminals in proportion to their moral culpability for harming others. Any effort to do so will confront very serious problems of knowledge, interest, and power.

Consider, for example, the knowledge problem. Assume we settle on punishing people in proportion to the evilness of their intentions when they violate the rights of others. How are we to assess the evilness of intentions. Of course, extreme cases of viciousness on the one hand and pure accidents on the other may be quite clear. But, in my experience as a prosecutor, most criminals are somewhere in between. How are we to assess each criminal's mental state when the minds of others are necessarily hidden from us? In the criminal justice system we generally do this by grading offenses, not offenders, then allowing for mitigation of punishments within limits. But the fact that we do this, does not mean we do it very knowledgeably, any more than the fact that wage and price control schemes are implemented means that the "prices" set by central managers are knowledgeable. Referring to retribution as the

---

[21] "In eighteenth-century England the punishment for treason began with hanging; then the offender was taken down while still alive and his entrails were cut out and burned before his eyes; and then he was beheaded and quartered." Walter Kaufmann, *Without Guilt and Justice* (New York: Dell Publishing, 1973), p. 43.

[22] Though I am not ashamed of these feelings, neither am I particularly proud of them. And I agree with Walter Kaufmann that "[t]he belief that wrongs call for retribution is not primordial, instinctive, and universal—timeless truth inscribed in the hearts of all men that only moral nihilists and relativists dare to question. It is rather a belief that developed in historical times." Walter Kaufmann, "Retribution and the Ethics of Punishment," in Barnett and Hagel, *Assessing the Criminal*, p. 219.

"siamese twin" of distributive justice theories based on desert, Walter Kaufmann argues that "desert is incalculable. Not only is it impossible to measure desert with the sort of precision on which many believers in retributive justice staked their case, but the whole concept of a man's desert is confused and untenable. This claim is as fatal for distributive justice as it is for retributive justice."[23] "It would be simple," Kaufmann observes,

to make a list of offenses and to defy anyone to say what was the just punishment for each of them: rape, seduction of children, torture, mass murder, espionage, blackmail, embezzlement, fraud. There is really no stopping point because there is no crime at all of which it could be said that those committing it clearly deserve a particular punishment.[24]

And in this regard, retribution resembles distributive justice for

it is quite impossible to say how much income surgeons, lawyers, executives, or miners deserve; or what kind of housing each deserves, or how much free time per day, per week, or per year. It makes no sense to call any particular distribution of such goods among them "just."[25]

Notwithstanding this symmetry, "[s]peculation about the proportionate punishments after death gave rise to a veritable pornography of punishment and allowed the sadistic imagination rather free rein. Speculation about proportionate rewards, on the other hand, has remained a rather barren affair."[26]

All judgments of desert require knowledge of particular circumstances, the subtleties of local norms and expectations, and hidden mental states. In short, they require a personal and local knowledge of the same order as that which I discussed in Chapter 2. This suggests that the solution to this problem of knowledge lies in handling matters of deserved punishments and rewards in a highly decentralized manner. Persons and groups in a society governed by the liberal conception of justice may punish and reward within their respective domains, but these judgments should be made by the people with access to the information which such judgments require.

Partiality also presents a problem in assessing the seriousness of offenses. Consider the influence of the civil rights and woman's movements on the crimes of rape. Rape was once widely thought to be a more serious "offense" when committed against white women than against black women, or by black men than by white men. The seriousness of rape was also thought to depend on the sexual history of the victim. Though traditionally rape was considered

[23] Kaufmann, *Without Guilt*, p. 64.
[24] Ibid. 71. "But is not the death penalty a perfectly proportionate punishment for murder? Yet it meets the eye that being killed suddenly, unexpectedly, is altogether different from a protracted trial and a long period of imprisonment under sentence of death; and usually the mode of execution bears no resemblance to the method of the murder. To this one might also add the difference in the family circumstances, the age, and the attitude toward life of the original victim and the criminal." Kaufmann, *Without Guilt*, pp. 226–7.
[25] Ibid. 71.   [26] Kaufmann, "Retribution and Ethics," p. 228.

less serious than murder, even this has begun to change. I am not contending that any of these changes is less than salutary, but rather showing how attitudes towards rape—both before and after these changes—reflect the partiality of judgments of moral harm and desert.

Above all, however, retribution severely exacerbates the problems of enforcement error and abuse. Retribution will obviously greatly increase the cost imposed on the innocent accused, both those who did not do the acts for which they are accused and those whose actions do not merit punishment. As you read these words, innocent people are being tortured and mutilated in the name of retribution somewhere in the world, and in the United States are being wrongfully imprisoned. Some innocent persons have been and will be put to death. Can you imagine anything more terrible than your child being murdered by a stranger and then being wrongfully accused, prosecuted, and incarcerated, for her murder?[27] (If emotional examples like this one seem out-of-place in an academic discussion, then emotion-laden examples of criminals escaping their "just deserts" should not be used against restitution.) Yet, given the tens of thousands of people charged with crimes every year, in even the most reliable legal system, this sort of thing must happen every day.

Once legitimated by retributivists, the power to punish can be abused when it is knowingly applied to the innocent, to disfavored groups, and to those whose actions do not merit punishment. If you think this never happens, consider a saying commonly-known to public prosecutors throughout the United States: "Any prosecutor can convict a guilty person, but it takes a really great prosecutor to convict an innocent one." I do not believe that most or even many prosecutors take this attitude, but a willful disregard for the guilt of defendants does exist for some and is reflected in another saying commonly-heard around courthouses: "If he didn't do this one, then he did something else." Cognitive dissonance leads even good prosecutors to have difficulty admitting their mistakes and to continue alleging the guilt of accused persons long after their innocence is well-established.[28]

By "innocent," I refer not only to those persons who did not commit the offense for which they are charged, but also to those who are punished for actions that ought not be prohibited because they do not violate the rights of others. Tens of thousands of persons are incarcerated each year, for example, for violating laws prohibiting the possession and sale of some intoxicating

---

[27] For a case study of a wrongful prosecution by prosecutors acting in good faith that occurred when I was a prosecutor and which involved both prosecutors and defense attorneys of my acquaintance, see David Protess and Rob Warden, *Gone in the Night: The Dowaliby Family's Encounter with Murder and the Law* (New York: Delacorte, 1993) (detailing the wrongful prosecution, conviction, and incarceration of parents for the murder of their daughter).

[28] The national wave of prosecutions of day care workers (and parents) over the past decade for sexual abuse is, by all accounts, a massive example of wrongful and persistent retribution, encouraged and facilitated by social service agencies and other child abuse "experts."

substances. Whatever one thinks of the use and sale of intoxicants, it is undeniable that these people's lives have been ruined by law enforcement. Many have been separated from their spouses and families, their children to be raised without a father or mother, or by government agencies. The stigma of being a criminal will end their careers and forever cripple their employment prospects. Pursuant to "civil asset forfeiture statutes," homes, businesses, cars, and boats have been confiscated and sold at auction; the proceeds of which are used to pay the salaries and expenses of law-enforcement officials themselves. Many are killed trying to avoid arrest, or simply protecting their families from what they think is an illegal home invasion.[29]

What if the legal system is wrong about all this as it has been so often in the past?[30] One virtue of adhering to a rights theory of the sort I have defended here is that it helps avoid imposing these harms without the need for conducting "social experiments," especially considering that such "experiments" provide rich sources of income to the very experts and officials who are tasked with assessing them. Little wonder that few are ever deemed failures. A virtue of restitution is that it helps mitigate the inevitable errors and abuses that occur notwithstanding the theory of justice we may adopt.

Whatever harm is imposed upon the innocent by restitution, retributivism greatly enhances it. But retributivists typically advocate their position without regard to the suffering their approach unavoidably imposes on the innocent. Of course, retributivists do not *intend* that innocent people be punished. They simply advocate a theory of what should happen to a criminal *on the assumption that he is guilty*. And this is to overlook the problem of enforcement error and abuse. If men were gods, then perhaps imposing rewards and punishments on the basis of desert would be a workable theory, but then such a theory would hardly be necessary.

---

[29] See e.g. Malcolm Wallop, "Tyranny in America: Would Alexis De Toqueville Recognize this Place?," *Journal of Legislation*, vol. 20 (1994), p. 37. In this article, then-United States Senator Wallop discusses several instances of enforcement abuse including that of Donald P. Scott, a wealthy rancher suspected of growing marijuana. Scott was shot and killed by law-enforcement agents executing a search warrant when he responded to his wife's screams for help while carrying a rifle. Despite hours of searching, no marijuana was found. "Just before the raid, sheriff's deputies had done an appraisal of the ranch, complete with a marginal notation of recent nearby comparable sales. . . . The Ventura County District Attorney suggested afterward that the real purpose for the raid may have been to use forfeiture laws to acquire the Scott ranch. Rough justice." Ibid. 38. Scott had previously refused to sell his land to federal officials for a scenic corridor.

[30] See Barnett, "Bad Trip" (explaining how drug prohibition has wreaked havoc on individuals, families, law enforcement and the legal system, and why these consequences are predictable). See also Steven B. Duke and Albert Gross, *America's Longest War: Rethinking our Tragic Crusade against Drugs* (New York: Putnam, 1993) (detailing the historical origins and costs of drug prohibition).

3. Beyond Justice and the Rule of Law?

We are accustomed to thinking of rights as "trumps."[31] Once a right is established, then all other countervailing considerations cannot override these
rights. At the same time, in Chapter 1, I endorsed the view of Allen Buchanan
that "assertions of rights are essentially *conclusory* and *argumentative*,"[32] and
that a conclusion that a claim of right is valid "will usually be and all-things-
considered judgment, the result of balancing of conflicting considerations."[33]
Yet when we examine "the plurality of different kinds of considerations that
can count as moral reasons to support a conclusion of this sort,"[34] the claim
of right will likely seem less compelling. If we jiggle an assumption here, an
empirical claim there, we can undermine the idea of a right as trump altogether. Once the rationale for a particular scheme of rights is made explicit,
like eating the fruit of the tree of knowledge, there is always the fatal conceit
that we can go rights one better. We can supplement rights or replace them
altogether by an allegedly comprehensive analysis of what is often called
"public policy."

Public Policy vs. Rights

The public policy model of decision making has two necessary components:
(1) "public-policy experts" formulate "rational" solutions to "social" problems; (2) these solutions invariably require implementation by coercion,
either to mandate or prohibit citizen conduct or to dispense money collected
by taxation. The ideology of the public policy model is that policy makers
"weigh" the costs and benefits of human conduct as well as the costs and
benefits of legally regulating or prohibiting that conduct. The formation of
"rational" public policy is really a type of utilitarian decision making procedure that uses legal coercion in any way that will maximize some implicit conception of aggregate welfare.

  Of course, this ideology is based largely on a myth or fiction, for no genuinely comprehensive cost–benefit analysis is even attempted, much less
achieved. For example, no public policy analysis ever factors into its equations
the harm imposed on those who are wrongfully accused and punished for violating coercive mandates or the abuse and corruption that such regimes make
possible. Although the shortcomings of the public policy model are multifac-
eted, in all its guises, it is a form of central planning and suffers from all the
well-known deficiencies of this genre.[35] This is true even for so-called "decen-

[31] The metaphor is Ronald Dworkin's. See Dworkin, *Taking Rights Seriously*, p. xi
("Individual rights are political trumps held by individuals.").
[32] Buchanan, *Secession*, p. 151.   [33] Ibid.   [34] Ibid.
[35] See Ludwig von Mises, *Socialism* (New Haven: Yale University Press, trans. J.
Kahane, 1947); F. A. Hayek, *Individualism and Economic Order* (Chicago: University of
Chicago Press, 1948), pp. 77–208; Thomas Sowell, *Knowledge and Decisions* (New York:
Basic Books, 1980); Don Lavoie, *Rivalry and Central Planning*.

tralized" versions that shift some decision making authority to administrative agencies, "independent" government corporations, or states and municipalities (but not down to the level of private individuals and groups).

By contemplating the use of coercion to address the myriad problems facing individuals and groups on the basis of the expertise of public policy analysts, this model of decision making runs afoul of the pervasive social problems of knowledge and of interest. The problem of knowledge is the inability of public policy experts to know enough about the subject at hand to formulate consistently welfare-enhancing public policies. The gross generalizations and abstractions used by public policy experts to elide these factual particulars mask those experts' pervasive ignorance and the inherent riskiness of adopting their policy "prescriptions" into law. Moreover, although some versions of the model contemplate ratification of these prescriptions by popularly-elected officials, the electorate gets the bulk of its information from the proponents of the policies in question.

Ironically, the problem of knowledge is typically used by adherents to the public policy model of decision making as a weapon to advance their agenda. Before a particular policy is coercively implemented, predictions about its adverse effects are necessarily abstract and conjectural. Arrayed against such "speculation" are the ever-confident predictions of policy analysts that legal coercion will eliminate or greatly reduce a particular social problem. While the purported benefits of such bans or mandates are asserted by their proponents with certitude, the predictable harms are dismissed as merely speculative.

Emotions are also at work here. Enacting coercive measures is seen as "doing something" about a social problem and is depicted as being morally superior to "doing nothing." Legislators who vote for such policies are portrayed in the press and in popular fiction as caring and courageous (although their courage involves imprisoning others at public expense). Those who oppose such policies are considered to be old-fashioned, small-minded, and without imagination. They are called "soft on" whatever problem is supposedly being solved. Most damning of all, they are charged with being indifferent to the suffering of others. After all, if a policy initiative does not work out we can always end it. What harm is there in trying?

Plenty. Once enacted, if not before, such policies are subject to the problem of interest. Enacted public policy schemes create a conflict of interests between persons who directly benefit from the policies and those who must bear the costs of the policies. Experts in the field, regulatory and law-enforcement agencies, and politicians all directly benefit from such policies. Diffused taxpayers and those who are prosecuted for the offenses which have been created pay the price. The beneficiaries of such policies are constantly striving to recruit the public to their cause. They are adept at producing evidence showing either that current efforts are working or that the widespread failure of current efforts demonstrates the need for a massive escalation of funding. Whether continued or increased levels of funding are justified because current policies have succeeded or because they have failed will vary from expert to expert and from day to day. Those who benefit from public policies can always be relied upon to produce horror stories to illustrate the necessity of the policies in question. They are not above smearing or dismissing contemptuously those who oppose them and ignoring any expert or official commission that reaches the "wrong" result. In the world of public policy, there is no failed social program that would not work as advertised if only massive amounts of new "resources" were made available.

Although the public policy model usually takes a "do something" approach to a particular problem, professing concern for the problems of knowledge and interest, public policy experts reject the idea of individuals and associations taking a similar approach in their own lives. The choices of individuals and groups are portrayed as ignorant and partial, requiring second-guessing by impartial experts. This reveals the essentially elitist and paternalistic attitudes underlying the public policy model. Public policy experts and officials are competent to implement coercive schemes to deal with vastly complicated social problems, but ordinary persons are not competent to make decisions concerning some of their most personal situations.

The public policy model of decision making errs in the direction of enacting schemes of coercion that rarely if ever can be repealed, regardless of how useless and damaging they may turn out to be. Such repeal then only comes after costing countless persons their happiness and even their lives. What is the alternative? Ensuring that the harmful side effects of legal coercion are incurred only when such coercion is both necessary and proper requires not problem-by-problem experimentation formulated by public policy experts, but a commitment to what can only be called principle and a respect for properly formulated individual rights.

A commitment to principle was once considered a virtue. This attitude was a product of a more humble view of human knowledge and interest, as well as human power, than obtains today. The dominance of the public policy model of legal decision making has undercut this sentiment by promising clean precise solutions to intractable problems. Persons of principle are now commonly condemned—especially by academics—as "doctrinaire" or "ideologues." It would be nice if those who are skeptical of identifying the "right set" of rights were equally skeptical of finding the right set of public policies.

The abstract rights I have identified are by no means perfect guides to conduct. Based as they are on certain factual generalizations, they do not always yield favorable outcomes even within their respective domains, though where possible this typically leads to the formulation of general exceptions. Moreover, as products of human understanding, such rights may be imperfectly formulated, though they can be refined when they are shown to be deficient. Indeed, the rights I defend here are valuable guides to conduct precisely because exceptions have been recognized over time and formulations have been refined in light of ongoing experience.

Still, despite these imperfections, a legal system informed by the right set of rights can do a better job than a system that ignores these rights in favor of the public policy model. The wisdom of respecting these rights has been demonstrated by long and varied experience. In contrast to the formulation of "social problems" that abstract from the great diversity of individual circumstances, the generalizations on which these rights are based attempt to take those circumstances into account. They are bottom-up, rather than top-down.[36] And they are supported by the fact that they address the pervasive social problems of knowledge, interest, and power.

Given the critical tenor of these remarks, I should hasten to emphasize that there is nothing inherently objectionable about public policy analysis; some of my best friends do public policy analysis. Principles alone do not make us expert about any social problem; that requires the sort of information that good public policy analysis and some experience on the ground can provide. In this way, public policy analysis reinforces and sometimes helps reshape our principles. What is objectionable is enacting laws sanctioning the punishment of persons solely on the basis of such analysis—what I have called here the "public policy model of decision making"—unconstrained by the sort of principled analysis provided by the liberal conception of justice. The rights that define justice remind us of the inherent limitations of using legal coercion and enable us to predict with a fair degree of confidence when a legal scheme that looks attractive from a public policy standpoint is likely both to lead to damaging unforeseen results and to be difficult to reverse if that should occur.

The limitations of human reasoning and the complexity of the world in which we live make it hard to argue conclusively against any competing value overriding the requirements of justice. Yet these same considerations ought to make it equally hard to argue conclusively in favor of such an override. Given that the baseline favoring these rights is set by their ability to handle the pervasive social problems of knowledge, interest, and power, prudence suggests that no overrides be permitted. The analysis presented here both explains why and enables us to predict that overrides will lead to bad consequences, the particular nature of which we are better off not experiencing. We are better off thinking of rights as trumps.

Solving other Problems

Adherence to the liberal conception of justice and the rule of law is necessary to achieve a well-ordered society in which the problems of knowledge, interest, and power are handled. Of course, these are not the only problems facing persons living in society with others. What about the problem of providing food, water, shelter, and other material, not to mention spiritual, needs of life? Does not legal coercion have an important role to play in the provision of

---

[36] Cf. Matson, "Justice: A Funeral Oration," (contrasting natural justice or justice from the "bottom up" with artificial justice or justice from the "top-down").

these goods as well? By now, my responses to this type of challenge should be evident.

Altering the precepts of justice to pursue other social ends—even very important ends—is like taking from the foundations of a building to add more floors to the top. The foundation of a building is not an end in itself. And a little can be stolen from here or there without noticeable effect. Such is the resilience of a well-designed foundation. But, assuming the foundation was correctly designed in the first place, the structural integrity of the building is jeopardized by the very first taking. Moreover, the *principle* of taking from the foundation to build a higher building is most certainly a threat to the structural integrity of the building and, consequently, is a mortal threat to the lives and well-being of those who reside within.

One ought not to infringe upon the rights and procedures that make a well-ordered social life possible to address other pressing problems if doing so will seriously undermine our ability to address the problems of knowledge, interest, and power. Addressing these problems is a prerequisite to any hope we have of effectively handling the other problems of social life. A society that failed to deal effectively with the problems of knowledge, interest, and power would be in chaos. And a society in chaos cannot deal effectively with any social problem, however serious it may be. Any effort to do an end run around the rights and procedures described here will run into its own intractable problems of knowledge, interest, and power. For this reason, in Pufendorf's words, the "medicine [is] far more troublesome and dangerous than the disease."[37]

Most of the serious problems that we allegedly need to violate or limit rights to address can be handled by people and associations who respect those rights. Indeed, such goods as community, art, entertainment, religious inculcation, education, and the provision of food and shelter have, throughout history, been provided by people exercising their rights while refraining from violating the rights of others. Even rewards and punishments are best handled this way and for the same reasons.

The analysis presented here would predict that individuals and associations employing their personal and local knowledge in pursuit of their partial interests, while constrained by the boundaries of their jurisdiction to take into account the knowledge and interests of those around them, are likely to do a better job at these tasks than central managers and policy analysts who must confront the problems of knowledge, interest, and power. While I cannot guarantee this is true, the analysis of this book explains why the guarantees issued by those who would substitute coercion for consent, power for right, desert for justice, central commands for liberty, are illusory.

---

[37] Pufendorf, *De Jure Naturae*, p. 118.

4. The Limits of Criticism

When considering supposed deficiencies of the structure of liberty examined here, we must bear in mind that social theories have to be assessed comparatively. As with science, while open-minded persons will reconsider their convictions when given reason to do so, they need not reject them even if they agree that the objections to them are grave. To change, rather than reconsider, one's convictions requires that one be aware of a new and better conviction to take its place. Criticism simply is no substitute for the presentation of a potentially-superior alternative perspective.[38]

Nor is the ability to criticize or deconstruct a known approach the same as the ability to discover or build a better approach. Consider the art of "deconstructing" or demolishing buildings. Demolition is a valuable skill—a skill often worth paying for—but it is not the same kind of skill as that of architecture or structural engineering. Demolishing a building may be needed to make room for a new building, but the art of demolition will not build a replacement. There is not a building standing that cannot be demolished. The fact that someone can demolish a particular building establishes neither that the building is a bad one, nor that it is possible to build a better one. It certainly does not qualify a demolition expert to be an architect.[39]

The same is true, I suggest, for the ability to criticize a conceptual analysis such as provided by the structure of liberty. The fact that one is able to criticize severely a particular conceptual scheme establishes neither that the scheme should be rejected, nor that it is possible to construct a better one. It certainly does not establish the critic as capable of constructing a superior alternative. While both skills may be present in a single person, construction and "deconstruction" are two distinct skills, each with its own techniques and value.

In short, sheer criticism of the structure of liberty, however insightful and serious, is not enough. Given that the pervasive problems of knowledge, interest, and power must somehow be solved, how do the critics propose to solve them? Let us see *their* blueprints. We will not be content to see only an artist's rendering of their proposed building. (Artist's renderings are *always* beautiful.)

[38] See Thomas S. Kuhn, *The Structure of Scientific Revolutions*, 2nd edn. (Chicago: University of Chicago Press, 1970), p. 77 (even when confronted by severe and prolonged anomalies, "a scientific theory is declared invalid only if an alternate candidate is available to take its place.").

[39] The art of demolition will not even tell us much about how the replacement should be built. For, while it is true that we want a building that is strong enough to survive the forces that will be exerted on it during its use, we hardly design buildings to withstand deliberate demolition. An exception to this is when civility breaks down to the extent that some persons can be expected to try to destroy a building if given a chance. Under such circumstances we may have to take precautions against such acts of destruction. (Perhaps we may design, say, a barrier that would make driving a car bomb into a building more difficult.) The need to take precautions against acts of willful destruction does not, however, undermine the basic point of the analogy.

Let us examine how their proposed foundation and superstructure will support the weight, the needs, and the aspirations of the civilization that will inhabit the building they propose to build and that will be displaced by the building they propose to demolish. Only when we can compare schematics can we make the correct choice.

Until then, we can still profit from a fuller understanding of the function of justice and the rule of law—the structure of liberty—in solving the problems of knowledge, interest, and power. For by appreciating the tasks performed by these abstract rights and procedures that often seem to constrain us from doing what we desire, we may see how they can better be implemented. And we can resist the ever-present temptation to infringe upon or discard the structure of liberty that is essential to our survival and pursuit of happiness, peace, and prosperity.

BIBLIOGRAPHY

ABEL, CHARLES F. and MARSH, FRANK F., *Punishment and Restitution: A Restitutionary Approach to Crime and the Criminal* (Westport, Conn.: Greenwood Press, 1984).

ADDISON, ALEXANDER, "Analysis of the Report of the Committee of the Virginia Assembly" (1880), in Charles S. Hyneman and Donald S. Lutz (eds.), *American Political Writing during the Founding Era, 1760–1805* (Indianapolis: Liberty Press, 1983).

ALEXANDER, LARRY, "Pursuing the Good—Indirectly," *Ethics*, 95 (1985), 315.

ALSTON, WILLIAM P., "Teleological Argument for the Existence of God," in Paul Edwards (ed.), *The Encyclopedia of Philosophy*, viii (New York: Macmillan and Free Press, 1967).

American Law Institute, *Restatement of the Law of Conflicts 2d*, i (St. Paul, Minn.: American Law Institute, 1971).

AQUINAS, THOMAS, *Summa Theologica*, in Robert Hutchings (ed.), *Great Books of the Western World*, xx (Chicago: Encyclopedia Britannica, 1952).

ARISTOTLE, *Nicomachean Ethics*, trans. W. D. Ross, in Richard McKeon (ed.), *The Basic Works of Aristotle* (New York: Random House, 1941).

—— *Nicomachean Ethics*, trans. Martin Ostwald (Indianapolis, Ind.: Bobbs-Merrill, 1962).

ASHWORTH, TONY, *Trench Warfare 1914–1918: The Live and Let Live System* (New York: Holmes & Maier, 1980).

AUERBACH, JEROLD S., *Justice without Law?* (New York: Oxford University Press, 1983).

AXELROD, ROBERT, *The Evolution of Cooperation* (New York: Basic Books, 1984).

BANFIELD, EDWARD, *The Unheavenly City Revisited* (Boston: Little, Brown, 1974).

—— "Present-orientedness and Crime," in Barnett and Hagel (eds.), *Assessing the Criminal*.

BARNETT, RANDY E., "Restitution: A New Paradigm of Criminal Justice," *Ethics*, 87 (1977), 279.

—— "The Justice of Restitution," *American Journal of Jurisprudence*, 25 (1980), 117.

—— "Resolving the Dilemma of the Exclusionary Rule: An Application of Restitutive Principles of Justice," *Emory Law Journal*, 32 (1983), 937.

—— "Pursuing Justice in a Free Society: Part Two—Crime Prevention and the Legal Order," *Criminal Justice Ethics* (Winter/Spring 1986), 30.

—— "Contract Remedies and Inalienable Rights," *Social Philosophy and Policy*, 4 (Autumn 1986), 186–95.

—— "Squaring Undisclosed Agency Law with Contract Theory," *California Law Review*, 75 (1987), 1969.

—— "Curing the Drug Law Addiction: The Harmful Side Effects of Legal Prohibition," in Ronald Hamowy (ed.), *Dealing with Drugs: Consequences of Government Control* (San Francisco: Pacific Research Institute, 1987).

—— "Of Chickens and Eggs—The Compatibility of Moral Rights and Consequentialist Analyses," *Harvard Journal of Law and Public Policy*, 12 (1989), 611–35.

—— (ed.), *The Rights Retained by the People: The History and Meaning of the Ninth Amendment* (Fairfax, Va.: George Mason University Press, 1989).

BARNETT, RANDY E., "Introduction: James Madison's Ninth Amendment," in Barnett (ed.), *Rights Retained.*

—— "Introduction: Implementing the Ninth Amendment," in Barnett (ed.), *Rights Retained.*

—— "The Virtues of Redundancy in Legal Thought," *Cleveland-State Law Review*, 38 (1990), 153–68.

—— "The Sound of Silence: Default Rules and Contractual Consent," *Virginia Law Review*, 78 (1992), 821.

—— "Conflicting Visions: A Critique of Ian Macneil's Relational Theory of Contract," *Virginia Law Review*, 78 (1992), 1175.

—— "The Intersection of Natural Rights and Positive Constitutional Law," *University of Connecticut Law Review*, 25 (1993), 853.

—— "Bad Trip: Drug Prohibition and the Weakness of Public Policy," *Yale Law Journal*, 103 (1994), 2593.

—— "Getting Normative: The Role of Natural Rights in Constitutional Adjudication," *Constitutional Commentary*, 12 (1995), 93.

—— *Contracts Cases and Doctrine* (Boston: Little, Brown, 1995).

—— "Necessary and Proper," *UCLA Law Review*, 44 (1997), 745–93.

—— and Hagel, John, III, "Assessing the Criminal: Restitution, Retribution, and Legal Process," in Barnett, Randy E. and Hagel, John, III (eds.), *Assessing the Criminal.*

—— —— (eds.), *Assessing the Criminal: Restitution, Retribution, and the Legal Process* (Boston: Ballinger, 1977).

—— and Kates, Don B., *Under Fire: The New Consensus on the Second Amendment*, 45 (1996), 1139–259.

BATOR, FRANCIS M., The Anatomy of Market Failure," *Quarterly Journal of Law and Economics*, 72 (1958), 351–79.

BENN, STANLEY I., "Punishment," *The Encyclopedia of Philosophy*, vii (New York: Macmillan and Free Press, 1967).

BENSON, BRUCE L., *The Enterprise of Law: Justice without the State* (San Francisco: Pacific Research Institute, 1990).

BERMAN, HAROLD J., *Law and Revolution* (Cambridge, Mass.: Harvard University Press, 1983).

BERNSTEIN, LISA, "Opting out of the Legal System: Extralegal Contractual Relations in the Diamond Industry," *Journal of Legal Studies*, 21 (1992), 115.

BLACK, CHARLES L., JR., *The People and the Court: Judicial Review in a Democracy* (New York: Macmillan, 1960).

BOLICK, CLINT, *Grassroots Tyranny: The Limits of Federalism* (Washington DC: Cato Institute, 1993).

BORK, ROBERT H., *The Tempting of America* (New York: Free Press, 1990).

BOYLE, JAMES, "The Politics of Reason: Critical Legal Theory and Local Social Thought," *Pennsylvania Law Review*, 133 (1985), 728.

BUCHANAN, ALLEN, *Secession: The Morality of Political Divorce from Fort Sumpter to Lithuania and Quebec* (Boulder, Colo.: Westview Press, 1991).

BUCHANAN, JAMES, *Cost and Choice* (Chicago: Markham, 1969).

BUCKLE, STEPHEN, *Natural Law and the Theory of Property* (Oxford: Oxford University Press, 1991).

BUCKLEY, STEPHEN, "From Destroying Lives to Building Dreams—Housing Project is Foundation for Inmates," *Washington Post*, 10 Aug. 1992.

BUGLIOSI, VINCENT, *Helter Skelter* (New York: W. W. Norton, 1974).

BYOCK, JESSE L., *Medieval Iceland: Society, Sagas, and Power* (Berkeley: University of California Press, 1988).

CALABRESI, GUIDO and MELAMED, DOUGLAS, "Property Rules, Liability Rules, and Inalienability: One View of the Cathedral," *Harvard Law Review*, 85 (1972), 1089.

CHEATHAM, ELLIOTT E. and REESE, WILLIS L. M., *Columbia Law Review*, 52 (1952), 959.

CHEUNG, STEVEN N. S., "The Fable of the Bees: An Economic Investigation," *Journal of Law and Economics*, 16 (1973), 11–33.

CHILDS, ROY A., "The Invisible Hand Strikes Back," *Journal of Libertarian Studies*, 1 (1977), 23–33.

COASE, RONALD H., "The Nature of the Firm," *Economica*, 4 (1937), 390–1.

—— "The Problem of Social Cost," *Journal of Law and Economics*, 3 (1960), 1.

—— "The Lighthouse in Economics," *Journal of Law and Economics*, 17 (1974), 357.

COHEN, G. A., "On the Currency of Egalitarian Justice," *Ethics*, 99 (July 1989), 906–44.

COWEN, JONATHAN M., "One Nation's Gulag is Another Nation's 'Factory within a Fence': Prison-Labor in the People's Republic of Chance and the United States of America," *UCLA Pacific Basic Jorunal*, 12 (1993), 211.

COWEN, TYLER (ed.), *The Theory of Market Failure* (Fairfax, Va.: George Mason University Press, 1988).

DALBERG-ACTON, JOHN E., "Letter to Bishop Mandell Creighton" (5 Apr. 1887), in *Essays on Freedom and Power* (Boston: Beacon Press and Glencoe, Ill.: Free Press, 1948).

DIGGES, DUDLEY, *The Unlawfulness of Subjects, Taking up Armes against their Soveraigne* (n.p., 1644).

DUKE, STEVEN B. and GROSS, ALBERT, *America's Longest War: Rethinking our Tragic Crusade against Drugs* (New York: Putnam, 1993).

DUNCAN, DONNA, "ACA Survey Examines Industry Programs for Women Offenders," *Corrections Today*, Feb. 1992, 114.

DWORKIN, RONALD, "The Model of Rules," *University of Chicago Law Review*, 35 (1967), 22–9.

—— *Taking Rights Seriously* (Cambridge, Mass.: Harvard University Press, 1977).

—— *Law's Empire* (Cambridge, Mass.: Harvard University Press, 1986).

ELLICKSON, ROBERT C., "Property in Land," *Yale Law Journal*, 102 (1993), 1369.

EPSTEIN, RICHARD A., "A Theory of Strict Liability," *Journal of Legal Studies*, 2 (1973), 151.

—— "Defenses and Subsequent Pleas in a System of Strict Liability," *Journal of Legal Studies*, 3 (1974), 165.

—— "Intentional Harms," *Journal of Legal Studies*, 4 (1975), 391.

—— "Causation and Corrective Justice: A Reply to Critics," *Journal of Legal Studies*, 8 (1979), 477.

—— "Possession as the Root of Title," *Georgia Law Review*, 13 (1979), 1221–43.

—— *Takings: Private Property and the Power of Eminent Domain* (Cambridge, Mass.: Harvard University Press, 1985).

FARBER, DANIEL A., "Democracy and Disgust: Reflections on Public Choice," *Chicago-Kent Law Review*, 65 (1989), 161–76.

FARNSWORTH, E. ALLAN, *Contracts*, 2nd edn. (Boston: Little, Brown, 1990).

FEINBERG, JOEL, *Rights, Justice, and the Bounds of Liberty* (Princeton, NJ: Princeton University Press, 1980).

—— "The Nature and Value of Rights," in *Rights, Justice*.

—— *Harm to Others* (Oxford: Oxford University Press, 1984).

FIELD, RICHARD H., KAPLAN, BENJAMIN, and CLERMONT, KEVIN M., *Civil Procedure*, 4th edn. (Mineola: Minn.: Foundation Press, 1978).

FINNIS, JOHN, *Natural Law and Natural Rights* (Oxford: Clarendon Press, 1980).

FLETCHER, GEORGE P., "Two Modes of Legal Thought," *Yale Law Journal*, 90 (1981), 980.

FOOTE, PHILLIPA, "Morality as a System of Hypothetical Imperatives," *Philosophical Review*, 81 (1972), 305–16.

FRANK, JEROME, *Law and the Modern Mind* (New York: Tudor, 1936).

FREEDMAN, MONROE H., *Lawyers' Ethics in an Adversary System* (Indianapolis: Bobbs-Merrill, 1975).

FRIED, CHARLES, "Rights and the Common Law," in R. G. Frey (ed.), *Utility and Rights* (Minneapolis, Minn.: University of Minnesota Press, 1984), 231–2.

FRIEDMAN, DAVID, *The Machinery of Freedom* (New York: Harper Colophon Books, 1973).

FULLER, LON L., *Basic Contract Law* (St. Paul, Minn.: West, 1947).

—— "Positivism and Fiedelity to Law: A Reply to Professor Hart," *Harvard Law Review*, 71 (1958), 644.

—— *The Morality of Law*, 2nd rev. edn. (New Haven, Conn.: Yale University Press, 1969).

—— "The Forms and Limits of Adjudication," *Harvard Law Review*, 92 (1978), 353.

—— "Philosophy for the Practicing Lawyer," in Kenneth I. Winston (ed.), *The Principles of Social Order: Selected Essays on Lon L. Fuller* (Durham, NC: Duke University Press, 1981), 289–90.

FUNKE, GAIL S., WAYSON, BILLY L., and MILLER, NEAL, *Assets and Liabilities of Correctional Industries* (Lexington, Mass.: Lexington Books, 1982).

GALAWAY, BURT and H0 (eds.), *Restitution in Criminal Sanctions* (Lexington, Mass.: Lexington Books, 1975).

—— —— (eds.), *Considering the Victim* (Springfield, Ill.: Charles C. Thomas, 1975).

—— —— (eds.), *Victims, Offenders, and Alternative Sanctions* (Lexington, Mass.: Lexington Books, 1980).

—— —— (eds.), *Perspectives on Crime Victims* (St. Louis, Mo.: C. V. Mosby, 1981).

—— —— (eds.), *Criminal Justice, Restitution, and Reconciliation* (Monsay, NY: Criminal Justice Press, 1991).

GALES, JOSEPH (ed.), *The Debates and Proceedings in the Congress of the United States* (Washington DC: Gales & Seaton, 1834).

GASKINS, RICHARD H., *Burdens of Proof in Modern Discourse* (New Haven, Conn.: Yale University Press, 1992).

GEORGE, ROBERT P., "Natural Law Symposium," *Cleveland State Law Review*, 38 (1990), 1.

—— (ed.), *Natural Law Theories: Contemporary Essays* (Oxford: Oxford University Press, 1992).

—— "Symposium: Perspectives on Natural Law," *Cincinnati Law Review*, 61 (1992), 1–222.

—— "Symposium on Natural Law", *Southern California Interdisciplinary Law Journal*, 3 (1995), 455.

GOODRICH, ELIZUR, "The Principles of Civil Union and Happiness Considered and Recommended," in Ellis Sandoz (ed.), *Political Sermons of the American Founding: 1730–1805* (Indianapolis: Liberty Press, 1991).

GORDON, H. S., "The Economic Theory of a Common Property Resource: The Fishery," *Journal of Political Economy*, 62 (1954), 124.

GRAY, JOHN, "Indirect Utility and Fundamental Rights," *Social Philosophy and Policy*, 1 (Spring 1984), 73.

GROTIUS, HUGO, *De Jure Belli ac Pacis Libri*, trans. Francis W. Kelsey (Oxford: Clarendon Press, 1925).

HAMBURGER, PHILIP A, "Natural Rights, Natural Law, and American Constitutions," *Yale Law Journal*, 102 (1993), 907.

HARDIN, GARRETT, "The Tragedy of the Commons," *Science*, 162 (1968), 1243–8.

HARRISON, KEITH A., "Rebuilding Futures Inmates Work on Houses and their Lives," *Washington Post*, 26 Mar. 1994.

HART, H. L. A., *The Concept of Law* (Oxford: Oxford University Press, 1961).

HAYEK, FRIEDRICH A., "The Use of Knowledge in Society," in Hayek, *Individualism and Order*.

—— *Individualism and Economic Order* (Chicago: University of Chicago Press, 1948).

—— *Law Legislation and Liberty* (Chicago: University of Chicago Press, 1974).

—— *The Denationalization of Money* (London: Institute for Economic Affairs, 1976).

HEGLAND, KENNY, "Goodbye to Deconstruction," *Southern California University Law Review*, 58 (1985), 1203.

HELMHOLZ, R. H., "Assumpsit and *Fidei Laesio*," *Law Quarterly Review*, 91 (1975), 406.

HOBBES, THOMAS, *Leviathan* (Indianapolis: Bobbs-Merrill, 1958).

HUME, DAVID, *A Treatise Concerning Human Nature*, 2nd edn. (Oxford: Clarendon Press, 1978).

JOACHIM, HAROLD H., *Aristotle: The Nicomachean Ethics* (Oxford: Clarendon Press, 1951).

KANT, IMMANUEL, *Groundwork of the Metaphysics of Morals*, trans. H. J. Paton (New York: Harper & Row, 1964).

KAUFMAN, WALTER, *Without Guilt and Justice* (New York: Dell Publishing, 1973).

—— "Retribution and the Ethics of Punishment," in Barnett and Hagel (eds.), *Assessing the Criminal*.

KENNEDY, DUNCAN, "The Structure of Blackstone's Commentaries," *Buffalo Law Review*, 28 (1979), 211.

—— *A Critique of Adjudication* (Cambridge, Mass.: Harvard University Press, 1997).

KIRZNER, ISRAEL M., *Competition and Entrepreneurship* (Chicago: University of Chicago Press, 1973).

KISSEL, WILLIAM, "Behind Bars for Rape and Murder, Covicts Vie for the Chance to Cut and Sew for Sportswear Labels," *Los Angeles Times*, 16 Jan. 1992, E1.

KLEIN, DANIEL B., "Convention, Social Order, and the Two Coordinations," *Constitutional Political Economy* (forthcoming).

KRONMAN, ANTHONY T., "Mistake, Disclosure, Information, and the Law of Contracts," *Journal of Legal Studies*, 11 (1978), 1–34.

KUFLIK, ARTHUR, "The Inalienability of Autonomy," *Philosophy and Public Affairs*, 13 (1984), 281.

KUHN, THOMAS S., *The Structure of Scientific Revolutions*, 2nd edn. (Chicago: University of Chicago Press, 1970).

LAVOIE, DON, *National Economic Planning* (Cambridge, Mass.: Ballinger, 1985).

—— *Rivalry and Central Planning* (New York: Cambridge University Press, 1985).

LAWSON, GARY and GRANGER, PATRICIA, "The 'Proper' Scope of Federal Power: A Jurisdictional Interpretation of the Sweeping Clause," *Duke Law Journal*, 43 (1993), 267–336.

LIGGIO, LEONARD P., "The Transportation of Criminals: A Brief Political-Economic History," in Barnett and Hagel (eds.), *Assessing the Criminal*.

Locke, John, *Essays on the Law of Nature*, ed. W. von Leyden (Oxford: Clarendon Press, 1952).

—— *Two Treatises of Government* (1690), ed. Peter Laslett (Cambridge: Mentor, 1963).

Logan, Charles, *Private Prisons* (Oxford: Oxford University Press, 1990).

Lomasky, Loren E., *Persons, Rights, and the Moral Community* (New York: Oxford University Press, 1987).

Lutz, Donald S., "The Bill of Rights in the States," *Southern Illinois University Law Journal*, 16 (1992), 256.

McConnell, Terrance, "The Nature and Basis of Inalienable Rights," *Law and Philosophy*, 3 (1984), 43.

McLean, Iain, *Public Choice* (Oxford: Basil Blackwell, 1987).

Macneil, Ian, "Power of Contract and Agreed Remedies," *Cornell Law Quarterly*, 47 (1962), 495.

Madison, James, *The Federalist*, No. 10 (New York: Modern Library, 1937).

Maggs, Gregory E. and Weiss, Michael D., "Progress on Attorney's Fees: Expanding the 'Loser Pays' Rule in Texas," *Houston Law Review*, 30 (1994), 1929.

Magnusson, Magnus and Palsson, Herman, trans., *Njal's Saga* (London: Penguin Books, 1960).

Mardon, Steven, "Inmate Jeans Catch on in Oregon," *Corrections Today*, July 1992, 29.

Mashaw, Jerry L., "The Economics of Politics and the Understanding of Public Law," *Chicago–Kent Law Review*, 65 (1989), 123–60.

Matson, Wallace, "Justice: A Funeral Oration," *Social Philosophy and Policy*, 1 (1983), 94.

Meyers, Diane T., *Inalienable Rights: A Defense,* (New York: Columbia University Press, 1985), 13–15.

Mill, John Stuart, *On Liberty*, in Robert Hutchings (ed.), *Great Books of the Western World*, xliii (Chicago: Encyclopedia Britannica, 1952).

Miller, William Ian, *Bloodtaking and Peacemaking: Feud, Law, and Society in Saga Iceland* (Chicago: University of Chicago Press, 1990).

Mises, Ludwig von, *Human Action*, 3rd edn. (Chicago: Henry Regnery, 1963).

—— *Socialism*, trans. J. Kahane (New Haven: Yale University Press, 1947).

Moody, Ernest A., "William of Ockham," in Paul Edwards (ed.), *The Encyclopedia of Philosophy* (New York: Macmillan and Free Press, 1967).

Morse, Stephen J., "Blame and Danger: An Essay on Preventive Detention," *Boston University Law Review*, 76 (1996), 121.

Murphy, Jeffrie, and Coleman, Jules, *The Philosophy of Law* (Totowa, NJ: Rowman & Allanheld, 1984).

Nance, Dale A., "Civility and the Burden of Proof," *Harvard Journal of Law and Public Policy*, 17 (1994), 647.

Neely, Richard, *Why Courts Don't Work* (New York: McGraw-Hill, 1983).

Newman, Oscar, *Community of Interest* (Garden City, NY: Anchor Press, 1980).

Nicholas, Barry, *French Law of Contract* (St. Paul, Minn.: Mason, 1982).

Nozick, Robert, *Anarchy, State, and Utopia* (New York: Basic Books, 1974).

O'Driscoll, Gerald P., Jr., "Professor Banfield on Time Horizon: What has he Taught Us about Crime?" in Barnett and Hagel (eds.), *Assessing the Criminal*.

Peller, Gary, "The Metaphysics of American Law," *California Law Review*, 73 (1985), 1168.

Polanyi, Michael, *The Logic of Liberty* (Chicago: University of Chicago Press, 1951).

—— *Personal Knowledge* (Chicago: University of Chicago Press, 1962).

—— *Knowing and Being* (Chicago: University of Chicago Press, 1969).

POTTS, JEFF, "American Penal Institutions and Two Alternative Proposals for Punishment," *South Texas Law Review*, 34 (1993), 500.

PROTESS, DAVID and WARDEN, ROB, *Gone in the Night: The Dowaliby Family's Encounter with Murder and the Law* (New York: Delacorte, 1993).

PUFENDORF, SAMUEL, *De Jure Naturae at Gentium Libri Octo* (1672), trans. C. H. and W. A. Oldfather (New York: Oceana Publications; London: Wildby and Sons, 1964).

RASMUSSEN, DOUGLAS B. and DEN UYL, DOUGLAS J., *Liberty and Nature* (La Salle, Ill.: Open Court, 1991).

RAWLS, JOHN, *A Theory of Justice* (Cambridge, Mass.: Harvard University Press, 1971).

—— *Political Liberalism* (New York: Columbia University Press, 1996).

RAZ, JOSEPH, *The Authority of Law* (Oxford: Oxford University Press, 1979).

—— *The Morality of Freedom* (Oxford: Oxford University Press, 1986).

RIZZO, MARIO J., "Time Preference, Situational Determinism, and Crime," in Barnett and Hagel (eds.), *Assessing the Criminal*.

ROBACK, JENNIFER, "The Political Economy of Segregation: The Case of Segregated Streetcars," *Journal of Economic History*, 46 (Dec. 1986), 893–918.

ROBERTSON, D. H., *Control of Industry* (New York: Harcourt, Brace & Co., 1923).

ROTHBARD, MURRAY N., "Punishment and Proportionality," in Barnett and Hagel (eds.), *Assessing the Criminal*.

—— "Robert Nozick and the Immaculate Conception of the State," *Journal of Libertarian Studies*, 1 (1977), 45–57.

SAMUELSON, PAUL A., *Economics: An Introductory Analysis*, 6th edn. (New York: McGraw-Hill, 1964).

SANDEL, MICHAEL, *Liberalism and the Limits of Justice* (Cambridge: Cambridge University Press, 1982).

SCHAFER, STEPHEN, *Restitution to Victims of Crime* (Chicago: Quadrangle Books, 1960).

—— "Restitution to Victims of Crime—An Old Correctional Aim Modernized," *Minnesota Law Review*, 50 (1965), 246.

—— *Compensation and Restitution to Victims of Crime* (Montclair, NJ: Patterson Smith, 1970).

SCHAUER, FREDERICK, "Easy Cases," *Southern California Law Review*, 58 (1985), 399.

SCHELLING, THOMAS C., *Micro and Macrobehavior* (New York: W. W. Norton, 1978).

—— *The Strategy of Conflict*, rev. edn. (Cambridge, Mass.: Harvard University Press, 1980).

SCHMIDTZ, DAVID, *The Limits of Government: An Essay on the Public Goods Argument* (Boulder, Colo.: Westview Press, 1991).

SCHNEIDER DENENBERG, Tai and Denenberg, R. V., *Dispute Resolution: Settling Conflicts without Legal Action*, Public Affairs Pamphlet No. 597 (New York: Public Affairs Committee, 1981).

SCHWARTZ, BERNARD, *The Bill of Rights: A Documentary History*, i (New York: Chelsea House, 1971).

SEN, AMARTYA, "Equality of What?" in Stephen Darwall (ed.), *Equal Freedom* (Ann Arbor, Mich.: University of Michigan Press, 1995).

SHERRY, SUZANNA, "Natural Law in the States," *Cincinnati Law Review*, 61 (1992), 186.

SINGER, JOSEPH WILLIAM, "The Legal Rights Debate in Analytical Jurisprudence from Bentham to Hohfeld," *Wisconsin Law Review*, 1982 (1982), 980.

—— "The Player and the Cards: Nihilism and Legal Theory," *Yale Law Journal*, 94 (1984), 7.

SKAPERDAS, STERGIOS and SYROPOULOS, CONSTANTINE, "Gangs as Primitive States," in Sam Pelzman (ed.), *The Economics of Organized Crime* (Cambridge: Cambridge University Press, 1995).

SMART, J. C. C., "Utilitarianism," in *The Encylopedia of Philosophy*, viii (New York: Macmillan and Free Press, 1967).

SMITH, ABBOT EMERSON, *Colonists in Bondage: White Servitude and Convict Labor in America, 1607–1776* (Chapel Hill, NC: University of North Carolina Press, 1947), 366.

SMITH, ADAM, *The Theory of Moral Sentiments* (London, 1759; Indianapolis: Liberty Classics, 1976).

—— *The Wealth of Nations*, 5th edn. (London, 1789), in Robert Hutchings (ed.), *Great Books of the Western World*, xxxix (Chicago: Encyclopedia Britannica, 1952).

SMITH, GEORGE H., "A Reply to Critics," *Journal of Libertarian Studies*, 3 (1979), 453.

—— "Inalienable Rights," *Liberty*, 10 (1997), 52.

SMITH, KATHLEEN D., "Implementing Restitution within a Penal Setting: The Case for the Self-Determinate Sentence," in Hudson and Galaway (eds.), *Restitution in Criminal Justice*.

SOLUM, LAWRENCE B., "On the Indeterminacy Crisis: Critiquing Critical Dogma," *University of Chicago Law Review*, 54 (1987), 462–503.

SOWELL, THOMAS, *Knowledge and Decisions* (New York: Basic Books, 1980).

SPEIDEL, RICHARD E., "The New Spirit of Contract," *Journal of Law and Commerce*, 2 (1982), 193.

SPENCER, HERBERT, *Social Statics* (New York: Robert Schalkenback Foundation, 1970).

STEINER, HILLEL, "The Structure of a Set of Compossible Rights," *Journal of Philosophy*, 74 (1977), 767–8.

—— *An Essay on Rights* (Oxford: Blackwell, 1994).

SUGDEN, ROBERT, *The Economics of Rights, Co-operation and Welfare* (Oxford: Blackwell, 1986).

TOUHY, JAMES and WARDEN, ROB, *Greylord: Justice, Chicago Style* (New York: Putnam, 1989).

TOULMIN, STEPHEN, *Human Understanding* (Princeton, NJ: Princeton University Press, 1972).

TREITEL, GUNTHER H., "Remedies for Breach of Contract," in Arthur T. Mehren (ed.), *International Encyclopedia of Comparative Law*, vii (Paris: J. C. B. Mohr, 1976).

Trial of Queen Caroline, ii (London: J. Robins & Co., 1820–1).

TUCK, RICHARD, *Natural Rights Theories: Their Origin and Development* (Cambridge: Cambridge University Press, 1979).

VANDERVELDE, LEA S., "The Gendered Origins of the *Lumley* Doctrine: Binding Men's Consciences and Women's Fiedelity," *Yale Law Journal*, 101 (1992), 775.

VEATCH, HENRY B., *For an Ontology of Morals* (Evanston, Ill.: Northwestern University Press, 1974).

—— *Human Rights: Fact or Fancy?* (Baton Rouge, La.: Louisiana State University Press, 1985).

WALDRON, JEREMY, "Rights in Conflict," in *Liberal Rights* (Cambridge: Cambridge University Press, 1993).

WALLOP, MALCOLM, "Tyranny in America: Would Alexis de Toqueville Recognize this Place?" *Journal of Legislation*, 20 (1994), 37.

WEBER, MAX, *The Theory of Social and Economic Organization* (New York: Free Press, 1964).

WEINTRAUB, RUSSELL J., *Commentary on the Conflicts of Laws* (Mineola, NY: Foundation Press, 1971).

WEITEKAMP, ELMAR, "Recent Developments on Restitution and Victim-Offender Reconciliation in the USA and Canada," in Gunther Kaiser, Helmut Kury, and Hans-Jorg Albrecht (eds.), *Victims and Criminal Justice: Legal Protection, Restitution, and Support* (Freiburg: Max Planck Institute, 1991).

—— "Can Restitution Serve as a Reasonable Alternative to Imprisonment? An Assessment of the Situation in the USA," in H. Messmer and H.-U. Otto (eds.), *Restorative Justice in Trial* (The Netherlands: Kluwer Academic Publishers, 1992).

WENDELL HOLMES, OLIVER, JR., "The Path of the Law," *Harvard Law Review*, 10 (1897), 459.

WHITE, LAWRENCE H., *Free Banking in Britain* (Cambridge: Cambridge University Press, 1984).

WILLIAMS, GLANVILLE, "The Concept of Legal Liberty," in Robert Summers (ed.), *Essays in Legal Philosophy* (Oxford: Blackwell, 1970).

WINTER, RALPH, "Private Goals and Competition among State Legal Systems," *Harvard Journal of Law and Public Policy*, 6 (1982), 128–9.

WONNELL, CHRISTOPHER T., "The Contractual Disempowerment of Employees," *Stanford Law Review*, 46 (1993), 87–146.

WRIGHT, JAMES and ROSSI, PETER, *Armed and Considered Dangerous: A Survey of Felons and their Firearms* (New York: Aldine de Gruyter, 1986).

WRIGHT, M., *Justice for Victims and Offenders: A Restorative Response to Crime* (Philadelphia, Pa.: Open University Press, 1991).

ZUCKERT, MICHAEL, *Natural Rights and the New Republicanism* (Princeton, NJ: Princeton University Press, 1994).

INDEX